THE STORY
OF THE
CONFEDERACY

THE STORY
OF THE
CONFEDERACY

By ROBERT SELPH HENRY

NEW AND REVISED EDITION WITH A FOREWORD BY
DOUGLAS SOUTHALL FREEMAN

KONECKY&KONECKY

KONECKY & KONECKY
72 AYERS POINT RD.
OLD SAYBROOK, CT 06475

ISBN: 1-56852-253-3

PRINTED IN THE USA

CONTENTS

CONTENTS—Continued

FOREWORD

RECENT students of the Confederacy have been so engrossed in its history that they often have neglected its interesting historiography. Some of us have not realized how the literature of the conflict has been developing or in which directions. A few, but only a few works of major importance from the pens of those who shared the battles of the South have been printed since 1900. The *Autobiographical Sketch and Narrative of the War between the States,* by Lieutenant-General Jubal A. Early, was published in 1912. Colonel Charles Marshall's *An Aide-de-Camp of Lee,* admirably edited by Major-General Sir Frederick Maurice, was issued as recently as 1927. Both these books, however, with others of less importance, had been written a generation before, and were posthumous contributions to the concluded first period of the literature of the conflict, the period of memoirs by major participants in the battles of the South.

Before that era of Confederate historiography had been finished, the second was well advanced with the publication of source material and the writing of monographs. The initial volume of the *Southern Historical Society Papers* appeared as early as 1876; the forty-eighth volume is in preparation. That greatest of all publications of Confederate source materials, the *Official Records of the Union and Confederate Armies* bears imprints from 1880 to 1901. Naval operations were covered by subsequent volumes. As successive parts of this indispensable collection—so adequately compiled and so dispassionately edited—were made available, they were the basis of a multitude of special studies. Indeed, General Longstreet and several other general officers of the Confederacy were able to cite early volumes of the *Official Records* in their narratives.

The time is at hand for the third and final labor of Confederate historiography—that of integrating the memoirs, monographs and official correspondence and reports. This integration may be undertaken now in the reasonable belief that substantially all the essential evidence is available and that, unless the correspondence of Judah P. Benjamin should unexpectedly be brought to light, judgments deliberately formed by competent students who survey the corpus of existing source material, are not apt to be modified in any appreciable degree by after-discovered records.

It was one of the many distinctions of Robert Selph Henry to realize in 1926 that a beginning could be made in the writing of the definite history of the Confederate States of America. The researches which he then undertook with admirable method culminated in the publication, in October, 1931, of *The Story of the Confederacy*. A fellow student, who was wrestling at that time with some of the problems in the career of a pre-eminent Southern commander, may perhaps be permitted to record here the delighted satisfaction with which he breathlessly read the first edition of Mr. Henry's book. The end-sheets themselves were evidence of the soundest possible approach to the strategy for the war, for Mr. Henry wisely had made these sheets into maps of the Southern railways, which meant more than mountain-ranges and scarcely less than the great rivers in determining the lines of advance and defense. As an experienced railroad executive, Mr. Henry advanced a new and invaluable point of view in the interpretation of military operations. With this was joined a singular precision of detail, a wide knowledge of the civil history of the Confederacy, and a penetrating judgment of personalities which, in the War between the States, had extraordinary influence on results.

So often and so confidently have I turned to Mr. Henry's book for a better understanding of such co-ordination as existed in the confused grand strategy of the desperate Confederacy that when I learned a new edition was about to appear, I asked the privilege of expressing in this foreword my appreciation of his work. I regard *The Story of the Confederacy* much as John Addington Symonds did the *Autobiography of Benvenuto Cellini*—at present the book with which to begin one's study of the period it covers and the book to which to return when everything else on the subject has been read.

DOUGLAS SOUTHALL FREEMAN.

The Story of the Confederacy

CHAPTER I

"REBELLION" AND REVOLUTION

THE Confederacy was a belated attempt to exercise the right of a state to withdraw from the United States of America.

Because it was belated, because it opposed a mere right in the abstract to the concrete force of economics and the inevitable trend of history, because it was burdened with the defense of the anachronism of slavery, it failed.

Its short life was lived in war—it *was* war, with all that war can mean of waste and destruction, of misery and anguish, but, too, with all that it can mean of shining gallantry, of steadfast devotion. These the Confederacy had—but it met a spirit as sturdy and unbending, and one backed with greater power. And so, at the end of four years of struggle as human and moving as men might make, it failed.

With its failure the United States of America that we know was born. The South, they said, rebelled. To crush the "rebellion" the North wrought a revolution. The old union of states federated together for specific and limited purposes died, to be succeeded by a new nation in which the states, North and South alike, have contentedly sunk from the sovereignty they so jealously maintained in 1787 to become little more than convenient administrative subdivisions of government.

The men who through the long hot summer of 1787, by conflict and compromise of ideas, hammered out the Constitution of the United States thought that they had created a Federal Union. The men of the state conventions, which ratified this strange new form of government, with misgiving and some trepidation insisted upon being reassured on that point. Hamilton, great advocate of the national idea, and Madison, more than any one man the draftsman of the Constitution, did so assure them

11

through the columns of the *Federalist*, and the instrument was ratified. But all that, by 1860, had been a long time ago. The thirteen states had ratified an instrument which by the necessities of the case left open a great many questions for the answers of the future. During seventy years new forces, new ties had been writing those answers. Thirteen separate and individual sovereignties, although there had been no change in the letter of the organ of government, had in fact become a nation.

It was against this new sense of nationhood, the very existence of which was scarcely suspected by the leaders in the secession movement, that the Confederacy fought. The states which first seceded and formed the new government at Montgomery, persuaded themselves that their departure was of no real concern to the people of the Northern States, who would be at liberty to carry on the old government if it suited them. An entirely logical position—there were never better logicians than the early secession leaders—but it ran against a state of mind, the most stubborn sort of fact. With many thousands in the North, devotion to the Union, and a Union of continental proportions, had passed beyond logic to become an emotion, almost mystical, a religion.

The growth of the Union to the proportions of a continent had been due to efforts of both North and South—efforts in which the vision, courage and determination of southern statesmen and soldiers, exercised frequently in the face of bitter opposition from New England and northern leaders, had played a large part. To the seaboard strip of the original thirteen states, George Rogers Clark and his Virginia and Kentucky riflemen at Vincennes added the old Northwest Territory. Thomas Jefferson purchased Louisiana, and Andrew Jackson's soldiers at New Orleans perfected the title to that great empire. Meriwether Lewis and William Clark, through their explorations, established the claim of the United States to the Pacific Northwest. Stephen Austin and Sam Houston brought in Texas, and James K. Polk Winfield Scott and Zachary Taylor, through the War with Mexico, added California and the great Southwest. The South had reason for pride in its achievements in the building of the United

States, but to southern leaders of thought the country was just that—States united, not an integral nation.

One of the tragedies of the War between the States while it lasted and for many years afterward, was that neither side could realize or appreciate for what the other was fighting. To many of the North, the war of the South was a wicked and causeless rebellion undertaken to keep black men and women in slavery; to the like-minded in the South, the war of the North was a design of conquest and subjugation, hypocritically masking itself as a crusade for freedom. In this poisonous atmosphere of distrust, in this clamor of the vocal extremists, there was scarcely chance for the men of moderation to be heard, and less for them to be heeded.

The question to be decided being what it was, and men being what they are, it is difficult to see, even now, how that armed struggle called by the victors the War of the Rebellion, and by the losers the War between the States, could have been avoided.

There was a question that had to be settled. It was a bed-rock question, going to the very nature of the government. It happened, finally, to be forced to an issue on certain questions about African slavery in the South, but that was not the first time that it had arisen, nor the only form in which it had appeared. Less than fifty years before the Civil War secession had received serious discussion and considerable support in New England, because of bitter resentment of the effect upon the commerce of that section of the War of 1812 with Great Britain; less than thirty years before, South Carolina's attempt to nullify the operation of a tariff law in that state had sharply raised the question; only fifteen years before, New England men had again advocated leaving the Union because of dissatisfaction with the annexation of Texas and the policy of the War with Mexico.

The fundamental question of the relation of the states to the government they had created was the same each time, but each time a final answer was avoided. Such questions as tariff duties and embargo acts might involve reason and principle and self-interest, but not even self-interest moves men strongly enough to make them seek the final answer to a question which can be answered finally only by war. *That* requires an emotional base—moral indignation, passionate conviction of right on each side, rankling resentment of wrongs, stinging epithets taken to heart, flaming phrases of orators and editors.

Forty years of agitation against slavery, growing more intolerant and impassioned year by year, had effectively killed the movement in the South for the gradual emancipation of slaves. During the first generation after the adoption of the Constitution this movement made much headway, and would, doubtless, have made more had it not been for difficulties about what to do with the negroes after they were freed—difficulties that meant little to the ardent and sincere abolitionist five hundred miles away, but were very real to the southern planter who had the responsibility of meeting the problem at short hand.

These difficulties were not lessened, nor the movement for emancipation strengthened, by the sweeping and inconsiderate attacks of the more zealous abolitionists not only on the institution of slavery but also on the motives and character of the people who owned slaves. Men bitterly attacked will justify themselves with bitterness.

In their resentment at what they considered slanders of themselves and their states, those who had regarded slavery as an evil inherited by the people of the South and had sought to lessen it, began to defend the institution itself. Within a generation many in the South, and especially in the Lower South, convinced themselves that slavery was not an evil, tolerated only because it existed and there seemed no safe and practical way to do away with it, but was in itself a positive good for both races. The churches and ministers found not only justification but direct command for it in the Bible. Abraham, the father of the faithful, was a holder of slaves, said they, and Isaac and Jacob, Job and all the patriarchs. Slavery was authorized by the Levitical Law, and, though it existed all about Him at the time of His ministry it was not condemned by Jesus Christ, while Saint Paul expressly recognized it—so ran the reply to those who looked on slaveholding as the summation of all human iniquity, and who, because the Constitution of the United States recognized the institution, denounced the Constitution as "a covenant with death and an agreement with hell."

The tremendous acclaim in the North for *Uncle Tom's Cabin*, the martyr's crown for John Brown, with his insane scheme for making Virginia another San Domingo—these and a thousand lesser indications were taken by the sensitive South to show the attitude of the people of the nation toward them.   The roots of secession and the Confederacy are to be found in this human resentment—an emotional impulsion to action a thousand times stronger than carefully reasoned constitutional arguments on the nature of the compact under which the states had entered the Union and its violation by the states of the North, or learned and ingenious theories as to the ultimate sovereignty of the state.   The statesmen and leaders argued the constitutional questions, of course, argued them at immense length and wrote about them in great and illuminating detail, but the moving reason for action was not of the mind.   It was of the emotions.

Slavery had existed throughout the colonies. For many years after the formation of the government it continued to exist in some of the Northern States, where its final disappearance was due to its unprofitableness under northern conditions, as well as to the rise of the strong moral sense against property in human beings which led to the abolition movement. Virginia ceded to the general government the great empire of the old Northwest Territory with slavery for ever prohibited—and there was no objection, north or south. Slavery had not yet become an issue in politics, and did not become one until more than thirty years later, when in the fight over the admission of Missouri as a state, whether slave or free, it flamed up. From that time, for forty years, through a bewildering series of compromises and provisos and settlements the agitation never died out, the question was never forgotten. Sincere and earnest statesmen worked to bring about accommodations, only to have them all wrecked sooner or later on the stubborn intractableness of the convinced extremists of one side or the other, or of both. It was, truly, an "irrepressible conflict" so long as the nation tried to exist "half slave and half free"—and especially so long as no man knew whether, at the last, his final allegiance was due to his state or to the Federal Union of States.

"I speak to Cobb," said Lewis Cass, Secretary of State under Buchanan, "and he tells me he is a Georgian; to Floyd, and he tells me he is a Virginian; to you, and you tell me you are a Carolinian. I am not a Michigander; I am a citizen of the United States."

Both sides were right. Just a matter of difference of emphasis—but out of that difference came four years of war, a dozen years of bitter reconstruction and a new nation.

CHAPTER II

FROM SECESSION TO SUMTER

THE South did not secede all at once. It was April of 1860 when the definite movement for secession began, during the Democratic National Convention in Charleston. It was December of that year when the first state, South Carolina, seceded. It was in February of 1861 that the Confederate States of America were formed—but there were only seven of them then, and no more joined until Fort Sumter had made war inevitable, and President Lincoln's call for troops had shown that the war was to be carried into the South. Then, and not until then, four more states joined the Confederacy. It was not until June that Tennessee finally and formally withdrew from the Union and so completed the list of the Confederate States.

For the first year of that fifteen months not many really expected war, even with preparations going on about them. The issue had been acute before—never so acute as now, it is true—but each time an accommodation of some sort had been found. There were extremists on both sides who welcomed the prospect of war eagerly enough, but not many people of the North believed through the winter of 1861 that some way would not be found to bring back into the Union in peaceable fashion the seven states which had declared themselves out of it. In the South, many of the leaders in the movement for secession, convinced that they were merely exercising a right and not starting a revolution, persuaded themselves that their departure would be recognized and accepted.

There were spokesmen in the South, however, and even in that deep South where secession started and to which it was confined until after the call of President Lincoln for troops to invade the South, who recognized what it all meant. Most conspicuous among them was old Sam Houston, Governor of Texas. He had fought with Old Hickory; he had fought for Texas; he had served that Republic as· its President and had brought it into the United States. He loved the old Union; he knew that secession meant war, and that war meant the end of slavery. "Are the people mad?" he asked.

But even those who expected war could not have imagined the reality. President Lincoln's estimate of its extent may be gaged from his call for seventy-five thousand men for ninety days. On the southern side the President did call for men for a year's service, over stout opposition in his Congress, but in general Confederate arrangements were such as "might have implied a pact with Mr. Seward that, should war unhappily break out, its duration was to be strictly limited to sixty days." In fact there were not lacking people in the South who were comfortably sure that the "shopkeepers" of the North would not fight for the Union, and that if they did, the southern soldier could "whip the Yankees with children's pop-guns."

"And we could have done it, too," said one after the war, "but, confound 'em, they wouldn't fight us that way!"

Three thousand miles from the fevered seat of the trouble, on Alcatraz Island in San Francisco Bay, a young Lieutenant of Engineers saw that this was not to be a "pop-gun" conflict.

"This war is not going to be the ninety days affair that papers and politicians are predicting," wrote James B. McPherson, of Ohio, graduate of West Point of the class of 1853, on April 20, 1861, to his younger friend, Lieutenant E. P. Alexander, of Georgia, who had graduated in 1857. "Both sides are in deadly earnest, and it is going to be fought out to the bitter end. . . . For your cause there can be but one result. *It must be lost.* Your whole population is about eight millions, while the North has twenty millions. Of your eight millions, three millions are slaves who may become an element of danger. You have no army, no navy, no treasury, and practically none of the manufactures and machine shops necessary for the support of armies, and for war on a large scale. You are but scattered agricultural communities, and you will be cut off from the rest of the world by blockade. Your cause is foredoomed to failure."

No one of the ten thousand volumes since written about the war then just beginning has better outlined its course and result than the powerful prophecy of young Lieutenant McPherson— a course in which his leadership was to play a brilliant part, and a result that he was not to live to see. In little more than three years, riding out of the pine woods about Atlanta, he was to meet death at the hands of soldiers commanded by Hood, his West Point classmate.

Young Alexander, to whom the letter was addressed, was on his way back from remote Fort Steilacoom on Puget Sound to resign from the Army of the United States and follow the fortunes of his state into the Confederacy. He shared a great deal of McPherson's opinion about the result of the conflict, but devotion to Georgia was with him as strong as devotion to the nation with McPherson.

A state of actual war—or "rebellion," to use the northern term—existed from the beginning of 1861, but it was not until April and Fort Sumter that it was recognized in the popular, or even the official, mind for what it was. Hostile shots were fired as early as January ninth, when South Carolina shell struck the steamer *Star of the West*, attempting to carry supplies to Fort Sumter, but at that time no other state had seceded, the Confederate States had not been organized, Mr. Buchanan was still President, the Congress of the United States was busy with plans for compromise, the Virginia Legislature had called an unofficial "Peace Convention," and the mind of the country was not yet ready to receive the fact of war.

Fort Sumter made war certain—and determined, four years in advance, its outcome. To capture the fort with its little garrison of one hundred men was a slight military advantage; to fire on it, in the existing state of affairs, was a political blunder almost incredible, a disaster to southern hopes more serious than the loss of many battles.

The beginning was in politics. In April, 1860, the Democratic party met in National Convention in Charleston. There had been nothing sectional about the party. Pennsylvania and New Hampshire had been Democratic strongholds. The slavery agitation, however, had been driving deep into the organization for two decades and, finally, at Charleston the wedge split it.

William Lowndes Yancey was the voice of secession. In a land where oratory was the supreme art, he was preeminent among orators. Starting in public life in South Carolina as a vigorous Union man, following the lead of Andrew Jackson, he had, after his removal to Alabama, come to believe that separation from the old Union was, finally, to be the only way for the states of the South to find peace and security for their peculiaɟ institutions. For fifteen years before 1860 he had devoted all his high and dangerous gift for moving men to the preaching of this doctrine—extreme, and like most extreme positions, simple and therefore fit subject for eloquence. He had been a little heeded young man fifteen years before, but in 1860 he went to Charleston as the leader of Alabama's delegation, under instruction from his state convention to demand the extreme southern position as to the right of the slave-owner to go with his property into any of the common territories of the government, "territories bought with the common blood and treasure."

Yancey's was not the only voice for the extreme southern position at Charleston. There were fiery spirits from other states along the Gulf; there was the able Rhett, of South Carolina, who, for the time, took no active part because of the position of his delegation as dignified and courteous hosts to the gathering; there was great booming Bob Toombs, of Georgia, with something of the look and the manner of Danton—and something of the spirit, too.

Failing—by a narrow margin—to secure the adoption of their views, the delegates of the Cotton States withdrew from the convention. The Convention, hobbled by the two-thirds rule of the party, made no nomination and finally adjourned, to meet again in Baltimore in June. The group which withdrew called a convention for Richmond, which was finally held in Baltimore, also. Two Democratic nominations resulted. The northern wing put forward Stephen A. Douglas, of Illinois; the southern, John C. Breckinridge, of Kentucky. A third party was born, made up of remnants of the old-line Whigs, the "Know-nothings," and a few other assorted elements, which nominated John Bell, of Tennessee, and Edward Everett, of Massachusetts, on a platform of "the Union, the Constitution and the enforcement of the laws."

Meanwhile, in May, the Republican party, a collection of varied and assorted political elements and shades of thought, with opposition to slavery as its one common point of cohesion, met in a turbulent mass convention at Chicago. The organization, which had started only four years before as a party of moral protest, had been taken in charge by competent politicians. For good and sound political reasons Abraham Lincoln, an ungainly and little known lawyer from the capital of Illinois, became its nominee on the third ballot. The platform adopted was non-committal, if not actually evasive, on the issues of the slavery contest.

The result of the election was almost purely sectional. Lincoln, receiving not much more than one-third of the popular vote, carried every Northern State but New Jersey; Douglas carried only one slaveholding state, Missouri; Breckinridge carried the lower South; while Bell carried the Border slaveholding States of Virginia, Kentucky and Tennessee.

Abraham Lincoln had not yet become one of our national heroes. The people of the lower South knew him only by most partizan report—although, for that matter, it was a report not greatly different from that by which he was known to many of the North. He was judged in the South by the utterances of his extreme abolition supporters. In the calm light of to-day it is easy to see the needlessness of the wave of alarm and resentment that swept the Cotton States at his election; with the light that was before them, and in their then state of mind, their action is understandable, indeed inevitable.

The Legislature of South Carolina, in session, called a convention of the people of the state to take action on their relations with the Federal Government, such a convention as had been called more than seventy years before to ratify the proposed Constitution for the new United States of America.

The new "sovereign" Convention met on the morning of the seventeenth of December in the Capitol at Columbia. It was an elderly body. Half its members were more than fifty years old, three-fourths were over thirty-five. Four had sat in the Senate of the United States; one had been Speaker of the National House of Representatives; five had been Governors of the state; there were judges, lawyers, clergymen, manufacturers, merchants, planters. Three things were done the first day. The Convention organized, adopted a resolution to appoint a committee to draft an Ordinance of Secession and adjourned to reconvene the next day in Charleston, because of an outbreak of smallpox in Columbia.

At four o'clock the next afternoon the Convention reassembled in Institute Hall, in Charleston. Within the hall all was decorum and order, as if the delegates were consciously showing to the world the dignity that should accompany so solemn an act as a second declaration of independence. Outside, streets and squares were thronged with excited people, wearing the blue or the palmetto cockade, and clamoring for quick passage of the Ordinance.

Not until noon of the twentieth, with details disposed of, was the Convention ready to adopt the brief Ordinance, declaring "that the Union now subsisting between South Carolina and other States, under the name of 'The United States of America,' is hereby dissolved": yeas, one hundred and sixty-nine; nays, none.

The Convention, which had held its final session in St. Andrews Hall, moved in solemn procession to meet the Governor and the Legislature of the state at Institute Hall at seven that evening. The hall was packed; the galleries were crowded with ladies waving their handkerchiefs. In the presence of the authorities of the state the members of the Convention signed the engrossed copy of the Ordinance. Two hours it took to get all the one hundred and sixty-nine signatures. As the last name was signed, the President announced that fact and proclaimed the "State of South Carolina an independent Commonwealth.'

The city went wild with excitement. Bells began to ring,

artillery was fired, round after round. The Charleston
Mercury, with true journalistic enterprise, was on the streets
with an extra, containing a copy of the Ordinance, fifteen minutes after the adjournment of the Convention. Houses were
illuminated with candles and lamps in the windows; the military organizations of the city paraded, with bands of music
at their heads; the people shouted and shouted. South Carolina, come what may, was once more free, independent and
proud.

Four forts of the United States guarded Charleston harbor:
Castle Pinckney, a small round brickwork of obsolete pattern
near the lower end of the city; Fort Johnson, on the south
side of the main channel, used as a quarantine station; Fort
Moultrie, on Sullivan's Island, on the north side of the channel,
famous from Revolutionary days; and Fort Sumter, a frown-
ing pile, standing fifty feet high on a ledge in the channel, a
mile from one shore and two-thirds that far from the other, and
so commanding its entire width. Work had been going on on
this fort, in desultory fashion, since 1829, but it was not completed when South Carolina seceded in 1860, and the United
States garrison in the harbor, less than one hundred officers
and men, was still quartered in old Fort Moultrie.

As soon as South Carolina seceded, commissioners were dispatched to Washington to demand of the government the surrender of these forts and other public property, upon the
understanding that the state was to make proper payment for
them. In the meanwhile, the South Carolina congressional
delegation had, or thought they had, an agreement that the
status quo in the harbor was not to be disturbed pending these
negotiations.

The harbor defenses were under command of Major Robert
Anderson, a Kentuckian, whose sympathies were with the South
in the disagreements leading up to secession, but whose duty
as a soldier was to hold the works until ordered to deliver them.
His orders, oral orders delivered to him by Major Don
Carlos Buell, were "to avoid every act which would needlessly
tend to provoke aggression," but he was also authorized to oc-

cupy any one of the forts which would increase his power of resistance whenever he had "tangible evidence of a design to proceed to a hostile act."

These orders had been given on December eleventh, before the Ordinance of Secession had been adopted, but after it was perfectly clear to every one that it would be. Major Anderson and his garrison were in a decidedly ticklish position. Fort Moultrie, never designed to be defended from the land side, was absolutely indefensible. Fort Sumter was not completed, but work on it was being pushed, and as soon as it was ready it would afford a far stronger position of defense.

There were two difficulties about moving over: a mile of water, and orders not to make such a change. But there was a saving clause in the orders. He could move on evidence of hostile design. By Christmas Day, five days after Secession, Major Anderson was sure that there was such a design. For one thing, the channel between the forts was patrolled at night by steamers bearing parties of the South Carolina military organizations, the Washington Light Infantry and the Charleston Rifles.

The Major determined to insure the safety of his command by transferring it to Sumter. Weather prevented the change on Christmas Night. The night after, with much skill and a great deal of luck, he made the transfer across the broad belt of moonlit water, secretly and without opposition. The next morning the South Carolinians awoke to find that Fort Moultrie was empty, its guns spiked, their carriages burned, the flagstaff felled, and the garrison ensconced in the formidable work in the harbor.

That same morning the South Carolina commissioners arrived in Washington to be greeted with the news of the changed state of affairs in Charleston harbor. They lost their diplomatic balance, and from the start adopted a tone that would have made it difficult to treat with them even if President Buchanan had been disposed to do what they wished.

So affairs hung in Charleston harbor, growing graver day by day, while the secession movement spread westward through the Cotton States. Mississippi seceded on January 9, 1861; the next day, Florida; the day after that, Alabama. Old Bishop Cobbs, the venerable churchman who stoutly opposed Yancey in the movement for secession, was granted his fervent wish that he should never live to see Alabama leave the Union. He died at his home in Montgomery that morning; Alabama seceded later in the day—and, ultimately, the Bishop's sons were found in the Confederate Army.

On the nineteenth Georgia seceded, after a long debate between the giant Toombs, ardently for secession, and the frail and emaciated Alexander H. Stephens, a thoroughgoing believer in state's rights—a belief that he was to carry over into the government of the Confederate States,—who nevertheless believed that for Georgia the path of wisdom lay within the Union.

A week later Louisiana, in convention at Baton Rouge, seceded. There, as elsewhere, the movement had opposition to overcome. The New Orleans *True Delta*, representing the "conservatives," denounced it as a movement "to hasten the secession of Louisiana, right or wrong, cause or no cause, from the Federal Union, and every praise-God-bare-bones in the pulpits of the State, in rivalry of their pious brothers in fanatical and treason-loving New England, will bless their endeavors and sanctify their proceedings." On the day before the Ordinance was adopted, the *True Delta* characterized the movement as the result of "schemes of politicians, the rantings of pharisaical pulpit shouters and the machinations of unreasoning fanaticism . . . insane enough to engage in a destructive civil war." In spite of opposition and warning, however, the convention adopted the Ordinance, making Louisiana the sixth state to secede.

Representatives from these six states, at the suggestion of South Carolina and the invitation of Alabama, met on February fourth at Montgomery to organize a new confederation. A seventh state, Texas, seceded on February first, but distance and difficulties of travel prevented her delegates from reaching Montgomery until after the new Provisional Government of the Confederate States of America (Thomas R. R. Cobb of Georgia wanted to call it "The Republic of Washington") had been organized.

On Saturday, February ninth, Jefferson Davis of Mississippi, late Senator from that state, formerly Secretary of War in the Cabinet of President Pierce, Colonel of the First Mississippi Rifles during the War with Mexico, graduate of the United States Military Academy at West Point, was elected President of the new government. On the same day Alexander H. Stephens, who had fought to the last to keep his state in the Union but had loyally followed it out when secession came, was elected Vice-President.

Mr. Davis was not at Montgomery.

He was at "Briarfield," his plantation home on an island in the Mississippi below Vicksburg, where he had just arrived after resigning his seat in the Senate of the United States, and whence he hoped to be called to military command and not civil place. He had already been made Major-General in command of the Mississippi state troops, and was not averse to the command of the Confederate forces in the field should it be tendered him.

Since December he had been working with the special committee of the Senate appointed to seek a compromise. Half a hundred plans had been offered, the most promising being the elaborate one of Senator Crittenden of Kentucky. Nothing came of them, nor of the deliberations of the unofficial Peace Convention, called by the Legislature of Virginia, which met in Washington with the venerable John Tyler of Virginia, former President of the United States, in the chair, and with representation from twenty-one states. The Border Slave States, most earnest of seekers after peace, sought in this conference to find a basis of accommodation, but the seven states which had already seceded were not represented. They were gathering on the same day in Montgomery to organize the Confederate States.

On the evening of Saturday, February sixteenth, one week after his election, Mr. Davis reached Montgomery. There, from the balcony of the Exchange Hotel, Mr. Yancey presented the new President to the cheering throngs that filled Fountain Square. His phrase of introduction, almost at the close of his career of eloquence, will be remembered:

"The man and the hour have met!"

On Monday, in the Grecian portico of the Capitol of Alabama, the man was inaugurated as Provisional President of the Confederate States of America, as yet a government of but seven states.

Inauguration Day was "genial, serene and clear"—in contrast to a second inauguration day, when the same President was to be inducted into office after his election as "permanent" President. It was "ushered in by the thundering of cannons, discharged by the different military companies quartered in various parts of the city"—some there on the way to Pensacola, where Alabama and Florida troops were watching Fort Pickens, others to celebrate the day. In the middle of the morning the Columbus Guards marched into the triangular space before the Exchange Hotel and "entertained several thousand of our citizens by the display of their skill in military evolutions"— the sort of fancy drill that was then considered adequate train- ing for war.

Before noon, upon the firing of a signal gun, the procession formed—"red jackets, bottle-green jackets and gray jackets formed a mingled ground, above which the brazen epaulets, gleaming swords and bristling bayonets flashed in the sun- beams."

The President, drawn to the Capitol in a carriage with six beautiful grays, delivered a "short, manly and pithy inaugural address," was sworn in by Howell Cobb, of Georgia, President of the Provisional Congress.

On January twelfth, nearly a month before the Provisional Confederate Government was organized, state troops of Florida and Alabama had seized Fort Barrancas, guarding the channel leading into Pensacola Bay, the most commodious harbor on the Gulf and the United States naval base in those waters. The Union garrison had withdrawn from Barrancas to the more iso- lated and defensible position of Fort Pickens, located on Santa

Rosa Island, just as Major Anderson, two weeks earlier, had put his men into Fort Sumter.

As other states seceded they seized arsenals and forts within their limits, always with the declaration that they would make settlement with the United States Government for their value. By the time the Confederate States were organized the seven states which composed it held sixteen posts within their limits, mostly cavalry posts in Texas, while the United States held but four of consequence—Sumter, Pickens and the forts at Key West and the Dry Tortugas, in the Florida Channel, neither of which could be reached except by a formidable naval expedition.

The new Confederate Government inherited from each of its constituent states their differences with the Union about these properties. Commissioners, sent to Washington to negotiate with President Buchanan on the subject, arrived so late in his administration that they determined to wait for the inauguration of the new President before presenting their views.

On March fourth, in the city of Washington, Abraham Lincoln took the oath of office as President of the United States.

A little more than fifty years before the two Presidents, Union and Confederate, had been born in the same state, Kentucky, within a hundred miles of each other in distance, and less than a year apart in time. Lincoln's people, obscure, almost submerged, had migrated northward to Indiana and then to Illinois; Davis', substantial people but not wealthy, had gone southward to Mississippi. Lincoln had educated himself; Davis had the advantage of a course at Transylvania College in Kentucky, and at West Point. Five years after his graduation there the two young men met for the first time, when Lieutenant Davis, as mustering officer of the United States Army, swore in Captain Lincoln and his company of volunteers for the Black Hawk War—a meeting that made no recorded impression on either man. Ten years later, in the Twenty-ninth Congress, both sat in the House of Representatives for a session.

Fifteen years more, and they were to meet again—not in the flesh but in the supreme clash of war.

President Davis was head of a government having nothing,

with everything to provide. President Lincoln had the immense advantage of heading the "going concern," but it was a government sadly torn and disrupted by the uncertainties of the last few months of the administration of President Buchanan.

The old President's weak indecision and vacillation at a critical time have for seventy years been held up to public scorn. His part was pathetic, not heroic, and yet, looking back, it is difficult to see that he would have done better to have done differently from what he did—which was to hang on to the posts left to the government within the Seceded States and await developments. This "Micawber policy" was savagely criticized by the gentlemen of the North who cried aloud for "action," but just what "action" he could have taken is not made to appear. He had left but two months of office when states began to secede. The United States, as has so often been the case at critical times, was caught unprepared, with a tiny army of sixteen thousand men scattered over thousands of miles of frontier. A determined effort, with the forces at hand, to retake the fortified places that had been seized could have had but one result—war, and war brought on in such fashion as would not have enlisted the support of that very large element in the North who, before the Confederates fired on Fort Sumter, were willing enough to see the "erring sisters depart in peace."

President Buchanan may have followed his course simply because he did not know what to do, but the most profound wisdom and foresight could scarcely have done more for the ultimate preservation of the Union than his passive policy.

On March third, the day before Lincoln was inaugurated, the military situation about Charleston changed. Brigadier-General Pierre Gustave Toutant Beauregard, newly appointed in the Confederate States Army, arrived at Charleston and took charge of the preparations for the protection of the harbor from expected attack by United States vessels, and for the reduction of Fort Sumter, should that post not be surrendered.

Major Beauregard he had been, in the Corps of Engineers— a studious and capable officer, as well as a most gallant one, attested by citations of his service in Mexico, and by his appointment as Superintendent of the Academy at West Point just before Louisiana seceded; slight, erect, bronzed, military in every act and thought, punctilious in his courtesy, ardent in his cause; the very man to win the enthusiastic support of the Carolinians.

Artillery was to be provided or improvised and so emplaced as to command the channels leading to Fort Sumter and the fort itself. Another young soldier of the French race—or, at least, the Corsican—had started his rise to military fame with the skilful emplacing and handling of the artillery at Toulon, and his maxims and methods had no more zealous student than the new Confederate commander at Charleston harbor.

For a month he worked in a fever of haste, getting his batteries emplaced and in order, and doing it well. By the beginning of April the harbor was so fortified that it could probably have resisted even the serious attack of a relieving force from the sea—as it did, afterward, successfully withstand most determined sieges by combined land and naval forces.

As Buchanan had done, Lincoln waited. He waited throughout March, and on into April. General Beauregard's batteries had effectively closed Charleston harbor, and made it a major undertaking to attempt to reenforce or relieve Major Anderson. Anderson's provisions would be gone by April fifteenth, even if the men were put on short rations. Events pressed for a decision. Most of President Lincoln's Cabinet favored giving up the post. The President's sound political sense recognized in it not merely a little garrison in a detached work on a ledge in a South Carolina harbor, but a symbol and an opportunity. He ordered the fort reprovisioned.

The Confederate Government at Montgomery had a more difficult political situation to meet. South Carolina had been independent for more than three months, but she still saw her principal harbor dominated by a work flying the flag of a power that she regarded as "foreign." There was much impatience at what the Carolina leaders looked on as the pacific and temporizing policy of the Montgomery government, and more than a little chance that if that government did not order the reduction of Fort Sumter the state government would. In a measure the situation forced the hands of the Confederate Cabinet.

Moreover, they felt that to provision a fort lying within the limits of the Confederate States, and still held against that government in spite of demand for its surrender, was an act of aggression, justifying the Confederate Government in using force. Granting their premise of the independence of South Carolina and of the Confederacy, so it was—but the distinction, logical enough to them, was too fine-spun to register in the northern mind, which persisted in regarding the firing of the first gun as the opening of the war.

The Confederate Government, after three days of correspondence and negotiation, sent telegraphic orders on April eleventh to capture the fort. Formal demand for surrender of the post was made in the early afternoon.

Major Anderson had no hope of successful resistance. He knew the caliber of Beauregard. By one of those ironies so common in the Civil War, it was Anderson who had taught artillery to Cadet Beauregard at West Point. So apt a pupil had he been that, on his graduation, Anderson retained him as assistant instructor in the same subject. For more than a month now, the Major had been noting in his diary the evidences of military competence and skill shown by the beleaguering force under his old pupil and associate. Only a day or so before the demand for surrender he had noted, with misgiving, a battery of two forty-two- and two thirty-two-pounders which had been secretly erected on the upper end of Sullivan's Island in such position as to render untenable the barbette guns on the parapet of Sumter, the best and heaviest armament in the fort. This "masked battery" had been built behind a house, effectually concealed and only unmasked by the destruction of the house just before the engagement was to open.

With no hope of the result, but determined on resistance, Major Anderson declined to surrender. That night final preparations were under way for the bombardment. The people, thrilled by rumors of the engagement, packed the Battery and every other point in Charleston which offered a view of the lower harbor. They waited until midnight. Nothing happened. Most of them straggled home and to bed. At half after four in the morning, after due notice to Major Anderson, a signal gun was fired from Fort Johnson. Immediately, a shell was thrown into Sumter by the heavy mortar battery on Morris Island, and the bombardment was on.

During the same early morning hours of April twelfth the relieving fleet arrived off the bar of the harbor. At six o'clock in the morning the fleet started in. Only one of the vessels got within the bar, and it was driven back by the shore batteries, without making any very serious attempt to come up to Sumter. At seven o'clock the men in the fort, who had been kept in the deep bomb-proof casemates by order of Major Anderson, came up and began to reply to the fire of the Confederate batteries, which continued throughout the day with surprising accuracy and effect.

On the morning of the thirteenth, wooden barracks and store buildings within the brick walls of the fort took fire. Magazines had to be closed, and most of the powder that had been left in the casemates, being in danger of explosion from the raging fire, had to be thrown out into the water surrounding the fort. In the afternoon, just to show that they had not surrendered, the garrison fired a few rounds—a demonstration of spirit cheered by the Confederates at their batteries. After some misunderstanding, principally the result of unauthorized nego- tiations by a volunteer aide, Major Anderson surrendered the post at seven o'clock in the evening of April thirteenth, after two days of bombardment. The Charlestonians, and the thou- sands of citizens from up the state who had come in by train to see the great sight, spent that night, Saturday, with much rejoicing and enthusiasm. The next morning, Sunday, Major Anderson paraded his garrison in the sadly battered fort, raised the United States flag to receive the national salute allowed by the conquering Confederates, and started to fire the one hundred guns. On the fiftieth round a gun burst, killed Private Daniel Hough and wounded five—the first casualties of the bombardment, and so of the war, suffered not in battle, but in formal salute to a flag.

The flag was lowered. The Confederate States gained complete control of Charleston harbor. They demonstrated that they were in earnest about separating from the Union. So doing, they did for the Lincoln administration what it could not do for itself—set and solidified the wavering and divided spirit of the North.

Never was so costly a victory so easily won.

CHAPTER III

A NATION WITH NOTHING

THE day after Fort Sumter surrendered President Lincoln called on the several states for seventy-five thousand militia for ninety days' service.

The troops were to suppress "combinations too powerful to be suppressed by the ordinary course of judicial proceedings, or by the powers vested in the Marshals by law," a curiously legalistic phraseology probably adopted in an attempt to bring the proclamation under the Acts of 1795 and 1807 governing the calling out of the *posse comitatus*. "The first service assigned to the forces called forth will probably be to re-possess the forts, places and property which have been seized from the Union," continued the proclamation.

Amid immense enthusiasm, the established militia regiments in the eastern cities moved at once. Pennsylvania troops, a few companies, reached Washington the next day; Massachusetts troops came in within four days, in spite of the violent resistance to the transfer of the regiment across Baltimore between the railroad stations; New York's first regiment was but a day behind Massachusetts.

The effect in the Border States of the South, which had held off from the conflict until war had actually begun and a choice was forced, was as decisive and immediate. The Governors of Maryland, Virginia, North Carolina, Kentucky, Tennessee, Arkansas and Missouri sharply declined to honor the President's requisition for troops to be used against the seven states of the Confederacy. The Governor of Delaware reported that he had no lawful authority for raising troops.

Neither, for that matter, had President Lincoln, under strict construction of the laws. He met an emergency by emergency methods. In the tremendous game of war the Confederacy had made a bad move, and the President, if he was to take advantage

34

of it, must act at once, and on his responsibility alone. In his
first proclamation he called Congress into special session, but
not to meet until the Fourth of July, more than two and a half
months later. In the meanwhile, free from interference,
he drove ahead to organize his war, making laws or breaking
them as he had need to, creating armies, enlarging the Navy,
declaring blockades, exercising all the war powers of Congress.

Before the guns spoke at Sumter and the President answered
with his call for troops, there was everywhere, in the North, in
the Border States unhappily torn between loyalties, and even in
those states which had seceded, a strong party for peace. The
fire of Sumter swept away all that in the North; the call of Lincoln for troops, in the South. The New Orleans *True Delta*,
which had opposed secession and sought peace, "spurned the
compact with them who would enforce its free conditions with
blood"—an attitude that was general among those who were
not original secessionists.

Virginia, whose Convention had previously refused to submit an Ordinance of Secession, acted first. On the day after the
President's proclamation was received, the Convention adopted
the Ordinance and submitted it to an election, by which it was
overwhelmingly ratified a month later. Without waiting for the
result of the election, the state authorities on April eighteenth
seized the Arsenal at Harper's Ferry—or what was left of it
after it had been fired by its evacuating garrison—and the Navy-
Yard at Norfolk on the twentieth.

On the twenty-third, by authority of the Legislature, the
Governor appointed as Major-General commanding the military
forces of Virginia, Lieutenant-Colonel Robert E. Lee, to whom
the chief command of the Union Armies in the field had been informally tendered but three days before. The next day Virginia entered into a military alliance with the Confederate
States, to be followed by formal adhesion to that federation,
which, in June, transferred its capital from Montgomery to
Richmond.

In North Carolina and Arkansas, conventions met and very

promptly withdrew those states from the Union, without a popular election.

In Tennessee, which in February had voted against secession by a majority of two to one, the Ordinance was again submitted to popular election, and on June eighth was carried with enthusiasm and by a vote of three to one. In the meanwhile, anticipating the result, on May seventh the state entered into military alliance with the Confederacy.

When these states seceded there was no doubt about war, and not any such short and easy one as could be contemplated with the "joyous and careless temper" that prevailed in the early days of secession, when only a few of the staid and apprehensive anticipated any war at all.

The familiar figure of Robert E. Lee, pacing the floor of his chamber at Arlington in anguish of spirit, wrestling in prayer for guidance to the line of his duty, at the last coming out for Virginia and against the Union which he had so faithfully served and which offered him such brilliant military prospects, may be taken as the type of the struggle of the best and most conscientious men of the Border States. Their first fight was within themselves—a fight that did not always come to the same result as did Lee's. The noblest, and perhaps the ablest, of Union Generals, George H. Thomas, was a Virginian; the seaman who achieved most for the Union was David Farragut, a Tennesseean.

In Kentucky this inner struggle reached its greatest intensity. For a generation the state had been on the border-line of conflict. In every crisis its statesmen had worked for compromise. Through a confused internal struggle, half-political, half-military, the state government managed to maintain its neutrality from April to September, in 1861, but it could not last. The struggle most truly and literally became a war of brother against brother. Two sons of Senator Crittenden rose to high rank in the Union service; the other in the Confederate. John C. Breckinridge and his three sons went into the Confederate service; Robert J. Breckinridge was an outstanding leader on the Union side. Of his four sons two were in the Confederate

Army, two in the Union. At the battle of Atlanta, one of the Confederate sons captured his brother—a strange sort of family reunion, but one in which there was much warmth and no bitterness. Of the grandsons of Henry Clay, three went into the Union Armies, four into the southern. Mary Todd married Abraham Lincoln; her sister was widowed when Ben Hardin Helm fell on the field of Chickamauga at the head of a brigade of Kentucky Confederates. What was true of these distinguished families, was true of thousands of others in the unhappy state—a state which, in spite of its divisions, furnished seventy-five thousand men to the Union Armies, as many as Iowa or New Jersey, more than New Hampshire and Vermont together.

In Missouri, while the division of families was probably not so sharp, there was a fierce conflict of sentiment. Before the fall of Sumter there were four fairly distinct parties within the state: the ardent secessionists, headed by the newly elected Governor Claiborne Jackson; the equally militant Unionists, with Francis P. Blair, Jr., and Captain Nathaniel Lyon, of the Army, as principal leaders; the moderates of southern sympathies, led by former Governor Sterling Price, who had rendered distinguished service in the War with Mexico; and the Union moderates, best typified by Brigadier-General William S. Harney, a veteran of the Regular Army service and commander of the Department of the West, with headquarters at St. Louis.

Even after the fall of Sumter it appeared that Price and Harney might be able to keep the peace in Missouri. It was not until May tenth, after weeks of political maneuver and military preparation of a sort, that armed conflict began.

Early in May the state militia turned out for their two weeks' summer instruction at Camp Jackson, in Lindell's Grove, on the outskirts of St. Louis. General Harney was temporarily absent and Captain Lyon was in command of the Department. The Captain had fortified the United States Arsenal, the most important in the West, and was determined to hold it. The militia encampment, though it flew the flag of the United States and professed allegiance to the government, he regarded as a hot bed of secessionists and a "fearful menace" to the safety of the arsenal and the city.

This Captain Lyon was of the spiritual breed of old John Brown himself—a little man, hard-bitten of feature, red of hair and beard, with the burning eye of the zealot. In time of disturbance and revolution it is such men who come forward, fierce men, single-minded, simple. There was about him, too, something of the theatrical. To reconnoiter General Frost's little camp of militia—there were less than seven hundred of them, in a wide open and exposed position—he must borrow the dress of Blair's mother-in-law, muffle up his red beard in shawl and sunbonnet, and go through the camp in disguise.

More than ever convinced of its baleful character, he brought out from the city his troops, five thousand of them, surrounded the camp, and from the heights that commanded it summoned Frost to surrender. Frost had no choice. Resistance would have meant massacre. Massacre came, as it was. Lyon's volunteers marched their prisoners into the city through dense crowds of the curious—among them one U. S. Grant and one W. T. Sherman, ex-officers of the United States Army. A German regiment at the head of the line got into an altercation with spectators, opened fire. The firing spread down the line. Before it could be stopped there were twenty-eight dead, many more wounded. St. Louis that night and the next day was in a state of riot and terror, until General Harney returned, reassumed command of his Department, quieted and reassured the people.

The immediate result of the affair at Lindell's Grove was to drive fine old Sterling Price and his influential group from their position in favor of Union toward the Confederacy. Price, however, still working for peace, established a truce with Harney. It lasted less than three weeks, when orders from Washington removed Harney and put Lyon, promoted to the rank of Brigadier-General, in his place. Peace was the last thing that Lyon wanted. He would have none of a truce. Unconditional submission of the state to his orders, or war, was the choice.

Price withdrew from St. Louis and joined the Governor and the Legislature at Jefferson City. Lyon at once advanced up the Valley of the Missouri, drove the state government from the capital, and, on June seventeenth, at Boonville attacked and dispersed some thirteen hundred volunteer militia that Governor Jackson was trying to get together to oppose his advance. Lyon pushed on, driving the Governor and his half-organized and unarmed force to retreat from the rich river valley into the hill section in the southwestern part of the state.

Price, who was made Major-General of the Missouri State forces early in July, established himself at Cowskin Prairie, in the southwestern corner of Missouri, where he was in contact with the Confederate forces in Arkansas and the Indian Territory under General Ben McCulloch. Lyon established his headquarters at Springfield, the most important town in that section. Both sides went to work to arm, equip, organize and train their forces—a task in which Lyon had the immense advantage of possession of St. Louis and its arsenal, and of the backing of the Government of the United States.

While Lyon, with his half-improvised force, was making his advance and clearing a state, military preparation had been going on everywhere. There was so much to do, on both sides. Never was a nation less ready for war than the United States— except the Confederacy. The United States, though it had only a tiny Regular Army, had much more of the equipment and material of war than the South and, more important still, better means of manufacture.

The South had almost nothing except men. True, the men had, for the most part, led outdoor lives and were accustomed to the use of firearms, but it very soon appeared that the reliance of the South on these facts was misplaced. Hunting rifles and shotguns were of small value for military purposes. Their variations too greatly complicated an already nearly hopeless problem of ammunition supply. That Floyd of Virginia, Secretary of War, transferred rifles to southern arsenals between the time of the election and the inauguration of Lincoln is commonly believed. Arms were sent south to relieve crowded conditions at the Springfield Armory and elsewhere, but that was in 1859, before Lincoln was nominated, and even then almost all the modern rifled pieces remained in the North. Of the five hundred and thirty thousand small arms in the arsenals at the beginning of the war, but one hundred and thirty-five thousand were in the South, and of these all but ten thousand were old smooth-bore muskets, some of them of the flintlock pattern used in the War of 1812, which had to be altered for the percussion cap in use in the 'sixties.

From Texas to Virginia the people were trying, according to their abilities and resources, to prepare for war. The government at Montgomery, and later at Richmond, appears to have been overwhelmed with the difficulties and complexities of the job of organizing a government, a treasury, an army, a navy, and the industrial backing to sustain them, all from the bottom up. It was not until sixty days after it had become apparent that war was inevitable that an agent was dispatched to Europe to buy rifles—ten thousand of them, instead of the half-million that were to be needed!

The most dependable source of supply for good guns for the Confederates was the invading Union forces. Replacement recruits, reporting to Nathan Bedford Forrest on the field of battle, without arms in their hands, asked where they might get rifles.

"Just follow along here," said the General. "There is going to be a fight with those folks over yonder, and we'll get you some guns there."

Toward the last, however, the Union ordnance department played a scurvy trick on the Confederates. They introduced the vastly improved breech-loading rifle, arms which did the Confederates no good even if they had been able to capture them, because the southern armories, which could make fairly good paper cartridges and caps for the percussion muzzle-loading rifle, had neither the material nor the machinery to make brass cartridges for the breech-loaders.

The Confederate powder mills, armories and arsenals were inadequate to the enormous demands on them, of course, but

they were none the less a real achievement. They were created
from nothing and worked with improvised equipment and sub-
stitute materials—but they did produce enough usable military
stores to keep the armies of the Confederacy in the field and
fighting. In charge was General Josiah Gorgas, of Alabama,
father of the surgeon who, half a century later, led the United
States Army in the conquest of tropical diseases and so made
possible the Panama Canal.

President Lincoln on April nineteenth announced a blockade
of southern ports from Texas to South Carolina. On April
twenty-seventh, after Virginia forces had seized the arsenal and
the navy-yard, and North Carolina had taken the forts at the
mouth of the Cape Fear River, he extended it to the ports of those
states. In point of law there was no justification for the act,
just as there was none for the call for forty-two thousand volunteers or the increase in the Regular Army and the Navy, made
on May third, but war knows no law and the President was at
war. Ships of the Navy, such as were at hand, immediately stood
away to the southern ports to enforce the blockade, but it could
not be made really effective until well along in the fall of 1861.
Those were months of grace in which the Confederacy could
have sold, delivered and stored in Europe cotton and cotton and
yet more cotton, and bought ships and arms and equipment if
it had had a treasury, a currency or a credit with which to collect
and transport the cotton.

The foreign policy of the Confederacy, however, was based
on a delusion, a delusion so glittering and so plausible that it
blinded the eyes of the leaders. The Southern States had a
world monopoly of the production of cotton, the most important
of all textile fibers, and the one on which the great industrial
establishments of England, of France and of New England were
largely based. "Cotton is King" had been the boast of southern
orators for a generation—and the South believed it. The
world's need of the staple, their reasoning ran, would bring the
recognition of the Confederacy by the Governments of Queen
Victoria and of Louis Napoleon, such an intervention as would
decide the war and establish southern independence.

"Cotton is King" ran the thought of the Confederate Government, and their policy was based on that deceptive foundation—deceptive because there had been heavy crops in the years just before 1861, with a world carry-over so large that during 1861 and 1862 England actually shipped cotton back to the mills of New England. It was not until late in 1862 that the shortage of cotton became acute. By that time President Lincoln's shrewdly timed Emancipation Proclamation had made the issue of the war in European eyes one of freedom against slavery, and no British Government could afford to intervene on the side of slavery.

One thing more the statesmen of the South overlooked. Until the middle 'fifties the South and foreign nations reached only through the mouth of the Mississippi River had been the principal markets for the production of the great interior country of the United States. The West had floated its output of corn and pork and wheat and beef and whisky down the river to supply southern plantations absorbed in the production of the one staple crop of cotton, but in the middle of the decade before secession a new means of transport had penetrated the great valley of the interior. By 1860 the West was no longer dependent on the South for its markets, nor on the Mississippi for transport. Railroads connected St. Louis and Cincinnati with the seaboard. Economic currents were flowing, unnoticed, in new channels.

One of the ironies of the war was that the proud city of Charleston, reaching out before the war toward the Mississippi Valley to extend her sphere of commercial influence, had by her money and her leadership largely made possible the creation of the railroads which connected the Ohio River with Nashville, Chattanooga, Atlanta and the South Atlantic seaboard. Unwittingly, the very center and source of the Confederacy made possible the decisive campaigns of Sherman from Chattanooga to the sea, and, so doing, did more than any one thing else to destroy southern hopes.

But in the gay and joyous spring of 1861 all that was yet to be. There were men in the South of course, who saw just what Lieutenant McPherson foretold, but their forebodings were drowned in the rush of enthusiasm to get ready for the war. While in the North there were regimental camps, the South was dotted at first with the encampments of little companies. The court-houses, the schoolhouses, the scattered cross-roads villages became recruiting centers. Every county had its company, many more than one. There were the old social-military organizations, brilliant companies with their bright and shining uniforms—tail coats, braided trousers, cross-belts, shakos and busbies and fancy head-gear, buttons of gilt, white gloves on drill and duty; there were the new organizations, commanded by young lawyers and planters and merchants, with no uniforms, no guns, nothing but martial ardor. There were innumerable companies of "Grays"—not all of whom, by any means, wore gray; there were companies of "Rifles," not nearly all of whom had rifles; there were "Guards" of all sorts, and "Invincibles"; there were "Volunteers" and "Game Cocks" and "Tigers." The name of "Washington" was a favorite for the companies, and after the affairs in Charleston Harbor, there were the "Beauregards" and the "Sumters." There were fancy names, and plain names, and some fancy names that, by inspiration of the moment, became plain. Young Captain John B. Gordon—he was to become one of Lee's Lieutenant-Generals—thought to call his Georgia company the "Mountain Rifles," but a mountaineer in the ranks with a coonskin cap beat him to the christening, and they were the "Raccoon Roughs."

The Confederate Army forecast the great citizen armies of the World War. It was a complete cross-section of the military population of the South. Many a fire-eating oratorical captain who led out a local company in the spring of 1861 was back at home before the end of the summer, his place taken by some quieter man with more of the gift for fighting. Military rank depended far less on peace-time social position than is commonly supposed. In one fine company from Mississippi the son of the richest planter of the county, who had just spent four years at a famous old State University with a negro servant, a horse and a shotgun, put in four more as a high private, with a rifle but no servant and no mount, while the son of the village blacksmith became first a sergeant and then a respected lieutenant. A company from Tennessee asked and secured the pardon from prison of the man they wanted for captain, a man of courage, resource and capacity for leadership. Most of the high ranking officers of the Confederacy were West Point trained, but even into those ranks there rose men of small social position but of large military capacity. On the other hand, high connections did not necessarily bring quick and easy rank to the young soldier.

Young Robert E. Lee left school to join the Rockbridge Artillery as a private, and remained one long after his father became commander of the Army of Northern Virginia and the most famous soldier of his time. During the Seven Days about Richmond the son, a ragged cannoneer, begrimed with powder and sweat, asleep under a caisson, had to be poked awake with a rammer staff when his father came by the battery. At Second Manassas General Lee failed to recognize the same cannoneer, even more ragged and covered with Virginia mud and powder stains. At Sharpsburg, the Rockbridge Artillery lost three of its four guns. As the last gun was being withdrawn it passed the Commander. Captain Poague, of the battery, reported to General Lee for instructions, and was ordered back into the line to face the advance of McClellan's men across the Antietam. As the Captain left, young Robert Lee again spoke to his father.

"General, are you going to send us in again?" asked the boy.

"Yes, my son," he replied with a smile, "you all must do what you can to help drive those people back."

These incidents of Lee and his son are noteworthy for the very reason that they were not regarded as anything remarkable or unusual at the time. The war came close home to the South, from highest to lowest. To many of the North, too, it came as close as tragedy can come. Poor Mrs. Bixby of Massachusetts, proudly grieving for her five sons dead in the cause of their country, might be solaced with the immortal letter of

Lincoln, but the Union was never in such despairing need of men that, as a general thing, it must "grind the seed corn."

The President himself might, as he did, reserve his own son to complete his education at Harvard. That done, on January 18, 1865, with the war wearing almost to its weary and bloody end, he wrote to General Grant:

"Please read and answer this letter as though I was not President, but only a friend. My son, now in his twenty-second year, having graduated at Harvard, wishes to see something of the war before it ends. I do not wish to put him in the ranks, nor yet to give him a commission, to which those who have already served long are better entitled and better qualified to hold. Could he, without embarrassment to you, or detriment to the service, go into your military family with some nominal rank, I, not the public, furnishing his necessary means? If no, say so without the least hesitation, because I am as anxious and as deeply interested that you shall not be encumbered as you can be yourself."

Matching the straining effort of the South to prepare for conflict was the immense outpouring of devotion to the Union in the North. Washington was soon surrounded with camps. In fact, it became a vast camp, not only for the old militia regiments with their brilliant and showy uniforms, but for the new volunteer regiments formed on the call of the President, and for the regular commands. The city was perilously situated on the extreme frontier, even after Union forces had taken over, for all practical purposes, the government of Maryland. Confederate batteries on the south shore of the Potomac, below the city, could blockade the approach by water. By land there was the railroad line to Annapolis, where boats on Chesapeake Bay could be had; and the all-important line to Baltimore. From Baltimore separate railroads ran to Philadelphia, connecting to the East, and to Harrisburg, connecting to the West. Besides these, there was the Baltimore & Ohio line to the west— but that road ran for many miles through Virginia, and was subject to interruption by the forces about Harper's Ferry.

Northwestern Virginia, soon to be separated from the old

Commonwealth on tidewater to form a new state of the Union, was entirely out of sympathy with the secession movement. It was mostly a mountain region of small farm holdings, with its business and social ties along the Ohio River rather than across the Alleghany Mountains to the east and south. As to politics, for a generation the tidewater counties, controlling the Legislature, had used that power to restrict and limit the representation of the growing counties along the Ohio and its tributaries.

Civil war offered these communities their opportunity. Devotion to the Union and resentment at ancient political wrongs within Virginia were the mixed motives that brought the new state of West Virginia into being. With the double purpose of encouraging the Union sentiment in these counties, and of protecting the important line of the Baltimore & Ohio Railroad to the east, Union troops crossed the Ohio and advanced into Virginia as soon as it was known definitely and finally that the Old Dominion had left the Union.

That was on May twenty-fourth. Within the week troops crossed the Potomac from Washington and occupied Lee's home at Arlington and the old town of Alexandria, terminus of the railroad from the south; other troops, under Benjamin F. Butler, Massachusetts politician and lawyer whom the President commissioned as Major-General, advanced from Fortress Monroe up the Peninsula toward Richmond.

The advance across the Ohio, however, first showed results. This movement was under command of Major-General George B. McClellan—thirty-five years old, a soldier of rare technical proficiency and organizing skill, an individual of real charm, a general with but one serious fault, and that one fatal. He had graduated at the head of his class at West Point only fifteen years before; had served with real distinction in the War with Mexico; had followed the Crimean War as an observer, and made reports on that struggle which received the most flattering attention; had devised the saddle still in use in the Army; had resigned from the Army to become chief engineer of the Illinois Central Railroad, and then President of the Ohio & Mississippi; had been commissioned by the

Governor of Ohio to command the state troops, and accepted by the United States as a Major-General.

From the Ohio River McClellan followed the line of the railroad to Grafton. There he learned of a Confederate force, under Robert S. Garnett, advancing across the mountains toward the rail line. On June third advance parties of the two armies came together at Philippi, thirty miles south of Grafton. The night was dark, raining. On such a night the raw Confederate troops saw no need of standing a damp and uncomfortable guard. Before day they were surprised asleep, and fled south-eastward to Beverly, thirty miles away. The "Philippi Races" they were called locally, but in the newspapers the chase made quite a victory for McClellan's forces.

Beverly lies in the Tygart Valley, between Cheat Mountain on the east and Rich and Laurel Mountains on the west. The road from eastern Virginia, via Staunton, forked there, one hand going toward Wheeling, one toward Parkersburg. Garnett divided his forty-five hundred men and posted them to cover both roads, twenty miles apart as the roads ran. McClellan advanced cautiously. He was sure that there were as many as ten thousand Confederates in front of him—the first exhibition of what developed as a confirmed tendency to overestimate the strength of the enemy.

Moving southward from the railroad, with twenty thousand men, McClellan detached one of his brigade commanders, W. S. Rosecrans, to flank out the force posted on Rich Mountain. With difficulty, Rosecrans' men climbed through a supposedly impracticable mountain track. In a driving rain, they fell upon Pegram's flank on the afternoon of July eleventh. During the night Pegram fell back. Garnett, hearing of Pegram's discom-fiture, retreated also and left the road in front of McClellan clear. McClellan advanced with excessive caution.

Garnett, separated from Pegram and, as he thought, cut off from his main line of retreat, started on a long detour to pass around the northern end of Cheat Mountain and regain con-tact with his base. The next day, on July thirteenth, the little army made its escape, after a brilliant and successful rear-guard action at Carrick's Ford, in which Garnett himself was killed, just at the close of the fight.

Garnett, who had been commandant at West Point, was the first general officer to meet death in battle. At the extreme rear point of his rear-guard, with but ten raw soldiers who were showing nervousness, the General undertook to give them "a little example" by coolly walking back and forth along the line, exposed to the enemy's fire. Just as he was ready to retire a sharpshooter's bullet shot him dead. The knightly idea of war still prevailed in the early days of the Civil War, and it was not uncommon for officers to stand up and bid defiance to the bullets. By 1864 such "examples" were not needed. Men just as brave were taking advantage of every bit of cover they could find or make.

On the same day that Garnett was killed, Pegram, cut off from contact with his base, surrendered to McClellan what was left of the little force that Rosecrans had defeated on Rich Mountain. During that week Cox, another of McClellan's subordinates, most auspiciously started an advance by steamboat and road up the Kanawha Valley, an advance that was to take him beyond Charleston and on to the forks of the river at Gauley Bridge without serious opposition, and before the end of the month.

McClellan's campaign was a small affair, as judged by numbers, and was not particularly brilliant on either side, but it was a Union victory; it secured vast territory in western Virginia to the Union; it was supposed to have been conducted with dash and vigor; and it was to enjoy favorable contrast with the larger operations that ended, little more than a week later, in the battle to be known as Bull Run, or Manassas. It is not difficult to understand how a nation that was looking for a hero should hail the agreeable and appealing young McClellan as the Young Napoleon.

CHAPTER IV

MANASSAS—BATTLE OF BLUNDERS

ON THE afternoon of July sixteenth, under the spur of political clamor and the urge of the press, Major-General Irvin McDowell reluctantly and with misgiving left the fortified lines about Washington for the first great drive "On to Richmond."

Six days later, on the morrow of Manassas, the remnants of the army straggled across the bridges into the streets of the capital, worn and weary, pelted by a pouring rain.

Bull Run ended the ninety-day period of the war. Before that battle, war, for both sides, was still largely a matter of waving flags, of bright and variegated uniforms, of tender and romantic farewells, of sentimental songs about the camp-fire. Men *did* get killed and wounded in war, of course, but to the happy boys flocking to join the local companies forming throughout the South, or the larger and better fitted regimental camps in the North, that was a pretty remote and unreal possibility. It was all a great deal of a lark, a three-months picnic in the pleasant summer-time—and besides each one was sure that "our side" was to win and win quickly.

Bull Run changed all that. After that battle the ninety-day patriots went home—some of them actually "marched to the rear to the sound of the enemy's cannon" on the morning of the battle—and the North settled down to the long slow job of conquering eleven states.

The Confederacy, by resolution of its Congress in special session two weeks after Fort Sumter, had adopted a strictly defensive policy, asking to be let alone in peaceable withdrawal from the Union. That wish, of course, was not to be granted. It became the problem of the South to defend at all points and from all directions the immense territory stretching from the Potomac to the Rio Grande, open to attack by land and by sea, penetrated by great rivers, vulnerable at a hundred points.

49

The South's defensive policy gave to the North from the first the great advantage of the initiative, an advantage which their numbers and resources enabled them to use. The Confederacy felt itself compelled to stand watch and ward at all points, scattering its scant manpower and equipment in camps and fortified places from the outskirts of Washington all the way to New Mexico. It is not difficult to see the improvidence of such dispersion from a military point of view, but at the time and under the political pressure for "protection" it was doubtless never possible to bring about a concentration that might have been effective.

Political considerations, always important in war, were never more so than in the War between the States. The two capitals, which early acquired a value as symbols beyond their military importance, faced each other but a hundred miles apart. This fact, with its effect upon the imaginations and fears of the two governments, became one of the controlling elements in the Virginia theater of war where both sides put forth their greatest effort. Anxieties for Washington aborted some of the Union's best opportunities; Richmond, at the last, tied Lee to his trenches when sound military policy would have called him to the free and open field.

Virginia was peculiarly exposed to invasion. All along her northern and western frontier was the Ohio River, from which McClellan early launched his campaign; all along her eastern frontier was the Potomac River and Chesapeake Bay, with arms penetrating well into the state, controlled by the superior naval forces of the Union.

Even before Bull Run, Major-General Benjamin F. Butler, fresh from his achievement of overawing the civil government of Maryland, started an advance from a base at Fortress Monroe up the peninsula between the York and the James Rivers—the same route to be used the next year by McClellan. Butler's invasion ran into trouble at Big Bethel, where on June tenth a little Confederate force under Colonel John Bankhead Magruder stampeded his men back to their fortress base. The Confederates lost in the engagement one killed, Private Henry L.

Wyatt, of Colonel D. H. Hill's North Carolina Regiment—"first at Bethel."

At Fortress Monroe, about this time, General Butler added a new word to the vocabulary of the war. The government had ordered a strict regard for private property, and slaves were still property under the law, but the ingenious Butler noted that he was authorized to take and keep possession of such property as was contraband of war. He promptly applied the description to the negroes who came into his camps, on the theory that they gave, had given, or could give aid and comfort to the Confederates, and so they became, and remained during the war "contrabands."

Besides the Peninsula, three other lines of invasion remained: the advance by the Potomac to Acquia Creek, then the northern terminus of the Richmond-Fredricksburg Railroad; the line of the Orange & Alexandria Railroad, running southwest from Alexandria to Gordonsville, where it connected with the Virginia Central, extending from Richmond on the east through Charlottesville to Staunton, in the Shenandoah Valley; and the approach directly through that valley, with its fine stone pike road running from the Baltimore & Ohio Railroad southward to Staunton and beyond.

Joseph E. Johnston with eleven thousand men covered the lower end of the Valley for the Confederates. Sixty miles to the east, with the Blue Ridge between, was Beauregard, with some twenty thousand, facing the Union defenders of Washington. Beauregard's base was a little railroad junction, Manassas by name, where a branch line turned out to pass westward through a gap in the Blue Ridge into the valley of the Shenandoah—a vital link between the two major Confederate armies. Thirty miles still farther to the east, at Acquia Creek, Holmes with a small force guarded the third route to Richmond.

There was no one head to the three Confederate armies in the field. President Davis, in Richmond, was actively exercising his constitutional function as commander-in-chief, through the medium of General Samuel Cooper, the venerable Adjutant-General of the United States Army who had resigned to become the ranking military officer of the Confederacy and the Adjutant-General of its Army.

Two major Union armies were in the theater of action—that of Patterson, an aged veteran of the War of 1812 and of the Mexican War, recalled from civil life to face Johnston in the Valley; and that around Washington and Alexandria under Major-General McDowell, a big, kindly, vigorous, studious and capable officer, forty-three years old.

The Union Commander-in-Chief of the Army, under the President, was Lieutenant-General Winfield Scott, the grand old man of the Army, a Virginian who loved the Union and hated Jefferson Davis, a veteran of two wars and the leader in the American expedition from Vera Cruz to Mexico City—a brilliant feat of arms now nearly forgotten but then fresh in the minds of all men. The old General did not want to advance beyond the fortified lines about Alexandria. He preferred to wait until the enlistments of the ninety-day men expired and to reorganize his army for serious and prolonged fighting, but popular clamor and political pressure drove him on.

The two Union armies of Patterson and McDowell were decidedly superior in numbers and equipment to any combination that could be brought against them, and they were in close and easy communication by railroad. Instead of concentrating them, however, General Scott merely ordered Patterson to hold Johnston engaged in the Valley, while McDowell went out to meet Beauregard.

McDowell's thirty-five thousand men marched six miles on that first day out from Alexandria and went into camp. It was a motley army. Uniforms were variegated, gaudy, bizarre—the Turkish trousers, short bolero jackets and red fezzes of the New York Fire Zouaves, the cock-feather hats of the Garibaldi Guards, the Highland plaids of the 79th New York, the variety of blues and buffs, and even grays of the different militia organizations. Some of the troops were fairly well trained, as training was then understood. They knew the parade-ground tactics of the time—facings and marchings, evolutions of the drill ground, the prescribed method of loading and presenting the piece, the manual of arms, even, in some cases, the fancy "Zouave drill." Other troops, recently organized and arrived in camp, were scarcely trained at all but they were as far along as most of those they were to meet.

Almost by the time McDowell made his first camp, on the night of the sixteenth, Beauregard had word of it through his excellent secret service in Washington. On the morning of the seventeenth Richmond knew of it, through a telegram from Beauregard. Now was the time to bring Johnston from the Valley to join in meeting McDowell, a movement which Beauregard had been urging for some days, somewhat prematurely. There was some delay for consideration at Richmond, with loss of precious time, but during the night of the seventeenth John-

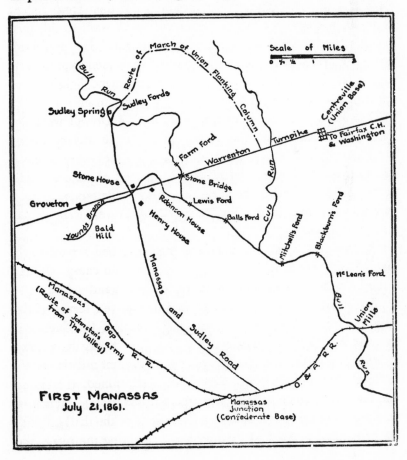

FIRST MANASSAS
July 21, 1861.

ston was authorized to give Patterson the slip and join Beauregard. Poor old Patterson, believing that Johnston had three times his actual force, was bluffed into a state of paralysis, while Johnston led his army to the end of the Manassas Railroad, put the infantry on the cars, and sent the artillery and cavalry by road.

Meanwhile McDowell's advance pushed slowly forward. The Confederate advanced posts fell back from Centreville to the southwest side of the little stream of Bull Run. Here Beauregard established his brigades to cover the various fords extending from Union Mills on the right, where the railroad crosses Bull Run, to Stone Bridge, on the left, where the straight turnpike from Centreville to Warrenton crosses. The whole front was more than seven miles, but it was not continuously and heavily held.

McDowell's advance was unduly cautious. His brigadiers, admonished by a sentence of McDowell's march order, felt their way forward expecting ambuscade by "masked batteries." Beauregard, it will be recalled, had put in a battery at Charleston masked by a house until it was ready to fire. The imaginations of the reporters, and even of the soldiers, populated the Virginia woods and hollows with like Confederate surprises.

The slowness of the advance gave time for Holmes to come up from Acquia Creek and, far more important, for Johnston and part of his force to join Beauregard on the twentieth, to play the deciding part in the battle of the next day. There had already been a clash along the line of the Run, about Blackburn's Ford, on the eighteenth—a little affair that the. Confederates call "Bull Run," as distinguished from the greater battle of "Manassas" on the twenty-first. In this affair Tyler, commanding a Union division, pushed a demonstration farther than McDowell had ordered and was repulsed, with bad effect on Union morale and elation among the Confederates.

Centreville, which became McDowell's base, is opposite almost the center of Beauregard's line along Bull Run, and little more than three miles north of it. Manassas lies about the same distance south of the Confederate right. McDowell, while he was bringing up and concentrating his troops about Centre-ville, felt for the best point of attack.   He gave up the idea of a frontal assault with raw troops after Tyler's repulse; figured on a turning movement around the Confederate right, but gave that up after reconnaissance showed the country too broken and the stream too difficult to cross in its lower reaches; and finally, on the afternoon of the twentieth, decided to turn the Confederate left.   One factor in the decision was the fact that such a movement, if successful, would put him between Beau-regard and Johnston, who was supposed to be still in the Valley, and on their line of contact.

Curiously enough, the aggressive Beauregard on the same afternoon decided that he would throw his right across the stream and attack the Union left, in the morning.   What would have happened had the movement been executed as planned is now nothing more than an interesting subject for speculation. Through the faulty staff work which played such an important part in the war, the orders for the movement miscarried.   Most of Beauregard's brigades on the right, outside of crossing and recrossing the stream three separate times during a day of confused and conflicting orders, played small part in the battle.

On the left, however, there was a different story.   McDowell's plan was one of those wide and elaborate turning movements that look simple enough on the map; that sometimes succeed when executed by trained troops, under experienced command-ers served by capable staffs; and that are next to impossible under the conditions that faced McDowell.

The extreme Confederate left, a demi-brigade under Colonel N. G. Evans, a soldier of the old service, was at Stone Bridge, considerably separated from the rest of the line and apparently clear out of the coming battle, much to the disgust of its soldierly commander.   Two miles farther up the stream, in an air line, there was a crossing of the Run at Sudley Springs.   From Sudley a direct road ran to the Con-federate base at Manassas, passing well behind the Confed-erate line.   From the turnpike near the Union base at Centre-ville there was a wandering woods road to Sudley, ten or twelve

miles as the troops must march. It was over this road that Mc-
Dowell decided to send his main force, to cross the Run at Sudley
and sweep down on the lightly held left flank of the Confederates.
The rest of his army was to make a demonstration at the Stone
Bridge to distract attention from the turning movement, and
then to cross to the attack as soon as the flanking divisions should
clear the bridge.

Instead of marching his turning divisions, Hunter's and
Heintzelman's, to their starting positions the evening before,
McDowell allowed them to remain in camp and to start at
two-thirty in the morning. It was a bright moonlight night,
but the way was long and crooked, the troops were new to that
sort of thing, and some troops of Tyler's division got in the
way on the roads. Instead of reaching their position of attack
early in the morning, it was nearly ten o'clock before the leading
brigade of the column was ready to strike.

Meanwhile Tyler had advanced to the Stone Bridge early
in the morning and started a noisy demonstration. Evans, with
a fine sense of soldiership, conceived that it was too noisy and
too tardy in its movements to be a real attack. Far away to
the northwest he saw great columns of dust above the trees, and
correctly judged the movement. He took the risk of leaving
but a small part of his force to hold the bridge, and with the
rest marched away to the left to meet the approaching menace
from that quarter. So doing, he saved the battle.

Almost at the same time, about half after eight o'clock, young
Captain Alexander, who had come all the way from the Pacific
Coast to fight with the Confederacy, looked out from his signal
station on a high rocky point a mile east of Manassas and saw,
eight or nine miles away, the movements of McDowell's marching
column. The newfangled system of signals by flags, since known
as wigwag, was then first used in battle, and with entire success.
A message sent to Evans, six miles away, confirmed him in his
diagnosis of the enemy's movements; another message sent to
Johnston and Beauregard caused Johnston to start toward the
threatened left the brigades of Bee and of Jackson, and the
Hampton Legion.

About ten o'clock the first of McDowell's flanking brigades struck Evans' little force, which had advanced a mile to the flank and was in position waiting attack. Evans, with little more than a regiment, put up a good fight and held the hill north of Young's Branch until Bee came up and prolonged the Confederate line. Besides the brigades in the turning column, which were attacking the Confederate force in front, the Union brigades of Sherman and Keyes managed to find a farm ford across the Run and fell upon the flank.

The Confederate forces broke and retreated, in considerable disorder, down the hill, across Young's Branch and the Warrenton Turnpike, and up the slopes of the plateau that is for ever known in history as the Henry House Hill.

On one side the hill slopes away to the little bottom where Young's Branch falls into Bull Run; on the other it is flanked by the sunken road running from Sudley to Manassas; in front, it rises from the turnpike on the north in a gentle slope to the plateau, some two hundred yards wide, with a fringe of young woods on the farther side. In the northeast corner of the area was the small frame cabin of the free negro Robinson; near the western side, above the Sudley road, fringed with old locust trees, was the small two story frame house of Mrs. Judith Henry. Her husband, half a century before, had been an officer of the United States Navy, under Truxton on the *Constellation*. To the eighty-five-year-old widow, bedridden and helpless, caught between the lines of battle at the fiercest point, death was to come, impartial, from the guns of the North and of the South.

As Bee's and Evans' commands, mingled, came back to the crest of the Henry House Hill, they found posted there two Confederate commands—the battery of young Captain John D. Imboden, half-concealed in a little swale just at the forward edge of the plateau, and the Virginia brigade commanded by a fiercely religious, sternly military Professor of the Virginia Military Institute, Thomas Jonathan Jackson by name. Jackson had drawn up his line at the rear of the plateau, just at the edge of the woods, a position where his men were sheltered from the Fed-

eral fire until the advance of their troops should expose them
to Jackson's at short and deadly range.

Brave Bee, having left Imboden's Staunton Artillery to hold
their advanced position until ordered away, rode among his
retreating troops as they swarmed across the hill toward Jackson's steady immovable line.

"There stands Jackson, like a stone wall," he cried. "Rally
behind the Virginians."

Bee, within the hour, was to be mortally struck, almost at
the spot where he conferred the immortal name of "Stonewall"
on the silent and secret genius of battle, Jackson. Jackson's
men were to stand; Bee's to rally behind them and return to
the battle; young Imboden to stay where he was until his battery was almost completely shot up, and other artillery came
and he was ordered back by Jackson. The battle was to sway
back and forth across the little space on the top and flanks of the
Henry House Hill, with short breathing spaces, all through the
noon of that hot and dusty July day.

Johnston, in command for the South, and Beauregard, second
in command, arrived at the scene of the fiercest fighting just
as Bee's men rallied on Jackson. Beauregard, as the junior,
remained in command there while Johnston returned to his
central position to direct and hurry forward the reenforcements
so desperately needed.

McDowell, too, came forward to take personal charge of
his turning column, but he had no Johnston in his rear to push
forward troops. While Johnston was sending in Cocke's brigade, and bringing up Early's and Holmes' from the right and
the reserve, and Kirby Smith's, coming in from the Valley by
train, McDowell was not only not bringing forward the reenforcements of which he had abundance on the north side of Bull
Run, but was even allowing some of the brigades on the south
to drift out of the battle at critical times and places. Of the
eight brigades he had on the central field of battle, four accomplished almost nothing.

After two hours of that sort of fighting, McDowell decided
on a final attack all along the line, with his fine artillery in

front. The two excellent regular batteries of Griffin and Rick-etts—both of them were to become Major-Generals before the war ended—were thrown forward to the Hill, and took position not far from the Henry House itself, with only one Zouave regi-ment to protect them from musket fire at short range. This protection proved to be weak and uncertain when a squadron of cavalry under a young Major J. E. B. Stuart, a happy war-rior, singing and laughing through his fine ruddy beard, swept into, over and through the supports. The batteries were left alone, coolly firing grape and canister into the smoke which marked the Confederate positions. A regiment advanced out of the smoke toward them. Major Barry, the Federal chief of artillery, thought it another Union regiment come to sup-port his batteries—a natural enough mistake, in view of the similarity of so many of the uniforms on the two sides, and the fact that by that time all uniforms alike were covered with yellow Virginia dust. Griffin thought that it was a Confederate regiment and wanted to open fire on them, but his chief held him back. The doubt ended when the 33rd Virginia, almost at shotgun range, blasted the batteries with a volley. Every gunner was down, most of the horses. Only three of twelve guns could be withdrawn. The others were left, surrounded with dead and wounded men and mangled horses, half-way between the two lines of battle.

Back and forth, charge and counter-charge, the battle swept through the afternoon hours. About four o'clock Beauregard made his final effort. The whole line pushed forward; the Federal guns near the Henry House were captured and turned on their retreating owners; the brigades of Early, coming up from the far right of the line, and of Kirby Smith, which had just left the trains at Manassas and marched to the sound of the battle, came into action on the Union right flank; the Union troops quietly started for home by the ways they had come, some going back around by Sudley Springs, some crossing the Run at the Stone Bridge and starting direct for Centreville on the turnpike.

The retreat was not yet become a panic-stricken rout. That

was to be a little later, but still long before dark, which comes late in July. The road back to Centreville over which the retreating army must pass, was already clogged with picnickers—correspondents, officials from Washington, Congressmen, ladies, who had driven out with their luncheon baskets to see the war ended with a glorious victory. As soldiers and Congressmen and picnickers streamed back across the bridge on the turnpike over Cub Run, a little stream in front of Centreville, a Confederate shell overturned a wagon on the bridge and choked it. The panic spirit, which had been growing, took possession of the retreat and made it into a rout, a rout that nothing stopped short of Washington.

There was nothing that could be called a real pursuit. In spite of confused and conflicting orders, some of the brigades on the Confederate right did cross the Run at the lower fords and started after the Union forces. They were recalled, through the error of some nervous staff officer, and were not again ordered forward. Nearly half the Confederate Army had not been engaged in actual battle, although all had been under arms since early morning and had marched and counter-marched across the creek. They were probably capable of pursuit, although the commanding officers then on the field, and President Davis who came on the field in the very hour of victory, did not think so at the time. Had they engaged in a real pursuit they might have accomplished much, although it is by no means certain. Not all McDowell's forces were in the rout. One whole division was not engaged in the battle, while parts of others held their organizations together.

Against them Johnston could have thrown the troops of Longstreet, Ewell and D. R. Jones, three brigades under excellent command, which were not engaged in the heavy fighting. It was not done, however, in spite of the opinion of Jackson. While the surgeons were dressing his wounded hand, he told President Davis that with five thousand men he could capture Washington. Then he was still just the somewhat eccentric Brigadier-General Jackson, not the famous "Stonewall."

That night the Generals conferred with the President, and

almost decided on a vigorous pursuit after Major R. C. Hill
came in and reported what he had seen of broken and abandoned
carriages, choked roads and utter rout. Almost—but not quite.
It was casually mentioned in conversation that Major Hill had
been known at West Point as "Crazy" Hill, a circumstance that
cast some doubt on his story. The nickname, it is true, had been
given merely to distinguish him from another Hill at the Acad
emy, had nothing to do with his sanity or the accuracy of his
observation, and was due to nothing more than an intensity of
manner "suggestive of suppressed excitement," but it served to
delay what might have been a fateful pursuit.

While the President and the Generals conferred and planned,
brave Bee lay dying. He had done his duty, all that could be
asked, but he could not die in peace. He had left Imboden to
hold an advanced and exposed position until ordered back.
Imboden had never received the order to withdraw, and, so
Bee heard, was resentful. Bee had sent the order in due time,
but the officer to whom it was charged had been killed on the
way to Imboden's position—a fact that kept Imboden there and
firing, with the result of delaying McDowell's advance up the
Henry House Hill, and so perhaps of saving the battle for the
Confederacy. But Bee wanted Imboden to know, and to know
from his own lips, that he had not been deserted and forgotten.
Messengers from the dying General scoured the battle-field
through the night, to find at dawn, asleep on a bag of oats in
a pouring rain, the young artillery Captain, bloody from his
wounds, begrimed from sweat and powder and dust, with one
sleeve ripped off by the bayonet of a fleeing infantryman whom
he had tried to stop and turn back into the line of battle. Imboden hurried to his chief, to find him unconscious, sinking
fast. In a few minutes he died—to live in the story of the
naming of "Stonewall" Jackson.

Manassas was a battle of blunders on both sides, no more
than was to be expected in the handling of new and raw armies
by commanders and staffs who, the best of them, had never seen
such forces brought together. The army that made the fewer
mistakes, and at the less critical times and places, won. In

the South, it was hailed as a great victory, which it was, and as foreshadowing the end of the war, which it did not. It bred undue elation and over-confidence. In the North, the effect was bitter disappointment, but not discouragement. The North settled down to real war.

CHAPTER V

THE FIRST AUTUMN

WHILE the North settled itself for greater efforts—the Congress authorized enlistment of five hundred thousand volunteers on the day after Bull Run,—the Confederacy, satisfied with its defensive policy, awaited the next move.

The troops who had won the great victory at Manassas again moved forward to Centreville, where they had spent the spring, and there went into quarters for the fall and the winter, with advanced posts thrown out to the hills on the south shore of the Potomac, within sight of the unfinished dome of the Capitol, and with batteries on the bank of the river at Cockpit Point maintaining a successful blockade of the stream below Washington. Johnston remained in command, while Jackson took the valley troops back across the Blue Ridge into the Shenandoah country.

On the day after Bull Run President Lincoln called young General McClellan from West Virginia to Washington, to take active command of all troops concentrated there. McClellan knew armies and the details of their training and organization. He was an engaging person, too, who aroused the admiration and excited the loyalty of his troops. For the first few months of his command of the Army of the Potomac, while the new regiments were pouring in from the North—they came in at the rate of ten thousand men a week that summer and autumn— everybody from the President to the soldiers in the ranks worked his bidding, sang his praises. The nation expected much of its new Napoleon of the West—too much.

On the same day that young McClellan arrived in Washington and took command, the Confederate Government found a use for Robert E. Lee. During all the months before Manassas he had not been an officer of the Confederate Army, his only rank being in the Virginia state troops which he commanded

His responsibility had been to raise troops in Virginia, organize and train them, and turn them over to the other officers who were defending the state for the Confederacy.

Affairs in western Virginia, growing steadily worse, largely because of the jealousies and bickerings of the Confederate commanders in that section, called for a commander who could assert and maintain authority over all of them. Lee was chosen for the job, and on July twenty-eighth set out for the mountains. The Lee who started on what he regarded as a forlorn hope—and it was—was fifty-four years old. All of his mature life he had passed in the Army of the United States, doing his duty as it came to him. The sentence, "Duty is the sublimest word in the language," so often ascribed to him, he did not write; its senti-ment he lived. He was a large man, a handsome man of com-manding presence, with a grave face, lighted by a rarely sweet and winning smile. Men looked up to him, loved him, fought for him. General Scott made no secret of his opinion that Lee was the best of American soldiers—and that long before the out-break of the War between the States. In the mountains of Mexico he had won much glory, and solid military reputation as well. In the mountains of West Virginia he was to do what could be done with the material at hand, but he was to win no glory, and was to return to Richmond to meet little but abuse.

It was all a confused and pointless sort of campaign. The Confederate forces were divided into four groups, each one grandiloquently called an army. Two of the commanders were military men of some competence; two were former Governors of Virginia, personally antagonistic, and neither one with more than a rudimentary idea of military subordination. The Confederate troops were in a country that proved to be hostile, seventy miles from their rail head, with the worst sort of mountain tracks leading back to their base; there was rain right through the summer; measles broke out, and mumps, the twin diseases that even in modern times are the worst enemies of new armies.

Movements were planned and failed, because of the failure

of subordinate officers to understand or to execute their parts. One especially promising surprise attempt on Reynolds at Cheat Mountain failed because a flanking force, with their ammunition wet by a mountain storm in the night, did not fire the concerted signal for the attack. Later, in September and early October, the Kanawha Valley was lost, and Rosecrans' army was allowed to escape from what might have been a predicament, largely because it proved to be impossible to get the two ex-Governor-Generals to work together whole-heartedly.

Lee came back to Richmond, when winter ended the campaign, to find the popular clamor against him led by the Richmond newspapers, which nicknamed him "Evacuating Lee." He paid no attention to the clamor. He might have justified himself; might have thrown the blame on some of his subordinates; might have explained his reasons for not risking a pitched battle at a point where victory could have meant nothing but the loss of the lives of a few hundred Confederates, but true to himself and to his cause, he did not. "I am sorry, as you say, that the movements of the armies can not keep pace with the expectations of the editors of the papers," he wrote his wife in October. "I know they can regulate matters satisfactory to themselves on paper. I wish they could do so in the field."

Before the first of November, Virginia west of the Alleghanies was definitely lost to the Confederacy. Missouri, while not finally lost, was almost entirely in the hands of Union forces, although what was left of the Legislature that Lyon had driven from Jefferson City, meeting in Neosho near the southwestern corner of the state, did formally secede from the Union and join the Confederacy.

Before that, however, brave Lyon had met death in the line of battle in the fiercely contested and bloody struggle fought at Wilson's Creek, ten miles southwest of Springfield, on August tenth. Lyon was opposed by Price, with some five thousand Missouri state troops, and McCulloch, with three thousand Confederate troops, under the general command of McCulloch. Lyon's force of about six thousand was unwisely divided in another of the wide and elaborate flanking movements so common in the early battles of the war. Franz Sigel, leading the flanking movement around the Confederate left, was sharply repulsed, and made his way back to Springfield without rejoining the main force. Lyon, in a final effort to gain the day, led a charge of his whole line, with the courage and resolution for which he was noted. When he fell, the fight, which had been wavering back and forth through the day, went against the Union troops, who retreated to Springfield, and then to Rolla, their rail head. This second real battle of the war was ranked by one of the Confederate officers engaged in it as a "mighty mean-fowt fight"—and so it was. The troops were not yet seasoned and steady, but they were rashly brave when well led, and losses on both sides were heavy.

In command at St. Louis at this time was John C. Frémont, whom Lincoln had unwisely made a Major-General. Frémont had some points of political availability. His wife was a daughter of the distinguished Senator Thomas H. Benton of Missouri; he had won some reputation in the exploration of the West, and was known as the "Pathfinder"; he had been the first nominee of the Republican party for the Presidency in 1856, when that party still represented the "lunatic fringe" in politics. In diplomacy and in war he was a blunderer.

After the battle at Wilson's Creek, McCulloch went back to Arkansas, and Price started north, along the western edge of Missouri, to regain the rich river valley. A month later, on September eighteenth, nineteenth and twentieth Price besieged Mulligan's Union force at Lexington, in the northwestern part of the state, with the result of capturing thirty-five hundred men shut up in a fort surrounding the Masonic College, besides three thousand rifles, seven guns and much other equipment.

The loss of the Missouri state forces was small, partly due to the fortunate adoption of the novel plan of "rolling breast-works"—wet bales of hemp pushed ahead of the troops in the final assault.

Missouri still had not seceded, formally, or been admitted

to the Confederacy. Relations between Price and McCulloch, commanding the Confederate forces in that theater of war, were not of the best, and McCulloch declined to advance to Lexington to cooperate with Price. On the other hand, Frémont was concentrating forty thousand men and one hundred guns against the little Missouri force. Price held Lexington ten days. His unarmed men he then sent to their homes; with his armed men, about seven thousand, he started southward again; marched to Neosho, the temporary "capital," and finally settled down for the fall and winter at Springfield, while negotiations were on foot to turn over the Missouri state forces to the Confederate Government.

While these operations were under way on the northern and western frontiers of the Confederacy, the United States Navy began to make its power felt on the seacoast. The blockade, nominally in force since April, could not be made really effective for some months. The South had four thousand miles of seacoast, with almost innumerable inlets and harbors, but only a few ports had satisfactory connection with the interior by railroad or rivers navigable for any distance—New Orleans, Mobile, Pensacola, Savannah, Charleston, Wilmington, Beaufort and New Bern, Norfolk. It was against these, of course, that the blockading squadrons were concentrated.

The Confederacy started the war with almost no navy. Very early the Congress authorized the issue of letters of marque—recalling the days of the War of 1812 with Great Britain when the Yankee privateersmen had played havoc with British commerce. About twenty small ships were fitted and armed under these letters, and took the sea to create consternation among northern shipping. One of the first war acts of President Lincoln was to declare them pirates, and their crews punishable as such, which they certainly were not. The crew of the first one of the little ships to be captured, the *Savannah*, was confined in the common prison in New York in June, 1861, and threatened with execution. The Confederate Government very promptly announced that it would retaliate in kind with the execution of a like number of Union prisoners of equal rank.

Calmer counsel prevailed and the story of the war was spared that blot.

Eastern North Carolina, the Sound country, where the wide shallow arms of the sea known as Pamlico and Albemarle Sounds, and their connecting channels and rivers are separated from the open Atlantic only by the barrier of the Hatteras Island and reefs, was an excellent base for the operation of the privateersmen, which could slip out through the inlets and, when pursued, return to the shallow water inside.

On August twenty-sixth, from Fortress Monroe, a combined naval and land attack sailed for Hatteras Inlet, the first passage south of Cape Hatteras, to start the reduction of the Sound country. The active Benjamin F. Butler was in command of the troops, Flag-Officer Stringham of the fleet. On the morning of the twenty-eighth the fleet, standing off just out of range of the Confederate guns, began bombardment of Fort Clark and Fort Hatteras, guarding the inlet. The superior guns of the fleet were able to throw their shell into the forts, whose missiles were falling short. In the meanwhile, a small force was landed on the island north of the forts. The next day the fleet resumed the bombardment, while the few men on shore advanced to Fort Clark. About noon of the twenty-ninth the forts sur-rendered. That afternoon the fleet sailed away with six hundred and seventy prisoners, leaving part of the land forces and three vessels to hold the forts and guard the inlet—the first footing of the Union forces on the coast south of Chesapeake Bay.

This footing, however, was of less importance than the establishment of a deep-water base for the blockading squadrons stationed outside Savannah, Charleston and Wilmington. The great harbor of Port Royal, in South Carolina, with ample depth of water and room for the whole Navy, only sixty miles south of Charleston and thirty miles from the mouth of the Savannah River, was the ideal base for these operations.

Late in October a most elaborate expedition rendezvoused in Chesapeake Bay, under sealed and secret orders for the taking of Port Royal. On October twenty-ninth with seventeen vessels of war and an immense gathering of transports and supply ships, Flag-Officer Samuel F. DuPont sailed out past the Virginia Capes and stood away to the southward. On board the transports were three brigades and auxiliary troops, about twelve thousand in all, commanded by Major-General T. W. Sherman—not William Tecumseh.

On November fourth, having ridden out a severe storm off Hatteras, and having been reenforced by ships from the squadron off Charleston, the fleet stood into the entrance to Port Royal harbor. To oppose its entrance the Confederates had three small converted river steamers, under command of the gallant Commodore Josiah Tattnall; Fort Walker on Hilton Head Island and Fort Beauregard on Phillips Island, the two sides of the wide channel.

Boisterous weather on the fifth and sixth delayed the attack, but on the morning of November seventh the fleet, formed in line of battle, swept up the channel, midway between the forts, firing on both, easily drove away Tattnall's river boats, turned and passed down, close to Fort Walker, and for four hours maintained a destructive fire on that work. At two in the afternoon, with but three guns left in working order, the little garrison of two hundred men withdrew from the fort, which was taken into possession by a landing party from the fleet. That night the six hundred men in and around Fort Beauregard abandoned that position, also, and retreated inland. During the next three days the fleet and army moved up the various rivers and inlets behind the harbor entrance, and took possession of the fine old colonial towns of Port Royal and Beaufort.

In command ashore in this first close battle between the fleet and the forts was Brigadier-General Thomas F. Drayton, of the Confederate States Army; afloat, in command of the *Pocahontas,* one of the ships in the attacking line, was his brother, Captain Percival Drayton, of the United States Navy—South Carolinians both. On the island for which they fought was the home where they were reared.

In the Gulf of Mexico the most difficult problem of the blockading squadron was the great port of New Orleans, with its numerous outlets through the passes of the Mississippi and Lakes Pontchartrain and Borgne. The first step toward solving that problem was taken in September when the Union Navy seized Ship Island, off the Mississippi coast, with its incomplete Confederate fortifications, and so secured a base near the job.

While all these events were taking place, affairs in Kentucky were engaging more and more the attention of both sides. The state's geographical position was such that so long as both sides respected its neutrality, the Union forces could nowhere come at the South between the mountains on the East and the Mississippi on the West. The balance between Union and Secession was so close in the state, and the feeling of state pride so strong, that for weeks neither side was willing to make any move that could be interpreted as a clear violation of neutrality.

Kentuckians were volunteering in considerable numbers for both armies. Because of political sensibilities the Union volunteers were accepted at camps north of the Ohio, opposite Louisville and at Cincinnati; while the Confederates established a similar camp for the recruitment of Kentuckians at Camp Boone, Tennessee, north of Clarksville. Within the state there were two militia organizations, one friendly to the Confederacy, one to the Union.

On May seventh, Anderson of Fort Sumter, a native Kentuckian, was made a Brigadier-General and assigned to the duty of raising Kentucky volunteers for the Union Army. He established his headquarters at Cincinnati, and by his tact and good judgment in dealing with the Kentuckians prevented unwise movements into the state that might have thrown it to the Confederacy. At the same time Lieutenant William Nelson of the Navy, a Kentuckian who became a Major-General in the Union Army, was actively at work within the eastern part of the state, where there was a strong Union sentiment. For two months the giant Nelson—he was six feet four inches in height, weighed three hundred pounds, was quick and active, physically and mentally—traveled back and forth, arming the Union Home Guards with the ten thousand muskets that had been placed at his disposal by the government.

Early in June Major-General Simon Bolivar Buckner, in command of the Kentucky state forces, journeyed to Cincinnati to hold conference with McClellan, there in command for the Union. It was agreed between them that there was to be no Union invasion of Kentucky unless the Confederates should occupy the state. In that event Buckner was to try to preserve the state's neutrality without Union aid; if he could not dislodge the Confederates he was to call for assistance. A similar agreement was reached between Buckner and Isham G. Harris, Governor of Tennessee. Except for the recruiting for the armies and arming of the Home Guards, the struggle in Kentucky was political, rather than military. The Congressional elections in June went for the Union, as did the elections for the Legislature in August.

Immediately after the August elections Nelson began to concentrate his forces at Camp Dick Robinson, between Lexington and Danville, for the purpose of an "expedition" into East Tennessee, where it was hoped that the process of arming the Union sympathizers which had been successful in eastern Kentucky could be repeated. The men gathering at the camp were nominally Kentucky Home Guards.

At the extreme western end of the state, in the short reach of the Mississippi River between the mouth of the Ohio at Cairo and the Tennessee boundary, is—or was—the commanding bluff at Columbus. North of Columbus, at Cairo, an obscure Brigadier-General Grant was in command of the Union forces. South of Columbus, along the river in Tennessee, Major-General Leonidas Polk was in command for the Confederacy. Columbus had a double importance. It was the northern terminus of the Mobile & Ohio Railroad, which stretched away clear to Mobile Bay, and it was safely above high water, which the Confederate fortifications about the point where the Mississippi loops around in the corner of Kentucky, Missouri and Tennessee were not.

On August thirtieth, the premature Emancipation Proclamation of Major-General Frémont in Missouri nearly wrecked the carefully laid and well executed plans of the Union forces to win Kentucky to their side. Many Kentuckians, willing to fight to preserve the Union, were not willing to engage in war to free the slaves. On September second, however, President Lincoln disavowed Frémont's acts, and upon his refusal to change them, removed him from command.

Fortunately for the Union, on the very next day there was a Confederate counter-irritant. Regard for the sensibilities of Kentucky had kept the Confederates away from Columbus all through the summer, but on September third, under the orders of Major-General Polk, they entered the state and seized the commanding position on the Mississippi.

From a strictly military point of view the move was sound; from a political, it was a mistake—and a mistake which was not helped by the replies of General Polk and President Davis to the official remonstrances of the state government of Kentucky. General Polk, cousin of President Polk and graduate of West Point, had early left the army to enter the Episcopal ministry, and for twenty years before the war had been Bishop of Louisiana. Recalled to service, he had been commissioned a Major-General and assigned to command the important line of the Mississippi, with headquarters at Memphis. He was a man of loftiest Christian character, of utter devotion, of fine ability and commanding presence, but there was about him a fixity of views and purpose that sometimes lessened his undoubtedly great value to the Confederacy.

With the seizure of Columbus, which the Confederates justified by pointing to the formation of Camp Dick Robinson, events moved fast in Kentucky. General Grant immediately moved from Cairo to take possession of Paducah, an important town at the mouth of the Tennessee River. General Anderson moved the Union headquarters from Cincinnati to Louisville on the seventh, and the Union troops all along the Ohio River crossed into the state soon after. On September eleventh the Legislature of the state demanded the unconditional withdrawal of the Confederate forces; on the thirteenth, Buckner, commanding the state forces, appealed to the government at Richmond to order Polk back, while Governor Harris of Tennessee made a similar appeal direct to Polk. The Confederate Government failed to gage the political effects of their refusal, and so lost the immense advantage of Kentucky's neutrality, though perhaps it could not have been much prolonged in any case.

In losing the protection afforded by Kentucky's neutrality the South did not gain any strong natural military frontier. The natural frontier was the Ohio; the political boundary was the Kentucky-Tennessee state line; the actual military frontier established was a zigzag line north and south of this boundary, vulnerable in several important particulars.

To command in the West now came General Albert Sidney Johnston, one of the great soldiers and lofty souls of the Confederacy. A Kentuckian by birth, he had passed most of his life in the Army of the United States, and of the Republic of Texas. At the outbreak of the war, fifty-nine years old, he was in command of the Second United States Cavalry, the regiment which had Robert E. Lee for its Lieutenant-Colonel, George H. Thomas and William J. Hardee for its Majors, and Earl Van Dorn, John B. Hood, E. Kirby Smith and Fitz Lee among its company officers—four full Generals, a Lieutenant-General and two Major-Generals in the Confederate service, all out of one regiment, besides one of the most distinguished of Union Army commanders. Johnston's ability and military capacity were great, but it was in a largeness of spirit that he was most truly distinguished. Like Lee, he never justified himself at the expense of a subordinate or of the cause of the Confederacy, even when he was being most bitterly assailed by press, public and politicians.

By the time that Johnston took command the political lines were drawn in the War in the West, and it was his duty to establish the best possible military line. From the mountain barriers about Cumberland Gap, the line to be defended stretched away more than three hundred miles to the Mississippi. On the right, to cover the road leading from Kentucky into East Tennessee, and to hold in observation the Union forces gathering at Camp Dick Robinson, he threw forward a little army under

George B. Crittenden of Kentucky, and Felix K. Zollicoffer, of Tennessee—devoted Confederates, but more experienced in political than in military matters. On the extreme left of the line, on the Mississippi, was General Polk at Columbus. In the center he advanced his headquarters and a good part of his totally inadequate force to Bowling Green, on the south bank of the Barren River, where the railroad from Louisville to Nashville crosses. From Bowling Green, beside the railroad line running back to Nashville and the southeast, there was another line running southwestward to Memphis. This line crossed the Mobile & Ohio at Humboldt, in Tennessee, and so afforded rail communication between Johnston's center and his left wing.

The vulnerable point of the arrangement was the fact that the railroad from Bowling Green to Humboldt and Columbus crossed the Cumberland and the Tennessee Rivers. To guard the crossings the Confederates, back in the days when they were tender of Kentucky sensibilities, had established two forts, Henry on the Tennessee and Donelson on the Cumberland, just within the boundaries of the state of Tennessee, at a point where the rivers are only twelve miles apart. Better positions for blocking the rivers could have been found farther down-stream (north), where the rivers come within three miles of each other in their parallel course into the Ohio, but these positions were in Kentucky and so out of bounds when the forts were built.

From the first of the war the Union Government had given attention to the matter of control of the western rivers by gunboats. Captain James B. Eads of St. Louis, the great engineer, had been commissioned to design and build ironclads; Colonel Charles Ellet, Jr., another civil engineer, to build steam rams. The fleets completed in record time were far superior in power, protection and mobility to anything that the Confederates with their limited resources were able to create. They played a most important part throughout the War in the West, and never more so than in the winter of 1861-62, when great floods in the southern waters enabled the gunboats to steam almost where they willed.

While Johnston was drawing his lines in Kentucky, ill health forced the retirement of General Anderson from the Union command. He was succeeded by William Tecumseh Sherman, who soon acquired a reputation of being "crazy," partly because he insisted to the Secretary of War that two hundred and fifty thousand men would be needed for the War in the West. Sherman requested to be relieved, and assigned to a command under Grant at Cairo—the beginning of a famous and fruitful combination. He was succeeded in Kentucky by Major-General Don Carlos Buell, a most accomplished soldier and gentleman, whose sound ideas of military policy and strategy and great capacity in the work of organization and training were to prove of much value to the Union.

In Missouri, Frémont was succeeded by Major-General Henry W. Halleck. Halleck was a good "book soldier," the author of the *Elements of Military Art and Science*, besides works on international law. He rose to the highest command, but was temperamentally unequal to the tasks imposed upon him.

Through the late fall there was but one operation of note in the western field, Grant's attack on the southern camp at Belmont, Missouri, across the river from Columbus. The battle lasted most of the day and ended in the repulse of the Union troops, who were driven back seven miles to the transports which had brought them down from Cairo, but it showed the fighting spirit of the man whom the President was to come to trust because "he fights."

With all this activity around the outskirts of the Confederacy—in Missouri, Kentucky, West Virginia, and on the seacoast—affairs in Virginia had been moving slowly and ponderously. General McClellan was engaged in the foundation work of organizing a great army, and it was a great army and well organized when he was through with his job. Joseph E. Johnston's force, tiny by comparison, lay at Centreville in their log hut winter quarters and watched him. Through the fall, in spite of some public impatience for an advance, the prestige of McClellan was enough to enable him to maintain his position that no advance should be made until he was ready. After the winter rains set in, the Virginia mud was an effective barrier to the movement upon Richmond through Manassas that was being pressed upon his attention.

On the Confederate side, too, there had been a great deal of discussion of an advance. Johnston had some forty thousand men about Manassas, organized into two corps, under Beauregard and G. W. Smith. On September thirtieth, at the request of the generals, President Davis visited the Army, and on the next day a lengthy conference was held on the advisability of a movement to cross the Potomac, cut the communications of Washington and carry the war into the North. The movement had much to commend it. True, the Army of the South was small, not yet well organized and not well equipped— but it was then more nearly equal to the Union forces in these particulars than it was to be again.

Recollections of the participants in the conference do not agree in all particulars, but a memorandum drawn up at the time by Smith, and signed by Johnston and Beauregard, is probably pretty nearly correct. The generals asked for reenforcements of the Manassas army—Johnston and Beauregard thought they should have a total of sixty thousand men, Smith, fifty thousand—and proposed an invasion across the Potomac. The President advised that he could not furnish the reenforcements asked for without "a total disregard of the safety of other threatened positions." The project was dropped and the policy of the dispersed defensive was continued, although it would seem that the Confederacy could better have sent some of the fine regiments that General Bragg was drilling and training about Pensacola, and detachments from other garrisons, to attempt a promising move.

Not until the spring of 1862 did either side move in Virginia, after the Union lines had been pretty well drawn about the beleaguered Confederacy, and the process of dismembering it had begun.

CHAPTER VI

FORT HENRY AND FORT DONELSON

THE rivers of the South ran the wrong way for the Confederacy. They did not afford communication between the sections of the South, but were open channels for invading armies, with their fleets of transports and supply ships, and their fighting convoys of gunboats which the Confederacy could not match.

The Mississippi in its north and south course separated Texas, Arkansas and most of Louisiana from the other states of the federation; the Arkansas and the Red Rivers penetrated the states of Louisiana and Arkansas; the Tennessee and the Cumberland opened the way into Alabama, Tennessee and northern Mississippi; the James and the York were tempting avenues of approach to Richmond. All these streams, as well as the open sea, from the early days of the war, were controlled by the superior power of the Federal Navy.

Almost from the beginning far-sighted Union leaders caught the importance of the control of the rivers, and of their use to carve the Confederacy apart. The most obvious of these movements, of course, was that down the Mississippi. General Scott, before his retirement from the service, strongly urged that the main effort of the Union be made along the Mississippi, with the Virginia operations secondary. General McClellan, also, while he was yet stationed along the Ohio River, seems to have entertained somewhat the same views, but after his transfer to Washington he proposed to the President, as his plan for winning the war, a fantastically immense combined land and naval expedition to move from Washington down the Atlantic coast, "crushing the rebellion in its very heart," capturing in turn Richmond, Wilmington, Charleston, Savannah, Montgomery, Pensacola, Mobile and New Orleans, with secondary operations along the line of the great river. It was a dream plan, with

77

the unrealities of a too-generous imagination. While he engaged in this dream of glorious conquest, a hard-headed, unimaginative, tenacious unknown took the first steps toward the dismemberment and final dissolution of the Confederacy.

McClellan was in command not only of the huge Army of the Potomac, gathered about Washington, but of the forces in the West also. These he unwisely divided into two departments: Kentucky, east of the lower Cumberland River, under Buell; Kentucky, west of that stream, and Missouri under Halleck. Between Buell and Halleck there was no concert of action, while the entire Confederate Department, from the mountains to the Indian Territory, was under one head, Johnston.

Halleck was expected to advance down the Mississippi; Buell was constantly urged, by both President Lincoln and General McClellan, to advance from the Ohio River into East Tennessee. It was a movement that had attractive political possibilities and aroused much sympathetic interest because of the strongly Unionist population of that section. From a military point of view it was totally impracticable, so long as Johnston held Bowling Green, Nashville and the line between.

Buell, an excellent soldier, a man of judgment, and on the ground, knew that with existing means of communication and transportation the East Tennessee plan could not be carried out and so represented to his superiors. Overruled, he followed instructions and started George H. Thomas forward from his camp in the edge of the Blue-Grass region of Kentucky, against the Confederate force under Crittenden and Zollicoffer. The two forces met early in the morning of January nineteenth, after a night march in the rain, at Mill Springs, near where Fishing Creek falls into the Upper Cumberland. Zollicoffer was killed early in the engagement and Thomas' little army, admirably handled, won a handsome victory. Congratulatory orders were issued to the command by President Lincoln, but for some reason never explained, unless it be by the explanation then current, that he was a Virginian, the name of Thomas himself was not mentioned in the orders. On the next day Crittenden abandoned the territory and fell back into Tennessee. Eastern

Kentucky was cleared of Confederate forces, except the small brigade under Humphrey Marshall which had been driven by a Union force under James A. Garfield into the upper reaches of the valley of the Big Sandy.

While Thomas advanced in eastern Kentucky, promising plans were on foot at the western end of the state. The idea of using the gunboats and the army in a combined attack on the forts guarding the Tennessee and the Cumberland seems to have been suggested independently first by Buell and then by Grant and by Flag-Officer Foote, in command of the flotilla. Halleck, having dismissed the plan when first suggested, suddenly adopted it and promptly put forces in motion to carry it out.

On January thirtieth Halleck ordered Grant to prepare for an advance up the rivers, in cooperation with the gunboats. On February second the expedition started from Paducah— two divisions of troops, one under McClernand, who had been Congressman from Lincoln's home district, and the other under the distinguished Charles F. Smith, former Superintendent of the Academy at West Point, where he had been the teacher of many leaders on both sides of the war. The transports were covered by Foote's gunboat flotilla, four ironclads and three wooden steamers. The whole expedition was brought up into good position four miles below the fort, where the troops were landed. Toward noon of February sixth the gunboats steamed up to engage the batteries.

Fort Henry was on the right or east bank of the Tennessee River, just where the stream passes from Tennessee into Kentucky. Twelve miles away, on the west bank of the Cumberland River, was the much larger work of Fort Donelson. Henry was miserably located, not well planned, poorly armed. The river was rising rapidly—the beginning of the great floods of 1862 that were to do such damage to the Confederacy—and it was apparent that in a few hours the main batteries would be under water.

Brigadier-General Lloyd Tilghman, the Kentuckian charged with the defense of the position, decided to send his garrison of some twenty-five hundred men overland to join the troops at Fort Donelson, while he remained in the fort with a band of less than a hundred artillerists to man the guns in their resistance to the advancing gunboats.

As Grant's two divisions floundered their way up along the banks of the river, hampered by the rising backwaters in the creeks, Foote's flotilla steamed up the stream with the four iron-clads abreast, in front, the wooden boats behind firing over them. It was the first use of the river boats in such close and determined formation against land fortifications. Foote's boats were built to fight best up-stream. They were well armored about the bow, only lightly armored on the broadside. Moreover, if disabled while fighting up-stream they would simply drift down out of range. Fort Henry was just such a position as they were best fitted to attack, lying on a low bank, without the advantages of plunging fire which the works at Columbus and at Fort Donelson enjoyed.

Tilghman, with defective guns and ammunition, with not enough gunners to man what he had, and with the water already rising into the lower batteries, kept up his fight with the gunboats for two hours, until he felt sure that the garrison was safely away, and then surrendered.

While not to compare with the results of the fighting at Fort Donelson ten days later, the capture of Fort Henry was of great value to the Union. It opened the wide Tennessee to their flotillas and made it possible for boats to move up at once, burn the bridge of the Ohio & Memphis Railroad at Danville and so cut Johnston's left away from his center, and pass on clear across the state of Tennessee into Alabama. It gave great reputation to the gunboats; not so much, as yet, to the commander of the troops.

His chance was to come at Fort Donelson. Waiting until the twelfth to give the fleet time to go down the Tennessee to the Ohio and up the Cumberland to Fort Donelson, Grant started his advance across the neck of land separating the two forts. Besides the two divisions which were at Fort Henry, he now had a third under General Lew Wallace, a distinguished civilian·

soldier, better known to a later generation as the author of
Ben-Hur. Included in Wallace's division was a brigade of
Buell's troops, which he had contributed on a hurried request
from Halleck.

Fort Donelson, in many ways, may be considered the critical
event of the Civil War. Its direct military results were immense: the opening of much of Kentucky and half of Tennessee,
including its capital, to the Union armies; the capture of nearly
one-third of Johnston's effective force; the establishment of a
firm base at Nashville, from which to push further conquests
in the South. The moral and political effects were perhaps even
greater. Deep discouragement in the South, in contrast with the
undue elation after Manassas; a new start and a fresh grip on
the war for the North, were some of the consequences. Another was the emergence of the man who, of all others, was to
win the confidence of the President and the nation to the point
where, all other means having failed, they were willing to support him in that last terrible campaign of attrition in Virginia
which, whatever its losses, did finally end the war.

Fort Donelson was a large work, much too large to be
occupied by the garrison available for it, as was the case with
so many of the early Confederate fortresses. Every engineer
sent to lay out a place of defense seems to have aspired to create
a "Gibraltar of the West"—all of which sooner or later fell.
The fort and its outworks occupied high bluffs on the left bank
of the Cumberland, including within its trace the little town of
Dover. Up-stream, to the southeast, were the important towns
of Clarksville, where the vital railroad line crossed the river,
and of Nashville, the capital of Tennessee, which in many ways
was to the West what Richmond was to the East, the major
depot of supplies and center of manufacture of arms, ammunition and equipment.

Johnston, all this while, had held his position about Bowling
Green, fortifying the line of the Barren River. He had never
had one-third the men he needed, or was popularly believed
to have, and had been unable to get more even after the most
strenuous exertions and private appeals to the Governors of the

states west of the mountains. For military reasons he had to keep his inadequacy secret, and the South behind felt no alarm with him on guard.

Johnston's was an extreme case of the situation in which the whole Confederate Government found itself during the first year of the war, and especially after the dazzling victory at Manassas. The government's labors to arm and fit itself for war were immense, its success considerable—but it was never able to take its people into confidence and tell them its difficulties and real achievements. This secretive policy of the government, secret sessions of Congress from which even the Departments had secrets, may have kept information of Confederate weak spots from the hands of the enemy; certainly they damped and chilled the earnestness and devotion which a fuller knowledge of the situation would have called out.

Beauregard had come out from the East to help, stopping on the way in Nashville, where Father Abram Ryan and the "Hero of Manassas" made public addresses of encouragement at the Masonic auditorium, and had been sent on westward to take command of operations in West Tennessee and Kentucky. Johnston was left alone with his problem.

He has been criticized for putting as many men as he did into the defense of Fort Donelson, and again for not putting more. The truth was that he had two armies to watch, either one equal or superior to his own, and both in position to advance against Nashville by converging lines, Grant following the Cumberland, and Buell the railroad from Louisville. To keep all his force at Bowling Green would have exposed Nashville and his rear to Grant; to have thrown everything into Donelson would have let Buell into Nashville, and between Johnston and the South.

His great mistake—and it was a mistake—was in his choice of commanders for the eighteen thousand men who were marched into Donelson to meet the advance of Grant's divisions. Brigadier-General John B. Floyd, one of the ex-Governors whose disagreements had so troubled Lee in Western Virginia, was first in rank of the three brigadiers; Gideon J. Pillow, veteran of the Mexican War and commander of the Tennessee forces while the state was in transition between the Union and the Confederacy, was second; Simon B. Buckner, West Point graduate and commander of Kentucky's forces during the time of neutrality of that state, was third. There was a great deal of confusion and uncertainty about the command, as well as about many other things.

Opposed to this divided counsel was a single-minded and direct man, tenacious to the last degree, filled with courageous common sense. Grant was forty. His life, so far, had been little better than a failure. Graduate of West Point and veteran of nearly all the battles of the Mexican War, he had retired from the Army and drifted through various unsuccessful sorts of business in the years before 1861. At the outbreak of the war, rescued from obscurity by the interest of the powerful Congressman Elihu B. Washburne, chairman of the Military Affairs Committee of the House, he had been given opportunity and was showing himself equal to it.

The attack on Fort Donelson began on the morning of February thirteenth. Troops on the landward side advanced through the thick woods and steep ravines toward the abatis outside the outer line of fortifications, Smith's division on the left, nearest the river below the fort; Wallace's in the center; McClernand's well over to the right, near the river above the fort. No effective resistance to this complete investment of the fort on the landward side was offered that day.

The next day, having landed additional reenforcements down the river, the gunboats steamed up to the fort. Remembering the easy victory at Fort Henry, the gunboats, whose metal greatly outweighed that of the fort, stood boldly up bow-on, to within a quarter of a mile of the water batteries; the batteries, elevated above the level of the stream, replied savagely and effectively. Foote's flag-ship and two others of the ironclads were disabled, and drifted off down-stream. The other boats were driven back, battered.

That night, February fourteenth, a sudden blizzard howled down from the northwest. Weather like spring was succeeded by a biting wind, with spits and flurries of sleet and snow—a bitter, freezing night. During the night, with the fleet out of the way, the Confederate commanders in council of war determined on a sortie, to open the road to Charlotte and Nashville and so to secure the escape of the garrison.

Early the next morning Pillow's division, holding the side of the fort up-stream and toward Nashville, moved out to the attack against McClernand's wing. The fighting was obstinate and protracted, but by a little after noon McClernand's men had been driven well away from the river and thrust back against Wallace's troops, who had themselves been forced to retire somewhat. The road to Charlotte and Nashville was open—but no plans had been made to use the open road when it was ready. Finally, Pillow's men were moved back within the works, no better off than they had been in the morning, while over on Buckner's side of the fort, the veteran C. F. Smith, in the confusion, had managed to effect a dangerous lodgment.

Expecting no battle, Grant had gone down-stream eight miles to the landing to which the gunboats had retired for repairs. After his conference with the wounded Foote on the flag-ship *St. Louis* he started back to the army. As he drew near, he passed stragglers from the divisions of McClernand and Wallace, drifting to the rear, and was met by an officer of his staff, "white with fear for the safety of the National troops," as Grant afterward wrote.

In that moment appeared the quality in Grant that made him. He dispatched Foote that, in his absence, there had been a "terrible conflict . . . which has demoralized a portion of my command, and I think the enemy much more so." Others might be demoralized, but not the imperturbable Grant. His common sense told him that not all the difficulties were on his side, and that aggressive counter-attacks by the army, supported by shell thrown from the fleet, would sustain the morale of his forces.

Darkness fell early on that bitter February night. Within the fort, at midnight, the three desponding brigadiers gathered in council. Outside, scattered about over the frozen fields where Pillow's men had fought that day, were wounded of both sides, freezing to death or, perhaps, dragging themselves to the remains of old campfires that the high north winds had fanned again into flame. It was the sight of these fires that had convinced the Generals that the way of escape to Nashville was again closed. Their power of resistance was at an end. The fort and its garrison must be surrendered. So ran their thoughts.

Colonel Forrest, commanding cavalry, was called to the conference. As to the state of affairs on the road toward Nashville, he wanted to *know*. Scouts sent out reported that there was a way open, but that it would require wading the back waters of a creek. Medical officers declared that the exposure would be fatal. This was still early in the war, it will be remembered, before it had been found out how much a Confederate soldier— or a Union one, either, for that matter—could stand.

General Floyd decided to surrender fort and garrison, but not himself. He had been Secretary of War under Buchanan, and had been indicted in Washington for alleged misuse of government funds. The partisan indictment had been *nolle prossed*, but General Floyd felt that in the then state of feeling in the North his capture would entail other than military consequences. He passed the command on to General Pillow, who hotly protested against surrender at all, but passed the command on to the third in rank, Buckner. Floyd and Pillow, together with Floyd's Virginia brigade, escaped across the river in steamboats before dawn and marched away to Nashville and safety; Buckner, believing that surrender was inevitable and escape impossible, accepted his responsibility as a commander and remained in the fort to surrender the garrison—all but Colonel Forrest, who marched his regiment and several hundred soldiers that attached themselves to him across the frozen creek, toward Nashville and his future fame.

In the darkness, a Confederate bugle sounded the parley. Request was sent to Grant for his terms of capitulation. "Unconditional surrender" was the firm reply—and the hitherto unknown U. S. Grant became, in the northern newspapers, "Unconditional Surrender" Grant—a bit of luck for which he could thank not the parents who had christened him Hiram Ulysses, but the registrar at West Point who had mistakenly entered his name as Ulysses Simpson.

The meeting at Fort Donelson was for Grant and Buckner a strange sort of reunion. They had been cadets together at West Point, and friends. Eight years before the war, learning that Grant was stranded in New York after his resignation from the Army, Buckner had hunted him out and advanced funds to take him home.

The surrender was made during the morning of the sixteenth, fort and garrison, some fourteen thousand men, with rifles and guns and other supplies that the Confederacy could not spare. No such victory had been won anywhere by Union arms, no such blow suffered by the Confederacy.

During the days that Donelson was besieged Johnston had been slowly falling back from Bowling Green toward Nashville, with Buell cautiously pushing on behind him. On Saturday, the fifteenth, the day of the nearly-successful sortie, Johnston had reached Edgefield, across the Cumberland from Nashville, and there had been cheered by premature news of a great victory. Within a few hours came the later news of the surrender. With the army he had, Johnston could not defend Nashville, and he could get no other troops. With the fall of Donelson, the whole of Middle Tennessee was opened. For Johnston there was nothing but retreat.

On a gloomy day of cold rain, Sunday, the sixteenth, his little army marched through the streets of Nashville, passing out to the southeast toward Murfreesboro, and leaving a small rear-guard to remove supplies. Nashville, which had been proudly confident, went into a panic. Every one who could, left the city; mobs took possession of the streets, pillaged the government storehouses before an opportunity was had to remove the stores to the South. Buell was a week in coming—in spite of hourly rumors of the arrival of his troops—and during that week, even with inadequate transportation, a great quantity of guns and ammunition, of meat and flour, shoes and blankets, was shipped south, but millions of dollars' worth were left behind, to the mob or to the Union army.

On the twenty-third Nashville passed into the possession of the Union arms, so to remain until the end of the war. With the capital of Tennessee in its hands, the United States organized a military government for the state, with Andrew Johnson, former Governor of Tennessee, and the only southern Senator who supported the Union, as the Military Governor. Johnson's power and zeal in that office, and his courage, were to win for him election as Vice-President under Lincoln, in 1864.

CHAPTER VII

GOVERNMENT, PROVISIONAL AND "PERMANENT"

ON THE birthday of George Washington and at the foot of his equestrian statue in Richmond the "permanent" government of the Confederacy was inaugurated, in 1862, all that had gone before having been merely "provisional."

The northern government had planned, also, a celebration of the birthday of Washington by a "grand advance" of all the armies in the field, as directed by the President's General War Order No. 1. However, the western armies had already advanced, before the patriotic date set by President Lincoln, while the eastern were not yet ready to make any move so that the only important notice of the birthday of the great Virginian whom both sides claimed as exemplar and inspiration, was the ceremony at Richmond, in which the Confederate President and Vice-President were installed in their "permanent" term of six years, of which they were to serve little more than half.

The War between the States has for us to-day almost totally eclipsed the nearly forgotten government that waged it for the South. Back of the figures in uniform, bearded and of venerable seeming, was a government of men, as well as of principles— alive, charged with political conflict and personal friction, burdened with immense and insoluble problems of policy, civil and military, foreign and domestic.

The members of this government, so remote to us now, marched in solemn procession from the hall of the House of Delegates of Virginia, just after noon of February 22, 1862, through spits of rain and snow, across Capitol Park to the noble statue of Washington, a representation of which was to become the center of the Great Seal of the Confederate States of America. The procession was headed, of course, by the Grand Marshal and his aides, followed by the band and by members of the Joint Committee of Congress on Arrangements.

Behind them marched President Davis, attended by the new President *pro. tem.* of the Senate, R. M. T. Hunter, of Virginia, who had served in the Senate of the United States with Mr. Davis. Behind the stately President and Senator Hunter came the frail Vice-President, Alexander Hamilton Stephens, weight less than one hundred pounds, with a voice weak and piping, with his strength and power in intellect and character. With the Vice-President was Thomas S. Bocock, of Virginia, Speaker of the House of Representatives.

The Cabinet of the Confederacy came next in the procession. There was one vacancy at the moment. Senator Hunter, who had become Secretary of State in the summer of 1861, when the ardent and impatient Toombs fell out with the President and left that place to raise and command a Georgia brigade, had just resigned to represent Virginia in the Senate, and no successor had been named.

The immensely industrious Judah P. Benjamin, able, versatile, politic, urbane, was still Secretary of War. He had been Attorney-General, the first in the Cabinet. When the first Secretary of War, Leroy Pope Walker of Alabama, resigned Mr. Benjamin had been called to fill that most important place. On March 18, 1862, he was to become the third Secretary of State, a post which he was to fill until the end of the Confederacy. By virtue of his position, and even more by virtue of his abilities, he was to be recognized as the outstanding member of the Cabinet. He was an easy worker, rapid in his mastery of facts and conclusions, facile in his judgments, suave and slightly smiling, qualities that excited a certain distrust among many of the more serious and determined of his associates. He knew President Davis and the President knew him—they had served together in the Senate of the United States—and almost from the beginning of the government at Montgomery Mr. Benjamin had become the President's chief reliance in the Cabinet.

Of English Jewish parentage, born on the British island of St. Thomas in the West Indies in 1811, reared in Charleston, South Carolina, and early admitted to the bar in New Orleans, the public career of Judah Benjamin was to carry him through the Senate of the United States, into the Cabinet of the Confederacy—and, at the end of everything, into a tossing open boat sailing from the coast of Florida to the Bahamas, and so to England. There, being fifty-five years of age, he began his fourth and final career. He took up in a foreign country the law that he had laid down for the stirring politics of the 'fifties and the war of the 'sixties. Within a year he was called to the Bar, soon to become Queen's Counsel and the leading authority in England on the law of Sales of Personal Property. At the age of seventy-three, he died in Paris, a British subject and an acknowledged leader of the Bar of Great Britain.

Mr. Benjamin was the second of six men to hold the portfolio of Secretary of War during the four years. When he left the post, less than a month after the inauguration, he was succeeded by General George W. Randolph, of Virginia, who served during eight months of increasing difficulties until November, 1862. When Randolph resigned Major-General Gustavus W. Smith was recalled from a long sick-leave to hold an interim appointment for three days. On November 20, 1862, James A. Seddon, member of the Provisional Congress from Virginia, was called to that most difficult Department. Mr. Seddon and President Davis worked together for more than two years, a longer time than the combined services of the five other Secretaries of War, but finally, in the last days of the Confederacy, he resigned and was succeeded by Major-General John C. Breckinridge, who had been Senator from Kentucky, Vice-President of the United States, a Democratic nominee for the presidency, and a fighting Major-General in the Confederate service.

The Secretary of the Treasury, Christopher G. Memminger, an orderly, precise Charleston lawyer, was in the group. Mr. Memminger was to hold his trying position until July of 1864, when he was to release an almost empty Treasury drowning in "Confederate money" to the keeping of George A. Trenholm, of the great Charleston banking firm.

Thomas Bragg of Alabama, who had succeeded Mr. Benjamin as Attorney-General, was in the Cabinet group also. Mr.

Bragg was to be succeeded in office by Thomas H. Watts, of the same state, and, after Mr. Watts' election as Governor of Alabama, by George Davis, of North Carolina.

Two members of the Cabinet on Inauguration Day had been members since the beginning, and were to remain in the same offices until the end—Stephen R. Mallory, of Florida, who brought to the work of Secretary of the Navy a knowledge gathered during his service as Chairman of the Naval Affairs Committee of the House of Representatives of the United States, and John H. Reagan, of Texas, the Postmaster-General.

Mr. Mallory showed considerable insight into the naval problems of the Confederacy by his ready approval of plans to convert into an ironclad ship of war a frigate, the *Merrimac*, which had been sunk at the Norfolk Navy-Yard. Judge Reagan, a native Tennesseean who had gone to Texas when that state was an independent republic, had already served on the bench and in the Congress of the United States. In the course of his long life—he lived well into this century—he was to become after the war chairman of the Committee on Interstate Commerce of the United States Senate, one of the leaders in the formation of the Interstate Commerce Commission, and, finally, once more to resign an important post with the government of the United States to go to the service of Texas when he conceived that duty called him to take the chairmanship of the newly organized State Railway Commission in 1891.

In the Confederate Cabinet it was Mr. Secretary Reagan's trying, indeed hopeless, task to organize a mail service for a territory of more than seven hundred thousand square miles, beset with enemies, with slight means of carriage and failing revenues. The large difficulties are easy to see, but there were many small and aggravating ones not so clearly evident. Even a thing seeming so simple as the supply of postage stamps presented to the "scattered agricultural communities" of the Confederacy, cut off from the world, a problem that was never solved.

There were, of course, United States stamps in every post-office in the South when the states seceded, but the postmasters, who were taken into Confederate service, were ordered to settle up their final accounts with the United States Post-Office, and return to them all unused postage. Meanwhile, the country being without so commonplace a necessity as stamps, the mail of the Confederacy moved upon the payment of money postage, that payment being noted by the local postmaster by endorsement on the envelope, or by use of a local stamp.

With every effort to find somewhere in the South engravers, die-makers, ink, paper, presses, mucilage and the technical skill necessary to produce stamps, it was not until the middle of October, 1861, that even an inferior lithographed and imperforated stamp was turned out. By that time the need of them, reported the Richmond *Dispatch*, "seriously taxed the public endurance." On October sixteenth, the first of the new five-cent Confederate stamps, "quite handsomely gotten up, of a green colour, and ornamented with a likeness of President Davis," as the *Examiner* reported, were sold in the Richmond Post-Office, but the supply was still most scant.

Agents had been dispatched to Europe to contract for and to bring back stamps and the plates, dies, paper and ink to manufacture them. In the same week in which the permanent government was inaugurated, the first shipment under this order was received—two million, one hundred and fifty thousand five-cent stamps made in London, bearing the likeness of President Davis, brought in by a blockade runner. There were other stamps imported, many of them, but millions more were intercepted and they, with their plates, destroyed by the blockading squadrons, or thrown into the sea. The making of stamps continued at Richmond, also at Augusta, Georgia, and, finally, in 1864, at Columbia, South Carolina. The Columbia plant, and the stamp plates, all of which had been sent there from Richmond for safe-keeping, were destroyed in the burning of the South Carolina capital city at the time of its occupation by General Sherman, in February, 1865, and there were no more Confederate stamps.

Besides the stamps bearing the portrait of President Davis, other issues and denominations showed the likeness of George

Washington, of Thomas Jefferson, of Andrew Jackson, and of John C. Calhoun—a conjunction of the living President with the departed statesmen of the South which was more than a little irritating to the political opposition to Mr. Davis, especially as his own portrait was used on the denomination most in demand for the mailing of ordinary letters. Of all sorts, however, there were never enough stamps to meet the need, and a practise of cutting them diagonally into halves, so that one twenty-cent might make two ten-cent stamps, for instance, became common, although the Post-Office Department warned that mail bearing such stamps would be sent to the dead letter office.

In spite of annoying difficulties with stamps, and the graver difficulties with transportation, the post-office did manage to handle the mails, and especially the soldier mail for the Virginia armies. Mail day was an event, a great event, in camp or the field. Each brigade, usually, had its own mail carrier, mounted, who carried letters from the brigade for dispatch at the nearest post-office, and there sought letters for soldiers of his unit. These were addressed merely to the military command of the soldier, not to any post-office, so that the mail orderly would finally find, at some office not too far from the army, all the mail for his outfit. The necessity of hunting for this post-office and the difficulties of travel made the arrival of the mail carrier with soldiers' letters an uncertain affair, but whenever he came, night or day, he was welcomed. Mail was sometimes distributed in this way on the march, as well as in quarters, and even just as the command was going into battle.

In the western armies, which swept over hundreds of miles in their advances and retreats, the mail service was less complete and satisfactory than that in the armies of the East, whose movements were in a more circumscribed zone.

Burdened with these and a thousand other difficulties and responsibilities, military, naval, diplomatic, political, administrative, President Davis stood at the base of the equestrian statue of Washington, facing an audience composed of members of his Cabinet, of members of the Congress, of Governors and Judges, of officers of the Army and Navy, of "the reverend clergy," the corporate authorities of the city of Richmond, and of the State of Virginia, of "the Masons and other benevolent societies," the "Members of the press," and, finally, of "Citizens generally," and there received the oath of office and delivered his second inaugural address.

Already, as the Confederacy was but a year old and its permanent government was just being born, there were signs of sharp conflict within the civil government. There were "national" men within the Confederacy, President Davis being the head and chief; there were state's rights men, just as obdurate in asserting the rights of Georgia or North Carolina or Alabama against a government at Richmond as they had been against the "Lincoln government" at Washington. There were critics in the Congress and among the press,—sharp critics, bitter, sometimes unfair, as political critics are apt to be.

Through the summer of 1861 there had been a deal of criticism of the government's "do-nothing" policy, criticism which the government had answered with Manassas. At the November elections the government had fared well, the President was elected for his permanent term without opposition, and with a friendly Congress. But in the days before the inauguration rumors of disaster had flown in Richmond, though there had been no definite reports made public.

And now, in the President's second inaugural address, there were ominous words: ". . . After a series of successes and victories, which covered our arms with glory, we have recently met with serious disasters."

The disaster uppermost in the mind of the President was, no doubt, the fall of Fort Donelson. That it was a military loss of the gravest consequence, involving the breaking of the Confederate line in the West and the loss of half of Tennessee, was obvious. That it was to have diplomatic results almost as serious was not yet apparent.

Considering the handicaps under which they worked, the diplomatic labors of the Confederacy in Europe had rather prospered in 1861. At the outset, the European nations, not acquainted with the dual and Federal character of the Constitution of the United States, had accepted the thought that the Southern States were mere revolting provinces. That fact and the difficulties of communication—news from southern sources usually reached the European capitals from two weeks to a month later than that from the North—made the work of the Confederate Commissioners peculiarly difficult.

One of the very first acts of the Confederate Government at Montgomery, a month before hostilities opened at Fort Sumter, had been to dispatch a Commission of three to Europe—William Lowndes Yancey, Pierre A. Rost and A. Dudley Mann. They were authorized to negotiate treaties of friendship, commerce and navigation—a delusive hope—and especially to press upon Great Britain the thought that the Confederacy was to be a nation devoted to the principle of free trade and low tariffs, with a "delicate allusion" to the probability of a failure of the cotton supply should the newly formed Confederate States become engaged in an extensive war.

The nation which they went abroad to represent was one of seven states. By the middle of the summer of 1861 it had grown to eleven states—as was duly related to them in the dispatches of Secretary of State Toombs—and then, in Secretary Hunter's first dispatch, came the glorious news of Manassas. The Commissioners, informally and unofficially, interviewed Lord John Russell and Monsieur Thouvenel, the British and French Foreign Secretaries, and pressed upon them not only the constitutional aspects of the Confederacy but also the point that the blockade of the long southern coast was not "effective" within the meaning of the Declaration of Paris of 1856, and was for that reason not binding on neutrals.

By the end of the summer, however, Mr. Yancey had resigned. Being an unofficial Commissioner of an unrecognized government gave but small scope for the play of his great power, oratory. He came home to become one of Alabama's Senators and for the short remainder of his life, one of Davis' bitter critics. It was decided to "disunite" the other two Commissioners, send one to Spain and one to Belgium, and supply their places at London and Paris with new Commissioners.

Then it was that diplomatic fortune smiled for the Confederacy. The new Commissioners chosen were James M. Mason, of Virginia, who had been in the Senate with President Davis and Secretary Hunter, destined to London, and John Slidell, of Louisiana, Judah Benjamin's colleague in the Senate of the United States, accredited to Paris.

In the first days of October the new Commissioners were at Charleston, waiting an opportunity to run the blockade. Their first plan was to use the Confederate cruiser *Nashville*, then in Charleston harbor being fitted out for her work as a commerce destroyer, but it seemed wiser to use a small steamer, the *Gordon*, privately owned. The blockading squadron had been strengthened, but at one o'clock in the morning of October 12, 1861, the little steamer, with Senators Mason and Slidell aboard, slipped away from the Charleston docks, silently steamed across the bar, and in a driving rain and a northwest wind, made her way southward, hugging as close to the shore as she dared.

The *Gordon*, safely past the blockade, sailed to Nassau, in the Bahamas, later to become the most regular of intermediate ports and transfer points for blockade runners. At that early date, however, there was no steamer connection with England, but it was learned that a regular mail steamer was to leave St. Thomas for Britain. The *Gordon*, starting for St. Thomas, ran low in coal and put into Cardenas, on the north coast of Cuba, whence the Commissioners made their way to Havana to board the next steamer for St. Thomas.

The Commissioners and their party embarked on the British mail steamer *Trent* on November 7, 1861. The next day, as the *Trent* made her way through the Bahama Passage, two hundred and forty miles east of Havana, the United States naval vessel *San Jacinto*, waiting in the middle of the channel, fired two shots across her bow, brought her to, put an armed party on board and over the strong objection of Captain Moir, took off the Commissioners, their secretaries and their papers and dispatches.

Captain Charles Wilkes, the naval officer who had conceived and executed this plan for the violation of British neutrality at sea, took his prisoners north to lodge them in Fort Warren, in Boston Harbor, and to become himself the popular hero of the day. Captain Wilkes doubtless enjoyed the glowing praises for his vigorous act, but he had raised up a problem for his superiors that brought the United States to the verge of war with Great Britain.

There was no question of the British rights in the matter, nor of the intensity of feeling aroused by their violation. On the other hand, the government at Washington was faced with the fact that to discipline Wilkes or disavow what he had done would bring offense to the zealous abolitionists in the country, and to the large section of press and public which traditionally found its delight in twisting the tail of the British lion. Meanwhile the Confederate Commissioners, worth far more to the Confederacy as prisoners than they would have been in Europe, remained in custody in Boston, while President Lincoln and Secretary of State Seward, adopting the principle of "one war at a time," worked their way out of the trouble into which their too-zealous Captain had brought them.

It was not until 1866 that the trans-Atlantic cable was finally completed and in working order. That fact, with its possibilities of delay in transmission of dispatches and demands, was the saving point in the difficult diplomatic situation of the North. It gave Secretary Seward time to wear the thing out, while popular enthusiasm cooled, and finally, on New Year's Day of 1862, quietly to deliver the Commissioners and their Secretaries to the British corvette *Rinaldo* at Provincetown, Massachusetts, to complete the voyage to England interrupted by Captain Wilkes two months before.

The *Trent* matter was settled before the time of the inauguration of the permanent Confederate Government, but the rancors it had aroused were not then all cleared up, and there was still a strong belief on the part of the Commissioners in London and Paris that either the British or the French Governments, or both in concert, could be brought to declare the blockade of the southern coasts raised. To accomplish this result they called for lists of vessels which had successfully run the blockade--

there were some hundreds of them at various ports and various times—and hoped for reports of victories.   Instead came the report of the fall of Fort Henry and Fort Donelson, and the breaking of the Confederate line in the West.

From Paris, Mr. Slidell wrote on February 26, 1862, that "the affairs of Somerset, Fort Henry and Roanoke Island (the latter yet wanting confirmation) are subjects of great exultation among our enemies here, and produce among some of our friends corresponding depression, a feeling which I do not share, but which can not fail to exercise for the time an unfavorable influence on public opinion."

On March tenth, referring to the "disastrous affair at Fort Donelson," he wrote, "I need not say how unfavorable an influence these defeats, following in such quick succession, have produced in public sentiment.   If not soon counterbalanced by some decisive success of our arms, we may not only bid adieu to all hopes of seasonable recognition, but must expect that the declaration of the inefficiency of the blockade, to which I had looked forward with great confidence at no distant day, will be indefinitely postponed."

Mr. Mason, from London, wrote that the "late reverses at Fort Henry and Fort Donelson have had an unfortunate effect upon the minds of our friends here, as was naturally to be expected."

Never again, not even at the end of the brilliant summer campaigns of 1862, was the Confederacy to have such diplomatic prospects as it enjoyed during and just after the *Trent* affair, and before the breaking of the main line in the West had its "unfavorable influence."   The Confederate Commissioners in those days could still claim, and with some show of reason, that the blockade was not "effective" in the sense of the international understanding of such matters—a sense that was to be widely stretched by the United States, which was exercising the right of blockade on a scale never before undertaken.   Later, after the blockade tightened its strangling hold, the Commissioners spoke less of "raising the blockade" and more of recognition on the part of foreign governments of the independence of the Confed-

erate States, based on their right to assert and their ability to
maintain it.

Throughout the war, and until after Appomattox, the Commissioners remained in Europe, in London, Paris, Brussels, for
a time at the Vatican, in Madrid and St. Petersburg, sometimes
hopeful, more often disheartened, finally despairing.   Theirs
was a trying task—in communication with their government
only by tedious and roundabout routes; without official status
abroad, confronted by difficult questions of neutrality and diplomacy; always hoping for the final and decisive military success that never came.

And always, far underneath the current of their negotiations, never to be brought near the surface until almost the
very end, after everything was hopeless, was the hidden obstacle—the fact that the Confederacy was committed to the
maintenance of an institution which the world had grown beyond.

CHAPTER VIII

THE WINTER'S LOSSES

WHEN the permanent Confederate Government was inaugurated, the main line of defense in the West had already been broken in the center at the Tennessee and the Cumberland Rivers; and the whole scheme of defense was gone. Nashville was to fall on the day after the inauguration at Richmond; Columbus was isolated, exposed to attack by superior forces from river and land. The remote right flank, in the mountains on the upper reaches of the Cumberland, had already been turned by the defeat variously known as Somerset, Fishing Creek, Mill Springs or Logan's Crossroads. Nothing remained to Albert Sidney Johnston but to establish a new defensive line, call Crittenden in from East Tennessee, draw Beauregard and Polk back, gather what strength he could to meet the Union advance.

The line of the Memphis & Charleston Railroad, running eastward from the Mississippi River at Memphis through northern Mississippi and Alabama, was obviously the next place where a serious stand could be made. Corinth, near the northeastern corner of the state of Mississippi, was chosen as the place of concentration. The Mobile & Ohio Railroad, crossing the Memphis & Charleston at right angles there, made it possible to bring back the troops from the advanced position of Columbus, to bring up reenforcements from the South, to move in those from the West, who would cross the Mississippi at Memphis. Johnston was right when he picked Corinth as the strategic center for the Confederacy in the West.

While Johnston was slowly marching southward to a crossing of the Tennessee River at Decatur, in northern Alabama, and then west to Corinth, Polk was compelled to evacuate Columbus and fall back along the railroad, first to Jackson, where Beauregard had his headquarters, and then to Corinth.

Halleck, at St. Louis, prompt to take advantage of the victories at Fort Henry and Fort Donelson, wired Washington asking to be put in command of all the operations in the West. "Make Buell, Grant and Pope major-generals of volunteers and give me command in the West. I ask this in return for Donelson and Henry." His request was granted, and the western operations were reorganized under one head. Buell, at Nashville, was to form the left of the grand advance into the South; Grant, operating up the Tennessee River, was to be the center; Major-General John Pope, who had been on small expeditions in northwestern Missouri, was to command the right, advancing down the Mississippi.

While this reorganization was going on in the main western theater, Halleck also had operations under way in the trans-Mississippi region. Major-General Samuel R. Curtis, who had been put in command of the four divisions of Union troops in southwestern Missouri, began his advance against the Confederate forces almost at the same time that Grant started toward the river forts. Having neither rivers nor railroads on which to move his advance was necessarily slow, and it was not until March seventh and eighth that the decisive battle of Pea Ridge or Elkhorn Tavern was fought in the Ozark region of northwestern Arkansas.

On the Confederate side there were again Price and Mc-Culloch, men of strong individuality and decided differences, but both now commanded by the new Major-General whom President Davis had sent out to take command of the region, Earl Van Dorn. Van Dorn was a West Point regular, with Mexican War service, and a brilliant record as a cavalry Colonel in Texas. McCulloch had been a hunter and trapper, had served under Sam Houston in the wars for the independence of Texas, had been Captain of a company of Texas Rangers. Price, a Virginian by birth, had commanded Missouri troops in the Mexican War and had been a most popular and respected Governor of his state. His troops were personally devoted to him—they had, really, no government to which to attach themselves—and followed him under the greatest difficulties as to arms, equipment, training and discipline. In this same Confederate Army were two other leaders of extraordinary individuality, followed by commands unique in the war: Brigadier-General Albert Pike, of Arkansas, orator, author and philosopher, and Stand Watie, the only Indian who became a Confederate Brigadier, with their force of Choctaw, Chickasaw, Cherokee, Creek and Seminole Indians.

On March sixth Curtis was drawn up in a strong defensive position near Elkhorn Tavern, or Pea Ridge, covering his line of retreat to Springfield. During that day and night Van Dorn, with Price's wing of the army, passed clear around his position to attack from the rear, while McCulloch and the Indian brigade moved up to attack on the right flank. Delayed by obstructed roads, the turning column failed to attack at the same time that McCulloch struck.

The fighting of the seventh was a mixed-up affair, isolated charges and counter-charges, flankers outflanked, all manner of confusion. Early in the afternoon McCulloch was killed. So was McIntosh, his second in command. The column was broken and driven from the field. Part of it made its way around the Union army to rejoin Van Dorn and Price, who had won considerable success that day, but had not been able to finish the job. During the night Sigel reenforced Curtis. In obstinate fighting on the eighth Van Dorn and Price were driven from the field. Serious Confederate operations in Missouri were at an end.

In these same early weeks of 1862, while great events were forward in the West and while McClellan continued his work of organizing his armies, pondering how best he might come at Richmond, the blockade of the seacoast was considerably strengthened.

On January eleventh a fleet of eighty vessels, ships of war, transports, supply ships, sailed at night from Fortress Monroe under secret and sealed orders. On board the transports were three brigades of excellent soldiers, twelve thousand men, commanded by Major-General Ambrose E. Burnside, a gallant officer who achieved much for the Union but who will be re-

membered most for the horror of Fredericksburg, and for the
distinctive style of his whiskers. It was a fine expedition,
well fitted and well commanded, and it managed to get
started without everybody in the United States knowing its
destination—that, in itself being no small achievement in those
early days of the war. Outside the Capes, the sealed orders
were opened, and the fleet stood away for Hatteras Inlet, to
complete the conquest of the inland waters of the North Carolina Sounds.

Confederate batteries on Roanoke Island, lying in the
narrow Croatan Sound between Pamlico and Albemarle Sounds,
were captured in gallant style on February eighth. The Confederate commander in this district was General Henry A. Wise,
the other ex-Governor of Virginia who had been so intractable
in the mountains during the autumn before. General Wise's
relations with General Huger, at Norfolk, in whose department
he was, and with Flag-Officer Lynch, commanding the Confederate "Mosquito Fleet" in those waters, were decidedly less than
cordial.

In connection with this disaster at Roanoke Island the
anti-administration forces in the Confederate Congress made
their first strong attack on the President. After an unsuccessful effort to have the House vote that Secretary of War
Benjamin had "not the confidence of the people of the Confederate States nor of the army," a special committee to investigate the affair was appointed. Its report, made after Benjamin
had become Secretary of State, laid the blame for the loss of
the position on the officers over General Wise, including the
"late Secretary of War"—who, in spite of all his brilliant
abilities, or perhaps because of them, was not popular with the
Congress.

Two days after the capture of Roanoke Island the Union
fleet steamed north across Albemarle Sound and captured Elizabeth City; and on February twelfth took Edenton.

A month after Roanoke Island, troops were landed below
New Bern, the most important of the Sound ports. After a
sharp fight on March fourteenth, Burnside captured that place,

and secured control of the terminus of the only railroad leading from the Sounds into the interior. On April twenty-sixth, Fort Macon, an ancient brickwork covering the inlet to Beaufort, North Carolina, surrendered after a siege of more than a month. With its fall the entire network of waters and inlets passed into Union control, leaving in Confederate hands only the port of Wilmington, on the Cape Fear River, destined to be the last southern port to fall.

Far more threatening was the position of the Union forces in Port Royal harbor. The seacoast between Charleston and Savannah is a maze of islands, surrounded by a network of channels and inlets, many of them navigable by light-draft vessels. Working in and among the islands, and through these intricate channels, it was possible for the Union forces to put troops and guns on the Savannah River above the defenses at the mouth of the stream, and into Charleston Harbor, inside the channel defenses. Moreover, the railroad from Savannah to Charleston was exposed to attack by advances up the Coosawhatchie, the Combahee, the Edisto and other coastal rivers.

General Lee, returned from his forlorn hope in West Virginia, was sent on another difficult and thankless task. He was in a cavalry regiment when the war opened but his training and experience had been in the engineers, wherefore he was given the task of so fortifying the various inlets and islands that inferior forces could hold them against the advances that might come at any point. It was done with good judgment and fair success. While Fort Pulaski, holding the mouth of the Savannah River, was captured on April 11, 1862, the cities of Charleston and Savannah, and the railroad between them, remained in Confederate hands until Sherman arrived from the landward side, in the very last months of the war.

Four months Lee worked on his task of fortification, still garbed in the blue uniform that he had worn in the old Army. In March, 1862, with the affairs of the Confederacy in low estate after eleven months of active hostilities, Lee was called back to Richmond, and on March thirteenth "assigned to duty at the seat of government, and, under the direction of the President, charged with the conduct of the military operations in the armies of the Confederacy."

At that time Joseph E. Johnston was in command of the army facing Washington; Stonewall Jackson, in the Valley; Magruder on the Peninsula, Huger at Norfolk; Albert Sidney Johnston, with Beauregard as second in command, in the country between the Alleghanies and the Mississippi, concentrating his forces about Corinth; Van Dorn, under Johnston, in the trans-Mississippi; Bragg, still drilling and training his forces at Pensacola, on the Gulf coast; others in command of garrisons and of outskirt operations, even as far away as Henry H. Sibley, inventor of tents and stoves that bear his name, pushing his small Confederate force on a disastrous expedition up the valley of the Rio Grande to Santa Fe. As a sort of Chief of Staff to the President, with a certain degree of responsibility for all of these armies but without any real authority over any one of them, it seemed that once more had Lee been assigned to a thankless and forlorn task.

CHAPTER IX

THE FIRST YEAR ENDS

THE first anniversary of Fort Sumter found the Confederacy in evil case.

Within the closing month of the first year of the war in the Southwest the last grip of the Confederacy on Missouri was lost; along the seacoast the blockade was tightened by the occupation of the Florida coast, except Pensacola, in March, and the sealing of the important port of Savannah by capture of Fort Pulaski at the mouth of its river early in April; in the Mississippi Valley the grand advance southward started, with Pope working down the great river itself, Grant pushing southward by steamer up the Tennessee River, and Buell marching overland from Nashville through Middle Tennessee.

In Virginia the long winter of inaction, busied with training, drill and preparation, was opening into the spring campaign which, it was confidently expected in the North, would end in the capture of Richmond and the collapse of the Confederacy.

Joseph E. Johnston, ordered back from his advanced position about Centreville and Manassas in March before the mud of the roads dried, had to leave behind him a vast store of supplies and valuable ordnance, which could not be moved.

In the same month McClellan gave his great army a practise march from Washington out to Centreville, occupied the abandoned Confederate entrenchments there, and marched back again. On March seventeenth he embarked his army on four hundred transports for the movement down the Potomac and Chesapeake Bay to the tip of the Peninsula between the York and the James Rivers, up which he hoped to make his triumphant advance to Richmond.

This movement, in one form or another, had been long in McClellan's mind. To it he had clung tenaciously, perhaps because it was not altogether favored by the President and the

Secretary of War, with whom the General-in-Chief's relations were becoming more and more difficult. Through the winter the transfer of the army had looked feasible, with the waters about the Peninsula firmly held by the fleet of the United States. But on a day in March, the eighth, just as McClellan was ready to trust his army to the waters, the strangest looking naval craft yet seen by man steamed slowly, very slowly, out from the shelter of the Confederate defenses of Norfolk and, in an afternoon, made obsolete the navies of the world.

The Union fleet securely held Hampton Roads—a noble sight, steam and sailing frigates mounting forty or fifty guns each, with towering wooden sides, stately masts, spreading spars, in appearance, except for unobtrusive smoke-stacks, not unlike the ships that had fought the War of 1812 with Great Britain. The squat and ugly *Virginia*, steaming toward them, had been just such a ship, the forty-gun steam frigate *Merrimac*, before she was burned and sunk at her berth when the Union forces abandoned the Gosport Navy-Yard in the spring of 1861. Of the *Merrimac*, though, nothing was left but the lower part of her hull, and the engines, wheezy and asthmatic before the destruc· tion of the ship and no better for having been burned and sunk. The hull, after being raised, was cut down so that the forward and after portions were awash. Amidships, ten guns were housed in a low penthouse of sloping sides covered with four inches of iron plates, backed with stout oaken timbers, and built up from the water-line to a height of seven feet above the old gun-deck. Moving on the water, she looked for all the world like a terrapin with a smoke-stack on its back. Her hull was invulnerable, as it proved, but she had two great weaknesses: her poor old engines which could get up no more than five knots speed, and her great depth of twenty-three feet.

Lieutenant John M. Brooke was awarded the honor of first suggesting the plan for such a vessel. Stephen R. Mallory, Secretary of the Navy, very promptly accepted the plans and ordered the work. Mr. Mallory knew that the *Virginia* and like vessels were the hope of the South on the water, and the only hope. To command her, he assigned Commodore Franklin

Buchanan, father of the Naval Academy at Annapolis, and one of the old Navy's distinguished officers. Second in command was Lieutenant Catesby ap R. Jones, who had superintended the placing of her armament, which included two rifles strengthened with steel bands shrunk on about the breech, a method then as novel as the ironclad itself.

About noon of March eighth, as the Union vessels swung lazily at their anchorage about Newport News and Old Point Comfort, and while workmen were still swarming over the *Virginia,* Commodore Buchanan started out for a little trial trip. As the ship steamed out of the Elizabeth River into Hampton Roads she spied the fifty-gun frigate *Congress* and the *Cumberland,* thirty guns, at anchor across the channel. The Commodore decided to make his trial trip a real trial of the theories on which the revolutionary vessel was built. He sent the workmen ashore and the crew to their battle quarters, and started across to the attack. It took nearly two hours for the slow moving *Virginia* to make her way across and plenty of time was given to receive her. The two heavy ships, a fleet of gunboats, and the shore batteries at Newport News all opened on the Confederate ironclad, without perceptible effect. The shot simply bounced from her sides and fell harmlessly into the water.

The *Virginia* passed close to the *Congress,* received a terrible broadside at close range with no material damage, poured a broadside into her, steered for the *Cumberland,* rammed her, cut a great hole in her side. She backed away, slowly turned— it took half an hour to turn the unwieldy and under-powered craft—and started for the *Congress.* The *Cumberland,* sinking fast, went down with her guns firing and the colors flying at the peak of her tall masts. The *Congress* slipped her anchor and attempted to escape, but grounded in shoal water. For an hour, in spite of ghastly losses, her crew kept up the fight with the terrible iron monster that was raking her with shell. Finally, her commander dead, she struck her colors.

In the fight with the *Congress* Commodore Buchanan was wounded. Lieutenant Jones took command and started down

the channel to meet the three heavy ships that had been anchored
about Old Point Comfort, seven miles away. They came up
to meet him, but the *St. Lawrence* and the *Roanoke*, steering too
far toward the north side of the channel to keep away from
the fire of the Confederate batteries on Sewell's Point, soon
grounded. The *Minnesota*, a sister ship of the *Merrimac* that
was, came within two miles and then went aground and stuck
fast—fortunately for herself, in water too shoal for the *Virginia*
to reach her.

The *Virginia* drew away to deep water and anchored, while
the burning *Congress* lighted up through the night the whole
broad sheet of water of the Roads, and the watching war-ships.
There seemed little doubt that the invincible *Virginia*, with
morning and the flow of the tide, would complete the destruction of the wooden fleet, beginning with the helpless *Minnesota*.

The news of the first day's battle had gone to Washington
where the President called a meeting of his Cabinet. Even
the indomitable Stanton was daunted by the news. " 'The
Merrimac,' said Stanton, 'will change the whole character of
the war: she will destroy, *seriatim*, every naval vessel; she will
lay all the cities on the seaboard under contribution. I shall
immediately recall Burnside; Port Royal must be abandoned. I
will notify the governors and municipal authorities in the North
to take instant measures to protect their harbors.' He had no
doubt, he said, that the monster was at this moment on her way
to Washington; and, looking out of the window, which commanded a view of the Potomac for many miles, 'Not unlikely,
we shall have a shell or cannon-ball from one of her guns in
the White House before we leave this room.' Mr. Seward,
usually buoyant and self-reliant, overwhelmed with the intelligence, listened in responsive sympathy to Stanton, and was
greatly depressed, as, indeed were all the members"—so wrote
Gideon Welles, Secretary of the Navy.

That was after the first day's battle. When the second
day dawned, however, and the *Virginia* started down the channel, there came forward to protect the towering *Minnesota* a
craft even lower in the water and more odd in appearance than

the *Virginia*. It was John Ericsson's *Monitor*, the "tin can on a shingle," a hull drawing but twelve feet of water, protected from the blows of rams by a wide overhang at and just below the water-line; a deck, just awash; on the deck, a revolving turret of iron, mounting heavy eleven-inch rifles; the most unseaworthy and most uncomfortable of craft, but the germ of the super-dreadnaught.

The United States Navy Department had not taken so readily to the idea of ironclads as had the Confederate, and had not acted so promptly. It was only after months of delay and rather ponderous consideration that anything had been done, and then the inventor Ericsson had received but scant encouragement. He did finish his *Monitor*, however, and it was with the greatest difficulty towed to the Chesapeake—to arrive on the night of March eighth.

The *Virginia*, steaming toward the *Minnesota*, met the *Monitor*. The vessels stood close in, fired into each other with all their might, passed, turned, passed again, still firing. For two hours the duel kept up, with no perceptible damage on either side. Lieutenant Jones, coming down into the gun-deck of the *Virginia*, inquired why some of his guns were not firing.

"Our powder is precious," answered Lieutenant Eggleston, "and after two hours' firing I find that I can do her about as much damage by snapping my thumb at her every two minutes and a half."

Determined Jones, unable to damage the *Monitor* by gunfire, backed away and attempted to ram her. The miserable old engines in the *Virginia* gave her just enough speed to bunt the *Monitor* about. Jones attempted then to board her, and with pistol and cutlass step from the deck of his ironclad back into the days of Stephen Decatur and John Paul Jones, but before the boarders could get away the *Monitor* sheered off and dropped astern.

Six hours the fight kept up, both sea monsters delivering mighty blows to no effect. Finally, as the tide was falling, the *Monitor* drew away into shoal water. The *Virginia*, drawing nearly twice as much, could not follow and withdrew to her anchorage.   The fight that revolutionized naval warfare was over.

Tactically it was a drawn fight, in its results a victory for the *Monitor*.   The blockade was saved; the *Virginia* was neutralized; it was safe for McClellan to come ahead with his army— although there was a great deal of uneasiness on the part of everybody so long as the *Virginia* was afloat and still in fighting trim.   Three times more, while the Confederates still held Norfolk, the *Virginia* steamed down to the Union fleet to seek battle with the *Monitor*, but each time the latter used her lighter draft and superior mobility to escape close contact.   There was then but one *Monitor*, and it would have been most unwise to risk her unnecessarily in battle, when her mere presence with the fleet was enough to prevent its destruction by the *Virginia*.

Finally, on the day after the evacuation of Norfolk, the *Virginia* was run ashore on Craney Island and burned; that winter, going south under tow, the *Monitor* went down in a gale off Cape Hatteras.

Relying on the *Monitor* to keep the terrible *Virginia* from getting among his four hundred transports and supply ships, McClellan moved his troops to the vicinity of Fortress Monroe, to start his slow and ponderous advance toward Richmond.

The grand advance in the West moved faster.   A week after Curtis gained his success at Pea Ridge, John Pope began to display that vigor and activity which so soon led him to high command, and to disaster.   When Polk evacuated Columbus, Confederate forces were left to hold the Mississippi farther down, in the neighborhood of the Kentucky-Tennessee-Missouri boundary.   The river runs southward from Kentucky into Tennessee, then loops back to the north into Missouri and finally turns again southward to form the boundary between the last two states.   In the bottom, or southern end, of the first loop lay the fortified Island No. 10, a Confederate stronghold.   At the top, or northern end, of the second loop, Confederate forces held New Madrid, an old Missouri town dating from Spanish times.   Pope could not come at New Madrid by river, because of the batteries of Island No. 10. but he was able to reach it overland, from the north and west, and very promptly did so.

With the capture of the town on March fourteenth the island fortress was almost completely isolated. Above it, the river was blocked by Foote's Union gunboats; down-stream by the batteries at New Madrid now in Pope's hands. Access from the South was blocked by the overflowed regions about the head of Reelfoot Lake, impassable when the river was up, and the river was rising. The fortress was isolated except for one road out to Tiptonville, but it was still a first-class obstacle to Union navigation of the stream.

On the other wing of the grand advance, Buell followed the retreating Johnston from Nashville southward through Middle Tennessee and then went toward the Tennessee River to join his forces with those of Grant.

General Grant's column, after their great victory at Fort Donelson, had moved by steamboat up the Tennessee River, and deep into the South. The column had moved, but not the General himself. He had incurred the displeasure of his department commander. On March fourth, just as the expedition was starting south up the Tennessee River, the victor of Fort Donelson found himself relieved of command, ordered to remain behind at Fort Henry, and to turn over the column to C. F. Smith. "Why do you not obey my orders to report strength and positions of your command?" wired the querulous and exacting Halleck, to whom the winning of victories was of less moment than the proper paper returns.

Steaming up the river, with Sherman's division in the lead, the expedition went into camp on the west side of the stream, in a rough and wooded country around Pittsburg Landing, nine miles up-stream or south of Savannah, the point to which Buell was ordered to march, and about twenty miles from Corinth, in Mississippi. General Grant, restored to command, had about forty thousand men. Buell's approaching army was almost as large.

Albert Sidney Johnston, during March, was gathering what was left of his force after the disasters of the winter in Middle Tennessee, and moving them toward Corinth. Popular clamor and outcry against him was extreme—so extreme that President Davis, his staunch friend, suggested that he should exonerate himself. There were few generals in either army who would not long before then have been engaged in publicly justifying themselves. Not so Johnston. From Decatur, Alabama, on March eighteenth, he wrote to the President a letter that shines out among so much recrimination, self-seeking and vainglory in the military correspondence of the unhappy time.

"The blow of Fort Donelson was most disastrous and almost without remedy," he wrote. "I therefore in my first report remained silent. This silence you were kind enough to attribute to my generosity. I will not lay claim to the motive to excuse my course. I observed silence as it seemed to me the best way to serve the cause and the country. The facts were not fully known, discontent prevailed, and criticism or condemnation were more likely to augment than to cure the evil. I refrained, well knowing that heavy censures would fall upon me, but convinced that it was better to endure them for the present, and defer to a more propitious time an investigation. . . . The test of merit, in my profession, with the people is success. It is a hard rule, but I think it right. If I join this corps to the forces of Beauregard (I confess a hazardous experiment), those who are now declaiming against me will be without an argument."

The forces to which he referred, and which he did join, were gathering at Corinth, where Beauregard had moved his headquarters from Jackson, in Tennessee, after the fall of Fort Donelson.

To him there he called Polk's garrison at Columbus, about thirteen thousand men, freed by the evacuation of that point. Strong representations made to the commanders of troops and Governors in the Gulf States secured a detachment of three thousand men sent from New Orleans and ten thousand brought from Pensacola by Bragg. Johnston himself brought up something less than twenty thousand men. A garrison of seven thousand was left in Island No. 10, and small garrisons in Fort Pillow and Memphis. The rest of the troops, concentrated in the vicinity of Corinth, were about forty thousand, with Van Dorn expected to bring fifteen or twenty thousand more from Arkansas.

To wait longer, however, was not possible, if the bold offensive plan of striking Grant at Pittsburg Landing before he could be joined by the army of Buell coming from Middle Tennessee was to be carried out.

CHAPTER X

SHILOH AND ISLAND NO. 10

IN THE drama of Shiloh, first great battle of the war, were all the elements of suspense and surprise and high tragedy. Soldiers, tens of thousands of them, from the North and from the South, for weeks moved by rail, by river, by country road, to meet in deadliest battle about a little log chapel in the woods, of no importance then, and unknown, now for ever to be remembered.

The field of Shiloh itself was of no particular value—no town, no "strategic point," just a few thousand acres of high wooded plateau, cut with hollows and ravines, stretching back from the Tennessee River at Pittsburg Landing to the little chapel of Shiloh on the ridge between the headwaters of Lick and Owl Creeks.

The issues of Shiloh, though, were not the possession of the field. They were the defeat of major armies and the possession of the Mississippi. The stake was immense; the valor and resolution of the new troops who fought were in keeping.

It was really two battles: one fought on an April Sunday, a day of bright sun and bracing winds, between the army of Albert Sidney Johnston and that of Grant; the other fought on the Monday, a day of gathering clouds ending in a night of storm, between Grant, reenforced by Buell's fresh army, and Beauregard, commanding the men who had the day before fought for Johnston.

The battle had in it the strain of suspense—on the first day Johnston pressing the attack to finish Grant before Buell can come up, Grant's men hanging on, grimly, waiting for night and Buell; on the second day, Beauregard, obstinately maintaining the unequal fight against the forces combined against him, hoping against hope to hear of Van Dorn bringing reenforcements from the West.

Bitterly fought at the time, the battle has been fought over and over since. It was a most personal sort of struggle. Partizans of Buell on the one hand, and of Grant and Sherman on the other, have had no end of controversy; among the Confederates, the same is true between Beauregard's supporters, and those who believe that Beauregard spoiled the battle plan of Johnston.

That the Confederacy did not win a complete and sweeping victory the first day is ascribed by many to the destiny that pursued the Confederate arms in battle. In the middle of that Sunday afternoon, Johnston was struck by a Minié ball— the most fateful missile fired during the war, if Jefferson Davis was right when he wrote that "the fortunes of a country hung by a single thread on the life that was yielded on the field of Shiloh."

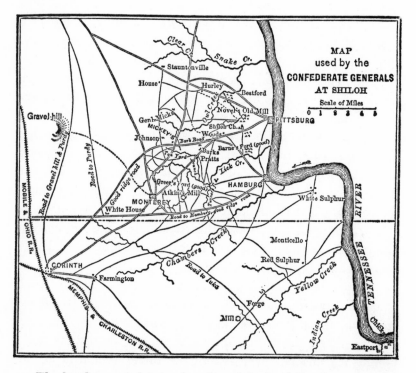

The battle opened just after five o'clock of Sunday morning, April sixth. Johnston had decided upon the advance from

Corinth to Shiloh shortly before midnight of April second. The movement was supposed to start on the third, but added to the natural confusion of moving forty thousand men over two narrow, crooked, execrably bad country roads, there was a great deal of standing still and blocking of the roads on the part of some of the corps. It was not until night of the third that the entire army was in motion, and not until late afternoon of the fifth that they were in position for battle. That meant that the fight must go over until the next morning.

One of the unaccountable facts of the whole war is that forty thousand men could leave Corinth, only twenty miles away, on a Thursday morning, march that day and the next and until the afternoon of Saturday, arrange themselves in order of battle in the woods, and then bivouac the entire night within two miles of the Union positions, and still, after all that, make an attack on the Sunday morning that bore every evidence of being a surprise. The men were about their Sunday morning tasks, the cooks busy with the day's meals. Sam Houston junior, of Texas, who scalded his arm snatching a joint of meat from a cooking pot as he went by, maintained that if the Union army was not surprised it was blessed with the most devoted cooks on record.

While both Grant and Sherman and their partizans afterward denied with no little heat that they were surprised, there is scarcely the slightest doubt of it. The five divisions of Union troops on the field of Shiloh had their camps scattered about in the woods with reference to convenience of camping, not of fighting. It happened that Sherman, who was a sort of unofficial second in command, was in the location farthest from the Landing, and so closest to the enemy, and should have been responsible for the service of security and information in that direction—but Sherman shows no sign of having taken the duty seriously, nor did Grant seem to worry about it. The fact was that these two, with all their natural capacity for war, had yet to learn the trade.

Not only had there been no real effort to observe the approach of the enemy; no proper steps had been taken to receive him should he come—in spite of the fact that Grant believed the Confederate force to be much larger than his own. Sherman said afterward that such a position as his troops held between Owl and Lick Creeks, would have been made impregnable in a night, with pick and shovel, later in the war. Then, however, no effort was made to build field entrenchments. Grant explained afterward that the men needed drill more than they did fortification work; Sherman, that he feared that to call on new troops to dig themselves in would have made them timid. Both excuses sound like afterthoughts. Certainly no such excuse would have been made, or listened to, by these competent Generals at a later date. It is not to their discredit to say that they did not realize, at that early stage, the value of the hasty entrenchment. It was later, and after much painful and bitter experience, that both sides were to learn the worth of such shelter. Soldiers who in 1862 would have scorned to dig a trench, by 1864 would scratch out a little hole with their bare hands, if no tool could be had. They had found that bayonets were more useful as entrenching tools, many times, than they were as weapons.

And so, on Saturday afternoon, Sherman, with no protection against forty thousand men deployed in the woods less than two miles from his camp, wrote to Grant, "I do not apprehend anything like an attack upon our position." Grant, as was his custom, went back down the river to his headquarters at Savannah, twelve miles from his front. Nelson marched into Savannah with Buell's leading division on Saturday. That afternoon, with Johnston right at his camps, Grant assured Nelson that he would send boats for his troops "Monday, or Tuesday, or some time early in the week," and that there would be no "fight at Pittsburg Landing; we will have to go to Corinth, where the rebels are fortified." That night he telegraphed Halleck, "the main force of the enemy is at Corinth. . . . I have scarcely the faintest idea of an attack being made upon us."

The intention of the Confederates had been to make a surprise attack. Orders to that end had been issued, but the young soldiers were hard to restrain. For two hundred miles, now, some of them had been retreating, and it was good to be moving forward again. They advanced in holiday mood, whooping and shouting at the rabbits and small game they stirred up in the woods. Both nights on the march there were torrential spring rains, and naturally there was a lot of unauthorized firing of rifles to see whether the wetting had ruined their paper cartridges. And then, on top of all that, an unwise reconnaissance sent out by Bragg's corps, had a brush with enemy outposts. It was inconceivable to the Confederate commanders that their presence was not known. In fact, so sure was the aggressive Beauregard that their plan must have been discovered that he urged its abandonment and a return to Corinth.

Twice was the matter discussed, informally, by Johnston with his corps commanders: once at a meeting in the road, little more than a mile from Shiloh Church; again, on the morning of the battle, at a gathering in the dawn about the General's camp-fire. Johnston ordered the attack to go on. While he spoke, at fourteen minutes past five, musketry fire from the front ended the discussion. The battle had begun.

To follow the detail of the movement of the battle across the field of Shiloh is difficult, and of small profit. The Union divisions, with their camps scattered about in the woods, formed line of battle as best they could. In the divisions nearest the Confederate advance the troops were surprised about their Sunday morning chores. The only division which had anything like proper outposts was that of Prentiss, not a trained soldier, who had with wise forethought sent out a regiment before dawn to find out what was the disturbance that his pickets had run into. It was this regiment that caught the first of the battle. Behind the divisions of Sherman and Prentiss, who were first struck, were those of McClernand, and, still farther back toward the Landing, of W. H. L. Wallace and Hurlbut.

The tactical disposition of the Confederate forces was faulty. Instead of arranging them in depth, so that there might be a chain of command and communication from front to rear on each part of the field, each corps was stretched clear across the field of battle, from Lick Creek on the right to Owl on the left. The first line was the corps of Hardee—the same Hardee whose *Infantry and Rifle Tactics* was the standard work on the subject for both Union and Confederate Armies.

A second line, also stretching across the field, was commanded by Major-General Braxton Bragg, also acting as Johnston's chief of staff. Half a mile behind Bragg's left came the corps of Leonidas Polk, while John C. Breckinridge's reserve division formed the rest of this third line, coming up behind Bragg's right.

Such an arrangement of battle would have been difficult to maintain with trained troops in an open field. In the close and broken country between the creeks, it was impossible. The lines became intermingled, pressing forward exultantly. They pushed through Sherman's camps, passed Shiloh Church, captured the camps of Prentiss, struck stubbornly defended Union lines formed by the different division commanders, flanked them, forced them back and pushed on. Before noon, on a front of three miles and a depth of two, the woods of Shiloh were filled with battle—not grand assaults by divisions and corps, but little isolated desperate fights, gallant affairs, sometimes futile, with waving of flags and encouragement to the charge, scattered and broken, but somehow always pressing forward.

"The Hornet's Nest" was a Union strong point. For more than four hours the divisions of W. H. L. Wallace and Hurlbut, on the flanks, with Prentiss in the center and a little forward, held up the Confederate advance, less than a mile from the steamboat landing. To their right, McClernand's division, bravely fighting, retired seven successive times in eight different positions. Sherman's division, badly broken, moved with them. Late in the afternoon Hurlbut and then Wallace were driven back. Wallace, who for that day commanded the division of the veteran C. F. Smith, ill in Savannah, was mortally wounded. Prentiss, whose vigilance in the morning had given first warning of the approaching storm, isolated and surrounded, was forced to surrender with some twenty-five hundred men. Their stubborn defense had given time for the preparation of a new position, protecting the very landing itself.

In the fighting in front of the Hornet's Nest General Johnston received his mortal wound. A chance ball cut an artery in his leg. With even unskilled attention it need scarcely have been serious. Absorbed in pressing his battle, the General did not notice or disregarded it. Within half an hour he was dead.

General Beauregard was second in command. His station was back at Shiloh Church, which had been within the Union lines in the morning and was now far behind the Confederate advance. To him went notification of Johnston's death, while Bragg, at the front, continued the pressure on the Federal troops in the center.

Time gained by the stubborn defense at the Hornet's Nest, and the forethought of Colonel J. D. Webster of Grant's staff, who had collected and strongly emplaced a great battery along the curving ridge just about the Landing, made possible the next and last defensive position of the day. The space about the Landing, under the protection of the high river bank, was filled with fugitives from the regiments and brigades broken during the day. It was through this mass of stricken and demoralized soldiers that the head of Buell's column, Ammen's brigade of Nelson's division, pushed forward just before the close of the day, to take place with the steady and determined lines of organized soldiers which still held together to protect the Landing.

About the time that the first of Buell's soldiers were coming up—they had marched all day through the swamps on the eastern bank of the river and had been ferried across at the landing—the Confederate brigades of Chalmers and Jackson, one of them with no ammunition and the other with little, crossed the deep ravine in front of the last Union position and prepared to attack. Darkness was at hand. General Beauregard, realizing the disorganization in his army, sent forward orders that the troops be withdrawn from battle, reformed and reorganized to carry on the fight the next day.

For that order Beauregard has been much and widely criticized in the South. Bragg, who surely was no rash and head-long fighter, at the front at the time, asked the staff-officer from Beauregard if the order to withdraw from the last attack had been given to the command. Told that it had, he answered, "If not, I would not obey it. The battle is lost."

Buell's fresh force poured across the Tennessee that night, a new army almost as large as Grant's or as the one with which Johnston had started the day before. Grant maintained in after-years that he was not defeated on the first day, and that with the arrival of Lew Wallace's division of his own army, which came up during the night after losing its way to the battle the day before, he would have been able to take the offensive Monday morning. Perhaps so, but the best evidence is the other way.

Grant had been at breakfast at the stately old Cherry house, on the bluff above the river at Savannah, when the sound of the guns, more than ten miles away, told him that battle had begun at Pittsburg Landing. Buell, also, was in Savannah that morning, but Grant started for the Landing on his dispatch steamer without seeing him. As the fire continued and increased, Buell decided to go to the scene of the fighting to find what was expected of his forces. About noon, a steamer bound down the river came alongside the one bearing Buell up, and delivered a letter from Grant. Two sentences in the letter stand out with evidential value: "If you will get upon the field . . . it will . . . possibly save the day to us. The rebel forces are estimated at over one hundred thousand men." That does not sound like the calm confidence of the result that Grant later professed to have felt.

Grant alone might have been able to take the offensive with effect Monday morning, but in fact the larger part of the troops under his command that day were those which came to the battle-field with Buell during the night. They formed the left of the line, Lew Wallace's fresh division the right, the rest of Grant's army or such of it as maintained organization, the center. Against this force Beauregard could oppose only what he had the day before. Messengers had been dispatched to Corinth to find if, by chance, Van Dorn had come up and, if so, to hurry him forward, but there was no Van Dorn.

There was nothing for the Confederates but retreat. It was a slow retreat, however, coolly conducted, almost "from tree to tree," and with such boldness of front that there was no break in the Confederate line, no rout, no pursuit worthy of the name.

Whatever *might* have happened at Shiloh—and that is a matter for interesting speculation and sharp controversy—the actual results were that the Confederate offensive from Corinth was checked and turned back; that Grant held his position on the flank of the line of the Mississippi; that the great-souled Albert Sidney Johnston, and four thousand other brave men, North and South, were dead and four times that many wounded; that never again could it be said by either side that the other "would not fight."

On the same day that Beauregard's army, fighting stubbornly, fell back from Pittsburg Landing past Shiloh Church and took up its weary and bleeding march through the pouring rain and the mud, axle deep, back to Corinth, John Pope closed in on Island No. 10, blocked the last road of escape, and with his force of nearly twenty thousand men secured the surrender of the forts, with their garrison of seven thousand. Union forces moved another eighty miles down the Mississippi in their progress of conquest, to be halted for the time by Fort Pillow, halfway across Tennessee.

The victory at Island No. 10 made good newspaper reading in the North, and a powerful appeal to the imagination. For a month before the surrender the situation had been at stalemate. Pope held the west bank of the river, but could not get across to block the one communication the fort had left with the outside world. Foote's gunboats, in the stream above the island, could not pass down by the forts, to put Pope's army across the river. However the river was very high, and it was discovered that a "canal" could be made through the flooded bottoms by cutting the trunks of the forest trees six feet under water. Light draft boats could pass through such a canal without running the gauntlet of the dreaded guns of the fort. With great ingenuity and much labor the canal was cut and certain boats and barges did pass through it to Pope, impatiently waiting at New Madrid, down-stream from the island. Just then, however, the *Carondelet,* one of the deep draft iron-clad gunboats, successfully ran the gauntlet, in a night of storm, to be followed in a night or so by other vessels of the fleet. When the large boats came down the river it was not necessary to use the canal, after all the labor spent on it, but the construction of such an unusual military work attracted much attention to the campaign and its commanding officer, General Pope.

Another Union General to whom much popular credit and acclaim came was Halleck. Vast results had been won by armies under his general direction. The presumption that these results were due to that direction was natural and was widely indulged, both in the popular and the official mind. It carried General Halleck to the highest command, where the defects of his temperament and military method were to weigh heavily against the Union armies.

After Shiloh and Island No. 10, on April eleventh, Halleck took the field in person. He called Pope's army to himself at Shiloh, and on April twenty-eighth, with more than one hundred thousand men, started the siege of Corinth—a slow, glacier-like forward movement of his huge army.

One lesson of Shiloh had been learned. Every night the Union army threw up entrenchments.

CHAPTER XI

CONSCRIPTION: THE SECOND SPRING

To THE thronging disasters that marked the end of the first twelve-month of war, the answer of the Confederate nation was a tightening of the belt, a bracing of shoulders, unbroken determination.

Almost on the anniversary day of Fort Sumter, the new Congress passed the first conscription law, "An Act to provide for the public defense." That act withdrew from the control of the states and placed under the exclusive control of the President of the Confederacy all male citizens over eighteen years and under thirty-five—a curious, almost ironic, negation of the whole doctrine of state's rights on which the Confederacy was founded, and one curiously and variously received by its people.

To Governor Joseph E. Brown, concerned with the sovereignty of Georgia and the right of her Governor to name the officers of Georgia troops, it seemed that "No act of the Government of the United States prior to the secession of Georgia struck a blow at constitutional liberty so fell as has been stricken by the conscript acts." To President Davis he wrote that conscription "encroaches upon the reserved rights of the State and strikes down her sovereignty at a single blow," while Linton Stephens, beloved younger brother of the Vice-President of the Confederacy, told the Georgia Legislature that "conscription checks enthusiasm; we are invincible under a system of volunteering, we are lost with conscription."

While not so outspoken in objection to conscription *per se,* the new Governor of North Carolina, Zebulon Vance, resented the Richmond government's control over the organization of the troops. "It is mortifying," he said to the Legislature of his state, "to find entire brigades of North Carolina soldiers commanded by strangers, and in many cases our own brave and war-worn colonels are made to give place to colonels from distant States."

Other anti-Davis leaders—there had grown up a distinct party of that description by the spring of 1862—were just as devoted to the abstract theory of state's rights as the Governors of Georgia and North Carolina, but they had a wider and clearer conception of the military necessities of a country invaded by superior force.   Robert Barnwell Rhett, the great South Carolina leader for secession, who had been "mentioned" for the Presidency of the Confederacy, and who in most things opposed Davis, stood solidly with him on the necessity of the conscript laws, as did "Pollard of the *Examiner*," the Richmond editor who during four years found but little of good in the President of the Confederacy.   Rhett and Pollard did not believe in Davis as President, but they were willing for the matter of state's rights within the Confederacy to rest until the nation itself could be established and peace restored.

Mr. Davis himself, during the War with Mexico, declined an appointment as Brigadier-General at the hands of President Polk, because of constitutional scruples as to the right of the President to appoint officers of the militia forces, and remained a Colonel under the commission of the Governor of Mississippi. Then, however, there was no such critical necessity as now confronted the Confederacy.

All men within the prescribed ages, with certain exceptions and exemptions, were conscripted for the rest of the war.   This action, taken just before the end of the enlistments of the twelve-month volunteers who had been in the armies since the spring before, had a double effect.   It kept the trained soldiers in the army, and it made them better satisfied to stay when they saw some of those who had been comfortably at home through the first year brought into the camps.

The Confederate conscript law, like that of the Union when it was passed the next year, sanctioned the abominable system of "substitutes," by which one drafted for service might hire another to fight in his place.   In the South, however, the hiring of substitutes was not as common as it became in the North—for the excellent reason, among others, that there were fewer substitutes to hire.   With all subject to service alike, it was difficult to find an "exempt" who would be accepted in lieu of his employer.   There was no stream of Irish and German immigrant boys, willing to soldier for a few hundred dollars.

It seems incongruous, too, that the owners or overseers of considerable numbers of slaves—twenty, at first, fifteen, later,—were exempted from military service in a war of which the controversy over slavery was one of the exciting causes. Such a man directing the labor of his slaves was probably more useful at home than he would have been in the ranks, and so the exemption was no doubt logical, but it was intensely unpopular.

Not with new conscripts, however, but with the men who had already put in their twelve months, Beauregard was to face Halleck about Corinth, and first Magruder and then Joe Johnston to oppose McClellan's advance up the Peninsula below Richmond. While these two major armies of the North were cautiously and scientifically creeping forward toward their objectives, the Union Navy struck, and struck swiftly and hard.

By April of 1862 the pressure of the relentless blockade was felt throughout the South, but nowhere as in her ports, and in no port more than in the greatest of them, New Orleans. Levees where river boats, rank on rank, and ships, sail and steam, from all the world had met to land and load their cargoes, were deserted, the cobble-stoned commercial streets of the town were grass-grown, the huge unfinished Egyptian custom-house was empty. Her young men had gone to Virginia and to Tennessee, to fight with Beauregard, many to die at Shiloh or on lesser and nameless fields, many more to die in camps and in the hospitals improvised by the Southern Mothers' Association and other relief organizations, of camp fevers and of the complications following on epidemics of measles and mumps.

For a while, in the summer of 1861, there had been a feverish sort of activity about the wharves, when the sea-going tugs, side-wheelers of great power and speed, were being converted into privateersmen and sent out under letters of marque and reprisal, to earn their keep on the sea by captures of Yankee commerce; and then there had been a little blockade running—but the strangling blockade had pretty well ended all that;

especially after the Union Navy had seized Ship Island, off the Mississippi Coast, a near-by base from which to patrol the passes leading into the salt-water lakes behind the city, and the mouths of the river.

New Orleans had, in a way, got used to the blockade close at hand, and the war a long way off. The place to defend New Orleans, they had been told, was on the banks of the Tennessee and the Cumberland—but outside the Passes of the Mississippi there were determined and dauntless naval officers who were to bring the war home to New Orleans.

Late in February there arrived at the base of the West Gulf Blockading Squadron, on Ship Island, the *Hartford*, flying the flag of David Farragut. Ship and man were of the "old" Navy, of pre-ironclad days. The ship was of wood, with tall masts and great spread of sail, that in a fair wind could drive her faster than her engines. The man was more than sixty when the war opened, the oldest commander to attain great distinction on either side. He had been afloat or in navy-yards since he was nine. He had fought in the War of 1812, on the Barbary coast in the Mediterranean, in the first "Mosquito Fleet," the one which stamped out piracy in the waters of the Caribbean. A salt of the saltiest, determined, inflexible, he was yet genial, jovial, with a kindly and winning smile—the sort of leader whom men follow devotedly and gladly.

Born in Tennessee, of a Tennessee mother and a Minorquin father, he had passed nearly half his short early life ashore in New Orleans. Adopted almost as a son by the famous Captain David Porter, he had sailed away from that port at the age of nine—to return more than half a century later, with a fleet organized at the suggestion of David Porter's son, and to the command of which he had been appointed upon his urging.

Captain Farragut he had been when the war broke out, stationed at Norfolk. Because of his southern birth and his southern wife, he was expected to go with the South, but his conception of duty called him to stay with the Union. He left Norfolk and retired to New York, whence he reported himself as ready for duty. And there he stayed, for the better part of a

year. There was, in some circles, a reluctance to put officers
of southern birth and connections in command in those days.
It was at the urging of the younger Porter that Farragut was
brought from his semi-retirement and sent to the Gulf, there to
become the most famous of American sailors.

After his arrival at Ship Island it was nearly a month before Farragut was ready to steam into the mouths of the Mississippi and start up the river, and it was nearly a month more
before the work of getting his heavy ships over the shallow bars,
and his mortar-boats in position to bombard the forts at the head
of the passes, was complete.

New Orleans relied greatly on these works, Fort Jackson
on the right bank and Fort St. Philip on the left, for its defense.
They were permanent fortifications, designed to command the
stream. Between them there stretched a barrier of hulks,
anchored, chained together. About seventy miles up-stream, as
the river winds, lay the city, with some inconsequential "inner
defenses" about it. The Confederate command was divided—
the army forces under Major-General Mansfield Lovell; naval
forces under Commander John K. Mitchell; the "River Defense
Fleet" of converted river steamers under neither Army nor
Navy in effect. Against them came a man singularly undivided.

After five days of bombardment of the forts by the mortar
fleet, under Porter, bold Farragut determined to run past them
at two o'clock in the morning of April twenty-fourth, and to proceed on up the river to the city. The fleet, in three divisions,
each division in line, steamed up the river, against the four-
mile-an-hour current, returning the fire of the forts. The ob-
struction in the channel broken, the fleet passed up beyond.
The Confederate naval forces—a handful of converted tugs
and river steamers, a home-made ram, the *Manassas*, and the
Louisiana, an unfinished ironclad that could only be tied against
the bank and used as a stationary floating battery—came down
into the darkness of the night, made darker by the thick smoke
of battle, little relieved by the lurid light cast by fire rafts.
When Farragut's ships came pushing past the forts, through the
clouds of smoke, there was little that the Confederate vessels

could do. Some did just that; others, with the greatest gallantry, went headlong into the fight, and to destruction.

The Federal fleet steamed on up to the city, which was evacuated by the military forces, demanded its surrender, and when that was not made by the city authorities, took possession and raised the flag of the United States over the public buildings. The forts below, isolated and cut off, surrendered also, and on May first the ubiquitous General Benjamin F. Butler landed with his troops, to garrison the city, while Farragut and the fleet steamed away up the Mississippi to take Baton Rouge, the capital of the state, and Natchez, in Mississippi. There was nothing to stop him.

Away up-stream, in Tennessee, the gunboat flotilla, under Flag-Officer Charles H. Davis who had succeeded to the command of the wounded Foote, was battering away at Fort Pillow, which was successfully holding its own, until events elsewhere were to force the withdrawal of its garrison.

That event was the evacuation of Corinth, which finally took place during the night before May thirtieth, after Halleck had spent a month advancing his great army from the field of Shiloh to the environs of Corinth, less than twenty miles.

Halleck's army, in this operation, was in some ways the most remarkable assembled during the war. Second in command was Grant. In command of the right wing, formerly Grant's army, was George H. Thomas; of the center, was Buell; of the left, John Pope. Sherman was there, commanding a division, and W. S. Rosecrans, while a young unknown, Philip Sheridan, who had come to Corinth as a captain of infantry on quartermaster duty, was rescued and put in command of a Michigan cavalry regiment.

To meet this force of more than one hundred thousand men Beauregard had the thirty thousand with whom he had got back to Corinth after Shiloh, and in addition the Army of the West, from Arkansas and Missouri, which came up under Van Dorn and Price; some regiments sent by Kirby Smith from his department in East Tennessee, and others by Pemberton from his command on the coasts of South Carolina and Georgia;

some new levies sent forward by the Governors of the Gulf States—in all, at their maximum, on paper eighty thousand men, of whom eighteen thousand were in hospitals with more coming down sick, and with only fifty-three thousand effectives present for duty.

Pushing forward by regular siege approaches, Halleck had his front parallels at some points within a thousand yards of Beauregard's entrenchments. Confederate sorties against his works had failed to drive him off or halt his advance. Under the circumstances there seemed nothing to do but to retire from Corinth and leave it to Halleck. With great skill and the strictest secrecy the evacuation was carried out. Supplies and ordnance were sent by train to Tupelo, fifty miles farther south in Mississippi, the sick were sent to the rear, and finally, during the night of May twenty-ninth, the troops quietly marched out and started south. Over on General Pope's wing they heard some unusual stir in the Confederate camps, but interpreted it as preparations for an attack the next day. By the time that Beauregard's departure was discovered, well into the daylight hours, his troops were safely away.

Beauregard had saved his army, which was the important thing, but had been forced to give up another great slice of Confederate territory. With the army at Corinth gone, Fort Pillow and Memphis had to be abandoned, and all of West Tennessee and northern Mississippi, and the great river itself down to the fortifications at Vicksburg, which alone kept the gunboat flotilla from the North from joining with Farragut's fleet coming up from the South.

Meanwhile Major-General O. M. Mitchel, whom Buell had left to garrison Middle Tennessee, had pressed on into northern Alabama, seized the Memphis & Charleston Railroad, established his headquarters at Huntsville, and displayed great zeal and activity, but not quite so much judgment. His temperament seems to have been variable—ranging from great expectations of conquest to dire fears of immediate disaster. His passion was destroying railroad bridges, some of which were to be needed later by his own side.

Under General Mitchel the first railroad raid was made—that one in which Captain James J. Andrews, a Kentucky Unionist spy, and twenty-one soldiers in disguise, stole the engine "General" on the line between Atlanta and Chattanooga and attempted to destroy the bridges of that vital line.

General Mitchel expected great things from the plan—and might have realized them had it succeeded. With Chattanooga's communication with the South broken, he planned to throw his force into that immensely important strategic center, for which a great campaign and costly battles were fought the following year. The plan, however, failed, for two reasons. One was that it was a day late in execution. The other was Captain W. A. Fuller, conductor on the state of Georgia's Western & Atlantic Railroad, in charge of the train from which the engine was stolen.

The plan was for Andrews and his men to rendezvous on the lower end of the line, near Atlanta, and to board the early-morning train for Chattanooga, at various points. At Big Shanty Station, where crew and passengers stopped for breakfast, the Andrews men were to seize the engine and one or two box-cars, and start north, cutting telegraph lines, burning bridges, spreading destruction. The movement was planned for April eleventh, a day on which, as it happened, the raiders would have had a clear track for their run. For what seemed good reason the movement was delayed one day—and ran into a flock of south-bound extra trains.

Even then, Andrews' boldness and ready wit, persuading trains to take siding and yield the main track to his train "hurrying powder to General Beauregard at Corinth," might have succeeded, had it not been for Captain Fuller and one Anthony Murphy, roundhouse foreman for the railroad. As they sat at breakfast they saw their engine slide away northward, with strange men scrambling into the box-cars. It took but a moment to find that the wires were cut—so these two, Fuller and Murphy, started on foot to pursue a score of men with a train. Meeting a hand-car, they impressed it and its crew.

At the crossing of the Etowah River, Andrews noticed a little

yard engine, the "Yonah," standing on a siding at the iron
mines there. The pause of a moment there, and the destruction
or disabling of that engine, might have saved the day for him,
but it was not done. He passed on up the road to Kingston,
where the branch line from Rome joins. There he found the
sidings and the main line blocked with extra trains going south.
With his men lying hidden in the box-cars of "powder for Beauregard" he bluffed and persuaded his way through the blockade
of trains—but it took more than an hour of switching and
"sawing by" to clear the line.

Meanwhile Fuller and Murphy and their hand-car crew came
flying along, as fast as a hand-car can fly. From Big Shanty to
the Etowah is mostly down-hill, from the river to Kingston is
more than a dozen miles, mostly up-hill—and pushing hand-cars
up-hill is a slow and laborious business. But at the river there
was the little old "Yonah," steam up and ready to run. They
pressed it into service and loaded it with soldiers.

Four minutes after Andrews left Kingston, Fuller steamed
in from the south. In shuffling trains to let Andrews by, however, the road was hopelessly blocked for Fuller. He abandoned
the "Yonah," came around the blockade, found the Rome train
on the branch line, headed the right way, commandeered it and
started in pursuit.

Four miles above Kingston Andrews stopped to tear up some
rail. Having no proper tools, his men were tugging at the
rail with their hands when they were startled by the whistle of
a locomotive *behind* them. Hurriedly they finished the job and
moved on. At Adairsville they met another south-bound train,
passed it with their usual story, and sent it on south, believing
that it must meet Fuller head-on and so effectively end any
pursuit.

When Fuller came to the broken rail he was blocked again,
but that indomitable man left his train south of the break, and
once more started on foot to pursue Andrews. In a little while
he met the train which Andrews had sent south from Adairsville,
impressed it into his service, backed it to Adairsville, threw the
cars into the siding by a flying switch and with his new engine,

the "Texas," and one car filled with volunteers took up the pursuit.

Never in the history of railroading or war has there been wilder running or greater courage than was shown by pursued and pursuers. Andrews, running over the crazy war-worn track, made the last nine miles into Calhoun in nine minutes, dashing up just as the last south-bound train he was to meet was ready to pull out against him. More explanations followed and persuasion, with time lost for Andrews. Finally, just as he got away to the north, and before the express train south could leave, Fuller and his "Texas," running backward and pushing a car at a mile-a-minute speed, raced into the station, and on north.

But Andrews was not through. He had cleared the last train opposing him, that at Calhoun, and he thought that Fuller was wrecked or in the ditch behind him. Between Calhoun and the bridge over the Oostenaula he stopped to tear up a rail—and two minutes before it could be done, found the terrible Fuller right behind him. Scrambling aboard, he started on a mad race northward. Two of his cars he dropped, hoping to delay the pursuit, but Fuller simply picked them up, shoved them across the wooden trestle and bridge at the Oostenaula, which Andrews had had no time to destroy, kicked them into a spur track at Resaca, and kept on. Andrews had cross-ties in one of his box-cars. Knocking out the end of the car he began strewing them along the track, hoping to derail his pursuers. Fuller had to slow down to get them off the track, but somehow he managed to keep up the pursuit, never giving Andrews time to get up a rail, or to burn a bridge, or to destroy the long tunnel at Tunnel Hill. The day before, when the raid was to have been made, was clear and windy; this day it was raining. The rain made it difficult to get fires started quickly on the wooden bridges, and the implacable pursuit gave no time to do it at leisure. On one of the covered bridges over the Chickamauga Andrews left his last box-car, burning, in the hope that it would catch the bridge from the inside and destroy it before Fuller could cross. The hope was vain. Through the smoke-filled bridge dashed Fuller, with his "Texas" running backward, to overhaul the "General," out of wood and water, just at the Georgia-Tennessee state line.   Andrews and his men, dressed in civilian clothes, scattered and took to the woods, but most were captured; some were executed as spies, some escaped from prison, some were exchanged.   Of all those most brave men and the locomotives they used, two survive: The "General" in honorable retirement at Chattanooga, the "Texas," at Atlanta.

CHAPTER XII

NEARLY TO RICHMOND

ON THE day that Beauregard gave up Corinth to Halleck, General McClellan's army was within five miles of Richmond.

To that position he had advanced by slow and laborious stages—beset all the way by cankering doubts as to his support at the hands of his own government, and by imaginative over-estimates of the strength of the enemy in his front.

There can be no better example of what the relations between a military commander and his civilian chief should not be, than those of McClellan and Lincoln. There was fault on both sides: McClellan was secretive with his chief, and condescending; he was without any conception of the importance of the political side of war; he lost sight of the necessity for keeping the government behind his plans. Lincoln and Stanton, his Secretary of War, interfered often and unduly with the plans of the young General to whom they had intrusted chief command, and frequently without so much as notifying him of what they were to do.

Wearying of inaction, Lincoln during the winter issued his President's General War Order No. 1, directing that all the armies of the Union advance on all fronts on February twenty-second, presumably as a patriotic gesture on Washington's birthday. Later, in March, was issued another order from the President, peremptorily ordering an advance by McClellan's army before the eighteenth of the month, distinctly threatening in tone. On March eighth, without discussion with McClellan, the President divided his army into corps and assigned commanders to them. On March twelfth, while McClellan was with his army, he saw in the newspapers the order relieving him from command of all the armies, and confining him to the Potomac Department—his first intimation of the change.

The President and the Secretary of War had finally agreed

to the movement by the Peninsula, most reluctantly, on the express condition that the fortifications of Washington be completed and heavily garrisoned, so as to leave no chance of a Confederate attack there while McClellan was away in his advance to Richmond. McClellan, with his mind and imagination enthralled by the vision of his Peninsula campaign, failed to take this requirement as seriously as he should. He made provision for the defense of Washington all right, but not such provision as removed uneasiness from the minds of the government. It was the success of the Confederates in playing upon this uneasiness that was finally to wreck McClellan's great campaign.

The government at Washington, having relieved McClellan of other command and confined him strictly to the operations on the Peninsula, now proceeded to divide the rest of the Virginia theater of war among three separate and independent commanders. The country about Washington and toward Fred-

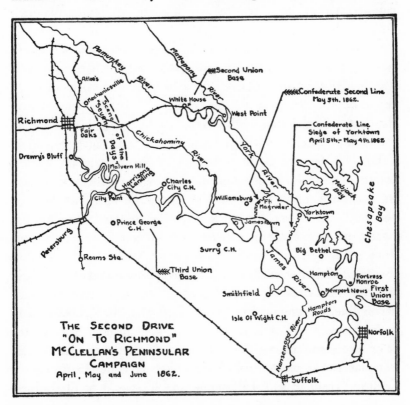

THE SECOND DRIVE
"ON TO RICHMOND"
MᶜCLELLAN'S PENINSULAR
CAMPAIGN
April, May and June 1862.

ericksburg and Richmond was put under McDowell; the Shenan-doah Valley country under Major-General Banks, former Governor of Massachusetts; the country west of the Shenandoah under Frémont, for whom a command had to be found because of what was described as political "pressure."

McClellan, bitterly disappointed and full of forebodings, landed on the Peninsula on April second. He had expected to have an army of one hundred and fifty-five thousand men for his operations, but after he left Washington the corps of Mc-Dowell had been taken away from him and kept about the capital. That, and other detachments, had reduced his force to about ninety thousand men—still a most respectable army, not far from twice as large as anything that Johnston could bring against it, and six times as large as its immediate opposition, the little force under Major-General John B. Magruder which held a line across the narrow Peninsula, extending from fortifications at Yorktown, on the north, along the little Warwick River, to the James on the south.

It was not only a large army but a fine one, well organized, well trained, splendidly equipped, but it did not accord with the picture that McClellan's active imagination had formed of the resistless progress up the Peninsula of his great force, flanked and supported by the naval vessels in the deep rivers on either side. A second disappointment, too, was the Navy. Flag-Officer Goldsborough, in command of the fleet at the Roads, told the General that he could not reduce the forts on the bluffs at Yorktown, or at Gloucester Point on the opposite shore of the York River, and that so long as the ironclad *Virginia* was afloat and in fighting trim at Norfolk he could not pass up the James.

To a General of McClellan's temperament there was but one answer, siege operations against the Yorktown-Warwick River line. From early in April until May, the elaborate and tedious siege operations went on. Magruder had at the start thirteen thousand men to hold five miles of line. He was somewhat reenforced, after Johnston came to Richmond with his army from the Rapidan, and his works were skilfully done, but there was no real reason why McClellan should not have pushed right on through him. Finally, just as all the huge siege batteries were ready to open fire, on the night of May third, Magruder evacuated the famous old Revolutionary village of Yorktown, and fell back up the Peninsula to Williamsburg, the colonial capital of Virginia and seat of the ancient college of William and Mary. On May fifth, in a smart fight through the town and the college grounds, Williamsburg was taken, and the Confederate retreat continued, through rain and mud and bottomless roads, as one said, neither by land nor by water, but by a mixture of half-and-half.

Meanwhile, from Yorktown, a portion of McClellan's army had been embarked on steamers and moved by the York and Pamunkey Rivers to the White House, a colonial home that had belonged to George Washington, now belonged to the Lees, and was occupied by Mrs. Lee and her daughter, Mary, "refugeeing" from Arlington. There, on the Pamunkey, where it is crossed by the Richmond & York River Railroad, McClellan established his base. He had intended to land and start inland in time to cut off the slow and toilsome retreat of the Confederates falling back from Williamsburg, but delays in embarkation and a sharp and unexpected attack from the Confederates under Major-General G. W. Smith prevented.

As he fell back toward Richmond, Johnston called on his government to collect troops from all directions to sustain the threatened attack on the capital. One result of the call was the order to abandon Norfolk, which was done after the evacuation of Yorktown. On May tenth the Union forces occupied the city; that night the *Virginia* was burned and the James River was open to the fortifications at Drewry's Bluff, only six or eight miles below Richmond. A naval attack on May fifteenth failed to pass that point.

However, the control of the James was to prove, a few weeks later, of the greatest importance. It could have been made even more decisive. Moving from the line of the James up the Appomattox, there was really nothing to keep the Union forces from taking Petersburg, the key to Richmond, holding the roads to the south. Three years later, after a desperate and bloody siege of nearly a year, Petersburg was to fall into the hands of Grant. In the spring of 1862 it was open to capture—but the opportunity was not recognized or appreciated.

The Confederate army with its back to Richmond was in command of Joseph E. Johnston, an able and experienced soldier. He had been a Lieutenant-Colonel in the old army, holding the same position in the First Cavalry that Lee did in the Second, but shortly before the war had been made Quarter-master-General, a detail which carried with it the brevet rank of Brigadier-General. When the Confederate Congress passed a law giving to all officers who joined the Confederacy the same relative rank they held in the old army that fact was to become of importance. If Johnston was to be placed according to his rank by detail he would be first of southern Generals; if according to his permanent lineal rank, fourth. When President Davis decided that his rank should be fourth a sore spot was created, a tiny sore spot, but one that festered and grew between two of the ablest leaders of the Confederacy—able, both of them, and high-minded, but lacking in that tolerant largeness that made so much of the greatness of Lee or Albert Sidney Johnston.

McClellan's campaign was based on the promise that Mc-Dowell's fine First Corps, detained about Fredericksburg, would be sent to him when the time came. There was nothing to prevent such a junction, except an insignificant Confederate force facing McDowell. Consequently McClellan, as he advanced up the Peninsula, constantly shifted the weight of his force to the right, both to cover his base at the White House and to be able to reach hands toward McDowell when the latter should start south.

There is a little stream, the Chickahominy, a lazy, wandering, swampy, wooded stream which cuts the Peninsula on the bias, from northwest to southeast. It heads up not far from the Pamunkey, on which McClellan was based, passes but a few miles east of Richmond and then wanders off southeastward into the James. It is but a trifling little stream, but it and Mr

Lincoln's change of plans with reference to McDowell finally wrecked the vast labor and plans of McClellan's Army of the Potomac.

Mr. Lincoln's change of plans, however, did not just happen. In Richmond, in charge of all operations under the direction of President Davis, was Robert E. Lee, facing the thankless task to which he had been assigned but a few weeks before. In the Shenandoah Valley was Stonewall Jackson. Between those two master brains of war a spark of genius struck fire. McClellan was obviously reaching out toward McDowell, expecting him to push southward from Fredericksburg along the railroad, join hands to the north and northeast of Richmond, and then with an irresistible force of nearly one hundred and fifty thousand men he would crush Johnston's army of one-third that number. To wreck McClellan's plan, why not detain McDowell about Washington? To detain him, what better than a threat against the capital, where the President and his advisers anxiously sat? To make such a threat, who better than the silent, praying Major-General in command in the Valley?

Jackson had, in the whole region of his command, about nineteen thousand men—eight thousand with himself, in the Valley proper, three thousand under Edward Johnson pushed out to the west to observe Frémont's approach from that direction, eight thousand on the east side of the Blue Ridge about the railroad junction of Gordonsville, under Richard Ewell.

Immediately opposed to him he had Frémont to the westward, with fifteen thousand men, and Banks, holding the lower or northern end of the Valley, with some nineteen thousand. At Fredericksburg, under McDowell, was a force of about forty thousand.

To understand the amazing thing that happened, consider the geography of the Shenandoah Valley. It extends from southwest to northeast, opening into the Potomac at Harper's Ferry. On the west it is bounded by the mountain ranges of the Alleghanies; on the east by the Blue Ridge, broken by a series of "gaps" through which roads run into eastern Virginia. Into the upper end of the Valley, to Staunton, came the Virginia

Central Railroad, through Rockfish Gap from Charlottesville; into the lower end, the Manassas Gap Railroad, to Strasburg making a short line to Washington.   In the floor of the Valley is the Shenandoah River, divided above Front Royal into a North Fork and a South Fork—which are, rather, northwest and southeast forks. Between these forks of the river, and extending fifty miles from Harrisonburg down to Strasburg, is the bold range of Massanutten Mountains, an isolated outlier, as high as the Blue Ridge itself. The Valley to the westward of Massanutten

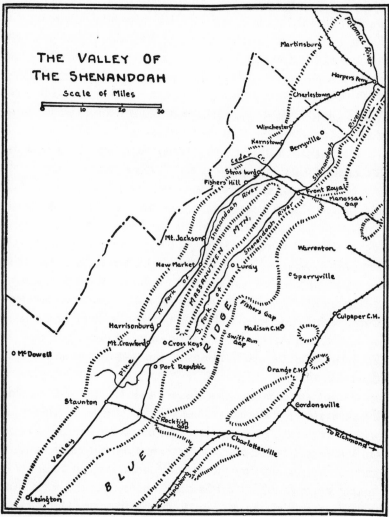

bears the name of Shenandoah; that to the eastward, a narrow valley along the South Fork of the river, is known as the Luray Valley. Through the western division of the Valley ran the Valley Pike, a good limestone macadamized road, from Staunton on down to Winchester and beyond.

At the opening of the great Valley campaign Jackson was at Swift Run Gap, the gap in the Blue Ridge nearest Gordonsville, where Ewell was camped. Secrecy, with Jackson, was a military passion, and one that, in a war where each army usually knew what the other was going to do, was one of the great elements of his success. From Swift Run Gap he marched down into the Valley, crossed the South Fork, recrossed it and went into camp at Port Republic. It was a severe march over muddy and difficult roads. Details of men went along with each wagon to help drag it through the mud-holes, while "Old Jack" himself was found, occasionally, bringing rocks from the roadside to put in some of the worst holes.

Having marched from the ridge down into the Valley, he now turned and ostentatiously marched back across the ridge, to the eastward. That was on May third, the day that Yorktown was evacuated. "Going to Richmond!" said everybody, especially when trains were found at Meechum's Station, on the railroad, waiting for the troops.

That night, on board the cars, instead of going to Richmond the little army went back across the ridge and to Staunton. Meanwhile Ewell had moved up from Gordonsville to Jackson's old position about Swift Run Gap, where he could keep an eye on Banks in the lower end of the Valley. From Staunton Jackson pushed out to reenforce Edward Johnson's command. With the two commands together, he marched on westward across mountains two days to the little village of McDowell. There he encountered Frémont's advance under Milroy. Milroy, repulsed, retreated to Franklin, where forces sent by Jackson came up with him on the afternoon of the eleventh. Two days of skirmishing in the narrow mountain defiles showed no results. On the morning of the thirteenth Jackson marched away from Milroy, back through McDowell and on toward Harrisonburg.

Milroy and Frémont were scotched for the time.   Other business was calling Jackson.

On the sixteenth the command halted all day to observe the national day of fasting, humiliation and prayer proclaimed by President Davis.   The next day but one, being a Sunday, there was another all-day halt at Mossy Creek, with religious services for most of the command.

At early dawn on Monday they marched, and marched hard. They passed through Harrisonburg, on the Valley Pike, where Richard Taylor's Louisiana brigade, the advance of Ewell's division, joined.   General Banks was looking for Jackson, if he advanced at all, to come down the pike, and Jackson did start that way, but at New Market he left the main road, turned sharp to the right, crossed the Massanutten into the Luray Valley, and pushed on down that line, augmented by the rest of Ewell's command.

While Jackson was pushing Milroy and Schenck back against Frémont, Shields' division of eleven thousand men had been taken from Banks and ordered to McDowell, leaving Banks in the Valley with less than ten thousand—but then it was believed that Jackson was out of the Valley.

In the afternoon of March twenty-third, after a long, swift and secret march, Jackson suddenly burst upon Banks' advanced troops at Front Royal, where the two forks of the river join. In this brisk battle, in which the Federal forces, outnumbered and outflanked, were driven from the field, leading parts were borne on each side by two "First Maryland" Regiments—one Union, one Confederate.   As a file of prisoners were passing to the rear, a young Maryland Confederate hailed with affection one of the Union prisoners.   They were brothers.

Jackson pushed on against Banks at Strasburg.   The pugnacious Banks, unwilling to retreat, started to hold his ground, but better counsel prevailed and he drew back to Winchester. There he determined to make a stand.   On the morning of the twenty-fifth, Jackson brought to bear his overwhelming force against him, flanked him out and drove him in disorder back to the Potomac and so, early the next day, out of the Valley.

Two days Jackson's worn men rested in camp north of Winchester, the fine old town in the lower Valley that was home to a great many of them. Vast stores of small arms, ammunition, medicines and supplies of all sorts were captured at Winchester. Great wagon trains were made up and started south, wagons moving on the pike two and three abreast for miles, filling it from fence to fence. To protect this movement, Jackson advanced again, threatening the Potomac at Harper's Ferry.

On May twenty-ninth he started his retreat, just in time. The main object of the Valley Campaign had been won. The President had canceled McDowell's order to join McClellan, and ordered him to dispatch twenty thousand men to the Valley to catch Jackson. Frémont, at the same time, was ordered to advance into the Valley from the west, for the same purpose. It was time that Jackson, with his great capture of supplies, should fall back from the open country in the lower Valley—which he did, passing back between the two Federal armies by a narrow margin.

Frémont and Shields pursued, moving up on either side of the Massanutten. Jackson, his captures secured, retreated to the upper, or southern, end of this barrier, and then by a series of bewildering marches, with sharp fights at Cross Keys and Port Republic, held off Frémont and drove back Shields. Both Frémont and Shields fell back down the Valley leaving Jackson secure in the upper end, at the place from which he had started just a little more than a month before.

The men who marched and fought with Jackson in that wonderful First Valley Campaign never tired of recalling it. There were other marches, and other great fights, but this was the first; it was back in those gay early days before the war became grim and desperate and a thing of vast weariness; back when happy laughing Bob Wheat, soldier of fortune in foreign lands, follower of Garibaldi, and so soon to die at Cold Harbor, was still leading his battalion of Louisiana Tigers, recruited from the docks of New Orleans; and while Turner Ashby yet rode his milk white horse at the head of Jackson's cavalry. He bore a charmed life, they said, but the charm was broken, almost at the end of the campaign, by a Union bullet in a little affair of outposts two days before the battle of Cross Keys. Jackson mourned him as a "friend, one of the noblest men and soldiers of the Confederate Army."

McDowell had been prepared to march on May twenty-sixth from Fredericksburg, to brush aside the slight opposition of Anderson's Confederate brigade, and to join forces with McClellan in the immediate vicinity of Richmond. On the twenty-fourth, while Jackson was in the lower Valley, the idea of brilliantly capturing him caused the President to order twenty thousand of McDowell's men to the Valley; fears for the safety of Washington caused him to keep the rest at Fredericksburg, covering the capital. McClellan, bitterly disappointed, had to fight his battles alone. He had, however, at least three men to Johnston's two. But there was that Chickahominy River. It was not, ordinarily, much of a stream, but in time of freshet it became a serious obstacle. To get at Richmond, and at the same time reach out toward McDowell, he had got on both sides of the stream, three corps on the north side, covering the base at the White House, two on the south side making the direct westward movement toward Richmond. Wooden bridges were thrown over the river, which angled across the front of the army, to maintain communication between the separated wings.

When McClellan had word that McDowell was to be denied him, he regained a certain freedom of action, of which he did not take advantage. He could have transferred his base from the York to the James River, moving his immense depot of supplies by water, and so have placed his entire command south of the Chickahominy. It was a movement that commended itself to him, and one which he afterward executed under the greatest pressure and with infinite peril.

For two months, now, McClellan had been pushing his way up the Peninsula, without serious opposition, just as Halleck had been moving against Corinth. On May thirtieth Corinth had been given up, but that could not be thought of with Richmond. As the enemy's advance was within sight of the spires and sound of the church-bells of Richmond, Johnston made his counter-stroke—the first grand battle in the East, to take its name of Seven Pines from a clump of trees not far from Fair Oaks Station, on the railroad from Richmond to the York River.

General Johnston's plan of battle was good; but it was not written out or made clear to the subordinate commanders who were to execute it. Moreover, these commanders, recently assembled into one army, had not yet been organized into corps, and there was more or less uncertainty about who ranked and commanded on vital portions of the field. The execution of the plan of battle, almost inevitably, was halting and confused.

The confusion in the execution of the plan came, largely, from an almost incredible ignorance of the topography of the country just below Richmond—the same ignorance that was to hamper Lee's actions in the Seven Days' Battles later on. The oldest English-speaking settlements in America were on this Peninsula, at Jamestown. For more than three hundred years it had been settled and occupied, but of the labyrinth of roads and tracks and creeks within its depths the invading Union forces knew far more than the Confederates. The Confederates relied on local guides, who, as almost all experience showed in the war, were more often than not unreliable because ignorant.

Most arm-chair *ex post facto* military criticism, however instructive it may be, is in a way impertinent—the views of a man, long afterward, studying out the situation at his leisure, without responsibility or distraction, and with all the information on both sides carefully collected and made available to him. Things are not done that way in war, but it is fair criticism to say that the Confederate authorities lamentably failed in not providing worth-while maps of the environs of Richmond.

Johnston, expecting McDowell to join McClellan and not knowing that his orders had been canceled, hastened his preparation to strike before reenforcements could come up.

On the morning of May thirty-first, when the battle opened, McClellan's force was stretched along the left bank, or northeast side, of the Chickahominy from the Mechanicsville Bridge, on his right, southeastward to the Grapevine Bridge, where the line crossed the river, turned due south, crossed the railroad at Fair Oaks Station and finally ended with its southern flank resting on the White Oak Swamp. That part of the line north of the river was held by the corps of Fitz-John Porter, Franklin and Sumner. South of the river and between it and the swamp, the corps of Keyes was pushed somewhat forward, centering about Fair Oaks Station, with that of Heintzelman behind it, between Fair Oaks and the river at Bottom's Bridge. During the night of the thirtieth, the Chickahominy had risen and was threatening the bridges connecting McClellan's separate wings.

Johnston's plan was to crush the advanced corps under Keyes, and force it back on Heintzelman's. As Johnston's entire force was much inferior to that of McClellan, he must arrange for a quick concentration at the decisive point, leaving lesser forces to contain the balance of the Union army.

To accomplish this Johnston had three roads running eastward from Richmond—in the middle, the Williamsburg Stage Road, straight east to the positions of Keyes; above it, the New Bridge or Nine Mile Road, which started somewhat to the north but branched southeast and struck the Union position at Fair Oaks Station; and the Charles City Road, the most southerly, which passed through the White Oak Swamp. Johnston's plan was to send Longstreet's heavy division of fourteen thousand men out by the northern road; D. H. Hill's, of nine thousand five hundred, by the central road; and Huger's, of five thousand men, by the southern road, as far as it led in the right direction, and then across country to the battle. Behind Longstreet, as he marched out the Nine Mile Road, was to come Whiting's five brigade division, to take position as a reserve northwest of Fair Oaks Station, whence they could be moved into Longstreet's battle, or used to fend off McClellan's corps north of the Chickahominy, should they undertake to cross and start toward Richmond. In addition to Whiting's force intended to be used either way as circumstances determined, there was on this part of the field the division of Magruder, watching McClellan's right, all under command of Major-General Gustavus W. Smith. On the southern part, where the main battle was to be, Longstreet was in command. Unfortunately, however, the gray-beard Huger had been brought up from Norfolk but a short while before, and it was not made clear to him that this young Longstreet was in charge of his movements. The consequent misunderstanding was but one of a series of mischances and delays.

Johnston himself moved to the northern part of the field, to see that McClellan did not cross troops against Longstreet's flank, and waited for the battle to begin. He waited and waited. Longstreet's troops, which should have poured past him on the Nine Mile Road, were not to be seen. Whiting came up and took his pivot position at Old Tavern, ready to fight either way as things developed, but no fight started.

Away on the right, Longstreet, placed in his first large command, had sadly bungled things. He had not marched by the Nine Mile Road, but had divided his force between the Williamsburg Road and the Charles City, which should have been clear for the movements of Hill and Huger. Even there, misunderstandings between him and Huger delayed the advance of the troops on the Charles City Road, each group waiting for the battle of the other to begin.

Finally, after one o'clock in the afternoon, the dashing D. H. Hill went into battle on the Williamsburg Road with his four brigades, later supported by two of Longstreet's. Longstreet had four more brigades there, besides three of Huger's under his command, but they were not brought into action. Six hours of hard fighting in that quarter of the field resulted in driving back Keyes' corps a mile or so.

Meanwhile, brave old Sumner, disregarding shaky bridges and rising waters, began to put his troops across the river to go to the rescue of Keyes. Johnston dispatched Whiting to help Longstreet finish his job on the Williamsburg Road. The two columns met in one of the desperate fights of the battle, late in the afternoon. Just before dark, Johnston was severely wounded.

G. W. Smith succeeded to the command. Longstreet he ordered to renew his attack on the morning of June first, changing its direction slightly to the north, and so meeting the troops which Sumner had crossed during the night, and at the same time closing the gap that was developing between the Confederate wings.

Longstreet did make a feeble attack the next morning, but did not press it. His dispatches of the day showed that he was laboring under the apprehension that the whole Union Army was being concentrated against him. In fact, the Union corps on the south side of the Chickahominy were very glad to be left alone. After a day of desultory fighting the Confederates withdrew to their original positions. The loss in killed and wounded during the two days was about five thousand on the Union side, more than six thousand on the Confederate.

General Johnston's wound was serious. He was to be out of the war for months. At two o'clock in the afternoon of June first, while the battle of Seven Pines was dying away, Robert E. Lee was put in command of the Army of Northern Virginia.

CHAPTER XIII

THE "SEVEN DAYS"

IN THAT June of 1862 the fortunes of the Confederacy were low.

In the East, Union armies were right at Richmond, and two days of bloody battle had just failed to drive them back; Norfolk was gone, and the North Carolina Sounds; Savannah was sealed up, Charleston closely beset; Wilmington alone of the principal ports remained open—or, at least, open enough for the swift blockade runners to slip in and out in the darkness.

In the West, New Orleans was gone, and Nashville. Memphis fell on June sixth, after a naval battle in the Mississippi, and on all the great river only Vicksburg was held by the Confederacy. All Kentucky, more than half of Tennessee, important territory in northern Alabama and Mississippi, were in Union hands. Pensacola, last of the Florida ports, had surrendered on May tenth; Mobile, the only other port on the Gulf with rail communication to the interior, was closely blockaded.

But, fortunately for the Confederacy, General Halleck seemed satisfied with the enforced retreat of Beauregard and the capture of Corinth. Had he held his great army together and closely pressed the main Confederate force, the summer held immense possibilities of achievement for the Union in that field, but this he did not do. He scattered his forces in garrisons and side operations, important enough in a local way, some of them, but in no sense decisive.

In the West, the grace of the enemy gave the Confederacy breathing time—and in the East, there was Robert E. Lee.

McClellan, after the Seven Pines, shifted all his army but the corps of Fitz-John Porter to the south bank of the Chickahominy, nearer to Richmond, but farther from McDowell. He had about lost hope of having McDowell's corps sent to him. He was there to capture Richmond, but he did not believe that he could do it without heavy reenforcement, for which he importuned Washington. While waiting, warned by the near-disaster of Seven Pines, he entrenched his entire front from the Chickahominy to the White Oak Swamp. Reenforcements came, twenty thousand of them, bringing his strength up to about one hundred and five thousand, but Lee, he believed, had two hundred thousand. To this belief he was led by his own temperament, and by the reports of the Secret Service, an organization headed by the great detective, Allan Pinkerton. Military intelligence, it developed, was not the strong point of the Pinkerton organization.

Just what McClellan would have done after he got his troops all nicely entrenched and made his position south of the river unassailable is not clear, for while he waited to decide the initiative was taken from him by Lee.

Lee's first care, upon taking command, was to select and begin fortifying a line of battle about Richmond, a procedure that brought upon him once more the scorn of the amateur strategists who wanted aggressive battle. To most observers, it seemed that the quiet, dignified, reserved Lee would not have the audacity to run risks and take chances, as the commander of an inferior army must if he is to have any chance of success. To a few who had known him in Mexico, or in the West, there was no question about it. "If there is one man in either army, Confederate or Federal, head and shoulders above every other in *audacity*, it is General Lee!" said Colonel Ives of the President's staff.

Lee, though, was more than just bold and audacious. He wanted to know all about his enemy's arrangements and dispositions. For that purpose, on June eleventh, he dispatched General J. E. B. Stuart, with twelve hundred cavalry and a section of artillery, to see what was behind McClellan's front. Stuart rode north as far as Ashland. Officers and men thought they were bound for the Rapidan or the Valley, when suddenly they turned east, passed behind McClellan's right and far to his rear, created a vast commotion near the base at the White House, obstructed the railroad at Tunstall's Station, and secured information about the enemy's line of supplies.

That done, the venturesome Stuart decided that the long way around was the best way home. Instead of turning back by the road he had come he rode on south, clear across the Peninsula, turned back west toward Richmond, and on the third day rode into the capital by the James River Road, having been clear around McClellan's Army with the loss of but one man killed and a few wounded.

This bold feat of arms, accomplished with dash and vigor entranced the imagination of the South. A handful of troopers circumventing and taunting the great army of invasion, set a style in cavalry raids for the Confederacy, the "raid around the army." Stuart himself was rarely able to resist the slightest temptation to repeat the romantic performance—once, at least, with most unfortunate results, not to Stuart's cavalry but to the army for which they were supposed to furnish the eyes and the screen.

This first raid around the army, too, helped to make McClellan realize how vulnerable was his base on the Pamunkey, and started him to thinking in earnest about changing to the James, now that there was no longer any real likelihood of having to connect with McDowell coming down from the north. In fact, within a few days, McClellan took precautions. He sent numerous boat loads of supplies of all sorts, ammunition and subsistence, around by water to Harrison's Landing on the James. There he established an emergency depot. Moreover, he put his engineers to work mapping the roads and laying out routes. When the time came for the change of base it was the invading army, not that of the South, which knew most about the winding country roads and labyrinthine ways on which that vast movement was to be made.

About the same time that Stuart started on his famous raid, six regiments of troops under Lawton, just arrived from Georgia, and two brigades under Whiting, were loaded on the railroad cars at Richmond, rather ostentatiously, and shipped off to

Jackson in the Valley. The movement was promptly reported to Washington, as it was meant to be.

Arrived in the Valley, Lawton and Whiting reported to Jackson. Jackson, secretive as ever, sent them back to their troops at Staunton, to await orders. Whiting, as he told afterward, decided that Jackson was a fool. There he was, come all the way from Richmond, and apparently nothing for him to do. The next day, when orders came to go back east across the Blue Ridge to Gordonsville, Whiting *knew* that Jackson "hadn't as much sense as my horse." "Why," he said, "we just came through Gordonsville on the way here day before yesterday."

Being a soldier, though, he obeyed the order whether or not he saw the sense to it. He went to Gordonsville, where he found Jackson and the Valley army. From Gordonsville they might move toward Washington or toward Richmond, and no one except "Old Jack" himself and one other understood which it was to be. At Washington the anxious government, knowing that reenforcements had gone to Jackson in the Valley, and not knowing what had become of him since, was holding McDowell's corps, which might have settled the war had it been joined to McClellan.

On Saturday night, June twenty-first, Jackson and his chief of staff, Major R. L. Dabney, a Presbyterian minister before the war and professor in the University of Texas after it, shut themselves in a closed car on the railroad and started toward Richmond. At Frederick's Hall Station, fifty-two miles from Richmond, Jackson and Major Dabney left the train, about dawn on Sunday morning, to spend that day in seclusion and divine service. Just after midnight, it being then Monday, Jackson started for Richmond, traveling swiftly by relays of horses, and secretly, without escort or insignia of rank. Just after noon he came to the house where General Lee had summoned him, on the Mechanicsville Road, northeast of Richmond.

Major-General Daniel H. Hill was called to the same house. As Hill dismounted, a dusty officer leaning over the yard fence, tired and drooping, raised himself and Hill saw his brother-in-law, Jackson, whom he had thought far away in the Valley

Together, they went in to General Lee, who "courteously tendered refreshments." Jackson declined, but drank a glass of milk. In a little while, Longstreet and A. P. Hill came in. General Lee closed the door, and unfolded to these four principal lieutenants his plan of battle.

He had decided on a swift secret concentration of almost his entire army on the north bank of the Chickahominy, to crush the corps which McClellan had left there. Only the divisions of Magruder and Huger were to stand between McClellan's main army and Richmond. The risk was great, but a general in the position of Lee before Richmond has to take great risks to attain worth-while ends. And the end to be accomplished was worth while. With Fitz-John Porter's corps out of the way, the Union base on the Pamunkey and the line of communications by the York River Railroad would be wide open to Lee unless McClellan should hastily fall back. Of course, while Lee was attacking Porter, McClellan, closer to Richmond than Lee, might knock Magruder and Huger aside and march into the capital—but that was a risk that had to be taken, and Lee, knowing the bent of McClellan's mind, was willing to take the chance.

Lee left the subordinates to work out details among themselves. The tactical plan was that Jackson, approaching from the northwest, should strike on and behind the Union right flank; pass down behind it, rolling it up, and so clear the crossings of the Chickahominy over which the divisions of the two Hills and Longstreet were to advance. As Jackson had the longest march, and must be in position to strike the first blow, he was asked to set the time for the attack. "Daylight of the twenty-sixth," he answered. Longstreet suggested that he take one more day to make sure, but Jackson was satisfied that he could be in position then.

On that basis Lee issued his orders. Jackson was to advance toward Pole Green Church at three o'clock on the morning of Thursday, the twenty-sixth. General Branch, who held the extreme left of the Confederate line, seven miles above the Meadow Bridge, was to cross as soon as Jackson reached his front, and advance down the north bank of the Chickahominy toward Mechanicsville. As soon as these columns moved, A. P. Hill was to cross at the Meadow Bridge, almost directly north of Richmond, turn to the right and drive the enemy from Mechanicsville, so opening the bridge near that point to the passage of Longstreet's troops. Longstreet was to cross and go

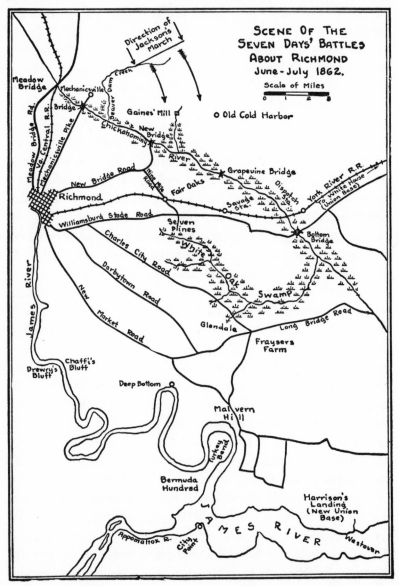

SCENE OF THE
SEVEN DAYS' BATTLES
ABOUT RICHMOND
June - July 1862.

to the support of A. P. Hill; D. H. Hill to follow Longstreet and join Jackson; all four divisions to sweep southeastward down the Chickahominy, with Jackson leading and bearing well to the left toward Old Cold Harbor.

Time and human weariness are inescapable facts in war. It takes time to move bodies of men, and vast weariness. To an extent weariness can be defeated and time denied—but only to an extent. Before the Seven Days, and after, men whom Jackson led showed a capacity for destroying distance and defying weariness that made them immortal as the "foot cavalry," but during the series of battles about to begin in the dark and tangled swamps of the Chickahominy Jackson lacked his usual vigor and drive. He was, say some, under a "spell," bemused. More likely it is that even his strength failed him after the ride to Richmond, which he would not begin on Sunday, the return to his command, the march to his starting position—more than three days and nights of continuous movement and strain. Weariness could no longer be denied.

The morning of Thursday, the twenty-sixth, came—and no Jackson. Finally, at three in the afternoon, the impetuous A. P. Hill, fearing to lose everything, decided to wait no longer. He forced his way across the river, drove the Union forces from the little plateau about Mechanicsville, down across the bottom of Beaver Dam Creek. D. H. Hill, nearest to the crossing, pushed over to join in the attack.

About dark, the Confederate forces advanced down the open and exposed slope to the creek, to find, to their terrible cost, that they were going against an impregnably fortified position, not known or shown on any of their maps. In those early days of the war—it was only the fourth grand battle of the whole struggle—it was still thought to be war to charge, with waving flags, against infantry and guns secure behind earthworks. Twenty-one Confederate regiments marched down the slope and into the face of that blasting fire. One regiment alone, the Forty-fourth Georgia, lost almost as many men as the entire Union force engaged, and fell back from the battle, a handful of shaken men without an officer.

That night, with more than two thousand Confederate dead and wounded scattered on the banks of Beaver Dam Creek, Jackson passed beyond the Union right flank, a day late. During the night Porter fell back to a second prepared position, on a curving ridge east of Powhite Creek. There, on the twenty-seventh, was fought the second of the Seven Days' Battles, known as Gaines's Mill.

It was two o'clock in the afternoon before the Confederate attack began. At that hour A. P. Hill's division desperately assaulted Porter's center and left, for two hours, to be repulsed, considerably broken and disordered. At four, Longstreet, to his right and closer to the river, went in to relieve the pressure on Hill, and then turned his feint into a real attack. Jackson, to whom D. H. Hill had been joined, came down from the north, from the direction of the old tavern, the smithy and the little cluster of houses known as Old Cold Harbor. He was well on Porter's exposed right flank, but the country was so dense, its woods roads so winding and devious, that much time was lost in getting into the battle and then, when they came in, they were badly scattered.

Meanwhile Porter, knowing that he had an army to fight, called for help. Franklin, the corps commander next to him across the river, sent Slocum's division. The other commanders on the south side, impressed with the strong demonstration of Magruder, feared an attack on their own fronts, and felt that they could spare no men. No one in the army could do a better job of demonstrating than "Prince John" Magruder.

At last, not long before dark, Porter's gallantly held line broke and retreated through the woods, to cross the Chickahominy. Darkness prevented an effective pursuit. The bridges were burned behind them, and Porter's corps was away.

What next? McClellan had four courses open to him: to advance and attack Richmond, while its defenders were north of the Chickahominy and farther away than the Union army; to fall back along the railroad to defend his base at the White House; to retreat by the way he had come, back through Williamsburg and Yorktown; or to shift his base to the south side of the Peninsula, on the James. The first course was too audacious for his temperament; the second, difficult and dangerous with Lee on his exposed flank; the third, too bitter a pill for his military pride. He chose the fourth.

Burnings and explosions within his line south of the Chickahominy during the night indicated that he was getting ready to retreat; destruction of the bridges on the York River route showed that he was not going to the base on the Pamunkey—but that left open two courses against both of which Lee must guard. If McClellan were going to retreat to Williamsburg Lee's army belonged on the north bank of the Chickahominy; if to the James, on the south.

McClellan started his great retreat—always referred to by him as the "change of base"—on Friday night. It was a masterpiece as a retreat, nearly a hundred thousand men, more than four thousand wagons, three hundred and fifty guns, immense stores, all crowded in between the Chickahominy and the White Oak Swamp, and all to be got out, across the swamp and on to the south, over narrow, winding country roads, exposed almost all the way to attacks from the rear or on the flank toward Richmond. That the retreat was successfully made speaks much for McClellan's abilities in that particularly difficult sort of warfare, and for the admirable training and steadiness of his troops. But even at that, the great army could not have untangled itself from the swamps and made its escape but for the persistent mishandling, delays and confusion of the Confederate subordinate commanders.

On Saturday, June twenty-eighth, Lee put his troops to work repairing the bridges across the Chickahominy destroyed by the retreating Federals, except Ewell's division which was sent down the northeast bank of the river to intercept any movement to recross to that bank and start toward Williamsburg.

All that Saturday the Union army was making its perilous passage of the White Oak Swamp. North of the swamp they were protected by their strong entrenchments thrown up after the Seven Pines; south of it, a short day's march away, was Malvern Hill, a great natural defensive position on which

McClellan's overwhelming artillery could be arranged tier on tier, sweeping the open ground over which any Confederate attack must come. Back of Malvern Hill was the James and safety. The critical point in the retreat was the passage from the swamp to the hill, on a road intersected by three running out from Richmond.

Keyes' corps crossed the swamp first, and early on Sunday morning took up position facing Richmond, while behind them filed the four thousand wagons and ambulances, the great train of the reserve artillery, the shaken corps of Porter, the herd of two thousand five hundred beef cattle assembled for subsistence of the army. That day Heintzelman, Sumner and part of Franklin's corps held the ground north of the swamp, acting as rear-guard.

Not until Sunday morning, the twenty-ninth, did Lee sufficiently divine McClellan's movement to be able to throw all he had to meet it. Meanwhile Stuart and his cavalry had gone again to the White House, where they were having a high and happy time destroying rich Federal stores, out of reach and of no more use until after the final battle of the campaign at Malvern Hill; Ewell was far down the Chickahominy on the north, or wrong, side and had to be brought back to the bridges to get across—but the rest of the army was in hand.

Lee's plan for using his resources against McClellan was designed to turn an orderly retreat into a rout—but the plan was not executed. Magruder was ordered to advance straight east on the Williamsburg Road, while Jackson and D. H. Hill were to cross the river on the Grapevine Bridge, over which Porter had retreated. The two forces were to attack the strong Union rear-guard north of the White Oak Swamp, flank and rear. Longstreet and A. P. Hill, meanwhile, were to march back up the river, the way they had come, cross on the upper bridges, circle around almost through Richmond itself and then, joined by Huger, to attack the Union troops as they filed out of the swamp on the south side and marched for Malvern Hill.

The plan failed in execution. Instead of a sharp and vigorous attack by Magruder and Jackson on the Union rear-guard,

Jackson spent the entire day rebuilding the Grapevine Bridge and did not attack at all. It was Sunday, and Jackson, withdrawn in communion within himself, did not push and drive as he could. Magruder, meanwhile, did not get into battle at Savage's Station until afternoon—the third battle of the Seven Days to start too late to accomplish its end. The Union rearguard held its ground, finished its work, and during the night crossed the swamp. Twenty-five hundred sick and wounded were left to Magruder, but most of the stores that could not be carried away were destroyed, the ammunition exploded, the railroad trains run full speed ahead off the end of the broken bridge into the Chickahominy.

By Monday morning, June thirtieth, McClellan, successfully through the swamp, destroyed the bridges by which he had come. Jackson came up about noon to the north side of the White Oak, to lose that day in an unnecessary rebuilding of bridges at places where his hardy veterans could have waded the stream. About the same time, Longstreet and A. P. Hill, finishing their circuit to gain the south side of the swamp, were ready to attack the corps posted to cover the tedious march of the retreating army. Huger, ordered in on their left, was having trouble with roads obstructed by felled trees, a trouble aggravated by a shortage of axes among the Confederates.

Away to the south, General Theophilus H. Holmes, just up from Carolina with a green division, had run into trouble in his advance down the river road toward Malvern Hill. The gunboats in the James opened on them, throwing the elongated shell that the Confederates called "lamp-posts" at the nervous troops, "mighty careless like." Just as panic threatened the deaf old General stepped out of the house where he had established temporary headquarters, cupped his hand about his ear and blandly inquired, "I thought I heard firing?"

Holmes was under orders to take and hold the position at Malvern Hill, but McClellan's advance was before him. Holmes called for help. Longstreet sent him Magruder. Before Magruder could get there, Longstreet himself had opened that battle against the flank of McClellan's line of retreat. to become known as Frayser's Farm, or Glendale; had run into trouble himself, and recalled Magruder. Before Magruder could get back to him, the short, bloody afternoon battle was over. Only the divisions of Longstreet and A. P. Hill attacked. Huger did not get up on the left. Jackson held his own troops and those of D. H. Hill north of the swamp, inactive. It was not like Jackson.

In spite of captures of guns and men, Frayser's Farm was a check to the Confederates. They were held off long enough for darkness to come, and for the Union army to make good its retreat to Malvern Hill.

Malvern Hill was Lee's great tactical mistake. An army unshaken, as we know now, held an impregnable position, backed by the fire of gunboats on the James. Against it, late in the afternoon of July first, Lee threw a badly organized, piecemeal attack of part of his force. With incredible gallantry and persistence, the Confederate brigades and divisions dashed themselves against the Army of the Potomac with its two hundred and fifty guns trained on them. It was a mad attempt, justified only, if at all, by the belief that the Union army was broken and in retreat, and that one more push would throw them back into the James. It was a mad attempt—and five thousand men, dead and wounded, men whom the Confederacy could not spare, were left on the slopes of the hill above the James at dark of the last of the Seven Days.

Richmond, from being closely besieged, felt herself free of the invader. Her joy, and that of the Confederacy, was in proportion to the despondency with which the spring had opened. Not since Manassas, now almost a year gone, had there been such cause for southern rejoicing. Only Lee, clear-headed, level-headed Lee, was not satisfied. He judged the Seven Days not by what had been accomplished—the raising of the close siege of Richmond, the capture of prisoners and guns, of small arms and supplies—but by comparison with what he had planned and missed, the rout and destruction of the greatest army of the North.

CHAPTER XIV

The Great Days of the Confederacy

THOSE summer days of 1862 were the great days of the Confederacy, when spirits drooping in June, high in July, were to soar as the triple offensive of the South got under way.

President Davis, tall, slender, erect, soldierly in his suit of Confederate gray, with his soft black hat, broad in the brim, might well have seemed less burdened as he responded with grave courtesy to the greetings of those he met as he walked through the grounds of the Capitol. Military affairs, to which his mind always turned, were going better. Of course there was less difficulty with Congress and the state governments and the whole political side of the Presidency, which he did not like and never mastered. His health was better, too. His inner enemy, a nervous dyspepsia, was not sending him from the office, home, "fasting, a mere mass of throbbing nerves, and perfectly exhausted," as the sympathetic Mrs. Davis described him. If there were any happy days for the proud and sensitive soul of Jefferson Davis during the martyrdom of heading the Confederacy, they were these.

Richmond, which had grown used to the sound of the guns to the east and north, drawing nearer and nearer, heard them no more after the Seven Days. This first and most emphasized of Union objectives was not again to be threatened seriously, until almost the very end.

Besides the drive against the Confederate capital and the maintenance of the unrelenting blockade, the forces of the Union had settled down to two main lines of effort: the opening of the Mississippi River and the occupation of East Tennessee, with its large Unionist population and its important railroad, the short line connecting Richmond with Chattanooga and the entire central South. It was toward these ends that Halleck directed his forces after the fall of Corinth and the retreat of Beauregard's army to Tupelo, farther to the south in Mississippi.

Nothing that the South ever did—or could do—made any real difference in the slow strangling of the blockade, never relaxed, but in the interior things were going better, almost everywhere, by the middle of the summer of 1862.

The main western army, under Braxton Bragg who had succeeded the ailing Beauregard, was still at Tupelo, restored in numbers and health, strengthened in training and discipline. The new commander was able, even, to plan an aggressive campaign.

Halleck, at the beginning of July, was himself still at Corinth, but he had scattered his great army over four states. Sherman, with a division, was at Memphis; Grant, with his own army and what had been Pope's, was holding West Tennessee and northern Mississippi, with a campaign against Vicksburg, following the railroad line southward, as his objective.

Facing Grant was Sterling Price, with part of that Army of the West which he and Van Dorn had brought across the Mississippi too late to get into the battle of Shiloh.

In Arkansas, Major-General T. C. Hindman, sent there just before the fall of Corinth, by his vigorous reorganization was doing much to raise Confederate hopes of holding that state, and perhaps, even, of going back into Missouri, in spite of the fact that Curtis, victor at Pea Ridge or Elkhorn Tavern more than six months before, succeeded early in July in taking and fortifying the important town of Helena, on the Mississippi, and so establishing a new Union base for the invasion of the eastern part of Arkansas by combined land and gunboat expeditions.

On the Mississippi, Vicksburg held fast, and so long as it held blocked the free use of the river by Union forces. Van Dorn, with a command separate from that of Price, was in charge of the land defenses there, but in the summer of 1862 the only serious effort made against the place was by the Union Navy, operating from above and from below. Confederate batteries crowning the bluffs above the river, and the Confederate Navy in those waters, consisting for the most part of one iron-clad ram, the *Arkansas,* offered successful resistance.

Vicksburg, on its bluffs on the Mississippi twelve miles be-low the mouth of the Yazoo, attracted a vast deal of attention from the Union Navy and the nation that summer.   While the gunboat flotilla, now under Davis, was working its way down from Memphis in June, Farragut's fleet, with which he had captured New Orleans, Baton Rouge and Natchez, appeared before Vicksburg from below.   On June twenty-eighth, after a bombardment of two days from Porter's mortar-boats, or "bom-bers," Farragut repeated his famous tactics of "running the forts."   The fleet, all but three vessels, got by all right, but did no real damage to the forts and received none of conse quence themselves.   Lying in the great river above Vicksburg Farragut's Western Gulf Squadron was joined by the gunboat flotilla, under Davis, and the rams, under Ellet, which had worked their way down-stream after the capture of Memphis. On July second Farragut reported that "the forts can be passed," but intimated that nothing substantial could be done without troops to take the land defenses.

All this time, while the mortar fleet under Porter was bom-barding the forts at Vicksburg each day, as a slight foretaste of what was to come the next year, and while the fleets were lying in the river above the town, the troops with the expedition were attempting to cut a canal across the narrow point of land opposite the city and so turn the river into a new channel, through which ships and transports could pass at will without being exposed to the fire of the forts.   Four thousand men worked on the canal, night and day, but the river fell faster than they could lower the bottom of the ditch, and it was never possible to turn the water into it.

Meanwhile, at Yazoo City, an ingenious and indomitable former Lieutenant of the old Navy, Isaac N. Brown, was at work on a home-made, iron-clad ram, the *Arkansas.*   Never was a ship of war built under more difficult conditions—the ship-yard far up a blockaded river, without experienced shipwrights, without materials, equipment or armament except such as could be hauled in by ox teams from the railroad twenty-five miles away. Within five weeks, such was the driving spirit of Captain Brown and his force, the *Arkansas* was ready to run, or as ready as ever she would be. Like all the Confederate naval vessels, her engines were crazy and unreliable at best, impossible at worst. Everything was improvised, including the crew, most of whom were cavalrymen from the Missouri irregulars of General Jeff Thompson. On July 14, 1862, Brown started out of the Yazoo to engage the thirty-seven Union men-of-war that he knew were in the vicinity of Vicksburg.

Early on the next morning, as she was approaching the main channel of the Mississippi, the *Arkansas* met three Union gunboats, one of them the ironclad *Carondelet*, commanded by Henry Walke, who had been a messmate of Brown's in the old Navy. The *Arkansas*, in spite of her rickety engines, stood for the little flotilla, and with superior weight of metal drove them before her. Finally, after a sharp fight, the Union boats were forced to retire disabled for action, using their superior speed and lighter draft to escape. The *Arkansas* continued down the Mississippi, to the place where a forest of masts and smoke-stacks showed the anchorage of the Federal fleets. In spite of the heat in her iron-sheathed boiler and engine-rooms, where men could work but a few minutes until they were exhausted, and in spite of her slow speed and poor maneuverability, the *Arkansas* stood for the fleet. She shaved the line of them along the levee so closely that no Union ram could come out with enough speed to hurt her, while much of the gunfire from the Union vessels did more harm among their own fleet than on the hull of the *Arkansas*, crawling along the line, and delivering broadsides which at that range could not miss some mark.

By the time the *Arkansas* had shaved her way past what seemed an interminable line of enemy ships, she was sadly battered, and her boilers and engines were failing fast, but she made her way on down to Vicksburg, and the protection of the land batteries, sent half her crew ashore, dead or wounded, and went to work with a will on temporary repairs. Before these could be finished, just at sunset, part of the enemy fleet steamed down the river, to pass the forts and take up station below Vicksburg. For the third time that day the *Arkansas* went into action, emptying her broadside into each ship as it passed between her and the glow of the western sky.

The *Arkansas*, controlling the stretch of river in front of Vicksburg, was able to threaten the upper or the lower fleets, and to force their vessels to keep up steam in the intense heat of mid-July on the lower Mississippi. To destroy this constant menace, two of the best of the Union river vessels, the *Essex* and the *Queen of the West*, made a most gallant attempt to ram and destroy her as she lay under the land batteries. The *Arkansas*, with a crew reduced by then to twenty men, stood her ground and made good her resistance. Before the end of the month, Farragut's fleet weighed anchor and stood away for the south, while the river fleet steamed back north. The naval siege of Vicksburg was raised, as much by the desperate gallantry of the fighting of one little ten-gun home-made boat as by the power of the batteries ashore.

A week later the brave vessel ended her brief career by self-destruction. Ordered from Vicksburg to cooperate in the land attack of August fifth against Baton Rouge, she had to push her crazy old engines too hard on the run of three hundred miles at top speed. Arrived just above Baton Rouge, which General Breckinridge was to attack from the landward side, the engines failed entirely, and the vessel became unmanageable. Able to bring but one gun to bear on the approaching enemy, it was decided to abandon and fire the ram, rather than to have her captured and used against the Confederacy. With the fire and the explosion of her powder magazines, the story of the *Arkansas* was ended.

The capture of East Tennessee, with its large Unionist population, the fourth major activity during the summer of 1862, was especially interesting to President Lincoln and Secretary Stanton for political and sentimental reasons. It was important, too, from the military standpoint, because of the railroad line running from Chattanooga through Knoxville and Lynchburg to Richmond and the East. Buell's advance toward this section, interrupted in the early spring by the necessity of going to the aid of Grant at Shiloh, was resumed in June, after the fall of Corinth.

Unfortunately for Buell, he had come under command of Halleck, who insisted that as he moved his troops eastward from Corinth toward Chattanooga he should rebuild the Memphis & Charleston Railroad as he went, and maintain it. During all of June, while McClellan was fortifying himself about Richmond, and Grant was standing fast in northern Mississippi, Buell was slowly pushing his way eastward across northern Alabama, building railroad as he went. The requirement was absurdly impractical, as the railroad line, which was the "frontier" between the territory held by the two armies, was liable to interruption almost in every mile as soon as it was rebuilt, and even when in running order could not be used to supply Buell's army from Memphis, because of constant raids and forays by small southern mounted parties.

June, when Chattanooga was held only by the small force of Kirby Smith, was wasted in this toilsome and creeping movement. By the end of the month, Buell had got permission to return to his original plan of advance, making Louisville his main base, with Nashville as an advanced secondary base, and using the railroad from Nashville to Chattanooga as his line of advance. He put his forces to work to repair the Nashville & Chattanooga Railroad, well within his lines and supposed to be secure from interruption. On July twelfth, so well did they work, a train was operated from Nashville through to the Tennessee River, the point of Buell's advance. Everything was now ready for the capture of the mountain-girt key position of Chattanooga, which would afford a base for the occupation of East Tennessee and a break-up in Confederate communications quite as important as the control of the Mississippi itself.

The night that the railroad was reopened, some fourteen hundred Confederates under Brigadier-General Forrest, the same who had ridden out of Fort Donelson with his men, were marching forty miles toward Murfreesboro, an important and well-garrisoned station, thirty miles southeast of Nashville

Before mid-afternoon of the thirteenth, Forrest's men had made prisoners of the garrison, about their own number, had captured and hauled off a considerable accumulation of supplies, and had so thoroughly broken up the railroad that it could not be used again for two weeks.

Forrest, with his handful of men, boldly remained within the territory held by Buell's army. Hard riders and hard fighters, under a leader who was to develop the qualities of a great general, they were a source of infinite trouble to Buell—and to many another Federal commander before the war ended.

Just after Buell got his communications south of Nashville in working order they were cut again, this time between Nashville and Louisville. John H. Morgan, a Kentuckian whose previous military experience had been that of a volunteer lieutenant in the Mexican War, crossed the Cumberland River at Hartsville and, on August twelfth, destroyed the twin tunnels on the Louisville & Nashville Railroad north of Gallatin.

And finally, before Buell was again ready to advance to Chattanooga, the situation there had changed. Kirby Smith, commanding the Confederate department of East Tennessee, had advanced to Knoxville, on his way to Kentucky. Bragg had moved into Chattanooga with his main army, transported from Tupelo by rail, around through Mobile and Atlanta to Chattanooga, and was preparing to advance into Middle Tennessee and Kentucky. Buell, before the summer ended, was compelled to stand on the defensive.

In Virginia, too, events in the summer of 1862 so shaped themselves that Lee was able to hold the offensive taken during the Seven Days.

Major-General John Pope, whose Island No. 10 campaign had won renown and commendation, was called to the East late in June to take command of a new Union Army, made up of all the forces of McDowell about Washington and of Banks and Frémont, whom Jackson had left in the Valley while he slipped away to take his part in the battles about Richmond. While McClellan's army was fighting the Seven Days, Pope was in

Washington, getting the lay of the land and acting as the un-official military adviser to President Lincoln.

After Malvern Hill, in a night of drenching rain, McClellan fell back to the James about Harrison's Landing, a region of gracious old colonial homes: "Beverly," where President William Henry Harrison was born; "Westover," the home of Governor William Byrd; "Shirley," seat of the Carters and the girl-hood home of Lee's mother, the "Brandons," Upper and Lower. There he settled down to begin his importunities for vast reen-forcements with which to make trial once more against Lee's "vastly superior numbers"; to write his complaints against the "Government that has not sustained this army," his vague in-timations that "persons in Washington" had done their "best to sacrifice this army."

President Lincoln was a patient man, and an eager and humble seeker after military competence and successful leader-ship. "Little Mac," whatever his defects of temperament, held and continued to hold the devotion of the great Army of the Potomac which he had built up. Lincoln recognized this and appreciated it. All that he asked was that McClellan use his army. He visited him at his new base, a visit that had but one definite result, the appointment on July eleventh of Major-General Halleck in McClellan's old place as commander-in-chief of all the armies. General Halleck, at that time, possessed the entire confidence of the President and, to large extent, that of the country. They had seen the sweep forward of the great armies in the West under his nominal command, and it was yet too early to see the results of the unwise dispersion of forces and scattering of efforts after Corinth.

Meanwhile Pope was busy taking over his new command, to be called during its short and stormy life the "Army of Virginia." He was greatly impressed with the difficulties of his problem. While McClellan was crying for reenforcements to be taken from Pope, Pope was calling for the transfer to him of McClellan's troops. Both of them were impressed with the superior strength of Lee, who lay between them and waited developments. The active D. H. Hill was sent to begin the fortification of Petersburg, the key to the approaches of Richmond from the south, whose importance and undefended condition had been noted; Jackson was sent back along the railroad to the junction at Gordonsville, a position where he could keep up the anxiety in Washington and at the same time be in quick reach of Richmond, should McClellan resume the offensive.

General Pope, held in Washington to advise with the President, decided that his soldiers needed an injection of the "offensive spirit," apparently—although their assigned task at that time was in no sense offensive, but was to hold Lee still until McClellan's army could be brought to reenforce them. Writing in reminiscent vein years afterward, General Pope told of the misgivings with which he, a stranger to the eastern armies and junior to the men over whose heads he was stepped, entered into his new command. If he felt any such diffidence at the time, it took strange form. "To the Officers and Soldiers of the Army of Virginia," he addressed from Washington on July 14, 1862, a pronouncement that is the classic of military bombast.

"By special assignment of the President of the United States," it ran, "I have assumed command of this Army. . . . I am about to join you in the field.

"Let us understand each other. I have come to you from the West, where we have always seen the backs of our enemies; from an army whose business it has been to seek the adversary, and to beat him when he was found; whose policy has been attack and not defense. . . . I desire you to dismiss from youı minds certain phrases, which I am sorry to find so much in vogue amongst you. I hear constantly of 'taking strong positions and holding them,' of 'lines of retreat' and of 'bases of supplies.' Let us discard such ideas. . . . Let us study the probable lines of retreat of our opponents, and leave our own to take care of themselves. . . ."

With this happy and tactful beginning the last campaign of Major-General John Pope opened. In the tug of ideas between the two army commanders, Pope won out, and on August third Halleck ordered the bitterly disappointed McClellan to break up his base on the James and send his troops by water to the vicinity of Washington. Burnside and Reno, from the North Carolina coast expedition, and Stevens, from Port Royal, with a total of sixteen thousand men originally destined for the neighborhood of Richmond, were also ordered to Pope. While all these reenforcements were on the move toward him Pope acted on his own dictum and started out to "seek the adversary."

Early in August with nearly fifty thousand men assembled along the Rappahannock, he pushed south of this river into the no-man's land between it and the Rapidan. Jackson was the adversary. He was about Gordonsville, south of the Rapidan, with some fourteen thousand men. As Pope moved, Jackson was reenforced by the division of A. P. Hill, bringing his strength up to about twenty-four thousand. On August seventh he advanced, also, crossed the Rapidan and moved north. On the next day Pope started Banks' corps and the cavalry south. On the afternoon of August ninth, the two forces met at the base of Cedar Mountain. Banks, brave and pugnacious, attacked, was driven back with heavy loss. Jackson, having struck, knew better than to pick a fight with Pope's whole army, double his own, with no other help near. He got back to the south side of the Rapidan to wait for news from Richmond; Pope pushed forward to the north bank of the river and encamped.

On August fifteenth the Union reenforcements from the Carolina expeditions joined Pope; at the same time Lee started the rest of his army to Gordonsville, leaving but two brigades in front of Richmond to watch McClellan pack up and depart. For a few days, while McClellan's corps were in transit, the armies of Lee and Pope were to be not far from equal in number. After that Pope could look for heavy reenforcements, Lee for none. He had all that the Confederacy, with its policy of the dispersed defensive, could give him.

South of the Rapidan rises a bold hill, Clark's Mountain. From it Lee looked out over Pope's vast and rich camp. Straightway to the north ran the Orange & Alexandria Railroad, his life-line of supply, well covered by the position of the army, but seven or eight miles away the rail line turned sharply toward the bridge over the Rappahannock, to the east of Pope's position and not covered by his army. Lee planned then and

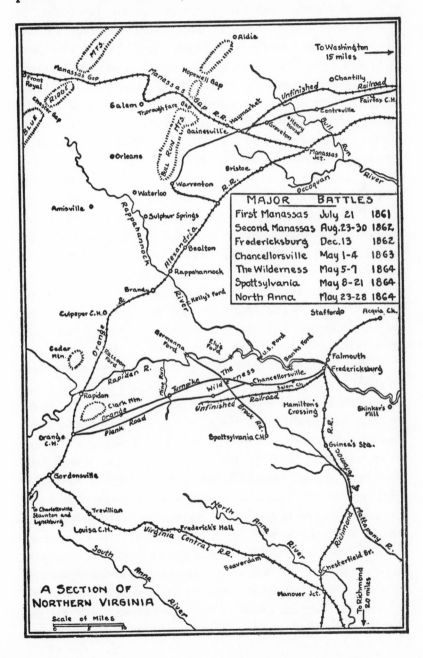

MAJOR BATTLES

First Manassas	July 21	1861
Second Manassas	Aug. 23-30	1862
Fredericksburg	Dec. 13	1862
Chancellorsville	May 1-4	1863
The Wilderness	May 5-7	1864
Spottsylvania	May 8-21	1864
North Anna	May 23-28	1864

A SECTION OF NORTHERN VIRGINIA

Scale of Miles

there a bold and simple movement. Jackson and Longstreet, with the body of the army, were to cross the Rapidan and strike Pope's camp, front and flank, while Stuart rode away to the east to destroy the railroad bridge and cut his life-line.

There was a good chance of the destruction of Pope's army, advanced, isolated and exposed, ignorant of Lee's plans—when a cavalry detachment, raiding south of the Rapidan, captured Stuart's headquarters dispatch book in which the whole plan was given. Pope took the alarm and hurriedly fell back to the north bank of the Rappahannock, and safety.

Lee, crossing the Rapidan, advanced to the south bank of the Rappahannock, where he planned another surprise for Pope: Jackson to cross by the fords above and fall on his flank, while Longstreet attacked in front. After Jackson had got Jubal Early's brigade across, there came torrential rains, a great freshet in the river. Not only was it impossible to get the rest of the corps across, it was with great difficulty that Early's brigade was got back from its exposed position.

Meanwhile, Pope, ordered by Halleck to "dispute every inch of the ground and fight like the devil till we can reenforce you," remained in a spread-out and exposed position, protected principally by high water in the river.

Toward the headwaters of the Rappahannock there were practicable crossings, freshet or no freshet, but they were miles away. To use them would mean a complete separation of the two wings of Lee's army, always risky, usually unwise. Lee, however, determined on the movement. It was one that the books would condemn as against the rules of war, but there were facts of local geography which made it not so risky as it might appear. Pope now had about seventy thousand men and reenforcements were coming in day by day. The boldest plan was, in this case, the safest.

Longstreet, with Lee, engaged Pope's attention in front with some twenty-five thousand men. Jackson, with about the same number, marched away on the morning of August twenty-fifth, to cross the Rappahannock at the upper fords. All that day the "foot cavalry" marched, not knowing where they were going, nor greatly caring. Jackson knew. They had no baggage, no wagons except those for ammunition and a few ambulances. Each man carried three days' rations, supposed to have been cooked, but in most cases half-raw because of the hurry of the start. The fresh-killed, unsalted and half-cooked beef soon spoiled in the haversacks in the August heat, and had to be thrown away. After that they subsisted on green corn and apples not yet ripe—a diet strongly conducive to straggling, in hot weather. And it was hot and dusty. But they marched, mile after mile, crossed the river—that was cool—and marched on, northwestward and away from the war. "Going back to the Valley!" said every one. That night they slept where they dropped, about the little village of Salem. At dawn they were up and away—southeast this time, toward the Bull Run Mountains, which lay between them and the fields about Manassas where the battle had been fought last year. Through Thoroughfare Gap, a narrow defile, they marched, and came out on the east side of the mountains and well in the rear of Pope's army. "Let us look before and not behind," Pope had said in his address to his soldiers. That day he had need to look both ways.

In the afternoon Stuart's cavalry, which had followed Jackson, came up to do in that campaign all that the most exacting could ask of cavalry. The Confederates struck Pope's railroad line about Bristoe Station, between the army and Manassas Junction, on the afternoon of the twenty-sixth, captured railroad trains, then turned north toward the Junction. There they found vast store of everything: a supply of good things the very memory of which years after would bring water to the mouths of old Confederates, who were young Confederates then. Capturing this great base of supplies, they rested there the next day, and reprovisioned and reequipped—shoes and boots and underclothing, trousers, blue but whole, bridles, saddles, food—all sorts of food, plain and fancy; drink, everything from lager beer, which was not a Confederate tipple, to whisky, which was; forage, mountains of it, everything. That night, having allowed each man to equip and provision himself, and having sent off in United States Government wagons, pulled by United States Government mules, thousands of barrels of flour and corned beef and sides of bacon, the vast supply base of the General who would discard the idea of "bases of supplies" was burned. Jackson's men marched off, picking their way northward by the glare of the fire.

Pope, who at first thought the attacks reported at Bristoe and Manassas just the work of small raiding parties, began to suspect something. During the twenty-seventh he abandoned the line of the Rappahannock and started to fall back toward Washington Ewell, who had been left at Bristoe to cover the force at work at Manassas, was driven away toward night. Pope, thinking that he had found Jackson's corps and had it on the run, gave orders to his various corps commanders to march "at the very earliest blush of dawn." There was still, in those days, a touch of poesy in the prosaic field order. He planned a concentration against Manassas, where he was sure he would find Jackson. When he got there, however, on the morning of the twenty-eighth, no Jackson was to be seen. He had marched away and again disappeared—bivouacked to the north in about the Federal position on the old battle field of Manassas. There his men were resting from their marching and labors, waiting for Lee and Longstreet to follow them around through Thoroughfare Gap and join them in falling upon Pope.

That morning, the twenty-eighth, one of Jackson's cavalry pickets captured McDowell's order for concentration at Manassas. It was sent to Jackson at corps headquarters—that being an angle of a worm rail fence, in the corners of which Stonewall Jackson himself and his two division commanders were peacefully sleeping on a hot August noon. Jackson woke up at once, and in a few minutes had his corps moving to a position to strike the turnpike on which Pope's marching divisions were to come. As they came by, late in the afternoon, Jackson attacked. In a desperate and inconclusive fight of an hour or so both Jackson's division commanders were wounded.

Pope, throughout this curiously mixed and muddled campaign, seems to have had a faculty amounting to genius for misinterpreting the facts that came to him. When night fell on the twenty-eighth, he thought that Jackson was retreating toward Thoroughfare Gap, and made his preparations accordingly. Jackson, instead, was staying where he was until Lee and Longstreet came.

Lee, in fact, was already east of the Gap that night, bivouacked in position to move promptly toward Jackson the next day. On the Union side, it was a night of vast effort and confusion, with great issuing of orders and marching and countermarching of divisions, until noon of the twenty-ninth. Pope seems to have had no idea of the Confederate positions and but the vaguest and most inaccurate of his own. His whole thinking and planning was based on the erroneous idea that Jackson was trying to escape back to the west of the Bull Run Mountains.

By afternoon of the twenty-ninth Pope got his forces together enough to attack, although he still had divisions scattered around fairly promiscuously. The battle was fought along the line of an unfinished railway cut and embankment, behind which Jackson took shelter. That valuable protection was, perhaps, the beginning of an idea that was to spread in the armies, to become at Spottsylvania and Petersburg the prototype of modern hasty entrenchment of the line of battle, as distinguished from more formal and leisurely fortification.

Pope's orders to his corps leaders show that he still thought, as late as the afternoon of August twenty-ninth, that he was in pursuit of a retreating fraction of Lee's army. To Porter, away on the left, he sent a rather indefinite order to attack Jackson's exposed right flank. Porter soon found that he had to deal not with Jackson's right "in the air," but with Longstreet. Wisely, he did not attack and so maneuvered his smaller force as to keep Longstreet out of the battle that day, a great service for which he was most shabbily requited by Pope and his friends when they sought a scapegoat for the failure of the battle and campaign. Charged with disobedience of orders and improper conduct in the face of the enemy, he was cashiered and dismissed from the service, to spend a quarter of a century in undeserved disgrace before he was reinstated in the time of Grover Cleveland.

On the morning of the thirtieth, Pope found that Jackson's line had again been withdrawn from the advanced position occupied at the close of the fighting of the twenty-ninth. Jackson had done nothing more than draw back to the strong line of his railroad embankment, but Pope's exuberant fancy soared. At noon he issued an order for a "vigorous pursuit" of the retreating enemy.

The Union forces occupied, as part of their line, the Henry House Hill, on which there was no longer a house, only ruins, and the grave of the Widow Henry. From this plateau they advanced northward against Jackson's men, facing them from across the pike—almost exactly reversing the movement of the battle of the year before. The battle was badly planned, and plans were changed for the worse as it progressed, but in spite of all that, in the middle of the afternoon, the Union forces made a most valiant and persistent attack on Jackson's line. At the critical time Longstreet's artillery came into action, enfilading the Union advance, and his infantry went forward, overlapping their exposed left flank.

Pope's troops fought well and bravely, although their General, who seems to have suffered from delusions of persecution as well as of grandeur, afterward laid the failure of his campaign to their poor fighting ability, and to jealous lack of support on the part of McClellan's friends. Beaten and beaten badly in the afternoon battle of the thirtieth, there was no imperative necessity for their retreat that night, with thirty thousand reenforcements coming close behind. However, one of the achievements of Lee and the Army of Northern Virginia was their power of impressing opposing commanders with their "over-whelmingly superior numbers," and under this impression Pope ordered his large and veteran army to retreat.

It was raining that Saturday night, as on the night of the First Manassas, and once more Union troops crossed the Stone Bridge and the fords of Bull Run, weary, defeated, disheartened, but this second retreat was no rout. The subordinate commanders retained their organizations fairly intact, in spite of darkness and defeat and the rain. Sunday they spent about Centreville, and the next day started to Washington. Meanwhile Lee advanced and tried to turn their right and cut off the retreat—an effort that was blocked late in the afternoon of September first by the troops of Kearny and Stevens at Chantilly or Ox Hill, a desperate clash, carried on right through a tremendous summer thunder-storm. Phil Kearny was killed and Stevens mortally wounded, brave and capable officers, both.

As the retreat to Washington continued, straggling increased. It was estimated that as many as thirty thousand men were strung out along the road from Fairfax Court House to Washington, making their way back to the capital. Pope's army, as an army, was in a fair way to disintegrate when the government took the unpalatable step of restoring McClellan to the command of the defenses about Washington and vicinity, including the troops of the short-lived Army of Virginia. McClellan rode forward to meet his retreating army, to be met with a moving enthusiasm that showed again the devotion of the soldiers of the Army of the Potomac to him. He had fatal military faults, but he had great virtues, and not the least was that he fought *for* his soldiers and his army, for their welfare, for their comfort, for their opportunity for success. And for that, his army loved him.

In Washington there was little less than panic—in spite of one hundred and ten thousand men available for defense, twice any force that Lee could bring against it. The streets were filled with stragglers, each one telling wild stories of disaster and rout. Government clerks were armed and sent to the defenses; surplus arms in the arsenal and the money in the Treasury, sent to New York.

And but two months before it had been the Confederate Government that for safe-keeping sent its records—it had no arms to spare and no money worth mentioning—away from Richmond.

CHAPTER XV

Flood Tide

WASHINGTON was not the only anxiety of the Government of the United States during those early days of September of 1862, when the Confederate cause reached its true high tide.

During the two months in which Lee had carried the war from Richmond to the neighborhood of Washington, the change in the state of affairs in the West had been quite as startling— so much so that Halleck was compelled, as he wrote McClellan, to give three-fourths of his thought and attention to developments there.

The army of Bragg, which in July Halleck had left well down in Mississippi, was in Kentucky, seriously threatening Louisville, by mid-September. The army of Kirby Smith, which in July seemed to have but a precarious hold on East Tennessee in the face of Buell's threatened advance, was at Lexington by the second day of September, enjoying the stores and supplies of that wonderfully well-favored Blue-Grass region, and frightening Cincinnati into closing her business houses so that men might work on the fortifications. Middle Tennessee, except Nashville and its immediate vicinity, was once more in Confederate hands by September.

While Buell's command was having the more serious difficulties, the other large Union army in the West, that of Grant, was not without its troubles in those early September days. Active cavalry raiders were into its rail communications, running back from northern Mississippi through West Tennessee to the base at Columbus, Kentucky. The Confederates under Price and Van Dorn, left in Mississippi to watch Grant, were on the move northward, also. Their offensive was to end in repulse in the fight at Iuka, on September nineteenth, and the two-day assault on the fortified position of Corinth a fortnight later, but it was successful in checking the transfer from Grant to Buell of heavy reenforcements to be used against Bragg.

In the far South, uneasiness about his position caused General Butler, late in August, to withdraw the Union garrison from Baton Rouge, which the Confederates promptly occupied, and to concentrate his forces at New Orleans. Having held only Vicksburg on the great river in July, the Confederacy now had command of a three-hundred-mile stretch, including the mouth of the Red River, the avenue into the interior of Louisiana and southern Arkansas. At the beginning of September, too, Hindman crossed the Arkansas-Missouri frontier and established a Confederate force about Newtonia, southwest of Springfield, a position they were to hold for nearly a month, with hopes of advancing farther.

With affairs in this happier state for the Confederacy, Lee determined to march into Maryland. There was really no other course to take. Pope's army had gone back into the defenses of Washington, some as organized troops, others as stragglers. The defenses were formidable, heavily armed, and even though Pope's army had been beaten there was no chance for fifty-five thousand men to take such defenses manned by more than twice their own number. Neither could Lee, safely or wisely, sit down before Washington and wait for the enemy to make the first move. Once more, the bold policy was the best and only one to take.

So, on September third, after a day's rest, the Army of Northern Virginia started for the Potomac. It was a strange and motley army. Supplies were scarce, in spite of captures, but then so were wagons to carry them and animals able to pull. Men were dressed in anything and everything. The fine militia uniforms of the year before had disappeared, and the regulation gray, which had a bluish tinge, was disappearing. Homespun jeans of the brownish butternut gray were, by force of numbers and circumstance, becoming the true "Confederate gray." After all, though, it was not rags and tatters that mattered so much at that season. It was the lack of shoes, a lack that the Confederate Army was never able to supply. Shoeless men were excused from keeping up with their commands on the march into Maryland, but many barefooted ones did manage to stay close.

Jackson's corps, closest to the river, led. On the fifth of September they marched to the unguarded fords of the Potomac, east of the Blue Ridge and close to Washington, pulled off shoes—those that had them—and trousers—such as they were— and started across on what is usually called the "invasion of Maryland." To the Confederates, it was in no sense an "invasion." Maryland, in their eyes, was one of themselves, wrongfully detained from full alliance by the military power of the government at Washington. They had a song *Maryland, My Maryland*—Confederate verses set to a stately old college Latin air. That was the song they sang as they waded the river, in column of fours, well closed up, each man with his trousers and his shoes hung about his neck. "The despot's heel is on thy shore," said the song, and they were on their way to lift that heel from the neck of their fair and suffering sister.

They were greeted with enthusiasm by many, with curiosity by more, with hostility by some, but the Marylanders did not flock to enroll themselves in the ranks of the lean, gaunt, unwashed scarecrows who came marching into their fat and smiling land. General Lee, by proclamation and order, made it plain that his army came as liberators, not as invaders, and the degree of order maintained among the Confederate soldiers was excellent—although the advance troops going into Frederick City did take ripe watermelons from freight cars on the railroad. In charge of the advance guard was a fine Confederate Marylander, Brigadier-General Bradley T. Johnson, a diplomat as well as a soldier. But still no great urge to join themselves to the armies of the Confederacy developed among the young men left in the state.

In fact there was some little defiance of the Confederates expressed around Frederick City, thirty-five miles northwest of Washington, where they first took up their headquarters. There was the minister of the Reformed Church who boldly prayed for the President of the United States right in the presence of Stonewall Jackson, but Jackson was soundly asleep, as was his wont at church. There was brave old Dame Barbara Frietchie, who was nearly a hundred years old and remembered 1776, and who did live in Frederick City, but not on the street through which Jackson's men marched; and who did wave the flag of the United States at a marching column, but it was after Jackson was gone and they were Union troops, and not Confederate, and so doing, all unconsciously achieved poetic immortality. But then there was another old lady, name unknown, of Confederate sympathies, who with upraised hands and tear-filled eyes called down on the column passing her doorstep that heart-felt descriptive blessing, "The Lord bless your dirty ragged souls!"

Going west from Washington through Maryland on the old National Road, one comes to the Monocacy River, flowing south into the Potomac, and then to the Catoctin Mountains. West of that range lies a narrow valley, bounded on the other side by the South Mountain, the local name given the extension of the Blue Ridge north of the Potomac. Westward again comes a wider valley through which Antietam Creek flows south into the Potomac. In this valley, really the northern continuation of the Shenandoah, lies the little village of Sharpsburg, with its back close to the Potomac, on the west, and its face to the east and the Antietam Creek. In the same valley, up toward the Pennsylvania border, is Hagerstown. Opposite the lower end of the valley, on the Virginia side, on a narrow point of land where the Shenandoah falls into the Potomac, lies Harper's Ferry, pressed close against the western foot of the Blue Ridge.

Lee's plans contemplated an invasion of Pennsylvania, perhaps the occupation of the capital of the state; beyond that, vast possibilities, military, political, diplomatic. On the military side he might threaten Philadelphia or Baltimore; on the political, strengthen the Copperhead movement for peace in the North; on the diplomatic, by a great victory on northern soil help secure that foreign recognition and intervention which was the will-o'-the-wisp of Confederate politics and diplomacy.

His line of communication and supply, which crossed the

Potomac east of the mountains and scarcely twenty-five miles from Washington, was too exposed for such an operation. Before all his troops were across he had established a new line to the westward, through the Shenandoah Valley. This new line necessarily passed through or between Martinsburg and Harper's Ferry, both of which contained sizable Union garrisons. It was desirable to clear away these possible threats to the line of communications, and besides, the capture of the garrisons themselves and their arms and supplies was a tempting project. Moreover, McClellan was again in command of the Union Army, under Halleck's general direction, and Lee probably did not look for any very rapid or vigorous advance of this force from Washington against him.

Considering all of which, Lee evolved one of the boldest moves of his audacious career. He had about Frederick not

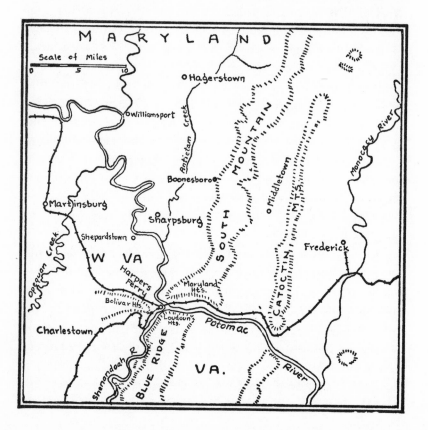

more than fifty-five thousand men. McClellan was bringing against him from Washington more than eighty thousand. Back of McClellan, in the capital, were seventy thousand more, of whom thirteen thousand were sent out early in the campaign to join McClellan. Back of Lee was nothing. In the face of that situation he decided to divide his army; to send one part to capture the garrisons at Martinsburg and Harper's Ferry, some twelve thousand in number; and with the remainder to delay McClellan until such time as the capture should be made and the whole Confederate force reunited.

To that end, on September 9, 1862, Lee issued his Special Order No. 191, outlining in explicit detail that portion of the campaign. The whole army was to be withdrawn westward from Frederick across the Catoctin and the South Mountains. Jackson was to make a wide sweeping march, cross back into Virginia clear beyond Martinsburg, capture that garrison or drive it into Harper's Ferry, advance to Bolivar Heights across the point of land on which that place stands, and lay siege to it. To cooperate with him, Walker was to occupy Loudoun Heights, across the Shenandoah from Harper's Ferry, and McLaws, Maryland Heights, across the Potomac. They were to capture the garrisons as quickly as possible and then to march northward to rejoin the rest of the army which, according to the order, was to await them at Boonsboro, just at the western foot of the South Mountain where the National Road crosses.

The movement so explicitly commanded began. Confederate troops marched away from Frederick on September tenth. The last troops left on the evening of the twelfth and by evening of the thirteenth had crossed the Catoctin Range, the intervening valley and the South Mountain, and were at Boonsboro. Longstreet, with the larger part of the force which Lee had retained with himself, went on beyond Boonsboro a day's march nearer Pennsylvania, to Hagerstown. Some of Stuart's cavalry, only, remained in and about the gaps through South Mountain.

About noon of September thirteenth, as the 27th Indiana Volunteers went into camp at Frederick, Private B. W. Mitchell found three cigars, wrapped about with a paper on which was written "Special Order No. 191." He took it to his First Sergeant, and he to the Colonel of the regiment, and so to headquarters and General McClellan.

The orders were directed to General D. H. Hill. Walker's copy of the same order had been securely pinned in an inside pocket; Longstreet's had been memorized and destroyed, but this one, used as wrapping paper by some careless courier, had never reached Hill.

No General ever had better fortune than McClellan here. An immediate advance through lightly guarded mountain passes would have put him in contact with a fraction of Lee's army, subject to defeat in detail before the other half could possibly come up. But McClellan, constitutionally unable to estimate Lee's force correctly, continued his cautious advance against the one hundred and twenty thousand men whom he believed Lee to have. He was going to take advantage of his lucky information all right, but would do nothing rash or precipitate. Meanwhile, Lee learned that McClellan, after his period of indecision and hesitation about Frederick, appeared to be about to make a direct and purposeful march westward to the mountains through which the Confederates had withdrawn.

There was about Lee nothing of McClellan's hesitation. Immediately he turned D. H. Hill back from Boonsboro to the gaps through South Mountain, and started Longstreet back from Hagerstown to support Hill in resisting the passage of the Union army. McClellan, having delayed marching on the night of the thirteenth, came up to South Mountain on the fourteenth, to find in his front not deserted mountain passes, but the troops of D. H. Hill and the cavalry of Stuart.

Of course they were but a small force to oppose the advance of the Army of the Potomac. A survivor of Hill's forces related that the sight of that great army, advancing on the roads across the Middletown Valley below them, and spreading out, right and left, over the fields at the base of the mountain, gave him a new appreciation of the simile of the Hebrew poet, "terrible as an army with banners." Although small, the Con-

federate force sufficed to hold McClellan east of South
Mountain all that day of the fourteenth, the day that the investing forces of Jackson, McLaws and Walker began to batter at
the defenses of Harper's Ferry.

One of the brigades marching against Hill as he held the
gaps of the mountain, was commanded by John Gibbon, who
but a few years before had been best man at the wedding of
the Confederate commander. North Carolinians, both of them,
and West Point graduates, Hill had gone with the Confederacy,
Gibbon with the Union, while Gibbon's brother was in the Confederate Army.

On the night of the battle of South Mountain, the
fourteenth of September, Lee with Longstreet and D. H. Hill,
some nineteen thousand men, fell back westward, crossed the
Antietam Creek and took up on the low hills along it a position
that included the little village of Sharpsburg and that had at
its back the Potomac, and beyond that, Virginia. Against this
position advanced the Army of the Potomac, pouring through
the gaps of South Mountain. All day of the fifteenth Lee, with
but half his little army, stood to await attack, while off to the
south the Union garrison at Harper's Ferry, cooped up and
ringed by artillery fire plunging from the heights above them,
was surrendering to Jackson. McClellan, however, did not
attack that day—although he could have put in line at any time
after noon sixty thousand effectives, more than three to one
against Lee. Nor did he attack on the sixteenth, except for
pushing Hooker's corps across the creek north of Lee's left
and marching them toward Lee's flank until, about dark,
Meade's division made contact with the Confederates, too late
to do more.

Lee's decision to stand and fight a vastly superior army
at Sharpsburg, with the Potomac at his back, is the most ques-
tionable of his career. It was bold to the point of rashness—
but Lee and the Confederacy were in a situation where boldness, and ever more boldness, was their only hope of success.
The consequences of defeat at Sharpsburg would have been
appalling, but the possibilities of victory, political and diplo-

matic, made it worth while to take the risk. And, besides, Lee and the Army of Northern Virginia had met this army coming against them before, and they could count, with reason, upon its being handled cautiously. In the existing situation, and with the combined military, political and diplomatic problem which faced Lee, it is likely that he did the wise thing by his decision at Sharpsburg to take risks with McClellan.

On September fifteenth, Harper's Ferry surrendered. Jackson left A. P. Hill to complete the surrender, handle the prisoners, eleven thousand of them, and gather up the spoils, while he marched at once to rejoin his chief at Sharpsburg. On the way there, he heard of McClellan's advance to the line of the Antietam. "I thought I knew McClellan," said Jackson to Walker, riding alongside, "but this movement of his puzzles me." Jackson did know his man—they had been together at West Point—but he did not know, then, of the lost order.

Of the tactical details of Sharpsburg, fought on September seventeenth, the bloodiest single day's fighting of the whole war, it is not necessary to speak. McClellan, having on the field more than two men to every one that Lee had or could bring up, was yet unable to drive the Confederates from their battle position. Divisions and corps crossed the Antietam and advanced through the corn-fields or pasture lands on its slopes; through the woods on either side of the little white brick Dunkard Church on Lee's left; and, finally, across that sunken road along the Confederate center which was that day baptized as the Bloody Lane—but it was as divisions and corps they advanced, and not as an army. Wherever they pressed too strongly, Lee pushed in his scant reserve to stiffen the bending line, hesitating not at all to bring men from the right to support the failing left, or from the last of his reserves to sustain either flank, as the need arose. McClellan, with heavy reserves available, cautiously kept them as reserves instead of using them at the critical time and place.

Finally, in the afternoon of this most terrible day, McClellan sent forward his left wing, on the southern end of the line, to cross the Antietam by the old stone bridge, since known as

Burnside's Bridge, and by the lower fords. At the bridge stood Toombs—Brigadier-General Robert Toombs he was now, and no longer a secessionist orator or the Secretary of State of the Confederacy. Almost had he been kept out of this battle. In the days before Cedar Mountain, while the troops were yet in Virginia, General Toombs had gone away one afternoon to call on one of his old Congressional friends living near by. While he was away, orders came from Longstreet, corps commander, for his brigade to move out and picket one of the fords of the Rapidan. Toombs, returning from his visit, found his troops moving, and moving on an order which had not come through him. Conceiving this to be in derogation of his military dignity, he peremptorily ordered them back to their camps, and left the ford unguarded. It was through this ford, it is said, that Pope's raiding cavalry got off with Stuart's dispatch book, giving away the first of Lee's plans. At any rate, Longstreet relieved Toombs of his command, and placed him in technical arrest. At the urgent entreaty of Toombs he was restored to command in time to take part in the battle, and right worthily he and his brigade stood and fought and held the line of the lower Antietam for an hour or more. And then when, after all, the weight of Burnside's corps pushed the Confederates back and up the hill and into the outskirts of the village, there came up through the corn-field to the south the division of Ambrose Hill, the "Light Division," which that day through September heat had marched from Harper's Ferry at top speed to take its part in the battle.

The division deployed as it came up and charged Burnside's corps in flank—a most demoralizing charge, with their red-shirted commander in front, joyous in the nick of battle. In peace this Hill, with his deep-set eyes and his beard of patriarchal proportions, was the mildest of men. In battle, he was born to fight—and, about Petersburg, to die. Is it any wonder that Jackson, in his dying delirium, and Lee, in his last breath, each called on Hill?

The battle was over, at fearful cost. Lee, with less than forty thousand men, lost about eight thousand that day; Mc-

Clellan, who started the day with seventy thousand, lost more than twelve thousand.

During the night and early on the next morning reenforcements numbering more than his losses joined McClellan. For Lee there were no reenforcements—but all through the day after the battle, with his shattered troops, he remained in position, inviting attack, and even considered a turning movement against McClellan's right flank. That night, however, urged by Longstreet and Jackson, he withdrew from his battle positions and forded the Potomac to the Virginia side, without any real molestation from the Union Army—then or for many weeks afterward.

CHAPTER XVI

THE TIDE TURNS

ON THE seventeenth day of September in 1862 the decline of the Confederacy began.

That day Lee, in Maryland, repulsed the great army of McClellan from Sharpsburg. On the same day, in Kentucky, Braxton Bragg captured the fort and village of Munfordville. So doing, he placed the main Confederate Army of the West in position to march to the Ohio River and capture Louisville, with consequences, military and political, that are incalculable.

On the next day, while Lee remained on the low hills along the Antietam, with the Potomac at his back, awaiting the attack that did not come, Bragg held his lines along the hills above the Green River, and "offered battle" to his opponent, Buell.

On the nineteenth of the month, Lee was back in Virginia, and Bragg, his offer of battle not accepted, began his eastward march toward Frankfort, abandoning the solid military advantage which two months of skilled maneuver and hard marching had placed in his hands, to go to the capital of the state and inaugurate a Confederate Governor of Kentucky.

Those days in September of 1862, not the July days of Gettysburg and Vicksburg in 1863, marked the definite point when the tide of fortune for the Confederacy turned and began its ebb. The turn came at the close of a summer of brilliant southern success. There were to be more battle victories for the Confederacy, and one or two successful campaigns, even yet, but it can be seen now that, regardless of these surface fluctuations, the ebb that then started never ceased its outward flow until the end. In the West there were to be no more offensives on any large scale; in the East, but the one campaign of Gettysburg. Brilliant defensive victories could only postpone the end, with the hope that the determination of the North would wear out, as it so nearly did, in the summer of 1864, or that the foreign powers would intervene on behalf of the South.

The advance into Kentucky had been under way a month when Bragg reached the position at Munfordville. Like the march into Maryland, the Confederates did not look upon it as an invasion. Kentucky, in fact, was considered the thirteenth of the Confederate States of America. Missouri was the twelfth, enrolled in the Confederacy through the action of the so-called "Rebel Legislature," which met at Neosho in the autumn of 1861. In like manner, an irregular convention, composed in good part of Kentuckians serving in the Confederate armies, had met at Russellville on November 18, 1861; declared the independence of Kentucky; formed a provisional government and taken steps to secure its admission into the Confederacy; and elected George W. Johnson as Governor. When Johnson was killed at Shiloh, in the following spring, the Provisional Council of Kentucky had chosen as his successor Richard Hawes.

The Confederates held that Kentucky was with them in spirit, and that only northern military force prevented her free association with the Southern States. There was more ground for the belief this autumn of 1862 than there had been a year before. The wise tolerance and forbearance of the men who dealt for the Union with Kentucky during the period of neutrality had not been entirely preserved. Many subordinate commanders in the Union armies acted as if they came as conquerors of a province in rebellion, in spite of the sacrifices that the "loyal" Kentuckians had made to hold their state within the Union. Such men as Buell and Anderson of Fort Sumter had a more correct idea, but there were lesser men in the Union armies whose haughty and oppressive disregard of the simplest rights of the population showed that they had no conception of the true relation between Kentucky and the Union.

Reports of these military outrages and repressions, perhaps magnified, had come into the South, and it was as liberators and restorers of popular government that the Confederate armies went into Kentucky, not as invaders of hostile territory.

They carried with them rifles to arm the large number of Kentucky recruits whom they expected to join their ranks. They carried, too, the provisional government of the state, which they were regularly to inaugurate. In their hope of recruits they were to be greatly disappointed, perhaps for the reason that most of the young men of Confederate sympathies in Kentucky had already left home and joined the southern armies. They realized even less on their political hopes. The Honorable

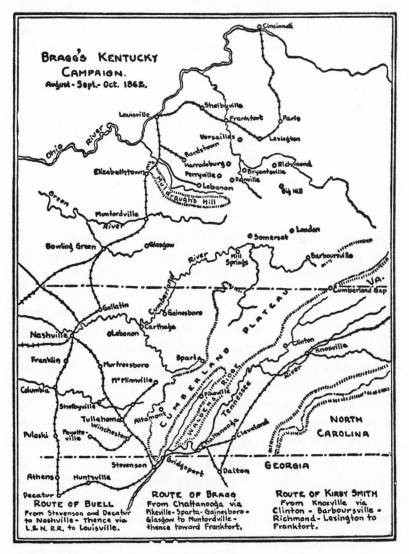

BRAGG'S KENTUCKY
CAMPAIGN.
August - Sept. - Oct. 1862.

ROUTE OF BUELL
From Stevenson and Decatur
to Nashville - thence via
L. & N. R.R. to Louisville.

ROUTE OF BRAGG
From Chattanooga via
Pikeville - Sparta - Gainesboro -
Glasgow to Muntordville -
thence toward Frankfort.

ROUTE OF KIRBY SMITH
From Knoxville via
Clinton - Barboursville -
Richmond - Lexington to
Frankfort.

Richard Hawes was formally installed in the old Capitol at Frankfort, but before the ceremonies could be concluded military necessity called away the army commanders. The administration lasted, perhaps, an hour—but the time lost and the positions sacrificed to go through the formality of inaugurating it, cost the Confederacy all the possible results of what promised to be a brilliant campaign.

Two generals, commanding separate and independent departments, conducted the Confederate advance into Kentucky. Edmund Kirby Smith, the junior, wounded at Manassas, had improved a long convalescence at Lynchburg by winning and marrying a young lady of that city, before he was returned to duty as commander of the new Department of East Tennessee. When Bragg, the senior, came from Mississippi into his department, Kirby Smith willingly waived his independent position, but even such harmony was not the same as the simple unity of command the operation needed.

The eastern column under Kirby Smith, some twenty thousand men, moved north from Knoxville about the middle of August. Finding the Union garrison at Cumberland Gap too strong, and too well fortified to be attacked successfully, Kirby Smith left Stevenson's division to watch them and with the rest of his army pushed forward into central Kentucky. At Richmond he met an army under bold Nelson, the gigantic naval lieutenant who had done so much to hold Kentucky in the Union and who was now a Major-General in the Army. Nelson's force was routed, scattered, and some forty-five hundred of them made prisoners—all on August thirtieth, the day that General John Pope started his retreat from Manassas back to Washington. From this heartening victory, Kirby Smith moved on to Lexington, principal city of the Blue-Grass region, which he occupied on September second. There, with active scouting and raiding parties out toward Louisville and Cincinnati, he rested and waited for the advance of Bragg's army.

Bragg started his advance from Chattanooga on August twenty-eighth, with an army of twenty-seven thousand men, in two nearly equal wings under Leonidas Polk and William J.

Hardee, who were to become Lieutenant-Generals and corps commanders in the Army of Tennessee, but who were never able to please entirely the exacting and critical Bragg.

Of the twenty-seven thousand men a considerable proportion were Tennesseeans and Kentuckians who had left their states in the great retreats of the winter before. They had spent the summer in Mississippi, had been as far south as Mobile Bay, and now were on their way back home. At Chattanooga they ferried the wide Tennessee, wound their way up the steep side of Walden's Ridge, dipped down into the deep and narrow Sequatchie Valley, climbed the Cumberland Mountains, all on bad and narrow tracks, and finally, on September third, went into camp at Sparta, right at the western foot of the mountains and in Middle Tennessee.

Buell, when Bragg started his advance, began to concentrate his scattered forces to meet the movement which equally threatened Nashville or Louisville. Northern Alabama and all Middle Tennessee outside the section about Nashville were denuded of their Union garrisons, and Buell's army was gathered at Murfreesboro, covering Nashville, which for political as well as military reasons must be held.

Bragg decided to go to Kentucky and started north along the Highland Plateau west of the Cumberlands. Buell, matching his movement, left a garrison in Nashville and with the rest of his army started a march, roughly parallel, along the railroad line from Nashville to Louisville. For ten days in September there was a great foot race for Louisville. At Munfordville, where the railroad crosses Green River, there was a Union fort and a garrison of more than four thousand men. The Confederate cavalry reached Munfordville ahead of Buell. Bragg hurried up his whole army from Glasgow and at two o'clock in the afternoon of September seventeenth received the surrender of the fort and garrison. The Confederates had won the race. They were between Buell and his base squarely on his line of march, and in position to fight or to march into Louisville ahead of the Union army.

In Louisville, there was the utmost excitement, almost consternation. The bold Nelson was in command, but was without much hope of successfully defending the place with the raw and untrained troops he had. It looked as if the game were in the hands of General Bragg.

The next day, September eighteenth, Bragg remained at Munfordville. That night, with some misgiving and uncertainty of mind, he decided to abandon his position and let Buell pass on to Louisville, safety and reenforcements, while he marched away to the east to join Kirby Smith in the political part of their mission in Kentucky.

General Bragg's decision, which cost whatever chance of success the campaign into Kentucky had, was based on his belief that "this campaign must be won by marching, not by fighting." The time came in the history of the Confederacy when her boldest Generals fought only when they had to, on the defensive, but that was after there was no chance of winning except by exhausting the patience of the North. In the glowing September of 1862, not only campaigns but the cause of the Confederacy depended on fighting, at the right time and place and in the right way. The establishment of a new government could not be achieved by mere marching, no matter how rich the region through which the marches should be made. Recognition could be had only upon definite victory—if then.

On the chance of winning such a victory, General Lee stood and fought at Sharpsburg. The same reasoning applied with even more force to the situation of General Bragg. His army was nearly as large as that of Buell, while only a hundred miles away was Kirby Smith, who could have spared perhaps as many as ten thousand men, a reenforcement which would have put Bragg on a substantial equality in strength with the Union forces opposed to him. In case of defeat, the Confederates would have had a fairly good line of retreat, the one they afterward adopted when they were forced to fight under unfavorable circumstances and were repulsed. Victory, so close to the Ohio River and so close to the November elections in the North, would have been most valuable.

While Buell marched on into Louisville unmolested, Bragg

pulled his army away northeastward, through Hodgenville, where Lincoln was born, and on to Bardstown, site of the *Old Kentucky Home*. Leaving the army there, Bragg with his staff rode to Lexington, conferred with Kirby Smith, and spent a week arranging for the inauguration of the Confederate Governor at Frankfort, on October fourth.

On the same day that Bragg established his command at Bardstown, Buell was in Louisville. Louisville was in a state of utmost excitement. The near approach of the Confederates—a detachment of Kirby Smith's cavalry had burned bridges within seventeen miles of the city—was enough, it would seem, but there was internal strife within the Union forces. On September twenty-ninth, the day that Buell's last division marched into the city, Major-General Jefferson C. Davis, of Indiana, shot and killed Nelson, in the Galt House at Louisville. Davis, who had been a lieutenant in Fort Sumter at the opening of the war, had recently joined the army in Kentucky, bringing his division from Mississippi. Nelson, who added a fierce and dictatorial temper to his real ability and exceptional versatility, had sharply reprimanded Davis for some act or omission in connection with the frenzied preparations for defense. Davis, feeling himself insulted, had gone to Indianapolis and enlisted the aid of Indiana's powerful War Governor, Morton. Together they returned to Louisville, and approached Nelson in the hotel. After an altercation in the lobby Davis followed Nelson toward his room, and in the hall shot and killed him. The affair caused such excitement and resentment, on both sides, that it was with difficulty that a clash beween the friends of the two Generals was prevented.

Buell, uniting to himself the forces at Louisville, had planned to march out of that city on September thirtieth to seek the Confederate army. On the day before he was to move out—it being the same day on which Nelson was killed—he received an order from Washington removing him and placing Major-General George H. Thomas in command.

Buell, though an excellent organizer and a good commander, had fallen back more than two hundred miles from northern

Alabama, and that was a thing Washington could not under-stand. Moreover there were strong political influences against him, and until toward the close of the war political influences were potent in the selection of commanders at Washington.

Thomas, notified of his appointment, told Buell that he in-tended to decline the command. Buell urged acceptance, but high-minded Thomas, feeling that the removal of Buell at such a critical time was an injustice, and that the army would suffer, wired that day to General Halleck, "General Buell's preparations have been completed to march against the enemy, and I there-fore respectfully ask that he may be retained in command."

In neither army was there a soldier less selfishly ambitious than "Old Pap" Thomas. He was a most competent soldier, who took counsel of his own knowledge of things and his own sense of right, whom neither enemy nor superior in rank and authority could stampede into making a move that did not seem to him justified. He lacked the pushing self-assertiveness and the sense of personal advertising that carried men of less ability and character to higher rank and greater fame.

Thomas' remonstrance, together with the earnest protest of the Senators and Congressmen from Kentucky, availed to keep Buell in command. On October first he marched east from Louisville. His northern column, under Sill, moved directly toward Frankfort, where Kirby Smith was; his southern column, the main army, moving on three roads, advanced south-eastward toward Bragg's army. Uncertainty as to which was the main attack, and which the feint, took possession of the minds of the southern Generals, whose troops were spread along a line of about sixty miles, running from the Kentucky River, opposite Frankfort, on the northeast, to Bardstown, on the southwest.

On October second, Bragg sent orders from Frankfort to General Polk, commanding in his absence, to bring the main army up toward Frankfort, and attack Sill's northern column. Bragg was busy with political affairs in Frankfort, and his order showed considerable ignorance of the exact military situation in front. Polk availed himself of a certain discretion left him and fell back southeastward toward the main Confederate base, located at Bryantsville, in the angle between the Kentucky and Dix Rivers. ,

On October fourth, with due and solemn form, the Confederate Governor of Kentucky was inaugurated at Frankfort. The need for formal legality, which was such a strong part of the mental background of the Confederacy, being thus satisfied, the new Governor cut short his inaugural address and the Generals hurried away to their armies—and none too soon. Buell, now with largely superior force, was advancing along four roads. Kirby Smith, thinking himself more seriously threatened than he was, called on Bragg for aid. Bragg sent him two good divisions, those of Withers and Cheatham, and then, after they were started, changed his mind and recalled them. Only that of Cheatham got back in time to be of help in the impending battle of Perryville.

Perryville, fought on October eighth, was a fight for water. All that country had been in the grip of drought for weeks. Marching armies must have water for men and animals, and the streams and springs of the parched region through which the armies were now maneuvering were about dry. In the Chaplin Fork of Salt River there were pools of water, not a great deal, but enough to supply an army that was using water for nothing but drinking purposes. The night before the battle of Perryville much of the Union army made a dry camp—not enough spare water to permit a tincup bath. The next day they engaged in what proved to be the deciding struggle of the Kentucky campaign, but the immediate object of the contention was the pools of water in the Chaplin River.

Perryville was tactically a Confederate victory. With about fifteen thousand men Bragg attacked and drove back parts of three corps of Buell's army. It is difficult to tell just how many men Buell had on the field, but he had there and near by something more than fifty thousand, of whom about one-half were actually engaged. The fighting was as desperate as was seen during the war, with a Confederate loss of more than three thousand killed and wounded, and a Union loss of nearly four thousand. At the end of the day's fighting the Confederates had forced their opponents back from the river on the right, and held them away from it on the left.

Regardless of temporary success, the Confederate forces, divided and weakened, could not hold their position in Kentucky. The forces of Bragg and of Kirby Smith were drawn back and united about Harrodsburg, eight miles east of Perryville. There they waited two days for an attack which did not come, and then withdrew toward East Tennessee.

One thing had been gained by the advance into Kentucky, the accumulation of great quantities of provisions and supplies, whose safe withdrawal to the South presented a major problem. The retreat began on October tenth. The movement of the great wagon trains over the difficult mountain roads of southeastern Kentucky, was slow, dreadfully slow, and the rear-guard had its work cut out to fend off the pursuit. Kirby Smith was rear-guard commander, with the bold and active Joe Wheeler in charge of the cavalry. There were days when the wagons could crawl and struggle but five miles, when the cavalry, dismounted, fought from behind stone walls and ditches, or drove back the enemy by savage counter-charges. Finally, after two weeks, the pursuit ceased, and the retreat continued unmolested.

It was a disillusioned and disheartened force that fell back into Tennessee. It was their first campaign under General Bragg—they were to have many others—and it had started out so well, and ended so badly. True they had managed to escape with their army and with vast supplies—and they had inaugurated that Governor—but the realization was so far short of the expectations they had on that September day when they stood between Buell and the Ohio River.

They marched south, east of the Cumberland Mountains, and then crossed and occupied Middle Tennessee, with advanced cavalry posts but ten miles out of Nashville. That, in itself, was a great achievement—the recovery of North Alabama and of two-thirds of Middle Tennessee, one of the fairest and richest regions of the South, and one they were destined to hold for nearly a year. It was immense, and would have been heartening, had they not expected so much more.

And their expectations were not unreasonable. On the day that General Bragg left Munfordville, had he but known it, Louisville was open to him, with Nelson under orders to evacuate the city if Bragg advanced. It was not, indeed, until Bragg was well away to the eastward of the line of march, and Buell was but a day's march from the city, that Nelson, with evident relief, telegraphed to General Wright at Cincinnati, "Louisville is now safe; 'God and Liberty.'"

Having taken Louisville, Bragg could scarcely have held it for any length of time—but the mere fact of taking it in that autumn of 1862 with the Army of Northern Virginia across the Potomac, might have had great political consequences, and perhaps diplomatic as well.

Diplomatic representatives of the South in the capitals of Europe were pressing upon the attention of those governments the fact that the North, so far from conquering the Confederate States, was itself standing on the defensive, with southern armies at and across the border. To those of the North who were weary of the war, with all its appalling sacrifice of life and treasure, there was the same appeal. After all, perhaps it would be best to let the Southern States go on and form their own government, for which they seemed so willing to fight— and so able to fight successfully.

It was in this dark time of crisis that President Lincoln once more showed that political discernment which he had in such extraordinary degree.

The subject of the emancipation of the slaves had been under consideration since early in the war. In the President's message to the regular session of Congress in December, 1861, he had suggested that slaves in the Border States remaining in the Union be freed, with compensation to their owners. Getting no response to this, he recommended by a special message, on March 6, 1862, that the United States "cooperate with any State which may adopt gradual abolishment of slavery, giving to such State pecuniary aid, to be used by such State in its dis-

cretion." In this message he estimated the cost of such emancipation in the four Slave States of Maryland, Delaware, Kentucky and Missouri, and in the District of Columbia, as equal
to the money cost of only eighty-seven days of war. Two conferences were held with Congressional representatives of these
states to enlist their help in getting the states to act, without
result. In point of fact, the people of those states did not
realize that the institution was doomed, and that their property
would soon be property no longer. Fearing the complications
of a large free negro population, they took the negative course
of doing nothing about the proposals of the President.

Finally, after making efforts to secure gradual abolition
in the Border States, the President, on September twenty-
second, with Lee barely out of Maryland and Bragg still in
Kentucky, issued his Emancipation Proclamation applying
only to those states in "revolt" against the United States.

So doing he changed the character of the war. It was, and
had been recognized by most foreign observers as, a conflict
between two systems of government, in neither of which had
people outside the United States any real interest. Now it
became a crusade for freedom in the eyes of foreign peoples,
and in the eyes of a good many in the United States, too.
Foreign intervention became impossible, the marching hymn of
John Brown's Body took on new meaning to the North when
the President issued his Proclamation of Emancipation.

CHAPTER XVII

MODERN WAR, MODEL OF 1862

THE great Confederate advance of the summer of 1862, at mid-September exultantly pressing forward, by mid-October had spent itself and turned back.

The Army of Northern Virginia, after the ordeal of fire at Sharpsburg, had first turned southward. Its retreat had been a leisurely and defiant movement into the Valley of the Shenandoah, where the whole army remained in camp about Winchester for nearly six weeks of rest, recuperation and refitment—all except the indefatigable Stuart and eighteen hundred of his men who on October tenth once more rode down the Valley, crossed the Potomac again, rode north through Maryland into Pennsylvania as far as Chambersburg, where they turned east and crossed the South Mountain, to return on the eastern side of that range and to ford the Potomac some twenty-five miles above Washington. This bold expedition, carried out with Stuart's joyous dash and skill, created a very considerable stir in Pennsylvania, and some perturbation in the minds of McClellan and of the authorities at Washington.

McClellan, who now had more than one hundred thousand men, content to have saved the nation by turning back the dreaded Confederate invasion, was reluctant to move into Virginia in the face of Lee's army, "greatly superior in number." He did reoccupy Harper's Ferry and fortify the heights about it, but went no farther in the pursuit of Lee, who was calmly encamped in the pleasant country about Winchester, a score of miles away. McClellan's army needed clothes, equipment, supplies of all sorts, he said, and especially reenforcements, to go against the ragged, ill-equipped Army of Northern Virginia, not much more than half its size.

President Lincoln and Secretary Stanton, who thought that one Union soldier ought to be the equal of one Confederate, were distinctly displeased at McClellan's tardy and timid course in Virginia. They were no better satisfied with that of Buell, who after Perryville, followed Bragg toward East Tennessee until both armies were well into the mountains of southeastern Kentucky. There, finding it difficult to subsist his troops, Buell called off the direct pursuit and marched to the Louisville & Nashville Railroad, to get back into Middle Tennessee ahead of Bragg.

The President was disappointed. He wanted East Tennessee invaded. It was his pet plan, and he did not care from what direction or by what route it was done. Buell's movement looked to him as if he were giving up the East Tennessee idea. To the President and the Secretary of War it seemed that if the Confederates could retreat through the mountains the Union army could follow them—a thought which took no account of the Confederate soldier's peculiar knack of living on less than most soldiers, and the fact that the passage of the retreating army denuded a country, poor at best, of what supplies there were. They could not truly understand the difficulties of the commander in the distant West who had to march his men over actual mountain tracks, not roads laid out prettily on the map, and feed them with real food, not statistical ration returns.

Buell was right in his refusal to lose his army in the mountains, but during the last week in October he was relieved from command and Major-General William S. Rosecrans named in his place. General Rosecrans was well thought of by his army associates, including old Regular Army friends now in Confederate service. In Mississippi he had just won considerable reputation by his aggressive fight against Sterling Price at Iuka, on September nineteenth; by his stubborn and successful repulse of the attack of Van Dorn and Price on the fortified position of Corinth, on October third and fourth; and by the vigor of his pursuit of the Confederate army retreating from this battle, a pursuit that carried him forty miles into Mississippi before he was recalled by Grant, the department commander. Within the month he was made an independent army commander charged with the special mission of vigorous pursuit.

Rosecrans, however, when he arrived at the scene of Buell's operations and learned the conditions of his problem, adopted the same plan: to continue to hold the railroad to Nashville, to remain there until the damage done to the rail line from Louisville could be repaired, to accumulate enough supplies to make the army independent of daily operation of trains, and then to advance against the rail junction of Chattanooga, rightly regarded as the key position in the war in the central South. Through threats of displeasure and intimations of removal from command, written him by Halleck, Rosecrans stood firm for the plan of campaign which he believed had a chance of success.

While Bragg was in retreat from Kentucky and Van Dorn from Corinth, the Confederate forces, in September in southwestern Missouri, were driven out of that state in a confused, scuffling sort of campaign in October. Part retreated southward through the Ozarks to the Arkansas River, below Fort Smith; part, including the brigades of Indian soldiers, were routed and driven into the Indian Territory. Hindman, who had been about Little Rock when the disaster struck, rushed back to his army, resumed command and started on the work of reorganizing his demoralized forces with the idea of again marching into Missouri—a march that pressure of events on the eastern bank of the Mississippi was to make impossible.

During the same week in which Buell was removed from command, McClellan managed to get started with his advance into Virginia—it could not be called a pursuit of Lee's army. He crossed the Potomac below Harper's Ferry, and to the east of the Blue Ridge, on October twenty-sixth. For ten days, with his one hundred and fifteen thousand men, he advanced cautiously into Virginia, to the neighborhood of Warrenton. His belief, always, and that of his friends, was that he was at last in position to defeat Lee, who at that time had the two wings of his army separated by nearly fifty miles of distance and the range of the Blue Ridge. There were moves open to

Lee, however, which would have checked any such plan for de-feating Jackson and Longstreet in detail.

On November fifth, President Lincoln wrote out with his own hand the order to remove McClellan from command of his army, naming in his place Major-General Ambrose Burn-side, an officer of entire devotion but with neither the abilities nor the temperament required to command an army with suc-cess. An officer took the order from Washington to the army by special train, and there, late at night, as McClellan was in his tent writing his wife, delivered it.

The order was a surprise to McClellan, to his army and to Burnside, who reluctantly assumed a command which he felt from the beginning was beyond his depth. The causes of the order go back almost to the beginning of McClellan's command; the immediate provocation seems to have been the fact that, as soon as McClellan started into Virginia, Lee put Longstreet's corps between him and Richmond.

When Burnside took over the command, Lee had Longstreet, with about thirty-two thousand men, on the south side of the Rappahannock, near Culpeper Court House, while Jackson's corps, of about the same size, was still in the Valley. Stuart's seven thousand cavalry were everywhere.

While Burnside, newly come to high command, was puzzling about just how he would destroy the army, or get to Richmond ahead of them, Grant's third major army of the Union, which held northern Mississippi and West Tennessee, started during the first week in November of 1862 the campaign against Vicks-burg, a campaign that was to meet checks and reverses, that was to assume various and unexpected forms, but that was to be driven forward with tenacious grip until the fall of the river fortress in the summer of the next year.

While Rosecrans was at Nashville, looking toward Chat-tanooga, and Grant at Holly Springs, starting for Vicksburg, Burnside decided on another "On to Richmond" movement. Instead of crossing the Rappahannock at some of the fords in its upper reaches, General Burnside decided to move down the north bank to Fredericksburg. Just what led him to the de-

cision is not clear, unless he hoped to forestall Lee at the crossing and, by seizing both banks of the river, establish a good
point of departure for his march southward along the railroad
from the Potomac to Richmond.   Such a movement, if it had
any chance of success, depended on promptness, a quality
which the huge Federal army did not possess.

On November fifteenth, a week after Burnside had taken
command, he had his army on the march toward Fredericksburg, to be supplied from a new base at Acquia Creek, on
the Potomac.   Two days later the first of the troops, the Right
Grand Division headed by loyal old Sumner, arrived at Falmouth, the village on the north side of the Rappahannock
opposite Fredericksburg.   Hooker, commanding the Center, and
Franklin, the Left Grand Division, followed promptly.   So far
the movement had been made in good time, but when it arrived
at Falmouth hesitation and uncertainty entered.   There was
nothing to prevent Burnside from crossing his troops and seizing the heights south of the town, except the fear that a rise
in the river would cut him off from his base before he could
get his bridges across.   Pontoon bridge trains, elaborate ones,
had been sent for, but their coming was much delayed for a
variety of inconsequential reasons—trifles of the sort that eat
up time, and so wreck campaigns.

Lee's own military preference was to allow Burnside to
cross the Rappahannock and advance southward to the next considerable stream flowing into Chesapeake Bay, the North Anna,
with the idea that defeat there, perhaps with Jackson striking
on the Union right flank, might be turned into rout and disaster.
It was finally decided, though, not to give up the territory between the two rivers, and so to make the stand at Fredericksburg.

By the time that Burnside got his pontoon trains, late in
November, Longstreet's corps had marched over and taken posi-
tion on the heights south of the river and above the town.   And
Jackson was coming up, marching from his valley, across the
Blue Ridge, down through Madison Court House and Orange
Court House and on through the dense and tangled Wilderness,

where there was a cross-road, a "big house," with its stables and outbuildings and cabins—Chancellorsville, they called it—to Guinea's Station on the railroad from Fredericksburg to Richmond. Once more, in the spring, was Jackson to pass that way, on his last march, from the field of Chancellorsville to the house at Guinea's Station—but that was the future, and the future was of no concern to Jackson. His unbending Presbyterian faith cared for that.

Jackson passed behind Longstreet, who held the Confederate left, and scattered his troops along the south bank of the Rappahannock for twenty miles, watching the places where Burnside might elect to throw his pontoons across. D. H. Hill and Jubal Early held the extreme Confederate right, down at Skinker's Neck, where there was reason to believe the crossing might be attempted.

The main Confederate position, however, was a line about Fredericksburg, some six miles long, occupying a range of hills that curved away from the river above the town and reached almost to the river below. Between hills and river in a wide cultivated plain, with fields and fences and, closer to the town, little gardens, lay the old colonial town of Fredericksburg. Across the river, where the Stafford Heights overcrowned river, town and the hills to the south, was the Army of the Potomac, with its one hundred and forty-seven guns commanding the town. To oppose this great army, Lee had a force less than two-thirds as large, and greatly inferior in artillery—so inferior that the Confederate guns did not even attempt to silence the northern batteries during the battle.

During the night of December tenth the men of the Washington Artillery of Louisiana, one of those brilliant old militia organizations which had been in the war since First Manassas, entertained with amateur theatricals. Sergeant John Wood—to meet death in the great battle that every one expected within a few days—was the impresario of the occasion. The show was good. So was the punch. The battalion and its friends were up late. It seemed that they had scarcely been asleep when two signal guns sounded from the front. That meant that the looked-for advance of the Union army had begun. The Confederate army went into battle position and peered from their heights down through the heavy morning mists that covered the valley. Nothing could be seen, not a target to shoot at. But down there along the river a fight could be heard.

Fredericksburg was almost the first of the "modern" battles, and one of the last of the old-style battles in the grand manner. Opposite Fredericksburg Sumner's men started to throw across two pontoon bridges. In the houses of the town, in the cellars, behind pits and barricades, were scattered Barksdale's brigade of Mississippi sharpshooters. Their rifle-fire, picking off the working parties, held up the pontoon bridges all that day of December eleventh, and most of the next—the first modern touch. To dislodge them, Burnside turned on the town the bombardment of his one hundred and forty-seven guns on the heights above, or of such as could be brought to bear. The Mississippians held on to the ruined and gutted town by going underground and keeping up their sharpshooting fire, until finally, in desperation, the effort to lay a formal pontoon bridge was abandoned.

The crossing was finally made by filling the pontoon barges with soldiers and rapidly pushing or rowing them across the river, to dislodge Barksdale's men by hard fighting through the quaint old colonial streets—Caroline, and Fauquier, and Princess Anne, and Charles Street, where George Washington's mother had lived. Bombardment, a fire-gutted town, street fighting in a ruined village—as modern as 1918.

Down the river, though, in front of the Confederate right, there was no village where snipers could find shelter in cellars, and the plain between river and hills was wider and more open. There the men of Franklin's Grand Division shoved their two pontoon bridges across on the first day, and came marching over, with a band and flags at the head of the first regiment. War in the old style—which almost proved disastrous as the men marching on the bridge unconsciously fell into rhythmic step and nearly upset and wrecked both floating bridges.

When Sumner's men could not get across because of the

sharpshooters in the village, most of Franklin's were withdrawn, leaving only a strong bridge-head held on the south bank. Finally, when Sumner did cross on the afternoon of the twelfth, Franklin's men crossed again, Hooker's came over and filled the gap between them, and everything was made ready for the grand assault on the Confederate position the next morning.

That morning was an eerie experience. Fog, dense, heavy, blanketed both armies and the plain between them. Bugles sang at reveille, and drums beat as troops moved back and forth into position down on the plain below, but not one thing could the Confederates on the heights see. Nor could the other army see them. Nearly two hundred thousand men could be heard moving about in the fog, invisible.

By noon the sun had sucked the fog up and away, and the assault began—as brave and determined an assault, and as hopeless, as was to be made during the war.

On the morning of the battle the divisions of D. H. Hill and Early, which during the night had marched up from Port Royal, eighteen miles away, were put in on the extreme Confederate right. Part of Hill's division was able to put down a flanking fire on the Union advance. Stuart's horse artillery was there, also, under that gallant boy, Major John Pelham, "the great cannoneer," whose single battery of brass "popguns" was to hold its own against half a dozen of the enemy's in this, his last great battle. Before the campaigns of the coming spring, and before his twenty-first birthday, he was to die in a skirmish at Kellyville.

As the fog lifted and the battle opened, a cavalcade of officers rode rapidly along the Confederate lines. Heading them was a man in a bright new uniform, a handsome uniform with the three stars and gold embroidery of a Lieutenant-General. It was not until he was well past each unit that the men realized that it was Jackson—realized it and burst into cheers. "Old Jack" in a new uniform! And they said Stuart— that gay and resplendent Stuart with his bright yellow sash and his beloved plumed hat—had given it to him! Interest in the coming battle was eclipsed by the buzz of comment on Jackson and his new uniform. And he had a regular General's hat, too, not the rusty old flat-topped cap that everybody knew!

In the plain below massed the forty thousand men of Franklin's Grand Division, with part of Hooker's troops, a force that properly driven home might have changed the result of the battle. Their orders were confusing and hampering, however, so that only some local successes were gained.

The division of Meade—a name to become tolerably familiar the next year—and of John Gibbon, the North Carolinian who fought for the Union, made a lodgment in the right of A. P. Hill's line with an assault that was somewhat favored by the local ground and trees. They broke one flank of Archer's brigade, but were checked and driven out by a local counter-attack in which Peter Turney, Colonel temporarily in command of the brigade, changed face to the flank and charged. As the difficult movement was under way a ball struck the Colonel in the mouth and passed out through his neck. Four men, carrying him in a blanket to the surgeon's hospital, were struck by an exploding shell. The Colonel was left on the field for dead—to be revived and saved to become Chief Justice and then Governor of Tennessee.

Burnside's right, which was to make the main attack from Fredericksburg against Marye's Heights on which stood the stately columned "Brompton," moved out from the protection of the houses of the town and started across the narrow open space leading up to the foot of the hill. "We will comb that space as with a fine tooth comb," said Alexander, commanding Longstreet's artillery. Just at the foot of the hill there lies a sunken road, and along the side of that road toward the enemy a stone wall, banked with earth. With banners flying, the red legs of the zouaves—they still had them that late in the war—flickering among the blue uniforms, with the bright shine of bayonets, with general officers erect on their horses, encouraging the lines of battle, an old-style army marched into "modern" war—a space shell-swept by guns from front and flank, with the spiteful crackling of rifle balls from the entrenched position

of the stone wall, that stone wall which stands out in every report of the battle in front of Fredericksburg. They marched into
battle, in the old grand manner. They halted, and formed and
dressed their lines and went forward, all as the tactics books
taught, because they were good soldiers—but the fire was too
much. Angry reports went back that their artillery was firing
into its own infantry—another touch of "modern" war—but
it developed that the fire was coming from Confederate guns
away to the right on the curving flank, where R. H. Anderson's
division held the heights.

Along the stone wall was but a small force, the brigade of
Thomas R. R. Cobb and part of Kershaw's. Cobb had been a
most successful lawyer before the war, in Georgia, not much
interested in politics until the question of the sovereignty of
his state became involved. On that he was almost fanatic,
giving to it the same intensity of devotion that he did to his
church.

He believed, as sincerely as man ever believed anything,
that the Confederacy was upholding the principles of government for which Washington fought—it was he who had urged
that the new nation be called "The Republic of Washington."
When war came, he left the Congress of the Confederacy to
enter its army. On this day of Fredericksburg, his service
ended at the doorway of a little white house along the stone
wall, where he quickly and quietly bled to death from a wound
in the leg. In the house, tending General Cobb and many
another Confederate soldier, was Mrs. Martha Stevens. Having
ample warning, she could have left. She insisted on remaining
to operate her own first-aid station, dressing wounds as long
as the cloth in the house and in her own voluminous petticoats
lasted.

Assault after assault the Union troops made, all to be
broken up and driven back before they reached the stone wall.
Darkness finally came, with twelve thousand five hundred
Union dead and wounded scattered about on the plain of
Fredericksburg. Darkness came, and with it the firing died
down, but the cold, bitter, freezing cold, came on. Men, dead,

froze stiff; the wounded, many of them, froze to death; the ground froze a foot deep; there were no fires, either in the open there or at the miserable bivouacs of the survivors in the streets and ruined houses of Fredericksburg. More "modern" war.

The next day, other Union troops moved forward, only to be forced down among the dead and wounded of the battle of the day before, there to lie through a most interminable day, literally pinned to the ground by Confederate fire. The Confederates behind the stone wall, and the larger bodies of them at the top of the hill, when not actually standing to arms on guard, were at rest and at ease, even those closest to the enemy. There was a card game going on in the road behind the stone wall—and that day, December fourteenth, was Sunday.

Burnside wanted to renew the attack, with himself at the head of his old corps, the Ninth, which he had brought up from the North Carolina expedition. He ordered the renewal, but the higher officers dissuaded him from what could have been nothing but another useless slaughter.

On Monday, too, both armies held their positions. That night, Burnside gave up the town of Fredericksburg for the possession of which more than twelve thousand men had been killed or wounded, retired to the heights on the north of the river and pulled back his pontoon bridges.

The Confederates returned to the river bank to find the plain dotted with dead, the houses of the town, where they had crawled or been carried to die, filled with them. One poor woman was found, still in her cottage home, with the bodies of six men lying about her feet as she sat staring through the smashed doorway. The town became a vast burying-ground— the yards, the gardens, the roadsides and open spaces, wherever trenches could be dug in the hard-frozen ground and bodies be thrust into them to be covered with the frozen clods. An empty ice-house was filled to the roof with bodies, to remain there through the rest of the war and finally, as unidentified dead, to be buried in the National Cemetery at Fredericksburg

CHAPTER XVIII

"HAPPY NEW YEAR"

WITH the fighting of Fredericksburg the war in Virginia entered into a long period of "winter quarters" for both armies. The winter before the Confederate Army had made itself fairly comfortable about Centreville. It was new then, and green— "a mob clamoring for leave of absence," was the way one high observer described them. In this second winter of the war, though, they were veterans, they had shed most of their "mess chests" and fancy equipment, they had worn out or lost their parade uniforms, they were down to the necessities—log huts, fire-wood, beef and bread, the standard Confederate ration, a little cooking equipment—but they had learned the veterans' art of comfort in the field.

Tents had long ago become rarities among them. Some of them may have looked back with amusement to the advertisements in the newspapers, along there in that first gay spring, telling how necessary to health and comfort were tents and extolling the merits of this or that cloth for their manufacture— but there was not much now of which tents could be made, and they were difficult to capture, and mighty bulky and heavy to haul off after they were captured, and wagons were scarce and teams scarcer and, anyhow, a man could get along pretty well with those contraptions the Yankee quartermasters had— "flies," they called them. They were about four by six, with buttons and buttonholes around the edges, fixed so that three men could button theirs together and make a really good shelter—if the open end was turned away from the rain. Or if a man hadn't been lucky enough to get one of the Yankee quartermaster flies, he and his messmates could build themselves a "shebang." All he had to do was to put up a couple of forked sticks, with a pole across the forks, and lean bushes against the ends and the side toward the wind. A shebang was better than nothing—but, if there wasn't time for that, or sticks and bushes were lacking, it wasn't so bad just sleeping out.

But in winter quarters there were huts, well fixed up, and even with all the drills and roll-calls and inspections and guard duty, there was a great deal of time for games—cards, especially poker, and chess and marbles and various sorts of ball. And snowball battles—regular battles, with the regiments formed and the flags flying and all manner of tactics and strategy used.

There was picket duty to be done along the Rappahannock, which was the "frontier"—but the pickets on the other side were pretty good fellows, at that, and a little conversation across the river, with maybe a swap of tobacco for coffee, or an exchange of newspapers, wouldn't hurt. It was right troublesome, though, getting the little bark boats that carried the tobacco over and the coffee back to sail across, without upsetting and spilling their loads, or drifting off down the river and out of reach.

Over there on the north bank they were having a lot of talk and trouble about their commanding General, too. That was one thing the men in the Army of Northern Virginia never worried about. Those politicians down at Richmond might do lots of foolish things, but there never was any idea, anywhere, after the Seven Days, of changing commanders for the army in Virginia.

Out in the West, now, it was different. Van Dorn, who had been beaten at Corinth, was relieved of command and Pemberton—he was a Pennsylvania man in the Regular Army who had gone with the South—was made a Lieutenant-General and sent out from Charleston to Vicksburg to take command. There was a great deal of friction in the Army of Tennessee, too, between General Bragg and his two corps commanders, Polk and Hardee—and there was going to be more.

But old Joe Johnston, who had been in command of the Virginia army, and was wounded at the Seven Pines—he had a most unhappy way of getting wounded in battle, not only in this war but in Mexico—was well now and had been sent

out to Chattanooga late in November, to take command of everything between the mountains and the Mississippi River.

That meant, mostly, Bragg's army of a little more than
forty thousand men, now in Murfreesboro, facing Rosecrans'
army of about the same size, looking southward from Nashville;
and Pemberton's force of thirty thousand or so, holding Vicksburg and Port Hudson, on the river, and fortifying Grenada,
in central Mississippi, against Grant's approach southward.

Rosecrans, still accumulating advance rations and supplies
at Nashville so that another of Morgan's railroad raids might
not imperil his whole army, was not yet ready to move out
against Bragg.   Grant was moving southward against Pemberton and had been since November.   Major-General Banks,
with a fleet of transports, had been sent to New Orleans in November, also, to supersede the obnoxious Butler in command
there, and to advance up through Mississippi to meet Grant
coming down. Pemberton needed reenforcements and called
for them.

Johnston's position, at Chattanooga, was unsatisfactory.
He was responsible for a vast stretch of territory, and the one
in which the Union Government was more interested than any
other one thing, save Richmond itself.   Both his Tennessee and
his Mississippi army were threatened; neither, he felt, should
be weakened for the other.   The solution, as he saw it, was in
the Arkansas army, under the aging Holmes, which was not
actively engaged in operations of any moment, nor threatened
with any.   But that army, which he believed could spare reenforcements for Pemberton, was not under Johnston's command.

On November eleventh, two weeks before Johnston took
charge, the War Department at Richmond had directed Holmes
to send ten thousand men to the aid of Pemberton.   Holmes,
whose hold on his department and even his own army was of
the weakest, ordered Hindman, who had more than eleven
thousand fairly well organized troops in the Ozarks, to bring his
force back to Little Rock and transfer it to the east bank of the
Mississippi.

Hindman, who was planning another advance into Missouri, protested and objected to the order and, finally, decided that he would fight one more battle with the Union forces under Blunt and Herron before he complied. The battle, fought on December seventh, 1862, at Prairie Grove, not far from Fayetteville, resulted in a staggering defeat for Hindman, who retreated first to Van Buren and finally to Little Rock. There were no troops left to send east of the Mississippi.

That left the question of whether to reenforce Bragg from Pemberton's army, or Pemberton from Bragg's. During the Fredericksburg period, President Davis himself was in the West, visiting Bragg's army at Murfreesboro, Johnston at Chattanooga, and Pemberton in Mississippi—a visit that resulted in an order from the President, over Johnston's objection, to transfer Stevenson's division of eight thousand men from Bragg to Pemberton. Bragg was left with about thirty-seven thousand men to face Rosecrans' forty-four thousand—not a great disparity as Confederate armies went.

After the second battle of Corinth, in October, Grant was formally put in command of the army in Mississippi and West Tennessee—a command which he had been exercising informally since Halleck left in July—and given the special mission of the opening of the Mississippi from the North. Curiously, on October twenty-first, five days later, Major-General John A. McClernand, former Congressman from the President's home town, was given confidential and secret orders, not communicated to Grant, to go among the Governors of the Western States and raise a separate force for the same purpose, orders that were to cause a deal of friction between McClernand and the Grant-Sherman team, and no little mischief.

Vicksburg, the hill fortress on the Mississippi, was the immediate objective of Grant's orders, and McClernand's as well. Memphis is on a bluff on the eastern bank of the Mississippi. The next bluff on the eastern bank of the river is at Vicksburg, four hundred miles below as the river winds, about half that distance by direct rail line south from West Tennessee to Jackson and across to Vicksburg, on high ground all the way. Between these hills on which the Mississippi Central Railroad ran and the river itself is the fabulously fertile Delta of the Yazoo River, a region of slow and lazy streams, laced and interlaced among great forests. The Yazoo and its tributaries, some of which were really cross-cut channels between it and the Mississippi, offered several "back ways" to Vicksburg, but all of them difficult to negotiate with steamers and impossible overland.

General Grant's plan was to take his main army straight down the railroad, and at the same time send Sherman down the river with a fleet of transports, convoyed by the gunboat flotilla of Rear-Admiral David Porter. Sherman, after conference with Grant at Grand Junction, where the Memphis & Charleston and the Mississippi Central Railroads cross, returned to Memphis on December eighth and began preparations to put about twenty thousand men on river steamers, proceed down the Mississippi to Helena, in Arkansas, pick up about twelve thousand more there, paddle on into the Yazoo, and attempt to make a lodgment on the north side of Vicksburg at Chickasaw Bluff. On December eighteenth McClernand came to Grant with his orders to take command of the river forces against Vicksburg, which McClernand figured made him an independent army commander. Grant telegraphed to Sherman at Memphis to hold up his departure, but Sherman was already away down the river.

Grant's main base for his overland movement was at Columbus, Kentucky, using the rail line from that point south to Holly Springs, Mississippi, where a great secondary base was established. Two days after Sherman had sailed away from Memphis to make his attack, relying on cooperation from the land forces coming down the railroad, things began to happen in General Grant's rear, such things as forced him to give up the land movement entirely. Van Dorn, who had been replaced in his independent army command by Pemberton, and assigned to the sort of cavalry service for which he was so well fitted by temperament and training, burst into Holly Springs, on December twentieth, and wrecked General Grant's winter stores.

On the day before, the nineteenth, General Forrest had got on Grant's rail line, at Jackson, Tennessee, and started north toward Columbus, Kentucky, capturing garrisons and supplies, burning bridges and trestles, wrecking track. It was a common complaint of army commanders on both sides that cavalry could not be relied on to get down off their horses and do the hard heavy work necessary to wreck a railroad track so that it would stay wrecked, but Forrest's men were not orthodox cavalry. By Christmas of 1862, after a week's work, they had made the railroad from Jackson north useless for the rest of the war.

The two events, coming at the same time, convinced Grant that he could not rely on this line to supply the needs of his advancing army, and compelled a change of plans.

Meanwhile Sherman, knowing nothing of all this, made his attack on the Chickasaw Bluffs above the Yazoo on the last days of the year, and was repulsed, with sharp loss. The second movement against Vicksburg was blocked, largely by destruction of railroads in West Tennessee.

Forrest, who had no military training and had never read a military book, had an instinctive realization of the best move to make. Surrounded and hemmed in by the troops which Grant sent against him during the week he was busy wrecking Grant's line of communications, he did not attempt to make a run for the Tennessee River, with the chances that he would be caught and have to fight, half on one side and half on the other of the wide stream. He decided to thrust himself in among his pursuers, and by bold and vigorous fighting, while they were separated one from another, paralyze them into inaction while he marched to the river and crossed to the safety of Middle Tennessee. At Parker's Crossroads, while he was engaged with one brigade of about his own size, another Union brigade fell upon his rear. A detachment sent out to observe the approach of the second brigade had lost its way and failed to report. Forrest, for the only time, was surprised by the enemy.

It was at this battle, with enemies in front and behind, that one of the legends of Forrest started—that he ordered his men to "charge them both ways." He did almost that, too, and managed to draw off most of his force, and even some of the cannon he had that day captured.

This first West Tennessee raid of Forrest, aside from adding some useful supplies to the Confederate armies, including the complete arming of Forrest's own half-armed men, was of real military service. It helped to cause Grant to give up the direct overland approach to Vicksburg, and change to the immensely difficult and complicated amphibious operation along the river.

Two weeks before Forrest left for West Tennessee, the tireless John H. Morgan, whose troops had done valiant service in the retreat from their Kentucky home land, and in the march from East Tennessee to Murfreesboro, proposed to General Bragg that he be allowed to take his brigade, with some infantry help, march north forty miles to the Cumberland River, cross it and capture the garrison at Hartsville. Permission was reluctantly granted and away went Morgan and his men. Leaving Lebanon, on December sixth, they found the roads covered with a wet slush of snow and mud. It was proposed that the infantry and cavalry share the use of the horses by the "ride and tie" system. Cavalry were to ride first, while the infantry trudged along behind them through the liquid mud made by the churning of the horses' feet. The cavalry were then to leave the horses and march ahead on foot, while the infantry, coming up, were to mount and ride. The plan was fair enough—but when the infantry came to ride they soon found that their feet and legs, wet through with the slush in which they had marched, were freezing. They were glad enough to turn the horses back to the cavalry—but then it developed that the cavalry, soaking wet from their march, were to have the same trouble with freezing feet. The horses got mixed, too, and everybody cursed everybody else. It was never hard, in either army, to get the infantry and cavalry to cursing each other, that being the way of soldiers.

In spite of these difficulties, and of a rapid rise in the Cumberland, Morgan got his little force across the river and into position to attack Hartsville at daylight of December seventh. The attack lasted little more than an hour. It was done with such impetuous dash, such disregard of danger, that the Union commander, convinced that Morgan must have a large command at hand, surrendered his garrison of two thousand before relieving forces, three times as large as Morgan's, could march the few miles from Castalian Springs. With his captures Morgan started back, before noon, wading the icy river, fighting a severe rear-guard action. Within thirty-six hours Morgan's men marched forty-five miles, crossed the Cumberland River twice, and fought a battle.

Returned to Murfreesboro, Morgan stayed there a little more than a week before he started back to Kentucky, this time with serious intent against Rosecrans' rail communications with Louisville. During that week he received his commission as a Brigadier-General, and, on the last night in which he was to be at Murfreesboro was married.

No one who saw that wedding in the week snatched from war ever forgot it. There was the charming Miss Ready, the bride—so soon to be a widow—and the laughing, happy, exultant groom. There was General Bragg, in his uniform of a full General of the Confederacy, with his staff, and there was the stately presence of Bishop Leonidas Polk, who performed the ceremony, garbed in his uniform of a Lieutenant-General. There were a few of Morgan's staff and companions, remaining behind with him for the wedding—after which they were all to mount and ride to overtake the troops who already were on their way to another of their incredible raids, the "Christmas Raid" into Kentucky.

Four days after Morgan left, Rosecrans started his long delayed advance southward from Nashville. His railroad line to Louisville was in working order, although Morgan was to cut it again up near the Louisville end within the week, but he had accumulated enough supplies of all sorts to make it safe to take the chance of interruption.

Bragg had been weakened by sending Stevenson's division to Pemberton; and by sending both Forrest and Morgan away on distant operations. Wheeler was in command of Bragg's cavalry—"Fighting Joe," he was to be called, or sometimes,

"Little Joe," but he had not yet won with the Army of Tennessee the reputation that gave him those affectionate names. In fact, there was more or less resentment among the friends and followers of Forrest and Morgan that General Bragg in reorganizing his cavalry had named as chief of that arm neither of those fighters, trained only by experience, but had appointed this twenty-six-year-old West Pointer, Wheeler.

Rosecrans left Nashville on the day after Christmas of 1862 to march thirty miles southeast and there meet Bragg. He had about forty-four thousand men, organized in three corps, under Crittenden, Thomas and McCook. Bragg had about thirty-seven thousand, with two corps, under Polk and Hardee, and a separate division under McCown. As Rosecrans advanced, moving on three roads, Wheeler, with about two thousand five hundred cavalry, started out on a raid around the army, one of the most practical and successful of those operations. Starting on the night of December twenty-ninth, he made the entire circuit of Rosecrans' army, captured more than a thousand prisoners, destroyed all or parts of four wagon trains, with great quantity of supplies, and created such shortage of subsistence in the Union army during the three days' battle to come that men were reduced to eating the meat of the horses killed on the field. All that done within forty-eight hours, he rode up to the Confederate left at two o'clock in the morning of December thirty-first in time to take part in the great, bloody and indecisive battle opened that day.

On the field of Stone's River, two and one-half miles northwest of Murfreesboro, there was no hill, no outstanding topographical feature, nowhere to rest securely the flanks of an army. It was an open country, nearly level, with fields on which the last picking of the cotton was white, with patches of forest and cedar thickets, with outcropping ledges of limestone rock thrust up through the red clay. Through the field, almost parallel and close together, ran the railroad and the turnpike between Nashville and Murfreesboro, which was the axis of the advance of each army. Roughly parallel to them on the east, was Stone's River, between steep rocky banks, but fordable.

Both commanders formed the same plan, to be executed on the same morning—to advance the left and crush the enemy's right wing. Bragg, however, got under way earlier, and all through the first day the initiative lay with the Confederates. Hardee, that stout fighter, was in command on the Confederate left, with Cleburne's division and McCown's. During the darkness of the early morning hours he put his men in motion. By six o'clock, just good daylight at that time of the year, they were pressing forward in determined advance against McCook's corps, holding the Union right. Rosecrans had had some uneasiness about the position of that wing but had deferred to the opinion of the corps commander on the field and had devoted himself to the left wing, under Crittenden, which he was planning to advance early in the morning. Before Crittenden's advance could more than get started things began going so badly on McCook's side of the line that the attack had to be deferred and everything thrown in to stop what threatened to become a rout. By the middle of the morning McCook's line had been bent back at right angles to its starting position, and the center, under Thomas, was bending, too. Polk's corps, with the divisions of Withers and Cheatham, came into battle. Only the Confederate right, under Breckinridge, was not actively engaged.

Rosecrans met the emergency in soldierly fashion. He was everywhere, organizing the movement of reenforcements from the left to the threatened center and right, encouraging and sustaining his officers and troops in a situation truly critical.

Then, at the critical moment and the critical place, the division under white-haired Van Cleve came up from the left and held the pivot on which the Union army was bending back. Bragg sent to Breckinridge for fresh brigades to deliver the final blow, but Breckinridge, misled by reports of heavy movements of the enemy against his front and flank, did not send them. The offensive flickered down and stopped; the Union lines, bent but not broken, held.

Of revelry there was none that New Year's Eve. A cold

bright moon shone on the freezing field of Stone's River. "No fires" had been the orders but soldiers on both sides soon had them started and, by common consent, neither molested the other. General Bragg telegraphed to Richmond the news of the success of the day. "God has granted us a happy New Year," he wired, believing that the morning would find Rosecrans' army in retreat toward Nashville.

The morning, though, found Rosecrans and his stubborn army right where the close of the fighting had left them the day before—that New Year's morning and the morning of January second, also. About noon of the second, Bragg determined to dislodge the Union left, which held some slightly rolling high ground along the river and in front of Breckinridge. The assault was to be made late in the afternoon, at four o'clock, nearly dark, and orders were that the advance was to stop at the crest of the swell and entrench to hold the position. Breckinridge, who had been Vice-President of the United States and the southern nominee for the Presidency, and who was to be Secretary of War for the Confederacy, commanded the movement. The troops were of the first order, the Kentucky "Orphan Brigade" of Roger Hanson, to meet his death on the field, and regiments from Louisiana, Tennessee, Florida, Georgia, Alabama, North Carolina, most of whom had been through the war since Shiloh and before.

At four o'clock the attack started. The swell of ground was carried with a rush, but it was a rush that the officers could not stop when the new line was reached. The eager soldiers, in full pursuit of what they believed to be a beaten enemy, pressed on to drive them into and across the river—and as they did so exposed their left flank to the fire of a terrible battery of fifty-eight guns, seven batteries which Major John Mendenhall had secretly massed on a bit of high ground right on the flank of the advance, but across the river. The Confederate infantry, with their ranks mowed down from the flank by the fire of Rosecrans' artillery, which they could not reach, were shattered and driven back, leaving eighteen hundred dead and wounded within an hour in the little field alongside Stone's River.

The next day, January third, both armies remained in position, watching and wondering who had won the battle. The fighting had been close-quarter, stand-up fighting; the losses, on both sides, had been appalling. The Confederates, out of thirty-seven thousand men had lost ten thousand, of whom nine thousand were killed or wounded; the Union army, out of forty-four thousand, had lost thirteen thousand, of whom nearly ten thousand were killed or wounded. There have been few battles in which the proportion of losses was greater—and still no one knew, for sure, who had won.

During the night of January third, Bragg settled the question. He withdrew from the field, marched southward through Murfreesboro, and took up his winter quarters about Tullahoma, thirty-five miles south of Murfreesboro, but still blocking the way to the key position at Chattanooga. Rosecrans occupied Murfreesboro on the fourth, and made it his point of departure for future advances—which, however, were not to come for nearly six months more.

CHAPTER XIX

Afloat on Rivers and Sea

The Union Government concentrated the most of its efforts in 1863 on four major objectives: the opening of the Mississippi River by the capture of Vicksburg and Port Hudson; the break-up of Confederate rail communication in the central South by the capture of the critical junction point of Chattanooga; another "On to Richmond" movement, which General Lee, as usual, converted into one for the protection of Washington; and, on the sea, the unceasing, relentless blockade.

The blockade, of course, went on, winter and summer. On the land major military operations were at a standstill in Virginia and Tennessee through the winter months of 1863. Along the Mississippi, however, the persistent Grant-Sherman team, having abandoned the land and taken to the rivers, found themselves able to keep right on through the winter, patiently trying this plan and that until, finally, they were to find the hole in the armor of Vicksburg.

Sherman, disappointed in the arrival of Grant's column coming overland through Mississippi, on January 3, 1863, abandoned his attack on the bluffs above the Yazoo, north of the southern fortress. The next day McClernand, armed with his special orders from Washington for operations along the Mississippi, arrived and took command of the expedition, thirty-two thousand soldiers on a great fleet of river transports, convoyed by nine gunboats.

It appeared that there was nothing to be done at Vicksburg without Grant's overland column, which had had to go back to Tennessee to take a fresh start after Van Dorn destroyed its advanced base at Holly Springs and Forrest broke up its rail line. McClernand, athirst for results, cast about for something else to do with his fine large army.

The Arkansas River falls into the Mississippi more than

one hundred miles above Vicksburg. Fifty miles above the mouth of the river, at a bend known as the Post of Arkansas, was a Confederate work, Fort Hindman, placed there to guard the river approaches to Little Rock, capital of the state. Against this fort, garrisoned by five thousand men under Brigadier-General Churchill, McClernand led his army, with the Navy cooperating. The post made resistance—McClernand's loss in killed and wounded was more than a thousand—but it was reduced on January eleventh.

Before the end of the month, Grant, confirmed in his position as commander of all the forces operating on the Mississippi, came down from Memphis by steamboat to the region of hostilities and took charge. The army, now of fifty thousand men, was reorganized into four corps: Sherman's Thirteenth, McClernand's Fifteenth, Stephen A. Hurlbut's Sixteenth, and the Nineteenth commanded by the brilliant young McPherson. The troops and boats up the Arkansas River were recalled, and the whole force put to the main task—finding the way to capture Vicksburg.

The Mississippi River, twisting its way to the Gulf without regard to the points of the compass, flows northeastward through a long straight reach to strike the bluffs above Vicksburg, doubles on itself and flows away southwestward past the town. Opposite the town, between the two reaches of the river, is a long low spit of land. It was across this spit of land, five miles long, not more than a mile wide at its base, that the first Vicksburg expedition had tried to cut a canal. The attempt, if successful, would have turned the river into a new and shorter channel, avoiding the town and its fortifications.

Vicksburg itself is on bluffs, with dry ground to the northeast, the east and the south, but northward along the river, the way that Grant must come, there was nowhere enough dry footing for an army. The fortress could not be come at, directly down the main river, while Sherman's attempt had shown the impossibility of crossing the bottoms and marshes between the Yazoo and the hills northeast of the town in the face of determined Confederate opposition. There was, however, more than one "back way" through which, in times of high water, boats might work from the Mississippi into the Yazoo above the fortifications, and so take the defenses of Vicksburg in reverse. First and last, every one of them was tried by the tireless Grant and the resourceful David Porter, in command of the gunboat fleet.

The first attempt, started in early February but a few days after Grant arrived, was made by cutting the levee closing the Yazoo Pass, an old inlet connecting the Mississippi with the Delta country, and so, by inundating that section with the waters of the main river, to pass light-draft gunboats and transports through the creeks and bayous into the Coldwater, the Talla-hatchie and, finally, the Yazoo. The levee was cut without great difficulty, but for days boats could not pass through the gap, as the waters of the main river tore through in a rushing torrent into the bottoms, eight or nine feet below.

When the fleet—two ironclads, two rams and six "tin-clad" gunboats—finally got through and into the tortuous ways lead-ing from the Pass to the rivers tributary to the Yazoo, they found their way blocked by trees, cut to fall into and across the narrow channels. With immense effort they hacked and forced their way through the lesser streams and on down to the Yazoo, where, after more than a month of labor, they struck Fort Pem-berton, a little work hastily built of cotton bales and earth, mounting but three guns and manned only by Loring's brigade of fifteen hundred men.

Across the channel they found the hull of a steamer that, but two years before, had been famous, the *Star of the West*, against which the first shots of the war were fired in January, 1861, before the Confederate States were organized, when the *Star*, attempting to take reenforcements to Fort Sumter, had been turned back by South Carolina guns. Captured at Indian-ola, Texas, after the secession of that state, the steamer had been taken from the sea by the Confederates and put in river service, to come to her end as a sunken hulk blockading a channel. The blockade and the little fort were successful in turning back the expedition. Ross' division and Quinby's brigade had been brought up on transports, but troops could not be landed on the flooded bottoms, in the face of the determined fire of Loring's men—with "Old Blizzards" Loring himself, pacing the parapet of cotton bales, calling on them, "Give them blizzards, boys! Give them blizzards!" The flotilla made its slow and toilsome way back to the main stream, which it reached on April tenth, after two months' absence.

In March, Porter attempted another back route—passing from the Mississippi into Steele's Bayou, and so through Black Bayou, Deer Creek, the Rolling Fork and the Sunflower River into the Yazoo. The attempt was made with five iron-clad river gunboats. As they pushed their way through the narrow and sluggish streams, with the branches of trees almost brushing their upper works, it soon developed that the Confederates were felling trees behind them to prevent their escape. Porter, with the utmost difficulty, backed out of the hole into which he was driving, and made his way out to the Mississippi on March twenty-fourth.

Meanwhile, Grant and the army were engaged on another of the canal projects—a futile attempt to by-pass Vicksburg by turning the current of the Mississippi, which flows where it wills, into new channels. Time and immense labor were expended on this hopeful project, without result.

While the army tried to change the channel of the river, the navy decided to run the stream as it was. The *Queen of the West*, ironclad, under venturesome young Ellet, ran down past the batteries in March and began operations in the two-hundred-and-sixty-mile stretch of the river below Vicksburg and above Port Hudson, an important Confederate work on the east bank, in Louisiana, some forty miles above Baton Rouge. The importance of this stretch of the river was increased by the fact that into it flowed the Red River, penetrating the interior of Louisiana with its great supply of cotton and of sugar. Young Ellet passed into the Red, and through it into the Atchafalaya, the Têche, and other old channels which the high water opened to him, finally to meet capture at Fort De Russy, a Confederate work on the Red, below Alexandria.

The captured *Queen of the West* and a little converted tug, the *Webb*, under Confederate command, returned to the main river, attacked and captured the Union ironclad *Indianola*, and for a short while held control of the river between the two fortresses.

Meanwhile, on March thirteenth, bold Farragut brought the Gulf fleet up from below to run the batteries at Port Hudson. A cooperating land attack, organized by General Banks, failed to get into position in time to move with the fleet; the fleet's movements were discovered through the indiscretion of one small steamer that showed lights and rang bells; the forts opened a heavy bombardment in the darkness and smoke, sank one vessel and forced most of the others back; but Farragut himself with his famous flag-ship, the *Hartford*, and one other ship got by and passed up-stream toward Vicksburg.

On April sixteenth Porter ran eleven vessels down past the Vicksburg batteries, with a loss of but one sunk. Union control of the river above and below was once more assured, and the way was made ready for the hazardous plan of attack to which General Grant's earlier unsuccessful efforts finally led him.

While all this immense effort and great accomplishment went forward in Mississippi, the Army of the Potomac lay in winter quarters along the Rappahannock, facing the scene of their December disaster at Fredericksburg. Only once during the winter did they leave camp—in a futile effort to pass up the river, cross the fords above Lee and turn his left, an effort that ended in rain and mud, bottomless and hopeless, to become known as the "Mud March."

Burnside, obviously, would not be able to lead the army again, and a new commander must be named. Lively intrigues were afoot in political Washington to name the successor. Burnside himself brought the matter to an issue with his General Order No. 8 in which, subject to the approval of the President, he dismissed from the service Major-General Joseph Hooker and other officers, and relieved from duty with the Army of the Potomac still others, charging varying degrees of military disloyalty. The President did not approve, but in-

stead relieved Burnside from the Army of the Potomac and
sent him to the West.   The partizans of General Hooker were
able to have him named in the place of the man who had
ordered his discharge from the Army.

Joseph Hooker, the fourth commander to lead the Union
army against Robert E. Lee, had the misfortune to be known as
"Fighting Joe" Hooker.   Because of its swashbuckling implica-
tions, he did not like the name.   Hooker was quick, generous,
high-spirited, but of a variable and uneven temperament which
was to fare badly when pitted against the even constancy of
Robert E. Lee.

There were other changes among the Union Army commanders during the winter and spring of 1863.   Rosecrans,
still with his headquarters about Murfreesboro, was not disturbed, but in Missouri Major-General John M. Schofield,
whose cooperation with the conservative Union element in the
state, as represented by Governor Gamble, was not liked by the
fiercer and more radical Unionists, was replaced by Major-
General S. R. Curtis, the victor of Pea Ridge.   Missouri was
torn with the most bitter and unhappy internal strife—local
neighborhood fights, bushwhacking, all manner of violence and
disorder going under the name of patriotism for one side or the
other.   Under the provocative rule of Curtis this situation was
so intensified that he was relieved from command and loyal
old Sumner, who had been in Virginia and out of the local
fights, was taken from the Army of the Potomac and ordered to
Missouri to take charge.   When Sumner died on his way to St.
Louis, Schofield was recalled to the command of the Department.

On the Confederate side, also, there were changes in command and serious consideration given to others more important
which were not made—unfortunately not, as the event proved.
On January twenty-second, while Joseph E. Johnston was at
Mobile inspecting the new harbor defenses there, President
Davis telegraphed him to proceed at once to the headquarters
of General Bragg at Tullahoma, and there, on the ground, deter-
mine whether Bragg had so lost the confidence of his army that

he should be removed. Johnston made his investigation, recommended that Bragg be left in command, and went back to his
inspection at Mobile. While engaged there he was directed by
the Secretary of War to return to the Army of Tennessee, take
command, and send Bragg to Richmond for conference with the
War Department. Arrived at Tullahoma, Johnston found General Bragg devoting himself to Mrs. Bragg, supposed to be at
the point of death. Before Mrs. Bragg was enough recovered
for the considerate Johnston to feel that he should deliver the
order from Richmond, Johnston himself fell sick. The order
was never delivered, nor was the change of command made
for another year, after the disasters of 1863 instead of before.

West of the Mississippi the Confederates made many
changes during the winter months. Having found the difficulty
of handling affairs in that quarter from far-away Richmond, or
from Chattanooga where Johnston had his headquarters, the
Department of the trans-Mississippi was created, with Edmund
Kirby Smith, promoted to the rank of General, in charge and
headquarters at Shreveport. The vastness of his territory and
its remoteness from Richmond made of it almost another government, with Shreveport as its "capital."

Lieutenant-General T. H. Holmes, an aging Regular Army
soldier, had command, under Kirby Smith, in Arkansas. Conditions there were deplorable, really appalling, as Secretary
Seddon wrote to General Smith in March. Civil government
had largely disappeared, and military rule was not strong.
Bushwhacking, burning, pillage, assassination, violence of all
sorts were common. Holmes still held Little Rock but the
Ozarks were gone, and the northern and eastern parts of the
state, with Union gunboats on the rivers penetrating them.

In Louisiana, Major-General Richard Taylor, old Zachary
Taylor's son, without military training himself but with real
native military ability, sharpened by his experience commanding a brigade under Stonewall Jackson in Virginia, was pretty
well holding his own against the aggressive Banks, who during
the early months of 1863 was feeling about among the bayous
and old river channels west of New Orleans, the Atachafalaya,

the Têche, the la Fourche, hunting a high water passage that would let him into the Mississippi River above the Confederate batteries at Port Hudson.

In Texas was won the first Confederate success of the New Year of 1863. Lieutenant-General John B. Magruder had just come to command there, the lordly and bold "Prince John," a handsome fifty-year-old Virginian, of the old Regular Army, whose gallant defense of the line of Yorktown on the Peninsula in the spring of 1862 had added to his distinction. Establishing his headquarters at Houston, he found right at his door, fifty miles down Buffalo Bayou, a Union land and naval force holding the principal Texas port, Galveston. A mixed and motley expedition was organized to recover the port—a few hundred volunteers from Texas cavalry regiments, "mounted" on two crazy river steamers, armored only with cotton bales, and commanded by Colonel Tom Green, of frontier fame. The boats were handled by Captain Leon Smith, an old Sacramento River steamboat man. With this force they steamed down during the last night of the year, to attack at dawn of New Year's Day, with great gallantry and final success, the five naval vessels and the companies of Massachusetts troops which held Galveston harbor.

Among the killed was Commander Wainwright, of the Union ship *Harriet Lane*, and his second in command, Lieutenant Lea, of the Regular Navy. In the boarding party of the *Bayou City*, which stormed the decks of the *Harriet Lane*, was Major Lea, the Lieutenant's father.

"Nearly two years ago," said the Houston *Telegraph*, "the father, then residing in Texas, had written repeatedly to the son, then on the coast of China, saying that he could not dictate to one so long obligated to act on his own judgment; and that, decide as he might, such was his confidence in his high conscientiousness, he would continue to regard him with the respect of a gentleman and the affection of a father."

Choosing different sides, they were to meet again but once, as the son lay dying on the bloody decks of the *Harriet Lane*.

One week after the Confederates seized Galveston the blockade was renewed, with five war vessels, headed by the *Brooklyn*,
standing off the harbor entrance. Three days later, on January
eleventh, a strange vessel came into sight, such a ship as
might well be a blockade runner. Observing the fleet, and
seeing that the fleet observed her, the strange vessel turned and
made off. The *Hatteras* was sent in chase; the stranger, not too
fast, drew her on and away. Just at dusk the stranger turned,
announced herself the Confederate States cruiser *Alabama*, engaged the *Hatteras*, and in fifteen minutes sank her. The
Alabama picked up the crew of the sinking ship, struggling in
the water, and, with all lights under cover, stood away into
the Gulf of Mexico, escaping the pursuing fleet on the wings of
a howling "norther."

This most famous of Confederate cruisers had already been
in commission more than two months when she sank the *Hatteras*. She was built at Birkenhead, in England, as an unarmed
ship, and dispatched to the island of Terceira, in the Azores,
in that guise. There she was met by another steamer bearing
armament and supplies. The two vessels were lashed together,
outside the territorial waters of Portugal, the arms transferred,
and the new ship made into a man-of-war—a wooden ship of
little more than one thousand tons, two hundred and twenty
feet long, eight guns, with engines that could drive her at ten
or twelve knots, barkentine-rigged and with plenty of canvas,
whose use saved the coal supply.

There, on the open sea, the *Alabama* was christened and
commissioned for the Confederate States by her new commander, Captain Raphael Semmes. Semmes was an officer
of the old Navy, with battle experience in the Mexican War,
who was serving on the Lighthouse Board in Washington when
the war opened. He elected to follow his state, Alabama, and
offered his services to the Confederacy. His first command
was the first ocean cruiser of the Confederate Navy, the *Sumter*, which had been a steamer in the New Orleans-Havana line.
She was fitted out as a naval vessel at New Orleans, with great
difficulty. Early in July of 1861 she had successfully run the

blockade of the Passes of the Mississippi and started on a career
of commerce destroying which sent marine insurance rates on
northern ships sky high. Her cruise ended, after six months,
when she was laid up in the harbor of Gibraltar, and her commander, officers and part of her crew went to the *Alabama.*

There Semmes had twenty-four officers, of distinguished
Confederate connection, most of them, and one hundred and
twenty men, including a small nucleus of Confederate seamen
and pilots, but with a much larger number of sailors from
the seafaring nations of the globe. After a few weeks of
successful cruising about the Azores and as far north as New-
foundland, the *Alabama* ran down into the Caribbean Sea.

From northern newspapers found on board a prize captured,
the Captain learned that General Banks was to send an army
from New Orleans by sea to Galveston, there to land and to
invade Texas. He decided to run the *Alabama* into the Gulf
and to Galveston, with the thought that no one would be looking
for a Confederate cruiser in such a situation and that he could
make a night attack on the fleet of transports, steaming slowly
among them, discharging both batteries right and left, and
make his escape in the darkness. Arrived off Galveston, and
seeing that the Union blockading squadron was standing off the
harbor, he correctly divined that the Confederates had retaken
the town, abandoned his first plan and was forced to content
himself with luring one ship out from the Federal fleet and
destroying her.

That work done, the *Alabama* sailed to Jamaica, paroled
the prisoners picked up out of the water as the *Hatteras* sank,
coaled ship, and sailed on to the South Atlantic—thence to sail
in every sea in the eighteen months afloat left to her, and to put
an end, almost, to the carrying trade of the United States before
she came to her end in the English Channel.

While the *Alabama* was on her way from Galveston to
Jamaica, another Confederate cruiser was making her escape
from the port of Mobile. This ship had started as the British
steamer *Oreto*, which, after many vexatious delays, including
four months of proceedings in Admiralty at Nassau, had taken

aboard her armament and a shadow of a crew at Green Cay, an uninhabited island in the Bahamas. She had been christened the *Florida* by her new captain, Commander John N. Maffitt, an officer of the old Navy and of the Confederate Navy, who had a son midshipman on the *Alabama* under Semmes. Yellow fever broke out on the *Florida* almost at once, and still further reduced her scant crew. Touching at Cardenas and Havana, Captain Maffitt decided to make a run for Mobile to recruit his crew and complete the fitting of his ship.

The *Florida* succeeded in running the blockade into Mobile on September 4, 1862. There Maffitt found difficulty in getting the needed work done on his fever-infected ship, but did, at last, succeed in getting ready for the sea and recruiting a crew. Knowing that the *Florida* was in the bay, the Union squadron off Mobile was reenforced to seven vessels, specially charged to capture her. On the night of January 15, 1863, Maffitt succeeded in taking his ship out, passing right between two of the fastest of the blockading fleet. For more than six months the *Florida* cruised and, with her tenders created from captured vessels, spread consternation among shipping as far north as the Maine coast and across to the coast of France. Again in 1864, the *Florida's* cruise was to be resumed, not under Maffitt, broken by yellow fever and exposure, but under Captain C. M. Morris. The *Florida* was not to come to her end in battle on the open sea, as was the *Alabama*, but to be sunk in the neutral harbor of Bahia by the United States cruiser *Wachusett*—a violation of neutral hospitality for which the United States apologized to Brazil and court martialed the commander of the offending cruiser.

In the early winter days of 1863 another Confederate cruiser, the *Nashville*, stuck on a mud-flat near the mouth of the Ogeechee River, south of Savannah, ran afoul of the Union Navy. All through 1862, after the great South Atlantic naval base at Port Royal was established, that fleet had been busy seizing the undefended or lightly defended bays and inlets up and down the coast—St. Augustine, the mouth of the St. John's River, Fernandina, in Florida; St. Mary's, Cumberland Island,

St. Simon's Island, Brunswick, the mouth of the Savannah, in
Georgia. Fort McAllister, on Ossabaw Sound at the mouth of
the Ogeechee, however, resisted all attack. Behind the fort,
waiting an opportunity to slip out and renew her commerce-
destroying cruise, was the lightly built and unarmored *Nashville.*

Against the fort came the new monitor *Montauk*, commanded by the same Worden who had so ably handled the
original *Monitor* in the fight at Hampton Roads the year before.
Three attempts to silence or destroy the fort were made in
January and February, 1863. The fourth time Worden discovered that the *Nashville* was aground a short distance up
the Sound. On the last day of February, the monitor steamed
boldly up under the guns of the fort, which rattled their shot
harmlessly against her iron sides. With care and deliberation,
using her heavy Dahlgren guns, she destroyed the helpless
Nashville, half concealed across a bend in the river.

The attacks on Fort McAllister were in the nature of a dress
rehearsal for the grand naval attack on Charleston, which, in
spite of close watch by eight or ten vessels, continued to be a
port for the runners of the blockade. Earlier efforts to cork
up the harbor by sinking a fleet of barges loaded with stone in
the channels had failed. The new monitors looked to be more
promising.

Enthusiasm for them was high following the earlier skep-
ticism. Newspapers and orators and bureau heads were
confident that a fleet of them could steam into Charleston
harbor, batter down the forts, take the place—"punishment"
for "that hateful city" where secession was born. John Ericsson, who designed and built them was not so confident, nor was
Rear-Admiral Samuel DuPont, to whom was given the task of
fighting them in their first wholesale test.

DuPont had tried it out on Fort McAllister, with a fleet
of three monitors, accompanied by gunboats and mortar
schooners, and the little fort had withstood the attack. While
the monitors seemed to be impregnable to the fire of the fort,
their fire against the land works was not notably destructive.

Here was not one of those cases of running by batteries and passing into the clear zone above. The fleet that went against Charleston must drive forward into a ring of fire, increasing in power as the ship passed into the center of the harbor defenses. Beauregard had designed and installed them, and in neither army was there a military engineer more competent, nor one with a better eye to the uses of the artillery arm. Recovered from his illness, he had returned to Charleston in the autumn of 1862, to take charge of the defense of all South Carolina, Georgia and Florida, after Pemberton was sent to Mississippi.

In Charleston harbor, in April of 1861, Beauregard had achieved the first bloodless victory of the Confederacy. In April of 1863, two years later, the forces of the North returned to begin a series of attacks and sieges which, almost without let-up, were to last until the very end. The first attack was by the monitors, eight of them, with the *New Ironsides*, a broadside vessel, as DuPont's flag-ship. On the morning of April seventh, with a smooth sea, a favoring tide, calm and fair weather, the formidable fleet steamed up the main channel, to pass the batteries on Morris Island and go against Fort Sumter. The attack, made with great spirit and determination, was the first test of Beauregard's new installations and arrangements. Within little more than an hour the well-directed fire from the well-placed batteries drove back the ships, with a loss of one sunk and two disabled—"a sad repulse," reported the Rear-Admiral.

There was the usual outcry against the unsuccessful military commander from the people and the department which had expected the new monitors to batter and silence the Confederate works, but the fact that the Beauregard defenses of Charleston were able to beat back later and far more formidable attacks, combined land and water movements, is justification enough for DuPont's wisdom in withdrawing his ships while they yet floated.

Cruisers on the sea, a handful of them, and ports into which the swift ships of the blockade runners could slip, were but incidents. The cruisers might, as they did, drive the American carrying trade into neutral vessels, but still the trade went on. The United States had the world from which to draw men and supplies and arms and equipment of all sorts; the Confederacy, except for the little driblets that trickled through Mobile, Charleston, Galveston, far-away Brownsville, at the mouth of the Rio Grande, and, most important of all, Wilmington, had itself alone.

CHAPTER XX

"On to Richmond"; as Far as Chancellorsville

In April, with persistent Grant still hunting for a dry place to stand while he attacked Vicksburg, and with Rosecrans and Bragg feinting and thrusting at each other in Tennessee, General Joe Hooker launched his "On to Richmond" campaign.

McDowell had started to Richmond in the summer of 1861, to get no farther than the little stream of Bull Run; McClellan had spent the first half of 1862 getting his army within sight of the city, to be turned back in the Seven Days' Battles; poor Pope had never got fairly started, before he found himself at sea on the old battle-field of Manassas; Burnside had broken his army against the heights of Fredericksburg. There is no doubt, and can be little wonder, that the Confederate soldier of the Army of Northern Virginia believed in 1863 that his army, under his commander, could meet the Army of the Potomac anywhere and under any conditions and take its measure.

The first "On to Richmond" movement had tried to advance along the Orange & Alexandria Railroad and the Virginia Central through Gordonsville; the second had based on the York and the James Rivers; Pope's had never developed as an offensive campaign, beyond the movement toward the Rapidan under Banks; Burnside had tried to use the Potomac, at Acquia Creek as his base, with the rail line from that place through Fredericksburg to Richmond as his line of communications.

Hooker adopted a variant of Burnside's plan. He would do three things at the same time: send a large cavalry raiding expedition, under Major-General George Stoneman, to pass well to Lee's left, and attack his communications between Fredericksburg and Richmond; cross a large force over the Rappahannock at Fredericksburg and make a feint at an advance along the line chosen by Burnside; and, under cover of the excitement and diversion of these movements, march the larger part of his great army up the Rappahannock to cross that stream and the Rapidan above Lee's left and so strike heavily at his rear and his communications with Richmond.

The Rappahannock flows into Chesapeake Bay, generally from northwest to southeast. At a point a few miles above Fredericksburg, there flows into the Rappahannock, coming from south of west, the Rapidan. The two streams make a Y, with the open end to the west, the stem to the east, and Fredericksburg on the stem a little below the junction of the two legs.

At Fredericksburg the stream is not fordable, but five miles above, at Banks' Ford, it may be crossed. Another six miles up—more than that as the river winds—is the United States Ford, a mile below the junction of the two rivers. The north leg of the Y, the Rappahannock, could be crossed at Kelly's Ford; the south leg, the Rapidan, at Ely's and Germanna Fords. The territory in the angle between the two was held by neither army.

South of the Rapidan lay a dense and tangled country, scrubby second-growth timber that had sprung up in old "coal choppings" where wood had been cut out for charcoal, a few clearings, none large, broken ravines where small streams ran down into the rivers—"The Wilderness," the country was called. Through it there ran west from Fredericksburg the old Turnpike Road and, roughly parallel to the Turnpike and near it, the Orange Plank Road. North and south there were a few roads running to the fords across the rivers—neighborhood country roads through the woods.

Along the north bank of the Rappahannock General Hooker had one hundred and thirty thousand men—"the finest army on this planet," in the opinion of its commander, seven fine infantry corps, eleven thousand cavalry, eight thousand artillerists, with more than four hundred guns.

South of the river was Lee, with an army considerably less than half that of Hooker. Longstreet, with the divisions of Hood and Pickett, some fifteen thousand men, had been sent to southeastern Virginia, to the region about Suffolk, during the winter. They were called back when Hooker's movements began, but General Longstreet had his wagons absent on a foraging expedition into eastern North Carolina at the time and felt that he could not move without leaving them to the enemy, or, that if he did so move, his troops would be of little value without their transportation. Nearly a week after the end of the Chancellorsville campaign Longstreet reported back. Meanwhile sixty thousand men had fought and decisively defeated one hundred and thirty thousand.

The first stirrings of Hooker's campaign were planned for April twelfth, but heavy storms and a rapid rise in the rivers prevented the start of Stoneman's cavalry raid. Later in the month, from the twentieth to the twenty-second, Hooker's left wing made demonstrations as if to cross the Rappahannock at Port Royal, eighteen miles below Fredericksburg—a demonstration which drew the comment from Lee to Jackson, "I think . . . his present purpose is to draw our troops in that direction while he attempts a passage elsewhere. I would not, then, send down more troops than are actually necessary. . . . I think that if a real attempt is made to cross the river it will be above Fredericksburg."

On the twenty-seventh of April Hooker made his real start. Stoneman, with about six thousand cavalry, operating in two columns, was thrown across the Rappahannock and the Rapidan, well above and to Lee's left, and started on a raid to break his communications—a raid that was moderately destructive but ineffective so far as disconcerting Lee's defense.

On the same day the army started moving. The division of Gibbon, in camp at Falmouth in plain sight of the Confederate pickets at Fredericksburg, was left in position, as a blind, while the rest of the army marched. Two corps were to cross the Rappahannock at Kelly's Ford, twenty-five miles up from Fredericksburg, push across the no-man's land between the two rivers, cross the Rapidan at Germanna Ford, strike the old Turnpike Road some twenty miles west of Fredericksburg, and turn eastward toward that point. These corps, the Eleventh under Howard and the Twelfth under Slocum, started their march on April twenty-seventh. On the next day the Fifth Corps, under Meade, started. The Fifth, after crossing the Rappahannock, was to cross the Rapidan by Ely's Ford, lower down than Germanna, with a shorter distance to march.

While these three corps—nearly equal to the whole of Lee's army—were on the march, Hooker kept three corps, Reynolds' First, Sickles' Third, and Sedgwick's Sixth, demonstrating in front of Fredericksburg. On the twenty-eighth, Couch's Second Corps was started for the United States Ford, just below the junction of the two rivers. As the troops which had crossed at Germanna and Ely's Fords, higher up the Rapidan, pressed on eastward on the south bank, they uncovered the United States Ford and Couch's men crossed.

On the thirtieth of April Sedgwick crossed the Rappahannock by pontoon bridges three miles below Fredericksburg, and started a strong demonstration against Lee's right wing, while the rest of the Union army was moving toward its concentration point at Chancellorsville, ten miles west of Fredericksburg and so on Lee's left flank and rear.

By the night of the last day of April, General Hooker had his army on the south side of the Rappahannock, and had got it over with little fighting and light loss. The sanguine, exuberant phase of his temperament took fire.

"It is with heartfelt satisfaction the commanding general announces to the army that the operations of the last three days have determined that our enemy must either ingloriously fly, or come out from behind his defenses and give us battle on our own ground, where certain destruction awaits him," said Hooker in his exultant general order of premature congratulations. At that, the order was not unreasonable—except that the army in front which was to fly or to be destroyed was the Army of Northern Virginia, with Robert E. Lee in command, seconded by Stonewall Jackson.

Hooker's position had one element of weakness. His movement, brilliantly planned, had been executed with precision, but it had separated the wings of his army widely. Sedgwick was thirteen miles away by the direct road, with Lee on that road between them, while the actual line of communication, crossing and recrossing the Rappahannock by the United States Ford and Sedgwick's pontoons, was more than twenty miles. The difficulty was not serious, however, or would not have been had the personalities of the two leaders been reversed, because Sedgwick could well take care of himself with his twenty-four thousand men, while Hooker had enough men concentrated about Chancellorsville to have gobbled up Lee's army, if properly used. Moreover by an advance eastward along the Turnpike Road it was possible to capture Banks' Ford, the one closest to Fredericksburg, and so reduce the long line of communication between the two wings of the Union army to one but little longer than the interior line held by Lee. Hooker had every reason to anticipate the victory that he promised his soldiers in his flamboyant address.

The troops, too, and the subordinate officers were in high mood when they started on the morning of May Day the eastward move along the Turnpike and the Plank Roads and the road to Banks' Ford. The movement was late in starting but by a little after noon it had struck Lee's advanced troops, under Anderson.

On April twenty-ninth, the day that Hooker was crossing the Rapidan and starting his march toward his point of concentration on the south side, Lee had sent Anderson out from Fredericksburg toward Chancellorsville—which was not a village, as the name would indicate, but was a road junction and a large mansion, the Chancellor House, with its outbuildings. The next day, being the day when Hooker completed his concentration, Jackson's corps and McLaws' division, less one brigade, moved out to join Anderson.

When Hooker learned that his troops were meeting stiff opposition on the road to Fredericksburg, where he had expected none, the sanguine element in his variable temperament gave way to doubt and indecision. That afternoon, after some hesitation and vacillation, he decided to call back his advance.

take up the position about Chancellorsville which his army had occupied the night before, and there fight a defensive battle. "I have got Lee just where I want him; he must fight me on my own ground," he said to his second in command, Couch.

As Hooker's divisions drew back from their advance, Lee's force followed, pushed forward and maintained close contact. Lee himself and Jackson were well to the front that day of May first. When night came they bivouacked in a little pine thicket at the forks of a country road but a mile and a half from Hooker's headquarters in the Chancellor House. After a sleep of a few hours, stretched on the soft pine-needles and covered with their army cloaks, in the chill hours after midnight the commanders rose for their final conference on the battle, held over a little fire of twigs, with cracker boxes for seats, and no attendants near. It was to be their last military conference.

Lee's plan at Chancellorsville is one that the safe and conservative soldier would have condemned in advance, but the commander who must fight against odds of two to one in men and guns can not always do the safe thing. His one chance, sometimes, lies in a bold daring that stakes greatly to win—or lose. Lee's plan was to divide his army into three parts: Early's division, reenforced by Barksdale's brigade from Mc- Laws, to remain at Fredericksburg facing east toward Sedg- wick; Anderson's and the rest of McLaws' divisions to stay in battle position facing west toward Hooker at Chancellorsville; Jackson, with the divisions of A. P. Hill, of D. H. Hill com- manded by Rodes, and of Trimble, commanded by Colston, to march away from the others, pass westward by country roads along Hooker's front and around his army, to the Plank Road and the Turnpike west of the Union positions, and there to turn east, push down the two roads and through the woods, and strike Hooker's right flank while Anderson and McLaws at- tacked the Union left.

Jackson's corps, or the three divisions that were to follow "Old Jack" himself, marched early on the morning of May second. It was to be Stonewall Jackson's last flank march— and his most brilliantly successful. The column was to go by narrow country roads, cut through the thickets and the forests of the Wilderness, closely screened in by bushes and vines. The divisions were closed up, pushed forward, carried on at a swinging pace, filling the roads with men hurrying to battle. Near the front rode Jackson on "Old Sorrel"—Jackson thoughtful, withdrawn, lips pressed close, the old flat-topped cap pulled down over his eyes; the horse, like his master, sober, serious, intent on the business of getting over the ground with his long pacing stride, a beast of awkward seeming but most effective for the work in hand.

By the middle of the afternoon the head of Jackson's column, which in the morning had been on Hooker's left, was well out beyond his right and on the roads leading toward his flank, exposed and unsuspecting. By five o'clock in the afternoon the divisions were up, formed in three lines of battle: Rodes in front, Colston next and A. P. Hill as the third line. The lines stretched across the main roads, through the woods and dense thickets on either side, and lapped well behind Hooker's right and rear.

When all was ready, a little after five o'clock, the advance began, an impetuous rush, with the wild rebel yell, the high-pitched, individual battle-cry of the Confederate troops, so different from the organized unison cheering of the northern regiments. The lines burst through the woods, tangled with briers, brambles and undergrowth that tore the ragged clothes and scratched the faces of the eager attackers. The first troops they struck were the Eleventh Corps, commanded by Major-General Oliver O. Howard, who had his headquarters at Dowdall's Tavern, which was not a tavern at all but the private residence of the Reverend Melzi Chancellor, two miles west of Chancellorsville, and at a fork of the Turnpike and the Plank Roads. On the extreme flank was Devens' division, with the brigades of von Gilsa and McLean. Next, facing more to the northwest or rear, came the division of Carl Schurz, with the brigades of Schimmelfennig and Krzyzanowski, covering the hollow where the little Wilderness Church lay in a small clearing. The third division of the corps, von Steinwehr's, with the brigade of Buschbeck and the reserve artillery under Schirmer, was about Dowdall's Tavern, covering the road junction and facing more to the south. Cavalry, which should have been well out to the west observing those dense and impenetrable thickets, was elsewhere. The flank of the army was in the air, with no adequate feelers out.

Howard had assembled what might have been adequate reserves under Barlow, on the little ridge above the Wilderness Church when these were called for to cooperate with Sickles, commanding the next corps to the left, in an advance south to beat up the bushes through which it was suspected that Confederate troops were passing. The advance came too late to intercept Jackson, and just early enough to deprive Howard of the reserves that might have helped him.

It is not likely, however, that anything would have stayed the rush of Jackson's men when they struck the Union flank. Isolated bodies of troops resisted stubbornly, only to be flanked and nearly surrounded as units to right or left gave way in retreat. Within an hour the corps became a panic-stricken mass, flying along the roads, through the clearings, in the pathless woods. Finally, as dusk fell and reenforcements came from the left, the resistance stiffened—but not until after the Confederates had driven in the Union right for two miles and jammed the whole army into a cramped and impossible position about the Chancellorsville plateau, where its numbers were of little avail.

The two leading divisions of the Confederate attack had become broken and disorganized in their successful advance through the woods. Jackson ordered the rear division, A. P. Hill's, to pass through to the front. While the change was on foot, Jackson with part of his staff rode forward in the deepening darkness to make a close reconnaissance of the Union line. As he started up the rise in the road toward the Chancellor House, not more than a mile away, he was fired on by Union soldiers lying in line of battle. He turned and rode back toward the Confederates. Hill's new troops had come up and taken the front, not knowing that the General was out toward the Union lines. Seeing a party of horsemen dashing toward them in the deep dusk, they fired. The first volley, from a company south of the road, killed two of the party. The second, from the north side, wounded Jackson in three places. As his horse bolted into the bushes the General was swept from his saddle to the ground.

He lay between the lines, in the edge of the road. A. P. Hill rushed forward to his assistance, and an effort was made to carry him back within the Confederate lines. As the movement started, Union artillery opened, sweeping the road with shrapnel. One litter-bearer was struck and fell, the others laid their burden on the ground and took refuge in the ditches. As the storm of shrapnel veered, Captain James Power Smith, Jackson's aide, managed to half carry the wounded General from the road to the woods. A second party of litter-bearers was organized and once more the short march to the Confederate lines was started. Again a litter-bearer was struck, the corner of the litter dropped and the General fell to the ground, with great pain.

General Pender, from whose North Carolina brigade the fatal shots had come, came forward to inquire as to his wounds "I shall have to retire my troops to re-form them, they are so much broken by this fire," he said. Jackson, faint and weak, rallied his strength to give his last battle order:

"You must hold your ground, General Pender; you must hold your ground, sir!"

Finally, after agonizing difficulty, Jackson was got back to the field hospital, where at midnight his left arm was taken off at the shoulder. The next day, Sunday, while the great battle which Jackson had so vigorously opened raged, he roused to hear read a note from General Lee:

"Could I have directed events, I should have chosen, for the good of the country, to have been disabled in your stead. I congratulate you upon the victory which is due to your skill and energy."

"General Lee is very kind," said Jackson as he turned his face wearily away, "but he should give the praise to God."

A. P. Hill being wounded also, J. E. B. Stuart, the "gay cavalier," was put in command of Jackson's corps that Sunday and pressed against Hooker's contracted right—riding the lines, with his banjo-player Sweeny, like some court minstrel of old, and singing his invitation:

"Old Joe Hooker, won't you come out of the Wilderness?"

During Saturday afternoon Hooker, hearing that Confederate troop movements to the southwest across his front had been detected, jumped to the happy conclusion that Lee was in the predicted "inglorious flight" toward the rail junction at Gordonsville. By night, when Howard's broken corps came flying into the right of his position, he knew better. He decided then that Lee must have denuded himself of troops on the east to make the attack on the west flank, and sent a peremptory order to Sedgwick, left below Fredericksburg, to march to Chancellorsville, "attack and destroy" opposition, and be there by daylight on Sunday.

Sedgwick, who had twenty-four thousand men, received the order at eleven Saturday night. He had some thirteen miles to march before morning, with an enemy in his front. It was an impossible order. By daylight, when he was called for at Chancellorsville, he had gone no farther than the town of Fredericksburg—and there before him were the fortifications on Marye's Heights, with their memories of the horror in December. The heights were lightly held, with only Early's division and Barksdale's brigade spread thin on a long front, but it required two heavy storming attacks and almost all the morning to secure them and start the march toward the anxious Hooker at Chancellorsville—and then they still had Early's troops, intact, to drive back all the way.

At Salem Heights, about half-way, Jubal Early made another stand, along a little ridge marked by the old brick church of Salem—and with reenforcements sent by Lee was able to fend off Sedgwick until Lee completed his battle of Sunday against Hooker.

The Sunday fight was a strange affair—forty thousand confident men attacking and driving eighty thousand, led by a General despondent and uncertain in his mind. Locally, in spots, it was hard bloody fighting, at close quarters in the woods, torn by shell and shrapnel. In the main, though, it was a retrograde movement of the Union army toward new positions, closer to the Rapidan, which Hooker's engineers laid out.

By the middle of the Sunday morning, Hooker, chagrined at finding that his exultant boasts of having out-generaled Lee were so soon recoiled upon him, stood on the porch of the Chancellor mansion, watching his battle. A solid shot struck one of the porch pillars, split it and knocked a part against the commander. He remained in command for perhaps an hour longer, much stunned, lying on a blanket in the rear of the house, which was burning. Before turning over the command to Couch, he ordered a retreat to his new line, which was about all that could be done with an army as much out of joint as that of the Potomac.

Lee's officers, a great many of them, wondered at the time why he did not hurl them on Monday morning against the new line and drive Hooker's army into the Rapidan. Affairs toward Fredericksburg were the reason. Jackson's corps, under Stuart, was left in front of Hooker to demonstrate and hold his army in position on Monday, the fourth, while Lee and the rest of the troops marched to the assistance of Early, holding off Sedgwick at Salem Church. Sedgwick, from being the attacker became the attacked, and it was only by prompt movement and fast fighting that he was able to get his right flank to Banks' Ford, draw his whole force there, and form them in a short semicircular entrenched line covering the essential passage of the river.

On that night, midnight between May fourth and fifth, General Hooker, recovered from his stunning, assembled his corps commanders and announced that the army would recross the Rappahannock and return to its camps. During the day and night of the fifth, Sedgwick got back across at Banks' Ford, and Hooker's "finest army of the planet," which had been out just one day more than a week, marched back across pontoon bridges laid at the United States Ford into its camps at Falmouth and resumed its position on the Stafford Heights "covering Washington." Three days later Stoneman's weary troopers rode into camp back from their raid, and the Chancellorsville campaign was over.

Both sides had lost heavily—more than eleven thousand killed and wounded and six thousand prisoners, on the side of the Union; more than ten thousand killed and wounded on the Confederate side, with less than two thousand prisoners.

The Army of the Potomac had lost heavily in spirit and morale, too—was there *no* way to get over, through or around this Lee?—while the southern army had suffered its greatest blow in the wounding of Jackson.

On Monday, after Hooker had withdrawn from the battleground of Chancellorsville to his new position, Jackson was carried in an ambulance across the rear of the army to the Chandler home, near Guinea's Station, on the Richmond-Fredericksburg Railroad. His wife was there, and his baby, who had come just before the battle to see him; the best of southern surgeons were there, with every care they could give; the prayers of the southern people centered there—but on the next Sunday after the great battle which he had launched, on May 10, 1863, Stonewall Jackson, who but a few moments before in his delirium had been again calling A. P. Hill to come up into battle—the last movement he had ordered on the field—sank back, wearily and at peace. "No, no," he murmured, "let us pass over the river, and rest under the shade of the trees."

CHAPTER XXI

VICKSBURG

WHILE Hooker was planning the Richmond campaign which ended in the thickets at Chancellorsville, and while Rosecrans was still in Middle Tennessee facing Bragg, west of the Cumberland Mountains, General Grant found the way to Vicksburg.

He had started the search in November of 1862, just after Van Dorn and Price had been repulsed at Iuka and Corinth. The Confederates got a new commander in Mississippi just then, John Pemberton. He and Grant had served together in Mexico, when both were Lieutenants. Now Grant was a Major-General commanding an army, and Pemberton had just been made a Lieutenant-General when he was sent out from the Department of South Carolina and Georgia to relieve Van Dorn. Before Grant's advance reached the line of the Yallabusha, at Grenada, where Pemberton was busy throwing up fortifications, Confederate cavalry raids in his rear dragged him back, and forced the advance away from the straight overland route along the railroad to the rivers.

The Mississippi proved satisfactory as a line of supply, clear down to the bend where the guns of Vicksburg blocked the stream, but it raised a new problem: to find a footing on dry ground where supplies could reach the army and from which the army could reach Vicksburg. It was this problem that engaged Grant through the winter months, when everything tried north of Vicksburg failed, as did efforts to persuade the contrary Mississippi to enter a new channel.

South of the city, however, the main stream of the Mississippi itself comes right up against more than one usable bluff on the east side of the river. The problem, however, was to get troops past the city to those hills—and especially to supply them after they were there.

On the night of April 16, 1863, Confederate pickets in small boats patrolling the river in front of Vicksburg, found bearing down on them from above a darkened and muffled fleet. They gave the alarm and then, instead of making for Vicksburg and safety, they paddled for the Louisiana shore, held by Federal forces, where they fired houses in the village of De Soto, to light up the river for the Confederate gunners on the opposite bluffs. So doing, the courageous pickets not only ran the risk of capture, but put themselves in the direct line of fire from the Confederate batteries firing at the moving fleet as it passed between the guns and the light of the burning houses.

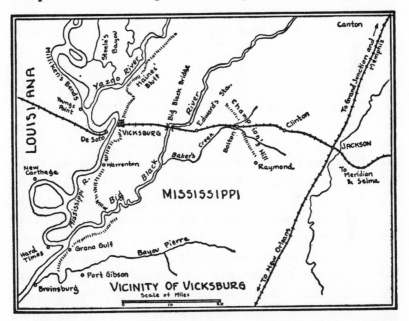

VICINITY OF VICKSBURG
Scale of Miles

Bold Porter was taking the first step in the solution of the problem of putting and keeping the army on the high ground below Vicksburg, to secure control of the river below, as well as above the city. Ten vessels got by that night, seven gunboats, a ram, two transports, protected with cotton bales on their decks and with barges of coal and baled hay lashed to the sides exposed to gunfire from the bluffs. One transport was sunk, burned to the water's edge. Six nights later, half a dozen more transports started down-stream, and five succeeded in running the batteries. By the last week in April Admiral Porter not only had entire control of the river downstream, but also had in his seven transports and their barges a fine fleet of ferry-boats with which to transport an army.

On the morning that Porter got his fleet into the reaches of the river below Vicksburg, Colonel B. H. Grierson, with some seventeen hundred Union cavalry, left La Grange, a few miles out from Memphis on the Memphis & Charleston Railroad, for a two-week cavalry raid through the length of the state of Mississippi and all the way to Baton Rouge in Louisiana. The raid had no particular immediate military results, beyond the destruction of a few railroad stations and bridges, but it did distract attention from the next move in Grant's main campaign, to get his army below Vicksburg.

Porter's exploits had shown that empty transports could be carried past the batteries, but some other way to move the troops must be found. Milliken's Bend is twenty miles upstream from Vicksburg, on the right bank. Landing from the upper transports there, Grant's men marched by devious ways seventy miles through the wide Louisiana bottoms, to strike the main river again at Hard Times, twenty-five miles below Vicksburg in direct line and nearly fifty as the river winds.

Just below Hard Times, on the Mississippi side, the Confederates had fortified Grand Gulf, at the mouth of the Big Black River. The works were held by Major-General John S. Bowen, Grant's old friend and neighbor in Missouri, with three small brigades. On April twenty-ninth, that being the same day on which Hooker was crossing the Rapidan, Porter attacked the little Confederate post without success. That night he ran down-river again, past Grand Gulf, while Grant marched his troops from Hard Times to a landing below Grand Gulf. There, on April thirtieth, the army and the fleet met, and the crossing of the river began. By night of the thirtieth, the same night on which Hooker completed his concentration at Chancellorsville, Grant was across the Mississippi, at Bruinsburg, with twenty thousand men.

Grant's orders from Halleck, far away in Washington, were

to effect a junction with Banks, working up-stream from New Orleans, join in the capture of Port Hudson, and then, with both armies, with the river fleet of Porter and the Gulf fleet of Farragut, come against Vicksburg.   Under this arrangement Banks, as the senior Major-General, was to be in command of the combined forces.

Grant's most immediate task, however, was to secure his footing on the bluffs above Bruinsburg, and to capture the bridge across Bayou Pierre at Port Gibson, from which roads diverged to Vicksburg, Jackson and to Grand Gulf, the location he wanted for his base.   As soon as the troops could be landed and supplied with ammunition they were pushed forward toward Port Gibson, where Bowen's little garrison from Grand Gulf met them and fended them off for a day.   The next day, May second, a home-made pontoon bridge was thrown across the Bayou Pierre; a home-made ammunition train, every sort of vehicle drawn by every sort of draft animal found on the farms and plantations, was gathered together and loaded, and the tireless Grant started on the last phase of the Vicksburg campaign—the campaign that was to give him his rank as General of the Army and his chief claim to consideration among the great soldiers.

The campaign was based on speed—speed, and light rations foraged off the country, and no baggage, nothing at the front but men and guns and ammunition, and no rear; no slackening of effort, no respite for the enemy until Vicksburg itself was invested and fell.

On May third, after a week of hard marching and one battle, Grant established himself at Grand Gulf, where he wanted to be.   There news reached him from Banks, away up the Red River toward Alexandria, that he could not reach Port Hudson until May tenth, and then with only fifteen thousand men. Grant's situation admitted of no delay.   Having started for Port Hudson, he changed his plan, abandoned his base at Grand Gulf, cut loose from his line of supplies, and boldly marched for Vicksburg by way of Jackson, capital of the state.

Even Sherman, who was to be chiefly remembered for a

like operation on a grander scale the next year, thought the step too venturesome, and remonstrated with Grant. That tenacious man, however, figured that a quick advance, before the Confederate forces could be concentrated against him would be worth more than any supplies or reenforcements he might hope for, while his men could live off the country through which they marched—as they did, though too much chicken and turkey and corn-bread palled before they got back to their regular diet of bacon and hardtack. He was favored, too, by the topography. As he advanced northeast toward Jackson he was able, at all times, to protect his left flank by seizing and holding the crossings of the Big Black River, flowing from northeast to south-west into the Mississippi at Grand Gulf.

More than all else, he was favored with a divided command among the Confederates. There were really three commanders: Pemberton, Joseph E. Johnston and President Davis.

Johnston, in general charge of all the West, believed in a quick concentration against Grant's army, perilously exposed, even if that meant the temporary abandonment of Vicksburg and Port Hudson. President Davis, following out the usual Confederate Government policy of the dispersed defensive of scattered localities, insisted that the river posts be held to the last—a plan that in the end meant the loss of the posts and of the garrisons shut up in them. Pemberton, torn between the radically different ideas of his immediate superior and his Commander-in-Chief, at times attempted to follow both plans, finally followed neither—and lost everything.

While Bowen was holding off Grant's advance on the road from Bruinsburg to Port Gibson, on May first, Pemberton telegraphed to Johnston that Grant was across the river and south of Vicksburg, and called for reenforcements. During the days that Grant was moving to Grand Gulf, bringing up Sherman's corps and the rest of McPherson's, to add to the twenty thousand men with which he had first crossed, and preparing cooked haversack rations to be carried by his men, there was great telegraphing back and forth between Pemberton, Johnston at Chattanooga and the Secretary of War at Richmond. On the morning of May seventh, with much misgiving on the part of his corps commanders, Grant cut loose from his base, abandoned communication with the North, and started after his enemy, with the corps of McClernand and Sherman bearing left against the Big Black, as far up as the point where the railroad between Jackson and Vicksburg crosses that stream, and McPherson bearing to the right, toward Raymond and Jackson itself.

Three days later, on telegraphic order from Richmond, Johnston rose from a sick-bed in Chattanooga and started for Jackson, to take personal command of the campaign. Because of invading armies on the direct route, he had to travel a round-about way through Atlanta, Montgomery and Mobile to Meridian and Jackson, over war racked railroads. It was night of May thirteenth when he arrived in the capital of Mississippi, to take up the work of defense.

That night there were about six thousand troops in Jackson, the brigade of Gregg sent up from Port Hudson, and of Walker, just arrived from the Department of South Carolina and Georgia. Maxey's brigade was supposed to be on the march up from Port Hudson, to arrive the next day, while Johnston had passed Gist's, on its way from Charleston by rail, and was expecting Ector's and McNair's, following him around from Tennessee. With them all in hand, he would have about fifteen thousand men to defend Jackson—part of whom had just been defeated, on May twelfth, by McPherson at Raymond.

Pemberton had some eighteen thousand men about Edwards' Station, twenty-five miles west of Jackson on the railroad to Vicksburg. Grant, with more than forty thousand men, had his entire force concentrated between the separated Confederate commands. Johnston, with intent to strike Grant's troops along the railroad, sent orders to Pemberton to advance against his rear, while Johnston moved out against his front. "All the troops you can quickly assemble should be brought. Time is all-important," ended the message.

One of the three messengers by which its triplicate copies were sent was a Union spy, who for months had posed as an extreme and rabid Confederate. The message was in Grant's hands as soon as it was in Pemberton's, and was acted on much more promptly by the Union commander than by the Confederate. In fact, Pemberton, after replying to Johnston that he would "move at once with his whole available force," weakened in his decision—there were those orders from President Davis to "hold Vicksburg at all hazard"—called a council of war at Edward's Station, and lost a day.

That was the day that Grant, prompt to the minute, moved. With knowledge of Johnston's plans he concentrated his forty thousand men against the handful in Jackson, on the morning of May fourteenth. It was not a long battle, nor one heavily contested. That night Grant slept in the room occupied the night before by Johnston, who had pulled off to the north with his forces, and halted at Canton.

On May fifteenth, leaving Sherman in Jackson to "destroy that place as a railroad center and manufacturing city of military supplies," Grant, who had been marching northeast to Jackson, turned west and headed back for the Mississippi River. Between Grant and Vicksburg was Pemberton, at Edward's Station, torn between conflicting orders from Johnston, and from President Davis, who sought to tie him to the fortress on the river.

Poor Pemberton compromised. He moved forward toward Johnston, not as far or as fast as that General had ordered, but farther than the President directed. His plan was to have strong defensive lines prepared where the railroad crossed the Big Black, fifteen miles east of Vicksburg, at the same time advancing against what he expected would be the rear of Grant, engaged with Johnston. His delay, however, had enabled Grant to dispose of Johnston for the time being, so that Pemberton, marching east of the Big Black, ran into the front of Grant's victorious army pressing west.

The battle of Baker's Creek or Champion Hill, fought on May sixteenth, resulted. It was a complete victory for Grant, who was able to throw seven divisions against the three divisions of Carter Stevenson, Bowen and Loring. After six or seven hours of confused fighting, with heavy loss for the Confederates, the divisions of Stevenson and Bowen retreated west to the Big Black; that of Loring, cut off, fell away to the south and finally, after a wandering march, made its way to Johnston at Canton.

The Federal pursuit continued, with the utmost vigor. On the next day, after a feeble resistance, the Confederate troops broke across the Big Black, some by the railroad bridge, some using the steamer *Dot*, moored across the river as a bridge. Quick work of the Confederate engineers, with the help of barrels of spirits of turpentine, burned the bridge and the boat before the pursuing troops could press across, while the Confederates fell back, disheartened and apparently demoralized, into Vicksburg.

In Vicksburg, however, were two divisions of Confederates not yet engaged—Forney's and Martin Luther Smith's. The destruction of the crossings of the Big Black had gained a little time, also, and given an opportunity to place the withdrawing troops in the fortified lines. Johnston, indeed, had sent orders to abandon the place and to fight out toward the northeast, one last effort to concentrate against Grant—but General Pemberton, partly because of his orders from President Davis to hang on to the fortress, and partly because he felt that "it was impossible to withdraw the troops from that position with such morale and material as to be of further service to the Confederacy," did not obey the order.

These troops, whose morale General Pemberton doubted, were to man the defenses of Vicksburg, invested, bombarded, starved, fighting for forty-seven days of unceasing danger, privation and effort.

A fortified line some seven miles long had been built among these ridges and ravines to the rear or east of Vicksburg, extending from the river above to the river below, and enclosing an area about four miles by two. The fortifications anticipated, in some ways, modern trench systems—detached strong points, connected by more lightly held fire trenches or rifle pits. Unoccupied for a year, the works had washed badly.

During the two days before Grant's army completed its investment, and the two months of the siege, there was constant
work on the lines—work that was made more difficult by the
limited supply of shovels. Bayonets could be used as picks,
after a fashion, but the total supply of "regular" shovels, but
five hundred to be distributed along a seven-mile line, had to
be supplemented by makeshift affairs of wood improvised by
the soldiers.

On May nineteenth Grant's troops struck the main line of
defenses. This was to be no run-over affair like that at the
Big Black. Determined resistance inflicted heavy loss as the
Union troops pressed forward in a first and a second unsuccessful charge. Two more days it took for all Grant's troops to
get up, and for his investing lines to be established, generally
about a half-mile outside the Confederate lines. Sherman, by
coincidence, held the very bluffs which he had tried to capture
from below just after Christmas of the year before. On the
twenty-first the line of supply by river was reestablished, and
that night the Union soldiers were relieved of their exclusive
diet of poultry and country produce, with corn-bread, and
were back on the old stand-bys of bacon and hardtack.

On May twenty-second Grant ordered his grand assault—
a most gallant attack, made in battle array, at ten in the morning, under cover of a whirlwind of fire from the artillery, and
of heavy shelling from the gunboats and the mortar fleet in
the river. Three times the assault was repeated. Waving flags
were planted on the parapets, in one or two places, only to be
captured as their bearers were shot down or driven back without making a lodgment. Finally, after the assault had ceased
elsewhere, McClernand, thinking that he had made an entry,
called for one more charge to create a diversion in his favor.
The assault was made—the last to be made on Vicksburg—
and repulsed with fearful slaughter.

More than three thousand dead and wounded Union soldiers
lay on the ground between the lines—the wounded dying in
agonies untellable, the dead rotting in the heat of the early
Mississippi summer. Three days they lay, stubborn Grant

refusing to ask for a truce for the treatment of his wounded and the burial of his dead, thinking that such a request would be an admission of weakness. Finally, on the afternoon of the twenty-fifth, after more than three full days of the horror, General Pemberton asked the truce, so that aid might be given to Grant's soldiers.

Regular siege approaches began: pick and shovel work; trenches, approach trench, parallels, saps run forward, mines run in under the Confederate works. Grant had disobeyed Halleck's orders in going to Vicksburg instead of Port Hudson, but Halleck recognized his achievement and began to send reenforcements from all the Union armies to Grant. Soon he had one hundred thousand men under his command, of whom seventy thousand were in front of Vicksburg, occupying a line nearly fifteen miles long—a double entrenched line, one front looking toward Vicksburg, where Pemberton's twenty-eight thousand men stubbornly defended themselves, and the other facing eastward toward Johnston, anxiously trying to get up enough troops to attempt to raise the siege.

Communication with the Mississippi River once reestablished and open, Grant's army had abundance of everything. The Confederates had only that with which they retired into Vicksburg. From gunboats and mortar-boats in the river, from siege guns and field guns on the land, shell rained into Vicksburg night and day through the siege. For the soldiers there was little rest from duty in the trenches; for the inhabitants nothing to do but burrow caves into the steep hillsides about the town, make themselves as comfortable as they might and watch the bombardment. They ate what they had; they went on short rations, then quarter-rations and finally a biscuit and a bit of bacon each day; they ate horse and dog and rat—and still they held on, hoping that the siege would be raised from the outside.

Away to the south, at Port Hudson, the same scenes were being enacted, on a smaller scale. Two days after Grant's fearful assault on Vicksburg, General Banks, as pugnacious as Grant, invested the lower Confederate fortress. Banks had some twenty thousand men; Major-General Gardner, defending, about six thousand. On May twenty-seventh, five days after Grant's assault, Banks tried to carry the works by grand frontal assault, to meet bloody repulse. At Port Hudson, too, matters settled down to regular siege operations, with the navy in the river, the army on the land, and starvation as an ally.

To the northeast of Vicksburg, Johnston hovered about, maintaining precarious communication with Pemberton, and trying to arrange for joint action from inside and out to raise the siege. At Jackson, on the day of its capture, he had but two brigades, Gregg's and Walker's. Later, toward the end of May and in June, he was reenforced by Gist's brigade from South Carolina, Maxey's from Port Hudson, Evans' from Charleston—the same Evans who had saved the battle of First Manassas—Ector's and McNair's brigades, Breckinridge's division and W. H. Jackson's cavalry from the Army of Tennessee. Finally he had collected twenty-four thousand men, but from shortage of rail transport had been unable to get up guns or enough horses for his cavalry. What material of war there was in Mississippi was shut up in Vicksburg.

The lack of equipment extended even to Johnston's mess gear. Lieutenant-Colonel Arthur J. L. Fremantle, of H. M. Coldstream Guards, who visited his bivouac north of Jackson during the days when Grant was completing the investment of Vicksburg, found that his "only cooking utensils consisted of an old coffee-pot and frying-pan—both very inferior articles. There was only one fork (one prong deficient) between himself and staff, and this was handed to me, ceremoniously, as the 'guest.' " The English Colonel, also, besides noting that Johnston's "officers evidently stand in great awe of him," recorded the General's willingness, when it became necessary to "wood up" the railroad engine behind which they were riding into Jackson, to "work with so much energy as to cause his 'Seven Pines' wound to give him pain."

By late June and early July, however, whatever opportunity to raise the siege that existed in May had passed. Grant was too strong in numbers, in position, in equipment and material, to be attacked with any hope of success, either from inside or outside his double fortified line.

Minor diversions were tried. Dick Taylor's little army of some four thousand men, over on the Louisiana side, attempted to break up Grant's base at Milliken's Bend, but was driven away by concentrated fire from the gunboats in the river. In Arkansas, Holmes, pressed to do something for the relief of Vicksburg, attempted to capture the fortified position at Helena, which had been in Union hands since mid-summer of 1862. The attack, not well made in concert, was repulsed with severe loss, on July fourth.

On that day Vicksburg surrendered. Negotiations for the surrender had begun on the morning of July third. Grant's first reply had been his usual "unconditional surrender," but an interview was arranged and terms were agreed on, by which the Confederate garrison was to be paroled at Vicksburg, without being sent North to prison or the regular station for exchange of prisoners.

Pemberton, a Pennsylvanian, of thirty years' service at West Point and in the Regular Army, who had sided with the South, found himself one of the most execrated of men. It was not so much that he had surrendered the fortress—that was recognized as inevitable after brave resistance—as that it had been done on July fourth. This, to some, proved that he had been a traitor to the South from the beginning, and had gone with the Confederacy just to humiliate the South and glorify the Union by surrendering Vicksburg on July Fourth.

Pemberton's reason for surrendering on that date was sound. In his peculiar position, he would have preferred to head a sortie and attempt to cut his way out. Instead, he offered to surrender on July Fourth. "I am a Northern man," he said to his council of war on surrender. "I know my people; I know their peculiar weaknesses and their national vanity; I know we can get better terms from them on the 4th of July than any other day of the year. We must sacrifice our pride to these considerations."

General Pemberton was to sacrifice more than his pride.

Realizing that there would never again be employment for him in his temporary rank of Lieutenant-General, he resigned and sought service in his regular rank of Lieutenant-Colonel of Artillery—an example that some other Confederate generals of high rank did not follow. In the defense of Petersburg he recklessly exposed himself in the handling of his guns, but was not struck. To enter the Confederate service, he had broken with his wealthy Philadephia family, and thrown away an inheritance, and last appears, after the war, seeking to establish himself and his family on a rented farm in the South. If a man's deserts are to be measured by his sacrifices no man deserved more of the Confederacy than Pemberton, who gave up his thirty years of career in the Army and his own people to follow the right as he saw it, and to win only the bitter distinction of surrendering Vicksburg on the Fourth of July.

General Pemberton and his garrison did not know, until after the surrender, that on the same Fourth of July the Army of Northern Virginia stood along a line of hills above the little Pennsylvania town of Gettysburg, looking across the valley at the heights they had tried for three days to storm—and failed; or that in the highlands of Tennessee, General Rosecrans had the night before occupied the position at Tullahoma which General Bragg had held for the South for half a year.

Down-river, the Fourth of July found General Banks wearing his six weeks' siege of Port Hudson toward its end. To maintain the investment there he had largely stripped his garrison at New Orleans, and the vigorous and enterprising Taylor, with a Confederate force of some four thousand men, was acting to raise the siege of Port Hudson by threatening to recapture that city. By surprise, Taylor had crossed the Atachafalya and captured Union garrisons on Berwick Bay; had made his way through the La Fourche country; had established light batteries on the Mississippi itself; and had so alarmed New Orleans that the level-headed Emory, Union commander there, on July fourth warned Banks that he must choose between continuing his siege at Port Hudson or losing possession of New Orleans.

Banks planned one more assault, which he felt would succeed. There had been three already: the first on May twenty-
seventh; the second, by night, on June tenth; the third, heavy,
to be heavily repulsed, on June fourteenth. The fourth, and it
was hoped the last, was to be on July ninth. On the seventh,
when the great news came down from Vicksburg, Banks tossed
a copy of the dispatch into the Confederate lines—they were
but a few feet apart in places. On the morning of the ninth,
after a defense as gallant if less famous than that of the larger
garrison above, and before the final assault was made, Gardner
and his men, fought out and starved out, surrendered.

One week later, on July 16, 1863, the river steamer *Imperial* tied up at the New Orleans wharf and began unloading
commercial cargo from St. Louis. The Mississippi was open.

CHAPTER XXII

Gettysburg

THE time came, in the early summer of 1863, for the Confederacy to take the offensive once more, for reasons military, political and diplomatic. The Army of Northern Virginia had shown a marvelous ability to confound invading enemies, but the South, blockaded and beset, threatened with a double dismemberment along the line of the Mississippi and again by Rosecrans' advance along the railroad toward Chattanooga, could not afford to stand always to receive battle.

Independence from the determined North and recognition by foreign powers were not to be won that way—not even by Fredericksburgs and Chancellorsvilles. To gain those political and diplomatic ends the South must strike back.

The diplomatic game in Europe was at crisis again, the last crisis in which there was any hope for the Confederacy. Since the late autumn of 1862, the Emperor of the French, pursuing his devious and tortuous path of diplomacy, had been smiling upon the Confederacy—a left-handed smile, it is true, but one that gave the buoyant Slidell, Confederate Commissioner at Paris, heady hope. With the knowledge and inferential approval of the Emperor the great French banking house of Erlanger & Company had underwritten the Confederate "cotton bonds," based on the pledge of government cotton to be delivered after the war at six pence per pound. The shipbuilding firm of Arman & Company, at Bordeaux, was at work on two ironclads, ostensibly for Italian service but really under contract to the Confederacy. Nowhere was Napoleon committed, but everywhere his inscrutable hand was seen—or suspected—favoring a Confederate alliance.

A great offensive victory, following Chancellorsville, was all that was needed to secure an alliance with imperial France, ran the thought of southern statesmanship—and it was an al·

liance with royalist France, they remembered, which had secured the independence of the United States of America.

How to win the victory, and where, were the problems. It was a close and difficult question. Even to-day, with our fuller knowledge of the position and situation of both sides, and after the event, it is not easy to say how best the South might have used its resources, fixed and dwindling, in that period of opportunity just after Chancellorsville. There simply were not enough men, enough guns, enough anything except high courage. There never were.

On the right of the Confederate grand line, extending a thousand miles from Virginia southwest through Tennessee to the Mississippi, Lee had some seventy-three thousand men at Fredericksburg, looking across the river to Hooker's army of more than one hundred thousand. There were thirty thousand more Union soldiers in southeastern Virginia, about Norfolk and on the Peninsula, with still another seventy thousand about Washington and in the lower Shenandoah and along the Potomac, while Confederate forces in Virginia, outside Lee's army, numbered not more than thirty thousand, including the defenses of Richmond, the garrisons in the upper Shenandoah, and Jones' little forces away in the southwestern part of the state, guarding the salt mines, the iron workings and the railroad to Tennessee.

In that state, where there had been no major movements since the great battle of Murfreesboro or Stone's River at the very beginning of the year, was the center of the Confederate grand line—about sixteen thousand men in East Tennessee under Buckner, and fifty thousand under Bragg, holding the southern half of Middle Tennessee, covering the vital rail center of Chattanooga. Against these forces could be brought Rosecrans' eighty-five thousand men based on Nashville, and nearly forty thousand more under Burnside, facing Buckner in upper East Tennessee.

During the first half of 1863, except for the one tremendous week of the Chancellorsville campaign, affairs had been quiet among the main armies on the right and center of the Confederate grand line. It was only on the left, where Pemberton held beleaguered Vicksburg and Johnston hovered about outside Grant's investing line, that the war was active. The immediate military problem, in the spring and early summer, was the saving of the crossings of the Mississippi. Whatever was to be done must have in view its effect on the siege of Vicksburg and of Port Hudson.

Resources for an offensive were not abundant at best. The ports of Wilmington, Charleston and Mobile, almost the only gateways of the South to the world, must be held. There were, however, lesser garrisons scattered about through the interior of the far Southern States which might, it would seem, have been brought into the main stream of military effort.

There was an even more important possibility of shifting considerable bodies of troops between the three major field armies of the Confederacy. At that time the South still controlled the direct railroad line running from Virginia through East Tennessee to Chattanooga, and on through Atlanta, Montgomery and Selma to Meridian and Jackson. The link between Selma and Meridian, in fact, had been built by the Confederate Government after the capture of the Memphis & Charleston line by Union forces early in the war, to establish connection between middle Mississippi and the railroad system to the east without the long detour by way of Mobile.

The use of this interior line of railroad to strengthen the Confederate center or the left for offensive action was urged upon the government at Richmond by Beauregard, by Longstreet, and by D. H. Hill, of the Army, and by Postmaster-General Reagan of the Cabinet. Their plans varied in detail, but each contemplated reducing the forces in Virginia, assuming the defensive there, and shifting troops to the southwest. Beauregard's plan, written from Charleston on May fifteenth, proposed that both the left and the right contribute forces to put Bragg's center in overwhelming strength for an advance northward to crush Rosecrans, recapture Nashville and all of Tennessee and move on north and west to the Mississippi, there to cut Grant's communications. The plan had about it a sweep of boldness that appealed to the strategic imagination of Beauregard, but not to the conservative War Department at Richmond, which rather distrusted the flights of their Gallic General.

Longstreet's plan, submitted to Secretary Seddon and to General Lee, as he afterward wrote, called for reenforcing Bragg for an advance northward from Tullahoma along the railroad line to Nashville, to Louisville and so on to Cincinnati.

Both the Beauregard and the Longstreet plans contemplated that the Confederate advance in the center would force Grant to raise the siege of Vicksburg. D. H. Hill and Reagan favored the reenforcement of Johnston in Mississippi for direct action against Grant's troops investing that city.

General Lee's plan, as finally developed and approved by the Confederate War Department, was to invade Pennsylvania by way of the Shenandoah Valley and its extension north of the Potomac, the Cumberland Valley. With the Army of Northern Virginia on the Susquehanna, he planned to act against Philadelphia, Baltimore or Washington as opportunity offered. He suggested, too, that scattered garrisons in the South be gathered up and organized into a new army, to be stationed southwest of Washington, preferably under the command of Beauregard, whose "presence would give magnitude even to a small demonstration"—a recommendation that was not carried into effect.

The plan presented a more difficult military problem than Longstreet's, especially in its supply arrangements, depending on a wagon haul of nearly two hundred miles from rail head at Staunton into the enemy's country in Pennsylvania, while Longstreet's proposed advance would have been along a working railroad line. It was less promising in its immediate military effect on the siege of Vicksburg, too, but for political and diplomatic reasons it was probably the wiser move to make. Confederate victories in the Valley of the Ohio would have meant little in Paris, where the eyes of Confederate statesmanship were turned, while even at Washington they would have had less effect than battles won in near-by Pennsylvania.

And so it was decided, little by little and under the pressure of events, that the Army of Northern Virginia should march north. It was a reorganized army, three corps instead of two. Longstreet kept the First Corps. There were two new Lieutenant-Generals, Richard Stoddart Ewell, who had Jackson's old Second Corps, and Ambrose P. Hill, who had the new Third Corps, made up of parts of the First and Second. Longstreet did not care for the rearrangement—perhaps because it somewhat diminished his own importance; perhaps, as he wrote afterward, because Ewell and Hill, Virginians, were preferred for the new commands over D. H. Hill, North Carolinian, and Lafayette McLaws, Georgian. It was felt by some that there was "too much Virginia" about the army command, wrote Longstreet—but that was after he had become embroiled in most bitter controversy with more than one of the "Virginians."

Longstreet did not believe in the Pennsylvania expedition. Finally, finding Lee's mind made up, he "then accepted his proposition to make a campaign into Pennsylvania, provided it should be offensive in strategy but defensive in tactics"— strange language from a military subordinate, "accepting" a "proposition" of his commander, with a proviso.

General Longstreet was a square, solid man, most tenacious in his opinion. His vanity was impregnable—in his memoirs he blandly and unconsciously refers to an army comrade as a "friend and admirer." He loved General Lee, for whom he named his son—but where Jackson declared that Lee was "the only man he would follow blindfolded," Longstreet felt upon himself the call to lead Robert E. Lee by the hand. He was singularly stubborn in self-justification, both before and after the event. Cassandra, no doubt, took a certain mournful satisfaction in the fulfillment of her prophecies—but it is not of record that she contributed to that end by the defects of her temperament, as Longstreet all unconsciously did at Gettysburg.

All that, though, was a month in the future when the movement north started from Fredericksburg on June third. Longstreet led off, marching westward to cross the Rapidan at its upper fords, and so on to Culpeper Court House. Ewell followed, to pass behind Longstreet's rear and march on through the Blue Ridge to the Valley, where, the year before, he had served under Jackson. Since Second Manassas, he had been away from the army, recuperating from a wound which had caused the loss of a leg. It was not until May twenty-ninth, only four days before the Pennsylvania march started, that he had returned to his troops, strapped to his saddle, but still able to ride with the best of them through field or forest.

Unlike Longstreet, Ewell's military weakness, if he had one, was too much reliance on authority, too little on his own judgment on the ground. "Why do you suppose President Davis made me a Major-General?" he would ask quizzically, explaining that he had spent twenty years on the western plains learning everything about a half-troop of dragoons and forgetting all about everything else. Of the military genius of "Old Jackson," as he always called him, although himself the senior by several years, he was perfectly assured, and of his lunacy as well, he used to say—especially after hearing Jackson insist seriously that he never ate pepper because of a weakening effect on his left leg. He never saw one of Jackson's couriers approach, he said, that he did not expect an order to attack the North Pole. And now, a Lieutenant-General himself, he was commanding Jackson's old corps, and leading it back into his old Valley.

As Ewell was passing Culpeper on June ninth, Hooker's cavalry, under Pleasonton, came across the Rappahannock on a grand reconnaissance, with ten thousand men. At Brandy Station they struck Stuart's cavalry of about the same strength, gathered together the day before for a great review and still assembled. After a day of fighting, in which there were true cavalry charges, lines of mounted men, boot to boot, with sabers out, using the shock and weight of the horse and the swordsmanship of the trooper in combat, Pleasonton fell back across the Rappahannock, while Ewell and his men marched on to the Valley. There, on June fourteenth, they drove their old opponent Milroy out of Winchester, with large captures. On the next day they crossed the Potomac, occupied Sharpsburg with its memories of the September before, and pressed on north up the Valley into Pennsylvania.

While Ewell marched through the corridor of the Valley, and Longstreet marched up along the east side of the Blue Ridge, A. P. Hill was left behind at Fredericksburg to see what Hooker would do. Hooker himself wanted to cross the Rappahannock and go to Richmond, but that Lincoln forbade in his famous letter of warning not to get caught like an ox jumped half over a fence, unable to kick one way or gore the other. Ordered to go after Lee's army, but not to uncover Washington, the harassed General left his encampments and started moving northward toward the Potomac.

A. P. Hill, then, on June fourteenth, followed after Ewell and Longstreet. Longstreet held and closed the lower gaps in the Blue Ridge; Hill passed behind him into the Valley and marched hard after Ewell. As Hill passed on Longstreet fell back through the Gaps, leaving only cavalry to hold them, and followed Hill north. There were cavalry fights, some of considerable size and fierceness, all along the eastern face of the Blue Ridge from the seventeenth to the twenty-first.

The last of the main Confederate army crossed the Potomac on June twenty-fifth. Two days later the extreme advance, Gordon's brigade of Early's division, was at the Susquehanna, where the railroad bridge from Wrightsville to Columbia was burned by retreating Union soldiers before the Confederates could seize it. The burning bridge set fire to near-by lumber yards and the entire town was threatened with destruction, to be saved by bucket brigades organized by Gordon's men. In appreciation, Gordon and as many of his officers as could attend, were graciously breakfasted by one of the staunch Union women of the town next morning, before they marched away toward Gettysburg.

While the main army was moving north through the valleys west of the Blue Ridge and South Mountains, Stuart and his cavalry went off on another raid around the army. The raid was not a disobedience of orders, but it was a most unwise exercise of the wide discretion left Stuart by General Lee. Hooker's army followed Lee across the Potomac on June twenty-fifth and twenty-sixth, but because of the dislocation of the Confederate cavalry it was not until late at night of the twenty-eighth, and then only through an independent scout who made his way through the Union army in civilian dress, that Lee had this vital information. Stuart and his raiders were far away, and out of touch. After a hard and dangerous ride, lost from the main army, they finally rejoined on the last day of Gettysburg, too late to be of use. Stuart did bring with him a captured supply train of two hundred wagons—small recompense for the loss of the services of his fine cavalry at the critical time of the campaign.

Late on the night of June twenty-eighth, Hooker was relieved from command of his army and Major-General George Gordon Meade was named. Meade was a serious, studious soldier, a man of fine attainments, high courage, physical and moral, not a self-seeker. He did not want the command, and preferred that it should have gone to John Reynolds. That brilliant and generous soldier, so soon to meet death at Gettysburg, and most of the other high officers, believed Meade the man. He had been the choice of the Secretary of War, even the year before when Hooker was named, but had been passed over for reasons of politics. Now, in supreme emergency, the choice was based on merit alone.

Meade, taking command at Frederick in Maryland, started his army north for Pennsylvania on June twenty-ninth, with his seven infantry corps spread wide to cover possible approaches to Washington, and his cavalry marching in the lead and on the flank toward Lee. On the same day, Lee began his concentration to meet the Union advance.

From Chambersburg, in the Cumberland Valley, a turnpike runs eastward through the defiles of South Mountain to Gettysburg. Cashtown, on this road just at the eastern foot of the mountain, became the focus for Lee's army. To this point Ewell was called back; Hill's corps moved in by short marches; Longstreet's brought forward. Stuart was lost, as far as Lee and the main army were concerned—struggling and fighting his weary way toward the Susquehanna, where he expected to find Ewell—and hanging on, all the while, to the two hundred

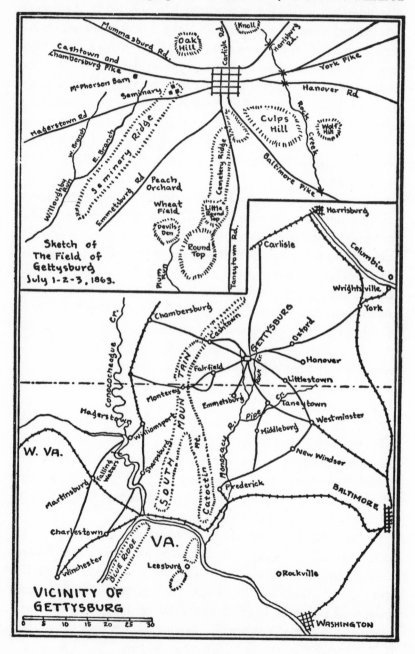

Sketch of
The Field of
Gettysburg
July 1-2-3, 1863.

VICINITY OF
GETTYSBURG

wagons of supplies he had captured almost in the suburbs of Washington. Supplies were never so plentiful in the Confederate Army as to be willingly abandoned.

On the last day of June, Heth, with his division at Cashtown, heard that there were shoes at Gettysburg, nine miles to the east. No Confederate commander could afford to overlook a chance of getting shoes, especially after the march from the Rappahannock mostly on stone turnpikes. Pettigrew's brigade, sent to Gettysburg for the coveted footgear, approached the little town in the afternoon of June thirtieth and found it oc-cupied by what appeared to be the advance of a large force. Pettigrew returned to Cashtown and reported.

The next morning, July first, the Confederate advance moved toward Gettysburg in force—Heth's division in front, followed by that of Pender. As they dipped down into the little valley of Willoughby Run and breasted the rise toward the high ground beween that stream and Gettysburg, they struck the Union advance. Two great armies, neither having any very definite idea of the whereabouts or intentions of the other, had come together.

That morning there was hard fighting on the high ground west of Gettysburg, with varying result. John F. Reynolds, commanding the advance for Meade, was killed before noon. Howard, coming up about noon, took temporary command, with Doubleday's First Corps in on the Union left and Howard's own Eleventh on the right. That afternoon the Eleventh Corps, which had had such unhappy experience of Confederate flank attacks at Chancellorsville, was to suffer again.

Ewell, hurrying down from the north, marching to the sound of battle, arrived on the field in the middle of the after-noon; threw the divisions of Rodes and Early against Howard's flank; broke it and drove it into and through the town. The rest of the Union line, pressed hard in front by Hill, withdrew in some confusion through the streets of the town. As Ewell's men pressed after them, the corps commander himself rode into Gettysburg. There he met young John B. Gordon, of Georgia, commanding one of the leading brigades. Gordon had passed this way as he went north and had had a smart fight on the heights east of the town where Evergreen Cemetery lay—the same heights where the Union troops were being rallied and emplaced by Major-General Winfield S. Hancock, whom Meade had hurried forward from his general headquarters to take charge of the advance. As the Confederate generals reconnoitered the position, which Gordon wanted to press on and capture, a Minié ball struck Ewell with a thud. "Suppose that ball had struck you; we would have had the trouble of carrying you off the field, sir," said Ewell to Gordon. "It don't hurt a bit to be shot in a wooden leg."

Ewell, with orders from Lee to avoid bringing on a general engagement until the rest of the Confederate army was up, and with his own third division under Edward Johnson not yet in reach, decided against immediate pursuit—a decision that may have been the turning-point of Gettysburg, and yet one entirely within the spirit of General Lee's directions.

Lee, with Stuart off he knew not where, was for once in the dark. He did not know, could not know, whether the troops that had appeared in front of him were the main Army of the Potomac, or mere detachments. Not knowing, he was not justified in committing his army to battle beyond recall.

R. H. Anderson, commanding one of Hill's divisions, tells of finding Lee on the first day of the battle, "intently listening to the fire of the guns and very much disturbed and depressed. At length, he said, more to himself than to me, 'I can not think what has become of Stuart. I ought to have heard from him long before now. He may have met with disaster, but I hope not. In the absence of reports from him, I am in ignorance as to what we have in front of us here. It may be the whole Federal army, or it may be only a detachment. If it is the whole army we must fight a battle here. If we do not gain victory, those defiles and gorges which we passed this morning will shelter us from disaster.'"

It was the whole Federal army, moving up by forced marches to occupy the position selected by Hancock, and approved by Meade after a moonlight reconnaissance at midnight of July first. The position was strong, a line of heights east and southeast of Gettysburg, shaped like a question mark turned backward. The dot at the bottom is Round Top, a roughly conical hill at the south end of the position, with its smaller neighbor, Little Round Top, just to the north. Cemetery Ridge continues northward, with a slight depression through it near the town, and finally curves east and then south to the height known as Culp's Hill. By short interior lines on the inside of the curve, the defenders could march reenforcements from one flank to the other, as needed, while the Confederates, holding the outside of the curve, had a long way to go from point to point.

The weakness of the position lay in the fact that Confederate troops, well posted on either Little Round Top or Culp's Hill, at the ends of the line, could make the whole position untenable. By nightfall of July first Union troops were busy entrenching Culp's Hill, but all that night and through the next day, until late in the afternoon, Little Round Top was held only by a signal station.

During the hot, sultry, moonlit night of July first, while Meade crowned the heights with troops and guns, Lee was disposing his army for battle. Ewell's corps held the left, around the head of the question mark; Hill's corps the center, along the Seminary Ridge west of Gettysburg; with ground on the right for the placing of the advancing corps of Longstreet.

Longstreet's movements that night, and for the two days following, have been the subject of most bitter controversy. It appears that his leading division, that of McLaws, camped four miles from Gettysburg that night. Hood's division, also, after marching until midnight, went into camp not far from the field. Law's brigade of this division, however, camped twenty-four miles away, rose in the middle of the night, and started their march to the field at three in the morning. Pickett's division was still farther back.

By night of July first Lee decided to attack Meade where he had found him, an attack that has been criticized as rash and unnecessary. Rash it may have been—most of the movements of an inferior army must be—but it was very necessary. To have retired without giving battle would have been to give up the campaign and any possible results it might have without fighting for them. To have passed around Meade's left flank, which Longstreet earnestly urged, might have forced the Union army to fall back toward Washington or Baltimore, but would merely have postponed the battle and brought it on away from the protecting defiles in South Mountain through which the Confederates might fall back if they were defeated. To wait for Meade to attack, here or elsewhere, was impossible. That precarious and insufficient supply line of wagons forced Lee to seek a decision while he still had ammunition, while his troops were concentrated and before he should have to scatter them for provisions. There was but one other course—to attack, and attack quickly, before Meade's corps to the rearward could march up. It meant risks, great risks and terrible losses, but it was the only plan that gave promise of any results commensurate.

The main attack of the critical second day of Gettysburg was committed to the right wing, under Longstreet, which had not been engaged in the fighting of the first day. Longstreet did not like this campaign, and especially did he not like this attack, which was to be made as soon as possible on the second, with the divisions of McLaws and Hood. The morning and the most of the afternoon passed with no attack. During the long delay Longstreet continued to urge his objections to making the attack and his reasons why the army should move around Meade's flank—while Union troops, all day long, were marching up from the south and into position on the ridge across the valley.

Of course there were reasons for the delay of the Confederate divisions—to move masses of men on crowded battlefield roads is not shifting pins on a map—but no one of them, nor all of them together, made necessary the delay of almost a whole day. Longstreet, the "War Horse," appears to have been less aggressive than usual, perhaps in the unconscious hope that the General might yet change his mind and avoid the pitfalls around which his anxious junior in command would steer him.

At the southern end of the Union position, where the attack was to be made, Major-General Daniel Sickles, through a misunderstanding that became a controversy, put his troops in advance of the main Union line, a salient thrust out from the main range of the Round Tops to the Peach Orchard on the Emmetsburg Road, nearly a mile.

Longstreet's two divisions were finally lined up, ready to attack, after four o'clock. Lacking cavalry, Law, who had the extreme right brigade of the Confederate line, sent out scouts to reconnoiter the wooded slopes of the Round Tops and the territory behind them. They returned with the startling information that the Round Tops were not occupied; that unguarded hospital trains were to be found in the level ground behind them; and that Meade's left flank and rear were wide open.

Law reported what his scouts had found—information that could not have been got by a long-range field-glass reconnaissance of the thickly wooded slopes. He asked permission to change the direction of his attack so as to include the Round Tops and the open ground behind them. Hood, his division commander, approved the change and referred the matter to Longstreet. Longstreet declined to use his large discretion, even when there had come to him such important information not in the possession of his chief, and ordered the battle to be made up the Emmetsburg Road.

In this obscure corner of the second day's battle, not in the famous charge known as Pickett's, Gettysburg was decided— and lost—for the South.

The attack did not get under way until nearly five o'clock. It was made fiercely, and stubbornly resisted, until Sickles' advanced and exposed salient corps had its lines crushed in and driven back from the Peach Orchard, and through the wheat-field, and over the boulder-strewn and wooded slopes of the Devil's Den, until finally, about sunset, the battle came to rest on the lower slopes of Little Round Top. The fighting was hard, desperate, bloody, and locally successful, but there above the Confederates was Little Round Top.

A few troops from Law's extreme right, after all, did make their way up the slopes of that key position. These few, clambering over the ledges and through the trees, met blue soldiers feeding in from the other side, on the run, with their muskets at the trail. General G. K. Warren, Meade's chief engineer, on his way to examine the position of Sickles had passed by the signal station on Little Round Top just before the Confederate attack began. He sensed at once that here was the most important point in the whole field of battle, and that it was wide open and exposed to attack by the flank. Troops called for in most urgent haste came up, a regiment at a time, to meet and finally overwhelm the Confederate regiments working their way up the opposite side. It was close bitter fighting.

On the far Confederate left Ewell's corps was to cooperate with the advance of the right. The attack, made after a cannonade of an hour, was late in starting and achieved little, except that Johnson's division did secure a lodgment in the entrenchments on Culp's Hill, which had been denuded of defenders to resist Longstreet's advance. Darkness, however—it was after eight o'clock—prevented Johnson's men from pressing their success or realizing its full extent. By morning, with affairs on his left stabilized and more troops up, Meade was able to concentrate enough men against Johnson to drive him from the hill.

The Union attack to dislodge Johnson's division from Culp's Hill opened the fighting of the third day of Gettysburg. By noon the attack was successful, the Confederates were driven off the hill, the fight died down. For an hour there was quiet— strange quiet on the field where three hundred guns and more than a hundred thousand men watched each other across the mile-wide valley in which lay Gettysburg.

The Confederates of the assaulting columns, self-described as "dirty, hungry and lousy," lay quiet waiting for the signal "to go up there where the enemy was and lick them or get licked," said Private William Griffin, of Archer's brigade.

"While lying there I heard the shot of a single cannon and noted with some interest a puff of white smoke as it rolled along the valley. It was the signal for opening of the battle"—a battle that, to Private Griffin, was a matter of marching up a hill toward a clump of trees; making his way to a stone wall which he could see below the line of waving Union flags; staying there if he could; getting back alive, if he could not; out of all of which he retained but one clear and vivid recollection, watching a large frog work himself out of a hole to the surface during the great cannonade, as if to see what all the disturbance was about.

This cannonade, opened with the firing of signal guns at one o'clock, followed by every gun in position, was in preparation for the final assault, to be made by Lee's right center directly against Cemetery Hill. Alexander, Longstreet's corps chief of artillery, was in charge, with instructions to watch the effect of his fire on the enemy and when the moment for attack came to advise General Pickett.

Alexander had planned for a cannonade of fifteen minutes—three days' fighting had dangerously depleted his ammunition supply—but at the end of that time there was no perceptible slackening of the reply from the Union artillery. Five minutes more, and ten, and then young Alexander, with heavy responsibility on him, sent a note to Pickett: "If you are coming at all you must come at once, or I can not give you proper support; but the enemy's fire has not slackened at all; at least eighteen guns are still firing from the cemetery itself"—a cemetery on whose gates was still posted the sign: "All persons found using firearms in these grounds will be prosecuted with the utmost rigor of the law."

Thirty minutes of bombardment, and then, suddenly, the Union fire began to slacken and the eighteen guns limbered up and left the cemetery. That was the sort of thing that the Confederates did to save ammunition, but it was the first time that Alexander had seen Union batteries do it. Five minutes longer he waited; no fresh batteries came to take the place of the three that had withdrawn; the cemetery position, studied through the glasses, showed a litter of dead men and horses and broken carriages—and Alexander sent a second note to Pickett: "For God's sake, come quick. The eighteen guns are gone; come quick, or my ammunition won't let me support you properly."

Pickett rode to his corps commander when the first note came, handed it to Longstreet. Longstreet read it, said nothing.

"General, shall I advance?" asked Pickett. No answer. Again he asked. Longstreet, unable to bring himself to give an order for what he believed would be a useless slaughter, bowed, with face turned away. Pickett answered himself, "I am going to move forward, sir."

Longstreet rode forward to the artillery positions, and found that ammunition was running low.

"Stop Pickett immediately and replenish your ammunition," he ordered.

"There is no ammunition with which to replenish," answered Alexander, "and, besides, if we wait for that we will lose all the effect of the fire we have had."

"I don't want to make this attack," answered Longstreet. "I would stop it now but that General Lee ordered it and expects it to go on. I don't see how it can succeed."

As Longstreet spoke, the advance of the infantry swept by— a charge as grand, as heroic and as hopeless as men ever made. Nearly a mile of open plain to cross, broken by substantial walls and fences; a long slope to breast, and on top of the slope, in the cemetery where the use of firearms was forbidden, thousands of blazing muskets, and the eighteen guns, which were run back into position as the gray charge started. Not only in the cemetery, but for a mile to the right, and to the left, a line of guns raking with cross-fire the ground over which the advance must come.

They marched out steadily as if on parade, close lines of battle, straight and well dressed, color-bearers proudly waving their banners, field officers mounted moving forward with the men—the way they still charged in those days.

Pickett's division, the three fine Virginia brigades of Armistead, Garnett and Kemper, which had not been engaged during

Gettysburg, formed the right of the attack. Pettigrew's division, which had been Heth's until he was wounded on the first day, was next to the left: Archer's Tennessee and Alabama brigade, which had lost its commander on the first day and was commanded by Colonel Fry; Pettigrew's own North Carolina brigade, under Colonel Marshall; Jo Davis's Mississippians; Brockenbrough's Virginians. To Pettigrew's left came part of W. D. Pender's division—Pender lay dying from wounds received in the first day's battle—now commanded by Isaac Trimble, two North Carolina brigades, Scale's and Lane's. And all together, Virginians, Carolinians, Mississippians, Tennesseeans, the one regiment from Alabama, they moved out in the charge known as Pickett's.

Dick Garnett—his cousin had been killed in West Virginia right at the beginning of the war—went down, dead; three of his five regimental commanders were killed, the others wounded. Kemper was seriously wounded; two of his regimental commanders killed, three wounded. Lewis Armistead, pressing on to the fence at the top of Cemetery Hill, and over the fence, to the "high tide of the rebellion," was shot dead, with a handful of his men about him, with four of his five regimental commanders killed, the fifth wounded.

Archer's brigade, the column of direction for the attack, made its way to the cemetery also and penetrated the line before it was driven back, leaving its commander on the field desperately wounded. Trimble, too, was wounded and captured; Scales who succeeded him in command, wounded. In the brigades of the left, which had the longer distance to go, there was the same sickening story of loss—officers and men, scattered up the slopes of Cemetery Hill, and down the slopes, too, where they finally fell back and made their way to the Confederate line on Seminary Ridge.

As the survivors drifted back in the wreck of battle, three brigades from the divisions of Hood and McLaws, which had fought the battle of the second day, advanced to cover their retreat, too late to be of help—and the battle of Gettysburg was over.

Over except for yet one more isolated battle of the disjointed series—the great cavalry fight of the late afternoon, when Stuart, up at last, moved against the Union horse off to the east of the main battle. It was a true cavalry fight, mounted charges, shock action, desperate saber fighting, but it decided nothing, accomplished nothing.

The battle had been lost on the second day on the flank, as we know now, and the tremendous attack in the center on the third day was, as Longstreet thought at the time, a mistake. Perhaps that was what General Lee had in mind when he greeted the broken groups of men returning from the charge. "It's all my fault," he said, "it's all my fault." That was not true, except in the sense that he was the responsible commander, but from Lee there was no word of censure, no thought of self-justification. Nor, as long as he lived, did he attempt to lay the blame for the failure of Gettysburg on any one but himself—unless his chance remark to two of his professors at the University after the war that he would have won Gettysburg had he had Jackson there could be so interpreted.

That remark, generally applied to Longstreet's alleged "slowness" on the second and third days of the battle, might have referred as well to Ewell's failure to exceed his instructions and press forward on the first evening—there was plenty of daylight left in the long summer day—to seize Cemetery Hill before it was a-bristle with guns and men. Jackson, with his inspired insight into battle, might have done that, and so have changed the course of the struggle.

While Lee himself, in his lifetime. did not abate his regard and affection for Longstreet, it is apparent now that the self-willed subordinate did not give him the full and cordial coöperation at Gettysburg that was his due. There was much and harsh criticism of Longstreet by his old army associates, especially after he accepted office under the Republican party, for his failure to move with his usual promptness, a criticism which he hotly repels. It is in his own impassioned memoirs, however, that Longstreet reveals the state of his mind on the critical days of Gettysburg. General Lee, he wrote, "had an-

nounced beforehand that he would not make aggressive battle
in the enemy's country" so that Longstreet "was not a little
surprised" at his orders to do so, nor did he like them.   When
Hood "appealed again and again" for permission to make his
attack to the right, "he was reminded that the move to the right
had been carefully considered by our chief and rejected in
favor of the present orders."   To have delayed the attack,
which for one reason or another had already been delayed most
of the day, and sought Lee's further orders in the light of additional information would have been "contumacious," says
General Longstreet.   "That he [Lee] was excited and off his
balance was evident on the afternoon of the 1st, and he labored
under that oppression until enough blood was shed to appease
him," wrote Longstreet, whose plan of battle was not accepted by
his commander—a remark that tells much of the state of mind of
the subordinate.

The whole matter is best summed up, perhaps, by General
Richard Taylor, who knew both Longstreet and Lee well.   Writing in 1877, when the controversy was at its height, he said:

"Now it nowhere appears in Lee's report of Gettysburg that
he ordered Longstreet to him or blamed him for tardiness;
but his report admits errors, and quietly takes the responsibility
for them on his own broad shoulders.   A recent article in the
public press, signed by General Longstreet, ascribes the failure
at Gettysburg to Lee's mistakes, which he [Longstreet] in vain
pointed out and remonstrated against.   That any subject involving the possession and exercise of intellect should be clear
to Longstreet and concealed from Lee is a startling proposition
to those having knowledge of the two men."

When Pickett's men, and Pettigrew's and Trimble's, came
back from the slopes of Cemetery Hill, Lee began his plans to
extricate the army.   His wounded, those who could travel, and
his trains were to be sent to the Potomac, moving through the
gaps in South Mountain just to the rear, and so down the
Cumberland Valley to the pontoon bridges left at the Falling
Waters.   It was four in the afternoon of the Fourth of July
before the train could be lined up and started—a procession

of agony, seventeen miles long, a few ambulances, hundreds of unsprung farm wagons, all crowded with men whose undressed wounds were rasped and torn by their blood-soaked and hardened clothing at every jolt of the wagons.

All that day the army remained on the ridge west of Gettysburg, facing it out with the Army of the Potomac, which remained in position. That night, in torrential rain and storm, the army started south, moving on another road but covering the retreat of the trains and ambulances. That retreat, writes Imboden, whose little cavalry brigade acted as train guards, taught him more of the horror of war than all his other service beside—wagons pressing on through storm and night, with orders to throw off to the side of the road any one that could not hold the pace and its place in the line, to stop not at all until the Potomac was reached; rough wagons jolting south with men lying on their loose and uncovered floor boards, men moaning and cursing and crying aloud, and praying for the mercy of death—which came to many.

The Potomac reached, it was found that the storms had put the river in freshet; that a raiding detachment from Harper's Ferry had cut the pontoon bridges; and that there was nothing for it but to wait until new bridges could be got up. It was an anxious wait, with wounded men and teamsters forming line of battle to stave off attack of enemy cavalry by giving an impression of strength that was not there.

The army, which had left two thousand six hundred dead on the field and had nearly thirteen thousand wounded, out of something more than sixty thousand men engaged, came up and formed to protect its trains and its crossing. Meade's army, which had suffered a loss slightly larger than the Confederates, out of about ninety thousand men on the field, came up in pursuit—a pursuit that, more vigorously pressed, might have had greater results. All through the week, though, Lee held a bold and bristling front to his enemy until the night of July thirteenth. On that night, just before a grand attack was to have been made, the Army of Northern Virginia slipped across the Potomac—as an army to cross that stream no more.

CHAPTER XXIII

THE CENTER GIVES

As LEE was crossing the Potomac to go to Pennsylvania, and while Grant with pick and spade was still driving forward the siege of Vicksburg, Rosecrans and his Army of the Cumberland, on June twenty-third, started the brilliant advance of the Tullahoma Campaign against Bragg, holding the center of the Confederate grand line.

The advance had been long deferred, since the battle of Stone's River, away at the beginning of the year. Bragg, with his headquarters at Tullahoma on the Highland Rim of Middle Tennessee, had his forces disposed on an east and west front through the valley of Duck River. Leonidas Polk had the left corps, around Shelbyville, with the cavalry of Van Dorn and Forrest out to the west about Columbia; Hardee, the right corps, holding Wartrace on the railroad, and the gaps in the range of hills north of that place, with Wheeler's cavalry spread well to the north. Morgan, acting independently as he usually did, was still farther to the north, with headquarters at McMinnville. Rosecrans, with his main base at Nashville, had his troops on a line roughly facing that of Bragg, running from Franklin on the west through Murfreesboro to the headwaters of Stone's River on the east.

And there, facing each other across a narrow strip of neutral territory, the two central armies had been for half a year. Between them they divided a region rich in grain and grass, in beeves, horses and mules, in meat and forage, one of the storehouses of the South. Through this region there had been no lack of minor activity since the last great clash—raid and counter-raid, thrust and feint. In February, Wheeler, with some of Forrest's men under his command, had gone again to Fort Donelson, lost to the South a year before, with the object of recapturing that fortress and interrupting Rosecrans' com·

munication by steamboat with the Ohio. The unwise attack, badly planned and not well executed, ended in repulse across the frozen February hills, with heavy loss, mostly among Forrest's men.

A month later, Rosecrans thrust. Colonel Coburn, commanding an expedition of infantry, artillery and cavalry, pushed out toward Columbia. At Thompson's Station, strung out on the pike, he met the Confederate cavalry under Van Dorn. After a lively fight, the issue of which was settled by Forrest with a wide flanking attack made on his own responsibility, half of the Coburn expedition, some one thousand three hundred men, surrendered; the rest fled. It was in this fight, at a critical moment, with the color-bearer of the Third Arkansas Cavalry shot and the flag down, that Miss Alice Thompson, aged seventeen, rushed from a near-by house to raise the colors and reanimate the wavering regiment.

Hers was one of the rare opportunities for heroism on the battle-field that came to the women of the South. To most, the war brought not so much an opportunity as an obligation for heroism in the home, less to be noted but more difficult to achieve. It has been commonly observed—and truly—that the devotion of the women of the Confederacy to the cause of southern independence was its chief sustaining force. It was, in retrospect, an incredible devotion—face to face with the grim day-by-day job of living in a wrecked and torn country, with the men away in the armies; with the children to feed and to clothe, and with little wherewith to feed and less to clothe them; with money, such as it was, going down to the ultimate vanishing point in value, and taxes, which after this summer of 1863 were to be collected in kind and not in the government's own money, going up; with nothing of the sustaining power of comradeship and stimulation of example which lighten the life of the soldier—with all this, the Confederate women clung to their dream of a nation independent, out-faced the facts of despair, and, through long months and weary years of absence and separation, of privation and danger, maintained their "front" to the enemy.

Living, terribly simple in some ways, became curiously complicated in others. "I have just procured leather for our negro-shoes," wrote the mistress of a plantation in Middle Georgia to a friend in England, "by exchanging tallow for it. I am now bargaining with a factory up the country to exchange pork and lard with them for blocks of yarn, to weave negro-clothes, and am dyeing thread to weave homespun for myself and daughters. I am ravelling up, or having ravelled up, all the old scraps of fine worsteds and dark silks to spin thread for gloves, which I am to knit. My daughters and I being in want of under-garments, I sent a quantity of lard to the Macon factory, and received in return fine unbleached calico,—a pound of lard paying for a yard of cloth. They will not sell their cloth for money. You see some foresight is necessary to provide for the necessaries of life.

"If I were to describe the cutting and altering of old things to make new, which now perpetually go on, I should outstep the limits of a letter, but I thought this sketch would give you some idea of our Confederate ways and means of living and doing.

"The photographs of the children I was so happy to see. You would have smiled to have heard my daughters divining the present fashion from the style of dress in the likenesses. Amid all the woes of the Southern Confederacy, her women still feel their utter ignorance of the fashions whenever they have a new dress to make up, or an old one to renovate. I imagine that when our intercourse with the rest of mankind is revived we shall present a singular aspect."

Not less remarkable than the spirit of the Confederate women was the attitude of the slaves. In wide stretches of the South, especially in the Mississippi Valley and the central South, there were years when there was, in practical effect, no law. It was debatable land, swept over by armies, back and forth, wherein the writ of neither government truly ran. The restraint of the presence of the white men was gone; there were no more "paterollers" on the highways at night; there was every reason, in a time of disturbance and excitement, with the heady talk of freedom in the air, for the slaves to desert their masters, and even, as had been preached to them by the John Brown sort, to rise in revolt and destruction against their master's homes and families. Many able-bodied young negroes did leave their quarters, as indicated by the large number of negro soldiers enrolled in the Union armies, and the refugee camps of "contrabands" that accumulated around garrisons, but there was nowhere in the South even the beginning of the servile insurrection that might have been expected—the highest tribute to the southern negro, and the southern white man, and the relations between them.

More of a menace to the safety of the women and children on the lonely and scattered farms over the immense area of the South than possible slave uprisings, were the maraudings of the bushwhackers—sometimes of one side, sometimes of the other, often of either, or both, as opportunity of plunder and destruction offered. With no effective civil government in the war-torn regions, and with the armies able to police only their immediate vicinity, the hills and forests, the bottoms and cane brakes of the debatable grounds in the South were infested with such skulking bands, made up of deserters from both armies, living by prey on the people. It was an evil that in early 1863 was just coming to notice. By 1864, and the desperate winter between that year and the year of the surrender, it was to rise to shocking proportions.

In the same month in which Coburn was repulsed, March, 1863, Forrest moved forward on a smart raid on Brentwood, behind Rosecrans' right and almost in Nashville, while a part of Morgan's cavalry, under Colonel Roy Cluke, operating from the Confederate right, was away in their home-land of the Kentucky Blue-Grass.

Late in April Rosecrans dispatched Colonel Abel D. Streight, of Indiana, a bold and able soldier, with a picked raiding expedition of two thousand specially mounted men, to pass well to the Confederate left by steamboat up the Tennessee River; to disembark in northwestern Alabama in territory held by General Grenville M. Dodge, under Grant; and from there to move across the mountain section of North Alabama to reach the railroad line between Atlanta and Chattanooga upon which Bragg depended for supplies, reenforcement and all connection with the South.

The mission was difficult, but if successful might mean such a break-up of Bragg's communications as would force him to retreat to or beyond Chattanooga without battle. The Streight expedition, off to a good start, slipped away from the covering forces of Dodge at midnight of April twenty-sixth, and started southeast toward Rome, in Georgia. Forrest, ninety miles away, had been ordered to North Alabama three days before, to oppose Dodge's eastward advance through the Valley of the Tennessee River. Arrived there he heard, one day late, of Streight's movement, instantly divined its purpose, and, with a handful of his cavalry, set out in pursuit. At sunrise of April thirtieth, and at the crest of Sand Mountain, Forrest overtook Streight, to begin a most amazing three-day running fight; to move one hundred and twenty miles across mountain and valley and stream; and to end not far from Rome in the surrender of Streight's command, worn out, exhausted, asleep in line of battle, to a force of little more than one third its own strength, but one so displayed as to make its appearance overwhelming.

The advantage of the running fight, of course, was with the pursued, who not only had the larger force but were able to scour the country for mounts, leaving only the sore-footed and broken-down animals for the pursuer whose horses might drop out. Moreover, they could ambush the pursuers, and force a certain caution in the advance, all of which advantages the capable Streight used. It was through the superior management of his men and horses that Forrest succeeded, and with the help of one brave girl, Emma Sansom who, with bullets cutting through her ample skirts, showed him a lost ford over Big Black Creek, deep, sluggish, with precipitous banks, with its bridges burned, without her help an "impassable" barrier for the protection of the pursued.

When Forrest returned from the capture of Streight, he found that Van Dorn had been killed in private quarrel at Spring Hill, and that he was in command of the cavalry of the left wing.

May passed without event on the whole central front, other than patrol actions. The nation was watching Chancellorsville and the movements toward Vicksburg. That month, and early June, saw a great revival of religion in the Confederate army in Middle Tennessee—camp-meetings, professions of faith, baptizings. General Bragg himself was baptized, on June second, in the church at Shelbyville by Bishop Elliott.

Bragg, called on to send troops to Johnston for use against Grant, weakened himself. Rosecrans' opportunity had come. On June twenty-third he started his Tullahoma campaign— brief, almost bloodless, brilliant in its conception, execution and results. At the opening of the campaign he had more than eighty thousand men, of whom about sixty thousand were available for mobile operations, the others being required to garrison his base and his line of supplies. To oppose him, Bragg had a strength of about forty-seven thousand, of whom nearly fourteen thousand were cavalry.

Rosecrans opened with a feint to his right, threatening to pass around the left flank of Polk's corps at Shelbyville. His cavalry, on the night of June twenty-fourth, filled all that countryside with camp-fires, as if there were heavy infantry forces advancing. During that day and the next the main Union army moved to the left, forced Hoover's Gap on the road between Murfreesboro and Manchester, drove the Confederates across the Garrison Fork of Duck River and, on June twenty-seventh, occupied Manchester, fairly on Bragg's right flank and but twelve miles from his base at Tullahoma. By midnight of the twenty-seventh, Rosecrans' leading corps, under George H. Thomas, was all up on the plateau where Tullahoma stands; McCook was half-way through Hoover's Gap; Crittenden, with the third Union corps, was toiling along behind over roads made bottomless by rain, rain and more rain—seventeen consecutive days of it.

That same night Hardee, with his infantry, had fallen back along the railroad to Tullahoma to meet the threat from the right flank, while Polk's infantry was on the march from Shelby- ville to the plateau town. At Shelbyville, the crossing of Duck

River, the Confederate cavalry was fighting off the cavalry of the Union right, to which was to be added, the next morning, the advance of Gordon Granger's reserve corps of infantry. Forrest's cavalry, which had marched over from Columbia on Bragg's call, was cut off that night from the rest of the army, and on the wrong side of the river, but by the time Granger arrived, in the morning of the twenty-eighth, Forrest had made his escape and was successfully covering General Polk's wagon train toiling along the sixteen miles of mud road to Tullahoma.

That morning Bragg had all his infantry in position at Tullahoma, facing north and west; Rosecrans was still closing up his army on a line between Manchester and Tullahoma; the rain was still falling. The next day, while Rosecrans feinted again at Bragg's line, he moved by the flank to the left toward the railroad bridge over Elk River, southeast of Tullahoma. Once more was Bragg fairly flanked out of his position, this time to abandon his headquarters for half a year, and to retire eighty miles through the Cumberland Mountains and across the broad Tennessee. From Chattanooga, a little less than a year before, the army had started, in that glowing summer of 1862, to carry the Confederacy to the Ohio River. To Chattanooga they returned on the afternoon of July third—the afternoon that the Army of Northern Virginia was making its last charge against Cemetery Hill, and that General Pemberton stood and discussed with General Grant the terms of the surrender of Vicksburg.

When Vicksburg fell, General Johnston's inadequate relieving force was between Grant's lines and the city of Jackson. Immediately upon the fall of the fortress, and even before Port Hudson surrendered, the indefatigable Grant sent Sherman to drive Johnston off. By July ninth, with some slight fighting, Sherman arrived in front of Jackson, to which Johnston had retired, and sat down for serious attack against the city. On the sixteenth, after a week of scattered skirmishing, the Confederates for the second time gave up the capital of Mississippi.

Grant, having drawn one dividing line across the Confederacy now proposed to cut off another section: to advance to Mobile; with Farragut's willing help and the cooperation of Banks from New Orleans to take that port, and establish there a new base of operations, from which to push inland and detach another state from the practical support of the government.

Fortunately for the Confederacy, President Lincoln and General Halleck intervened. "In view of the recent events in Mexico I am greatly impressed with the importance of re-establishing the national authority in western Texas as soon as possible," wrote the President to Grant. "I am not making an order, however; that I leave, for the present at least, to the general-in-chief." The General-in-Chief naturally and promptly did make it an order, and the solid benefits of establishing a firm base at Mobile, urged by Grant, Banks and Farragut, were sacrificed to the diplomatic necessity, such as it was, of planting the United States flag in Texas where the Emperor Maximilian, and his Imperial backer in France, might see it at close hand and be deterred from any Confederate alliance.

The great army which had captured Vicksburg, and which might well have moved eastward through the Confederacy, was broken up: the Thirteenth Corps sent to Banks to be used in the futile and nearly disastrous expedition to Texas; a few thousand sent north to Schofield, to be used against Sterling Price, in Arkansas; some sent to Natchez, to relieve Banks' men of guarding the river in that section; other troops scattered about in garrison duty or minor expeditions.

Grant himself, going to New Orleans in August to confer with Banks, was tendered a review by his former corps. Thrown by a vicious horse, he was most seriously injured, three ribs broken, one side paralyzed, even his mind affected by concussion of the skull, injuries that were to incapacitate him for more than a month and to give him great pain and trouble for many weeks after that.

Johnston, returning to his proper duty as commander in the West, called Hardee to the command of the forces in Mississippi, facing Sherman.

With Vicksburg in Union hands, and the Confederate attack

on Helena driven off the same Fourth of July, Major-General
Frederick Steele, commanding Union forces in Arkansas, began
his plans to push forward the conquest of the state. General
Blunt, in the far northwest, was on the Arkansas River, at Fort
Smith. During July, Steele made ready at Helena an expedition
to take the capital at Little Rock, defended by some eight
thousand men commanded by Sterling Price. On August fifth
the expedition started, gathered reenforcements later that month
at Devall's Bluff, on the White River, and moved with about
fourteen thousand men and fifty-seven guns across country to
Little Rock. There, after some little maneuvering and light
fighting, Steele turned and overlapped Price's fortified lines.
Price, late in the afternoon of September 10, 1863, evacuated
the place and fell back to the southwestern part of the state,
holding a line from Monticello through Camden and Arkadelphia, on the headwaters of the Ouachita, and on into Indian
Territory, where General Samuel B. Maxey with a brigade of
Texans and Indians held the extreme left flank. To Nashville,
Baton Rouge and Jackson had been added a fourth Confederate
capital in Union hands, and most of the state of Arkansas.

From Arkadelphia, however, Colonel Joseph O. Shelby,
with about eight hundred Missouri cavalry, and two little guns,
turned and started back to Missouri, on September twenty-
seventh. He crossed the Arkansas in the Ozark region, between
Little Rock and Fort Smith; entered southwestern Missouri;
captured Neosho and a string of lesser posts near the western
border of the state, and finally, on October thirteenth, reached
his old home at Waverly, on the Missouri River, where he had
been a manufacturer of rope and bagging before the war. Attacked near there by overwhelming forces, from two directions,
he was driven back, to retreat in utmost and painful haste along
the Missouri-Kansas border; to reassemble his scattered command on the Little Osage River in the Ozarks; and finally, late
in October, to recross the Arkansas at Clarksville, a dozen
miles from where he had crossed going north, thirty days before. During those days he had marched a thousand miles
over a country with poor roads, had had ten fights, besides

patrol actions, had put out of action as many men as he had, had destroyed a million dollars' worth of supplies, had lost a fifth of his own command and all his artillery. The major military value of the move, however, was that it kept busy in Missouri Union soldiers who might otherwise have been sent to Tennessee to furnish needed reenforcements to General Rosecrans.

In those days of thronging disaster for the South there was to come one more, from a cavalry raid. John Morgan and his men rode to Indiana, to Ohio, past Cincinnati, almost to Pennsylvania, to the "farthest North" of the Confederacy—and, the most of them, to prison or death. Their raid, a ride of utter rashness but one so bold that it became and has remained one of the epics of the South, started from Burkesville, Kentucky, on the upper Cumberland on July second. It was designed to create a diversion in Kentucky to assist in covering the retreat of Bragg's army, but Morgan, on his own responsibility and against orders, carried it across the Ohio.

More than a thousand miles they rode and fought. From the Cumberland, across the headwaters of the Green, they rode through the familiar towns of Lebanon and Bardstown. There, instead of turning east toward the Blue-Grass, they turned west to pass south of Louisville, to cross the Ohio at Brandenburg on July ninth, using two captured steamboats, and to strike up into Indiana.

From that point their difficulties multiplied. Their coming spread terror that was embalmed in a song:

"I'm sent to warn the neighbors, he's only a mile behind,
   He's sweeping up the horses, every horse that he can find.
   Morgan, Morgan the raider, and Morgan's terrible men,
   With bowie-knives and pistols are galloping up the glen,"

but the terror did not prevent the country from rising against them—militia and home guards and some regular troops, rising before and closing in behind them.

Through it all "Morgan's terrible men" pushed on, burning bridges behind them, taking the horses and the supplies they

needed, bringing to this pleasant country of southern Indiana
a touch of the reality of war. At Seymour they turned east,
through Vernon, and on to the little town of Milan. There,
spread along fence rows for four miles, Morgan's men, who in
ten days had ridden four hundred miles, crossed wide streams
and fought daily skirmishes, snatched a trooper's rest for a few
hours. The next morning, July thirteenth, they rose to make
their march to and beyond Cincinnati, a march never equaled
by a column of two thousand five hundred men, carrying their
sick and wounded, their wagons and supplies, scouting, occasionally a little brush of fighting, with the halts and delays
that must occur in a column—and yet, in thirty-two hours,
marching ninety-five miles, feinting to the north to draw off the
troops blocking their way, and passing through the very suburbs
of the city.

That was the high point for Morgan's Ohio raid. Weariness, and losses, and the rising countryside harassed his steps,
but in spite of all, on the evening of July eighteenth, he reached
the place on the Ohio River appointed for recrossing into Kentucky, Buffington Bar below Blennerhasset's Island—to find
it too strongly occupied, his way blocked and pursuers closing
in from everywhere. Some of his men escaped to the Kentucky
shore. Morgan could have gone with them, but returned to lead
his remnant on north, seeking to elude pursuit. There was
another week and two hundred miles more of weary marching,
continual skirmishing, north and northeast, back from the line
of the river, nearly to Steubenville, and then a devious course
always northward, seeking a hole to escape, until the final
surrender on Beaver Creek, near New Lisbon, on July twenty-
sixth, of Morgan and three hundred and sixty-four of his men,
to be scattered among northern prison camps.

Gettysburg, Vicksburg, Tullahoma, Morgan's failure—and
now another blow threatened the South in the disastrous July
of 1863. On the morning of the tenth the long expected combined land and sea attack on Charleston began—a bombardment that was to last, with little intermission, all the rest of
that summer and far into the autumn. Troops were landed

on Morris Island, on the southern side of the inlet to Charleston harbor, and on Folly Island, still more to the south; batteries were emplaced among the sand-hills with the greatest labor, and the bombardment of Battery Wagner, guarding the portals of the harbor, begun. The little work among the sand-dunes on Morris Island, exposed to bombardment from land and sea, and to siege operations, for nearly two months, until September sixth, "fought the enemy . . . with men, artillery, and with sand"—and then its garrison withdrew and left the wreck to the invaders.

While Wagner still resisted, other batteries were turned on Fort Sumter. A seven days' bombardment, from the seventeenth to the twenty-third of August, began the destruction of that work, crumbling its proud brick walls into sloping piles of débris—but with its indomitable garrison still there to resist any attempt to land on its ledge and take possession of the coveted work. Sumter, ruinous, harmless and all but indefensible, became a point of honor in the defense of Charleston.

On August twenty-first while Sumter and Wagner were under bombardment, General Quincy A. Gillmore, commanding the Union forces, demanded the immediate surrender of the two works, coupling with the demand the threat that noncompliance within four hours would mean the bombardment of the city of Charleston itself from a battery already emplaced and covering it. Surrender being refused, fire was opened on the city from the "Swamp Angel," a rifled Parrott gun most ingeniously mounted behind sand-bag protection in the marshes southeast of the city. Fortunately, the Swamp Angel burst as it was firing the thirty-sixth shell into the lovely old city, and was not replaced. The shells that fell within the city itself after that were, for the most part, "overs" aimed at the forts and batteries.

Charleston passed into a state of siege that lasted with slight interruption for the rest of the war. Fort Sumter was again, and even more heavily, bombarded in September, and again late in October. Desultory fire was kept up through the rest of the year, but there was nothing there now to shoot at but a pile of ruins, crowned with a Confederate flag, and with a defiant garrison which, somehow, had kept one little smooth-bore piece with which to fire their sunset gun.

In Virginia, after Gettysburg, there was rest and quiet among the armies through the late summer, and on into the autumn. Once safely across the Potomac, Lee fell back by slow marches, with Meade following, to the neighborhood of Warrenton. Later he crossed the Rappahannock and occupied the triangle of territory between that stream and the Rapidan. Finally, on September fourteenth, after Longstreet had been detached and sent to Bragg to strengthen the central army for the great struggle about Chattanooga, Lee gave up this territory and took up position behind the Rapidan, leaving Culpeper Court House to Meade for his headquarters.

In August, a month after Gettysburg, and after he had his army safely back in Virginia, General Lee wrote to President Davis suggesting the appointment of another commander for the Army of Northern Virginia—as Albert Sidney Johnston had done after the loss of Fort Donelson and Nashville.

"The general remedy for the want of success in a military commander is his removal," wrote Lee. "This is natural, and in many instances proper. For, no matter what may be the ability of the officer, if he loses the confidence of his troops, disaster must sooner or later ensue.

"I have been prompted by these reflections more than once since returning from Penna. to propose to your Exc'y the propriety of selecting another commander for this army. I have seen and heard of expressions of discontent in the public journals at the result of the expedition. I do not know how far this feeling extends in the army. My brother officers have been too kind to report it, and so far the troops have been too generous to exhibit it. It is fair, however, to suppose that it does exist, and success is so necessary to us that nothing should be risked to secure it. I therefore, in all sincerity, request your Exc'y to take measures to supply my place. I do this with the more earnestness because no one is more aware than myself of my inability for the duties of my position. I cannot even accomplish what I myself desire. How can I fulfill the expectations of others? . .

"I have no complaints to make of any one but myself. I have received nothing but kindness from those above me, and the most considerate attention from my comrades and companions in arms."

Lee had been in command of the army a little more than a year. He had come to it on the second day of the battle of Seven Pines, almost in the suburbs of Richmond; under him it had fought and won the Seven Days and relieved Richmond; had fought and won Second Manassas and thrown Washington almost into panic; at Sharpsburg had fought to a standstill McClellan's great army; had fought and won Fredericksburg and again Chancellorsville, throwing back each time a threatened movement on Richmond; had gone to Pennsylvania, had fought Gettysburg and failed to win, but had stayed a whole day in line, facing Meade, and made good its retreat to Virginia, unhampered and almost unmolested. There is no wonder, and can be no doubt, that "whatever General Lee did, his men thought it the best that could be done under the circumstances."

They knew that their dangers, their privations, their trials and sufferings were his. For himself, he asked nothing; for his army, every chance that the failing strength of the Confederacy could give—including a new and younger commander, if that was their wish or that of the government. There was about him and his headquarters nothing for show or impression— unless there be considered the occasion when, with visitors at the General's mess during a time of short rations, a four-inch hunk of "middlin' meat" mysteriously and unexpectedly showed up on his table, to be treated with ceremonious respect by the mess, because it had been "borrowed" by the General's servant "for the company."

Soldiers in the camps along the Rapidan, making themselves comfortable as experienced soldiers will, settled down to a quiet life. There were camp-meetings and revivals, such as there had been in the Army of Tennessee in the early summer. There was even a camp newspaper, *The Rapid Ann*, got out by soldiers with pen and pencil. Its circulation, as measured by the number of copies "printed," was not large—

paper was too scarce in the Confederacy—but there was never a paper whose every copy had more readers.

Neither battles that had been fought nor disasters to come, dampened the humor of *The Rapid Ann*. It revised *Hardee's Tactics*, and widened its application, by the publication of the

"TACTICS OF KISSING.—Recruit is placed in front of the piece. First motion—Bend the right knee; straighten the left; bring the head on a level with the face of the piece; at the same time extend the arms, and clasp the cheeks of the piece firmly in both hands. Second motion—Bend the body slightly forward; pucker the mouth, and apply the lips smartly to the muzzle mouldings. Third motion—Break off promptly on both legs, to escape the jarring or injury should the piece recoil."

Journalism was not the only outlet for the creative impulse in the camps along the Rapidan that autumn and winter. Patchwork became an art after one waggish genius appeared in ranks with a glowing heart of red flannel where there had been a hole in his trousers. A new fashion of decorative patching struck the Army like a rash—hearts plain, entwined or pierced with arrows, geometrical patterns, every sort of fanciful device. There was music, too—Bugler Crouch, blowing his calls over the wintry hills, was to write *Kathleen Mavourneen*.

Pickets along the Rapidan, during that long period of comparative peace, became downright friendly. Talking and joking, trading and "swapping" grew so common that it excited no comment—until, finally, fearing that such loose intercourse between the armies might result in the unwitting communication of important information, the high command determined to break it up. John Gordon, instructed to break up the traffic in his front, came up without warning on one of the Confederate posts, to note unusual commotion and confusion.

"What's the matter here? What's all this confusion about?" he asked.

"Nothing at all, sir. It's all right here, General."

"I expressed some doubt about its being all right," continues Gordon, "when the spokesman for the squad attempted to concoct some absurd explanation as to their effort to get ready to 'present arms' to me as I came up. Of course I was satisfied that this was not true; but I could see no evidence of serious irregularity. As I started, however, I looked back and discovered the high weeds on the bank shaking."

Ordering the weeds to be broken down, in spite of the soldiers' protest that there was "nothing the matter" with them, the General discovered a soldier, almost naked.

"Where do you belong?" he asked.

"Over yonder," pointing to the Union side of the stream.

"And what are you doing here, sir?"

"Well, General, I didn't think it was any harm to come over and see the boys just a little while."

"What boys?"

"These Johnnies."

"Don't you know, sir, that there is war going on in this country?"

"Yes, General, but we are not fighting now."

Assuming his sternest aspect, the General ordered the social visitor to stand up.

"I am going to teach you, sir, that we are at war. You have no rights here except as a prisoner of war, and I am going to have you marched to Richmond, and put you in prison."

"Wait a minute, General," interposed Gordon's men. "Don't send this man to prison. We invited him over here, and we promised to protect him, and if you send him away it will just ruin our honor."

With a twinkling eye, and lips twitching beneath his beard, the General turned to the Yankee visitor, and said:

"Now, sir, if I permit you to go back to your own side, will you solemnly promise me on the honor of a soldier, that——"

"Yes, sir," interrupted the swimmer, as he "bull-frogged" over the weeds and into the river, headed for his own side.

Even that instance of fraternity, however, does not equal the "amiable episode" of the Delaware lieutenant who accepted an invitation to a country dance urged upon him by young southern officers opposite, crossed the river, donned a borrowed suit of civilian clothes, and spent a most enjoyable social evening within the Confederate lines.

There were marches and counter-marches of the two armies in Virginia in October, when Lee's threatened advance toward Washington caused Meade to fall back all the way to Centreville, where the Confederates had spent the first winter of the war; and again in November, when Meade's threatening advance across the Rappahannock and the Rapidan brought Lee into line of battle along Mine Run, where, during the last days of the month the armies bristled toward each other until, on December first, Meade withdrew from what appeared to be an unprofitable undertaking and went into winter quarters between the Rapidan and the Rappahannock.

But it was about Chattanooga, and along a little stream named by the Indians Chickamauga, meaning the "River of Death," that the interest of both nations focused through the autumn months of 1863.

CHAPTER XXIV

CHICKAMAUGA, THE RIVER OF DEATH

WHILE Grant's great army in Mississippi was being dispersed, Rosecrans considered how he might best get Bragg out of the key stronghold of Chattanooga. He asked for reenforcements—every one else, it seemed, was getting them from Grant's troops—but none could be spared for him. Instead there came insistent proddings from Washington to get on down to Chattanooga, proddings which finally produced action.

His movement against Chattanooga, which started from Winchester, just at the western foot of the Cumberland Mountain, in mid-August, was as brilliant a bit of strategy as the war produced, as far as the occupation of Chattanooga without a fight. Carried too far, it led Rosecrans to the disaster at Chickamauga, to the starvation siege in the valley at Chattanooga, and to the end of his command over the Army of the Cumberland.

The unique and spectacular conjunction of abrupt mountains, winding river and deep valleys, where the wide Tennessee, flowing by bold Missionary Ridge and Chattanooga, turns into Moccasin Bend to sweep past the foot of Lookout Mountain and on into the narrow chasm cut in the mountains to the west—the whole making a noble prospect that has delighted two generations of tourists viewing the field of the campaign from the towering Point of Lookout—was not just scenery to the opposing Generals in the autumn of 1863.

To D. H. Hill, just promoted to be a Lieutenant-General and sent out to him from North Carolina, General Bragg remarked on the difficulties presented by the peculiar topography of mountain-girt Chattanooga. "It is said to be easy to defend a mountainous country," said the anxious commander, "but mountains hide your foe from you, while they are full of gaps through which he can pounce upon you at any time. A

304

mountain is like the wall of a house full of rat holes.   The
rat lies hidden at his hole ready to pop out when no one is
watching.   Who can tell what lies hidden behind that wall?"
pointing across the river to the mountains to the northwest.

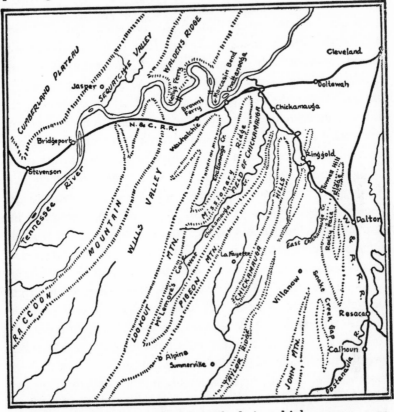

"That wall," most aptly described, is a high, narrow, precipitous ridge, with one break where the river, which from
Virginia and North Carolina flows southwest through the Great
Valley of East Tennessee to Chattanooga, turns abruptly northwestward and cuts its way through in a canyon—"The Suck"
it was called, and at another place "The Whirlpool," because
of the rapid and difficult current.   The ridge, known as Walden's Ridge north of the river and Raccoon or Sand Mountain on the south, lies between Chattanooga and the Sequatchie
Valley, wherein the river, after its hurried and tortured passage
through the mountain, again turns southwest and, in broad and

straight reaches, flows on into Alabama to pass through and around the stub end of the main plateau of the Cumberland Mountains.

Behind "the wall" Rosecrans' army was filing over the Cumberland Mountains into Sequatchie Valley, gesturing toward a crossing of the river that might be attempted anywhere within fifty miles above or below Chattanooga. There was reason to expect that it would be above, in the direction from which Burnside's cooperating advance from eastern Kentucky through Knoxville was to be looked for. Rosecrans, however, did the unexpected; threw his men across the river at and below Bridgeport, Alabama, thirty miles west of Chattanooga, where his railroad from Nashville crosses the stream; made Bridgeport his rail head and secondary base; marched over Raccoon Mountain, and down into Will's Valley, through which Lookout Creek flows northeast to empty into the Tennessee but four miles below Chattanooga. General Bragg, misled by the activity of detachments on the river opposite Chattanooga, and above, had watched the wrong hole in the wall.

With his troops well in hand in Will's Valley, on the same side of the river as General Bragg and but a few miles from him, Rosecrans began the second phase of the movement. He could have marched directly on Chattanooga, but that would have involved fighting his way along the narrow ledge between the northern "point" of Lookout Mountain and the Tennessee, where the railroad runs, or over bold Lookout itself. Rosecrans preferred to move across Lookout, by rough wagon roads through Stevens' Gap, twenty-five miles from Chattanooga, and Winston's Gap, twenty miles still farther south, and so to get in the rear of Bragg's army, and in position to threaten or break the Western & Atlantic Railroad upon which Bragg depended for his communication with Atlanta and the South.

Thomas' corps pushed through the first gap, marching down into McLemore's Cove, between Lookout and its lesser outlier to the east, Pigeon Mountain. McCook's corps was sent through the second gap, to debouch into the valley east of Lookout at Alpine. Either corps, or both, could push forward to Bragg's vital supply line, without serious difficulty or opposition. There was nothing for it but to give up Chattanooga and fall back to cover the railroad to Atlanta. As Bragg marched out, on September ninth, Crittenden's corps, held in Will's Valley for that purpose, marched in and occupied the much sought city, without a fight.

Rosecrans had won, brilliantly, the first objective of his campaign. Prudence would seem to have prescribed that he gather his army together at Chattanooga, consolidate his position and then start out, all together, to press Bragg still farther south. Instead, he seems to have become possessed of the idea that this army which he had turned out of Tullahoma in July and out of Chattanooga in September, which had already fallen back more than a hundred miles without serious resistance, was in full retreat.

General Bragg, though, had other plans. He retired in good order to Lafayette, in Georgia, about thirty miles south of Chattanooga, there to await the reënforcements that were hurrying to him from three directions. Buckner's corps was coming down from Knoxville, which on September second had been yielded up to Burnside's advance; Breckinridge was bringing troops from Mississippi; and Longstreet was on his way from Virginia with the divisions of Hood and McLaws. The Confederates at last were making the concentration in the center of their grand line which had been urged in the spring, but it was more difficult to make, now. The short line of railroad from Chattanooga through East Tennessee to Virginia had passed into Union possession with the capture of Knoxville. Longstreet's men must move by way of Petersburg, Wilmington, Augusta and Atlanta, with exasperating delays because of difference in gages of track and breaks in the line. Some of his infantry did not arrive until the morning of the last day of the impending battle; the artillery not until after the battle was over.

On September tenth General Bragg, whose information service was not of the best, found that from his central position at Lafayette he was closer to the isolated corps of Thomas in McLemore's Cove than was Thomas to either Crittenden, near Chattanooga, or McCook, at Alpine. Orders, not very explicit, were issued for Hindman to attack Thomas, on the tenth and the eleventh, and for Polk to attack Crittenden, on the twelfth or thirteenth. Whether because of uncertainty in the meaning of the orders, or "impossibilities" in the way of their execution, or the lack of supervision by Bragg himself, or the inattention of his subordinate commanders, all of which reasons were alleged, the orders to attack the scattered fractions of Rosecrans' army were not executed.

It was September thirteenth before General Rosecrans woke to the fact that this enemy whom he had been pursuing and flanking back for nearly a year was turning on him; that his own army was desperately divided; and that only quick concentration could save him.

Crittenden's corps was in the neighborhood of Lee and Gordon's Mills, where the road south from Chattanooga to Lafayette crosses the narrow Chickamauga, twisting and winding its way northward toward the Tennessee, between deep banks, through the densely wooded and sparsely settled country lying to the southeast of Missionary Ridge—still another range, paralleling Lookout and bounding on the east the valley in which lay Chattanooga.

Thomas, still in McLemore's Cove, was no closer to Crittenden than was Bragg's army. McCook and his corps were away to the south at Alpine. There was but one practicable way to get them back—to retrace their steps westward across Lookout Mountain, turn north in Will's Valley to the gap through which Thomas had crossed and again recross the mountain to the east—a trying march of fifty-seven miles, with two crossings of a difficult mountain, all to be done at straining, forced speed.

McCook got orders for this concentration march at midnight of the thirteenth. For the next three days, days that might have been golden for Bragg had that commander known the difficulties of his opponent, he was out of touch with the other Union corps. By September seventeenth, however, when Bragg was ready to move, Rosecrans had collected his forces, and that afternoon started moving them, cautiously, back toward Chattanooga.

On the eighteenth Bragg issued his order for battle and put his troops in motion to get between the Union army and Chattanooga. That day both armies moved north, or down the valley of the Chickamauga, the Union on the western side of the valley, between the little river and Missionary Ridge, the Confederate on the eastern side of the stream. The Confederate army bivouacked that night at the fords and rude country bridges of the Chickamauga, preparing to cross over in the morning and strike what General Bragg expected would be the open and exposed left flank of Rosecrans' army—an expectation blasted by Thomas' corps, which marched all night to become the extreme Union left and extend the line toward Chattanooga.

In the dark of this night before Chickamauga a group of young soldiers from Stewart's division, bivouacked about Thedford's Ford, made a raid on old Mrs. Thedford's potato patch. As a stern officer was driving them out the old lady—who was to be christened the "Mother of Chickamauga" by Buckner's corps—issued forth from her home. "Hold on, Mr. Officer!" she cried. "Those are my potatoes and my boys; let 'em take 'em." With two sons of her own in the Virginia armies, wounded, she made of her house and yard a hospital for the care of "her boys."

Early on the morning of the nineteenth, from right to left, Bragg's army began the crossing of the Chickamauga, to enter upon the great battle of the West, and the bloodiest two days of the war.

Chickamauga was a soldier's battle, fought with most headlong courage and admirable persistence on both sides, and with a minimum of direction from the high command. In general, the Confederates were the attacking force. Their attacks were scattered and spasmodic, however, so that for the greater part of the two days of fighting Rosecrans was able to shift reserves along his line, and to meet desperate and determined charges with counter-charges no less brave. In some ways it was Shiloh over again—woods, small fields, cabin homes scattered about in little clearings, not the sort of ground on which grand attacks could be organized or launched, just blind, headlong, short-range fighting against the enemy immediately in front. But this time the enemy was behind breastworks of logs and earth. No longer did brave soldiers scorn solid protection.

The shift to the Union left had put an enemy in front of Bragg's attacking right wing. Instead of striking an open flank, the Confederates struck lines of soldiers commanded by Thomas, good soldiers, well placed and well led. The fighting was desperate and doubtful from the start, and continued so through the day, with no concerted move to drive home the scattered Confederate attacks, obstinately made, but without central direction.

Night came on—a ghastly battle-field night, with dim and fitful moonlight to help the rescue workers, going to and fro with their little tapers, searching for the wounded in woods and thickets and field; thousands of wounded, and of dead, white-faced, except where their lips were powder-blackened from "biting cartridge." On the Union side, axes rang as Thomas' men worked on their log breastworks; on the southern side, there was marching and counter-marching, a rearrangement of commands.

During the night Longstreet arrived, riding in from the railroad at Ringgold where his last troops were leaving the cars. In the middle of the night and the midst of battle General Bragg undertook a most hazardous program of reorganizing his army into two wings: a right under Polk, made up of D. H. Hill's corps of two divisions, Cleburne's and Breckinridge's, of Frank Cheatham's division, and of W. H. T. Walker's corps, which had come from Johnston's army in Mississippi; and a left wing, under Longstreet, made up of Buckner's corps of three divisions, A. P. Stewart, William Preston and Bushrod Johnson, and Longstreet's own corps of two divisions, Hood's and McLaws', with Hood acting as corps commander. Wheeler's cavalry operated to the left on Longstreet's wing; Forrest's to the right, on Polk's.

Orders were for the attack to start with the right wing, at earliest "day dawn," and to be carried along the line from right to left. "Day dawn" came, and no battle. In the confusion of the night headquarters of commanders could not be located in the woods; orders had gone astray, or been misunderstood, or not acted on. Everybody blamed everybody else, afterward, but the battle did not get started until the middle of the morning, on a day when one more hour of fighting daylight would have been worth so much to the Confederacy.

And then when the fight did start it was a repetition of that of the day before—first the right wing fought itself out, for the time being, and then, with the Confederate right quiet, the left went in, after twelve o'clock. The attack by the right, however, had been driven so hard, right up to the log breastworks, that Thomas had called repeatedly for reenforcements. Rosecrans had ordered them to him, from the Union right. Through some strange lapse, in the shifting of divisions made necessary by this change, a gap was left for a while in the Union line, not far from the center. Into that gap Stewart's division thrust. By a "masterpiece of battle-field tactics" Longstreet was driving his attack forward by column of brigades at half distance, so that any break in the Union line might be improved by wheeling the Confederate troops either right or left, and so presenting them in regular line of battle. A force of eight brigades, massed five brigades deep, struck the weakened and wavering Union right.

Charles A. Dana, Assistant Secretary of War, was on the battle-field, representing Secretary Stanton. "Never in any battle I had witnessed was there such a discharge of cannon and musketry," he wrote. "I sat upon the grass and the first thing I saw was General Rosecrans crossing himself—he was a very pious Catholic. 'Hello!' I said to myself; 'if the General is crossing himself we are in a desperate situation.' I was on my horse in a moment. I had no sooner collected my thoughts and looked around toward the front where all of this din came from than I saw our lines break and melt away like leaves before the wind. Then the headquarters around me disappeared—the graybacks came through with a rush and soon the musket balls and cannon shots began to reach the place where we stood. The whole right of the army had apparently been routed."

Not quite the whole. Away to the right Wilder's Indiana brigade of mounted infantry, armed with repeating rifles purchased by their own funds, opened fire on the advancing Confederates—a fire which the new repeating breech-loaders made so brisk and heavy that it gave the impression of a much larger force. This little attack gave pause to the Confederate advance while that part of McCook's corps and of Crittenden's corps that had not already been sent to Thomas gave way with a rush, and rolled backward to the road across Missionary Ridge at McFarland's Gap, carrying with them in the rush their division commanders—Phil Sheridan was one of them—their corps commanders, the army commander and the Assistant Secretary of War.

Only Thomas, stout Thomas, remained on the field—Thomas, and, away to the left, the Reserve Corps under Granger covering Rossville Gap, where the other road to Chattanooga ran across Missionary Ridge. Thomas drew back his wings, took up a strong position on Snodgrass Hill, almost a horseshoe with the outer face toward the enemy, settled his troops for the fight, and, from that time until sunset, by stubborn and determined resistance, earned his fame as the "Rock of Chickamauga"—and saved the Union army.

Toward Thomas marched Granger, without orders but with sound soldierly sense. One division he left to guard his Gap; with two he pushed forward, thrust Forrest's cavalry to one side, and in the middle of the afternoon joined his force to that of Thomas. The reenforcement was just in time for, at last, the Confederates were to make one concerted attack on the position—Polk's wing to push forward across the Lafayette Road; Longstreet's wing, working at right angles, to push north toward Chattanooga. Late, about dark, the advancing wings met and joined with cheers whose ringing was never to be forgotten, while steady Thomas and his brave troops slowly fell back, during the night, to cross Missionary Ridge and go into the valley of Chattanooga.

The Army of Tennessee had one more chance. Half the Union army had gone into Chattanooga as a "panic-stricken rabble," according to Mr. Dana, whose dispatch to his chief opened with the ominous words that "Chickamauga is as fatal a name in our history as Bull Run." There was probably editorial rhetoric in that statement, but in sober truth the Union army in Chattanooga, hemmed in between mountains and river, was in most precarious position.

At dawn of the twenty-first, Forrest, nearest Chattanooga, rode with a rush to the spurs of Missionary Ridge, overlooking the valley, where Rosecrans' army could be seen below, as if on a map. With a pair of captured field-glasses, Forrest climbed a tree to get a better look. From the tree-top he dictated a dispatch to his wing commander, Lieutenant-General Polk, to be forwarded to General Bragg.

"We are in a mile of Rossville," read the dispatch, written on a leaf from a note-book, with the leather stirrup shield of a saddle as desk. "Have been on the point of Missionary Ridge. Can see Chattanooga and everything around. The enemy trains are leaving, going around the point of Lookout Mountain.

"The prisoners captured report two pontoons thrown across for the purpose of retreating.

"I think they are evacuating as hard as they can go.

"They are cutting timber down to obstruct our passage. I think we ought to press forward as rapidly as possible."

All that day, Monday the twenty-first, Forrest's little cavalry force held the Ridge, expecting the army to come up behind them. Nothing happened, the day was lost. That night Forrest went back to see the commanding general himself. He returned, late at night, exasperated, outdone. "What does he fight battles for?" was his comment.

It was a fair question A great victory had been won, at tremendous cost. Nearly sixteen thousand Confederates were dead on the field, or wounded, two thousand more missing, nearly one-third of all the troops with which Bragg had gone into battle.   Union losses, in killed and wounded, had been more than eleven thousand; in prisoners, nearly five thousand. The percentage of loss was not far from one-third on each side.   Some divisions and corps had lost nearly half their strength, the Tenth Tennessee regiment more than two-thirds of its roll.

Such sacrifice in battle was fruitless without adequate pursuit, which was not made.   Three days were allowed Rosecrans to get his supply wagons back to rail head at Bridgeport; to convert Chattanooga into a regular fortress capable of standing siege.   Then Bragg moved his army forward to invest the place, holding the heights above the town and a line across the valley of Chattanooga Creek.

General Bragg, as was his custom after a campaign, began disciplining his senior commanders—who were as little satisfied with his management as he with theirs.   Lieutenant-General Polk was relieved from duty, and Major-General Hindman. Brigadier-General Forrest, also, was deprived of his command, but not under charges of tardiness or neglect.

Lieutenant-General D. H. Hill, who had once served as a lieutenant in Captain Bragg's battery and had come out from Carolina sympathizing with him in his numerous quarrels with subordinates, changed his mind.   He prepared a petition to the President for the General's removal, signed by sundry of the higher officers.   Lieutenant-General Longstreet, too, had his objections to the management of affairs after the battle.

On October ninth, while the close investment of the Union army in Chattanooga continued, President Davis came to see about the troubles.   The higher commanders were called to meet him at General Bragg's headquarters.   There, in the presence of the commanding General, they were asked, in turn, their opinion of him as a commander.   The four active corps commanders present—Longstreet, Buckner, D. H. Hill and Cheatham, who had the corps from which Polk had already been relieved—were of the opinion that the General's usefulness lay elsewhere than with the Army of Tennessee, but for the second time General Bragg was left in command of his army, with only minor changes among his subordinates.   The President was accompanied by Lieutenant-General Pemberton, whom he suggested for Polk's place—a suggestion that brought out such a storm of protest, recalling Vicksburg, that the change was not made.   Instead Hardee was brought back from Mississippi to take Polk's old corps, while Polk was sent to Mississippi to succeed Hardee.   D. H. Hill was relieved of his command—he had been more outspoken and emphatic than any of the others at the meeting with the President—and returned to North Carolina.   Forrest, who flat-footedly and violently refused to serve longer under Bragg, was promoted to Major-General—without an army—and sent out to Mississippi to find himself another.

CHAPTER XXV

THE MOUNTAINS ABOUT CHATTANOOGA

WITH Confederate affairs about Chattanooga in this disturbed and unhappy state—a state which was not improved by the visit of President Davis—they were less happy for the invested Union army. Dana's despairing dispatch on the Sunday night of·Chickamauga, and later reports of the extent of that disaster, had shocked the Union Government awake to the necessities of Rosecrans' most difficult situation. Immense efforts for his relief were under way. From his rail head at Bridgeport there were four routes to Chattanooga: the railroad and the wagon road south of the Tennessee River, each about thirty miles, but both blocked and covered by the Confederate forces holding Lookout Mountain; the river itself, and a wagon road along the north bank, between it and the foot of Walden's Ridge, both covered by Confederate sharpshooters along the south bank as far as Brown's Ferry and Raccoon Mountain.

There was one other way, up the Sequatchie Valley from Bridgeport and across Walden's Ridge to come down to the river at Chattanooga out of reach of the Confederate batteries on Lookout Mountain or their sharpshooters on the banks of the Tennessee—a dreadful way, sixty miles of bottomless mud and steep and rocky mountain road, a way marked, before the end of the siege, by the skeletons of more than ten thousand army mules killed in the struggle to keep Rosecrans' men and animals supplied with the barest minimum of food and subsistence. In Chattanooga, starving soldiers would follow the wagon trains as they came in, hoping to pick up the few grains of corn that might fall in the road, while the feed troughs of the horses and mules had to be guarded to keep soldiers from taking the little allowance of grain that had to be given the animals to keep them going. The race was between starvation and reenforcements, hurrying from all directions.

The first to arrive were two corps sent from Virginia, the Eleventh and Twelfth, under Joe Hooker. They left the banks of the Rappahannock on September twenty-fourth, the day that Bragg moved forward in leisurely fashion to begin the siege of Chattanooga; entrained at Alexandria on the twenty-seventh, and, less than six days later, having moved by way of Cincinnati, Louisville and Nashville, began to detrain at Bridgeport, only thirty miles from Chattanooga. To cover that last thirty miles, however, was to take them sixty days. In truth, there was no need for them to go into Chattanooga at first—it would have meant just that many more men to starve— so they remained about the rail head at Bridgeport, waiting for the other reenforcements to come up.

On the twenty-third, Grant was ordered to send troops to the help of Rosecrans. Sherman was put in command of the relief column and started. Later Grant himself hurried from Vicksburg by steamboat to Cairo, and by rail to Indianapolis and Louisville to meet the Secretary of War. There, on October eighteenth, he was put in charge of the newly created Military Division of the Mississippi, giving him command of all Union forces west of the Alleghanies, except for Banks' force about New Orleans and in the Southwest. Rosecrans was relieved by telegraph of his command at Chattanooga; Thomas, who had once been Captain Bragg's first lieutenant of artillery, was put in command of the army facing him; and Grant himself, still on crutches and suffering great pain from his fall in New Orleans, started to Nashville and on to Chattanooga, to take direct charge of the relief of the Union forces.

A week before that, on October eleventh, Sherman had left Memphis to advance through Corinth and on to Chattanooga, three hundred miles away, handicapped, however, by orders from Halleck to repair and maintain the Memphis & Charleston Railroad as he advanced—the same impossible orders which had wrecked Buell's campaign for Chattanooga in the early summer of 1862.

Grant was activity itself. From Nashville, where he took charge, he telegraphed Thomas to hold on at all hazards. "We

will hold the town till we starve"—a not unlikely contingency—
answered the doughty Thomas. Arrangements were made for
advancing Sherman's march, and for moving Burnside down
from Knoxville. Grant himself went to Chattanooga, broken
as he was, over the excruciatingly bad road, learned his territory, his army and the depth of its need, and sent a dispatch to
Sherman to quit repairing the railroad in his rear and come on,
before it was too late. The dispatch reached Sherman at Iuka,
in Mississippi, on October twenty-seventh. That aggressive
commander left Major-General Grenville M. Dodge—who had
not yet won his fame as the chief engineer of the Pacific Railway—with eight thousand men to work on the railroad between
Nashville and the Tennessee River at Decatur, while he and the
rest of the army pushed on to Chattanooga by the shortest way.

Under Grant's orders, Hooker, who had been holding the
rail head about Bridgeport, crossed to the south side of the
Tennessee there and pushed forward toward Chattanooga, on
October twenty-sixth. At three o'clock the next morning, under
a most ingenious plan devised by Major-General "Baldy"
Smith, Thomas' chief engineer, eighteen hundred picked men
floated in pontoon boats eight miles down-stream from Chattanooga to a point opposite the Confederate picket posts at
Brown's Ferry. There, just before daylight, they rowed rapidly
across the stream and by a perfect surprise attack secured a
footing on the south bank—a footing so enlarged by reenforcements crossing during the day as to relieve that stretch of
the river, and the roads below, from the menace of the Confederate sharpshooters. Hooker, advancing up the south bank,
established himself in Lookout Valley on the next day, and the
starvation blockade was broken. Small steamers brought supplies from Bridgeport up to the lower end of the "Suck," where
the stream became too difficult for navigation, whence they
were hauled by a short road up the south bank to Smith's pontoon bridge across the Tennessee at Brown's Ferry. There
they crossed to the north bank and moved across the "foot"
within Moccasin Bend to a point opposite Chattanooga, where
they again crossed the river, safe from Confederate inter-

ference.   From Bridgeport to Chattanooga the line of supply
crossed the Tennessee three times—but it was a shorter, easier
and more effective way than the terrible road through the mud
of Sequatchie Valley and over the precipices of Walden's Ridge.

Meanwhile, with all this well-directed activity going on
below, Bragg began to scatter his forces.   Longstreet, with
about twelve thousand men, was sent off toward Knoxville to
recover that important point from Burnside.   Wheeler, with
his cavalry, who had played havoc with the Union supply trains
in the Sequatchie Valley during October, was sent along with
Longstreet.   They left Chattanooga on November fourth, moved
along the railroad to Loudoun, where they were halted by the
Tennessee River, and then, on November thirteenth, crossed
that stream and advanced to the siege of Knoxville.   So it
resulted that when Hooker came forward on the south bank,
and Sherman on the north bank of the Tennessee to reenforce
Thomas in Chattanooga, nearly half of the army with which
Bragg had fought Chickamauga was away on other missions.
Bragg's lines on the heights, reduced to skeleton proportions,
overlooked valleys where more than double his numbers were
in position to be brought against him.

And most skilfully brought, too.   Pontoons for another
bridge across the Tennessee were prepared and secreted in the
mouth of the North Chickamauga River, which flows into the
Tennessee from the north above Chattanooga.   When Sherman's
troops arrived they marched from rail head up the south side
of the river to the floating bridge at Brown's Ferry; crossed
and passed behind Stringer's Ridge, screened from the observation of Confederate stations on Lookout.

Sherman got in position on November twenty-second; the
day after one division of Buckner's corps had been sent off to
Longstreet at Knoxville, and while Cleburne's, the second division of the corps, was already at the Confederate rail head at
Chickamauga Station, boarding cars to follow him.   On the
twenty-third, Thomas, holding Chattanooga itself and the line
of entrenchments across the valley facing Bragg, pushed forward
almost a mile and placed his line near the foot of Missionary

Ridge. The following morning at two o'clock, Sherman **began** his swift and secret crossing of the Tennessee, with orders **to** seize the north end of Missionary Ridge, nearest the river, **and** advance down its crest while Thomas attacked in front. Away on the Union right, at the same time, Hooker was to push **his** force across the sloping toe of Lookout Mountain, between **the** precipitous palisaded Point at its crest, and the bluffs **where** the river sweeps by it.

The morning of November twenty-fourth, when Hooker began his advance and Sherman was crossing the river and occupying the heights, was dark, drizzly, with heavy mists rising from the waters and low-hanging clouds obscuring the slopes of the mountains—a circumstance that greatly favored the secrecy of the Union advance.

The Confederate forces on Lookout Mountain, holding the slopes about the Craven House, were reduced to a minimum by the constant drafts to go to Knoxville. Walthall's brigade of Mississippians, holding the most exposed position, fought magnificently, but they were only a little more than a thousand against the wing of an army. The whole defending force, scattered about in the impenetrable fog which has given to the struggle the name of "the Battle above the Clouds," was little more than two thousand men. With Hooker in possession of the slopes of the mountain, and with affairs going as they were on the main Confederate line on Missionary Ridge, the little garrison holding the crest was withdrawn during the night—a fact which does not lessen the bravery of Hooker's men who, in ignorance of that fact, undertook before daylight to scale the perpendicular cliffs leading up to the Point and fight their way out on top.

By mid-afternoon of the twenty-fourth, over on the other flank, Sherman was in possession of the extreme end of Missionary Ridge and ready to start his advance along the crest, only to find that there was a deep chasm about where the railroad tunnel goes through the ridge, not shown on his maps and not visible from below. On the other side of the chasm were the troops of Pat Cleburne, hurried back from the cars at Chickamauga Station just in time to meet this new menace. There was hard fighting all through the afternoon, ending with Cleburne holding his position, about the time that Hooker finished his fight and emerged into the Chattanooga Valley, to connect his line with Thomas' right.

The fogs of the twenty-fourth were gone on the next day, a bright day of clear sunshine. Grant was at Orchard Knob, near the center of his long line, running from the heights above the town to the heights below. Sherman was to attack along the Ridge on the Confederate right; Hooker was to march across the valley and to attack the ridge on the Con-deferate left; Thomas, as soon as Hooker was in position, was to assault in center.

Sherman's attack opened first, for hours without definite result. It was impossible to depress the Confederate guns enough to put an effective fire on his columns, but the artillerists, lighting the fuses, rolled bomb shells down the hill, to explode among them, while the infantry, when all other means failed, rolled stones and boulders. Hooker was delayed in his march because of the burning of the bridges across Chattanooga Creek. Sherman's condition was becoming critical. It was impossible to wait longer for Hooker to come up. Orders were given for Thomas' troops, in the center, to move out to the relief of Sherman, to take the Confederate line of rifle pits at the foot of the ridge, and there to re-form for the final assault.

Missionary Ridge, in its last phase, was again a soldier's battle. When Thomas' men had the Confederate rifle pits to which they had been directed, they simply kept going of their own accord, pressing up the steep slopes of the ridge so close behind the retreating Confederates clambering up over the ledges that the line of battle on the crest could make no effective fire. Line officers, dumfounded, at first followed the sweeping advance, and then, as they caught the meaning of it, led.

Grant, standing on Orchard Knob, saw the line rush forward beyond the place where it was ordered to halt. He turned angrily to Thomas.

"Thomas, who ordered those men up the ridge?"

"I don't know; I did not," answered Thomas in his slow Virginia speech. "Did you, Granger?"

"No," said Granger, "they started up without orders."

Confederate skirmish lines and Union line of battle went over the crest at the center of the ridge together. The Confederate defenses were broken; the center was routed, except for obstinate fighting groups here and there. On the Confederate right, Hardee's command, Cleburne's division and Cheatham's which had withstood Sherman's attacks, and on the left, part of Bate's division stood fast and prevented the broken retreat from becoming a headlong rout.

Across the Chickamauga by ten o'clock, the Confederate forces fell back, broken and dispirited, through the chill November night. At three in the morning, the ever-willing Cleburne received orders to hold the gaps in the little range of hills just below Ringgold, Georgia, on the railroad twenty miles southeast of Chattanooga, to give time for the trains and the artillery, and for the disheartened columns of foot soldiers as well, to pass the defiles of Taylor's Ridge to Dalton. The Arkansas brigade, under D. C. Govan, was put in the gap itself; Smith's Texas brigade to the north; Lowery's Mississippi and Alabama troops to the south; Lucius Polk's Tennesseeans and Arkansans, as reserve. That morning of November twenty-seventh, Cleburne's little division—there were only four thousand one hundred and fifty muskets—withstood the advance of the great pursuing army, while toiling wagons and marching men moved south behind them. With two little guns they held them off a while; with musketry a bit longer; finally, when the turn of the fight came, Colquitt's First Arkansas Regiment was fighting with clubbed muskets, with pistols—and with rocks. At noon General Hardee sent back word that the trains were safe through the ridge. Cleburne's withdrawal, cautiously made, went undiscovered until his men were safely away, and again in position covering the retreat of the army. With the check at Ringgold Gap the pursuit ended.

General Bragg's report of Missionary Ridge, made from

Dalton, Georgia, forty miles south of Chattanooga, which became winter quarters for the Army of Tennessee, was a document of chagrin. "No satisfactory excuse can possibly be given for the shameful conduct of the troops on the left in allowing their line to be penetrated," he wrote. . . . "Had all parts of our line been maintained with equal gallantry and persistence no enemy could ever have dislodged us, and but one possible reason presents itself to my mind in explanation of this bad conduct in veteran troops who had never before failed in any duty assigned them, however difficult and hazardous. They had for two days confronted the enemy, marshaling his immense forces in plain view, and exhibiting to their sight such a superiority of numbers as may have intimidated weak-minded and untried soldiers; but our veterans had so often encountered similar hosts when the strength of position was against us, and with perfect success, that not a doubt crossed my mind."

There is, of course, a reason which could not have occurred to General Bragg—the General himself. His is one of the tragic stories of the Confederacy. No soldier in the army was more devoted to Confederate success, more willing to sacrifice, more exacting of the fullest duty in himself. He was a brilliant and experienced artillerist, an "educated soldier," laborious, but critical, censorious, disputatious. It all went back, perhaps, to an intensely nervous dyspepsia—or, maybe, it was the disposition that was cause, and the dyspepsia, effect.

His discipline was harsh; his criticism biting. One of his ranking commanders he referred to, in public, as "an old woman, utterly worthless," and then kept him in command, because, as he said, he had no one better to replace him. His training—and it was extensive—simply taught him why things could not be done, not how they might be. From Tupelo to Munfordville, where he had thrown away the army's greatest opportunity; through Perryville, a bloody and barren tactical victory; to Murfreesboro, a drawn battle on the field followed by Confederate retreat; and in the other retreats from Tullahoma and Chattanooga, the Army of Tennessee had followed him—to turn and rend their adversary at Chickamauga; and then to see the fruits of that great victory frittered away in inaction, while the Confederate forces were being scattered and the Union armies from the whole West, and from Virginia, too, were massing against them. The Confederate soldier was too intelligent not to be disheartened.

On November twenty-fourth, the day that Hooker crossed Lookout Mountain and Sherman crossed the Tennessee River above Chattanooga, Longstreet had his besieging force at Knoxville ready to make an assault on that city, fortified by Burnside.

Forces inside and outside the city were not unequal—about twelve thousand or so of each. Burnside's line was well fortified, with only one place where an attack might be made with any chance of success, a bastioned fort at the northwest angle of the lines. Fort Sanders, it was called, named for the young Mississippi cavalry general, W. P. Sanders, who had been killed fighting for the Union a few days before.

The attack was ordered for sunrise on November twenty-fifth—the very day that Grant was to make his final attack on Bragg. It was to be a modern sort of attack, with artillery preparation and even a rudimentary barrage. By night of the twenty-fourth, however, it was learned that reenforcements were on their way from Bragg—the troops who left just as Grant was completing his concentration—and the attack was postponed to await them. With them came General Bragg's chief engineer, who was somewhat familiar with the terrain about Knoxville, and who advised assault at another point. Three days were wasted before it was found that General Leadbetter's plan was not practicable and the attack was shifted back to Fort Sanders. One more day it was postponed, because of rain, and then, finally, set for Sunday, November twenty-ninth.

The plan for the artillery preparation and accompanying fire was abandoned at the last moment, and a straight infantry assault substituted, to be made just at the first signs of dawn in the sky. It was made, with little light more than that given by the flashes of the guns, with the greatest gallantry and the utmost determination, but in vain.   Wire—not barbed wire, for that had not yet been put to use, but telegraph wire staked down—was struck in advance of the deep ditch and the parapet of the fort.   Through and over the wire the men went, and into the ditch—there to find that the steep and icy slopes in front of them could not be climbed.   Shells used as hand grenades were tossed among the men struggling in the ditch, while the few who managed to climb the frozen and slippery mud to the mouths of the embrasures were shot as their heads came up.   Forty minutes the assault lasted, to be drawn back and another prepared, with the magnificent courage that marked the troops of Longstreet's corps.

Before the second attack could be thrown forward, news of Bragg's disaster came, with orders for Longstreet to leave the siege of Knoxville and hasten to join Bragg below Chattanooga. The assault was abandoned, and plans made for withdrawing that night toward Dalton, but before the start was made word came that Sherman's force was between the two Confederate armies.   Longstreet decided to remain in front of Knoxville, threatening it as long as possible and so drawing Sherman up the Valley of East Tennessee and away from Dalton and Bragg. Finally, on the night of December fourth, as Sherman approached, the siege of Knoxville, which had lasted for little more than two weeks, ended.

Longstreet marched away up the valley, above Knoxville, in rain and darkness and mud, with horses mired to their knees, guns and wagons to the hubs, and foot soldiers, many barefoot, tugging at the wheels.   Four months, through the winter and into the spring, Longstreet held his position in upper East Tennessee, living off the country, and holding the last bit of Tennessee to remain in Confederate hands—the northeastern corner of the state, which, ironically, was of all sections of the South most devoted to the Union cause, and of which it is said that it furnished to the armies of the United States more soldiers than any other Congressional district.

Disaster at Chattanooga, repulse at Knoxville, and now in

Middle Tennessee a single note of high tragedy to mark the end of the Confederate year of 1863.

Sam Davis, private in the First Tennessee Infantry, riding south alone in Giles County in the late afternoon of November nineteenth, clad in a gray military jacket, with brass buttons, and a Federal overcoat that had been blue but had been dyed brown—there were tens of thousands like them in the Confederate service—was captured by Kansas cavalry. In his boot was a pass, signed by E. Coleman, captain commanding General Bragg's scouts, and a letter from Coleman to the General; in his saddle seat were maps and descriptions of the fortifications at Nashville, and an exact and correct report of the Federal troops in Middle Tennessee. Davis had been within the Union lines for ten days—ten critical days.

Taken to Pulaski, he was brought before Major-General Grenville M. Dodge, whose corps was hard at work rebuilding the railroad south from Nashville to the Tennessee River.

"I took him into my private office," said General Dodge, "and I told him that it was a very serious charge brought against him; that he was a spy and from what I found upon his person he had accurate information in regard to my army and I must know where he obtained it. I told him that he was a young man and did not seem to realize the danger he was in. Up to that time he had said nothing but then replied in the most respectful and dignified manner:

" 'General Dodge, I know the danger of my situation, and I am willing to take the consequences.'

"I asked him then to give me the name of the person from whom he got the information; that I knew it must be some one near headquarters or who had the confidence of the officers of my staff, and I repeated that I must know the source from which it came. I insisted that he should tell me, but he firmly declined to do so. I told him that I would have to call a court-martial and have him tried for his life and from the proofs we had we would be compelled to condemn him; that there was no chance for him unless he gave the source of his information. He replied:

" 'I know that I will have to die but I will not tell where I got the information. You are doing your duty as a soldier, and I am doing mine. If I have to die I will do so feeling that I am doing my duty to God and my country.' "

The court martial, on November twenty-sixth, "therefore sentenced him, the said Samuel Davis of Coleman's scouts in the service of the so-called Confederate States, to be hanged by the neck until dead" the sentence to be carried out the next day.

That night, in the jail at Pulaski, young Davis wrote to his mother at the family farm home at Smyrna, in Rutherford County, well within the Union lines: "I have got to die to-morrow morning—to be hanged by the Federals. . . . Mother, do not grieve for me. . . . I do not fear to die. . . . Mother, tell the children all to be good . . . do not grieve for me. It will not do any good. Father, you can send after my remains if you want to do so. They will be at Pulaski. I will leave some things, too, with the hotel keeper for you."

The next morning, Friday, November twenty-seventh, drums beat and a regiment of infantry marched down to the jail with a wagon, and in the wagon, a coffin. Davis, brought out, stood up in the wagon, looked around at blue sky and the bare November trees, caught sight of fellow prisoners at the barred window, bowed his farewell to them, took his seat on the coffin. The wagon, with its escort, moved away from the Public Square to a grove in the edge of the little town.

With fifteen minutes to live, Davis asked the news. Told of the defeat of the Confederates at Missionary Ridge, he expressed regret. "The boys will have to fight the battles without me," he added, wistfully, aside.

"I would almost rather die myself than to do what I have to do," said Captain Armstrong.

"I do not think hard of you; you are doing your duty," answered Davis.

Davis mounted the scaffold; the rope was before his eyes. One last effort General Dodge made. Captain Chickasaw of his staff, riding right up to the scaffold, once more offered Davis life if he would but name his informant.

"If I had a thousand lives I would lose them all here before I would betray my friends or the confidence of my informer," was Davis' proud answer. "Thank General Dodge, but I can not accept his terms."

To the Provost Marshal he turned, with his last words, "I am ready."

His age was twenty-one years, one month and twenty-one days.

CHAPTER XXVI

DIPLOMACY, POLITICS, WAR—AND LIVING

THE year 1864 was a political year.

The wiser southern soldiers no longer hoped for a military decision—Vicksburg, Gettysburg and now Missionary Ridge had ended all that—but the duty of the soldier is simple, to fight so long as the civil arm of the government wills.

Diplomatic hopefulness was about dead, too. Mr. Mason had packed up and left London during the autumn. Mr. Slidell, in Paris, was beginning to find the Emperor of the French more and more engrossed in his unhappy Mexican adventure, and less inclined to consider terms of amity with the Confederate States. Only Mr. Mann, who had gone from Brussels to the Vatican, was not downcast.

On November 13, 1863, he was received in audience by His Holiness—an "audience of forty minutes duration, an unusually long one," he wrote to Secretary Benjamin. "How strikingly majestic the conduct of the Pontifical State in its bearing toward me when contrasted with the sneaking subterfuges to which some of the Governments of western Europe have had recourse in order to evade intercourse with our Commissioners! Here I was openly received at the Department of Foreign Affairs, openly received by appointment at court in accordance with established usages and customs, and treated from beginning to end with a consideration which might be envied by the Envoy of the oldest member of the family of nations."

Colonel Mann, who had presented a letter from his President, was promised a "letter to President Davis, and of such a character that it may be published for general perusal." When the letter came, on December eleventh, the Confederate Envoy, who had been quite carried away by his interview, was simply transported, for, as he immediately dispatched Secretary

Benjamin, "in the very direction of this communication there is a positive recognition of our Government. It is addressed to the 'Illustrious and Honorable Jefferson Davis, President of the Confederate States of America.' Thus we are acknowledged by as high an authority as this world contains to be an independent power of the earth. I congratulate you, I congratulate the President, I congratulate his Cabinet—in short, I congratulate all my true-hearted countrymen and country. women—upon this benign event."

The clear-seeing Benjamin, however, was not so entranced. "The President has been much gratified at learning the cordial reception which you received from the Pope," he wrote on February first, "and the publication of the correspondence here has had a good effect. . . . As a recognition of the Confederate States we cannot attach to it the same value that you do, a mere inferential recognition . . . possessing none of the moral weight required for awakening the people of the United States from their delusion that these States still remain members of the old Union. Nothing will end this war but the utter exhaustion of the belligerents, unless by the action of some of the leading powers of Europe in entering into formal relations with us the United States are made to perceive that we are in the eyes of the world a separate nation, and that the war now waged by them is a *foreign*, not an *intestine* or civil war, as it is termed by the Pope. This phrase of his letter shows that his address to the President as 'President of the Confederate States' is a formula of politeness to his correspondent, not a political recognition of a fact."

That "utter exhaustion" spoken of by Mr. Benjamin was already at hand for the South, though the Confederacy was to fight on for fifteen months more. And, curiously, it was during that fifteen months of despairing, unreasoning, blind struggle that the South came nearest to achieving its goal of independence, not through military success—there was to be little more of that, unless skilful, resolute, unbowed defense could be so called—but through the political weariness of the opposing government. No one can say, now, how near the

South came to winning consent to separation, but there came a day, with Grant at stalemate in Virginia and Sherman not yet the victor in Georgia, when Abraham Lincoln was to face it not as a possibility vague and remote, but as an actual probability.

Politics—or, rather, the effect of the hope for victory, long deferred, on the 1864 politics of the North—might have saved the government of the Confederacy, but there was nothing in its economic state or military power that could do it.

The mere business of living had become enormously difficult in the South, strangled by blockade, dismembered by invasion, sucked dry by war. There was, perhaps, enough of food raised, what with the obvious need of it, and appeals of government to the patriotic duty of not raising cotton that might have to be burned to keep it from falling into the hands of the enemy and so finding its way to the mills of the world, as had happened with distressing frequency.

The breakdown was in manufactures, for which the South was not organized; and in transportation, with war-wrecked railroads working far beyond their capacity to supply the armies, with inland rivers controlled by northern armies, and the sea blocked off by northern cruisers; and, above all, in a medium of exchange. With paper dollars that by the beginning of 1864 were worth but six cents in coin, and by the end of the year were valued more nearly by weight than by the denominations shown on their faces; with the government issuing treasury notes, and then forcing their redemption or conversion into bonds by heavy taxation, and then issuing more notes; with states issuing their own promise-to-pay money, and so with all manner of banks; with railroads and bridge and turnpike companies, with cotton factors and mercantile houses, with almost anybody and everybody who had access to a printing plant issuing scrip of one sort or another in the form of money; with no established mart or basis of exchange anywhere, doing business in the Confederate States became a sort of lottery, wherein the only sure values were in things themselves.

Commodities, as measured by Confederate money, rose to fabulous, fantastic prices—and then could not be got often because they simply were not to be had. An austere Confederate father, discovering his nineteen-year-old daughter dressed in a black satin evening gown *in the afternoon*, sternly ordered her back up-stairs to dress properly for the time and occasion.

"I will have no daughter of mine so over-dressed while our soldiers are suffering."

"But, father," she objected, "this is all I have."

It was the literal truth. Workaday and ordinary clothes had worn out, with no way to replace them. The Confederate cloth mills were never able to supply the demands of the armies and the civil population as well, while the blockade cut off all but the most elaborate and expensive of foreign materials. The girl was reduced to one of her party dresses, made and worn in those gay days back in 1861 when she was seventeen and coming out, and the war—and the world—were young.

Many such dresses found their way back North—loot of raiding parties or of garrisons; some, even, were worn in the South by ladies, not their original owners, who had come down during quiet periods of the war to join their husbands—or others—on duty in garrison or behind the lines. Southern women who saw their last ham or side of meat taken from the smoke-house by bummers, or saw the army wagons drive in and strip their fields of ripening corn, forgave that long before they gave up their resentment at the violation of these belongings so personal to themselves.

Not every woman in the South, or anywhere else, then or now, had such dresses to fall back on; or even had meat in the smoke-house and corn in the fields. How they and their children lived, with husbands or sons in the army, drawing pay—sometimes—in money that by the time it could be got home was always worth less than when it was drawn from the paymaster, which never was enough for the most meager support, and which finally fell so low that a month's pay of a soldier would not buy one pound of bacon, is beyond imagination. It can only be noted that live they did, and live with an amazing little of complaining and an amazing much of fortitude.

The South, in truth, was a shell. The simplest needs were almost unobtainable—things as diverse as a sheet of paper, or an iron rail. As early as the spring of 1862, when the Confederates gave up Pensacola, they took up the railroad iron on the line from that port back toward Montgomery, and used it to lay a line to the port of Mobile, which they still held. That was the start of a practise that continued throughout the war—robbing this line, which could be spared for the time, to lay track on that line which must be had. Not only iron rails, but lesser articles of iron were desperately short, too. The army rarely had enough horseshoes and nails, even. Dead horses and mules were stripped of their shoes; sick and wounded, sometimes killed for them. At the siege of Knoxville the Union soldiers, holding the city, threw dead draft animals into the river, flowing down past the Confederate position. The Confederates fished them out, just to get the horseshoes they carried.

And yet Confederate life was not all gray, even in the latter days. General Jeb Stuart, tirelessly alive, used to be able to find gatherings at the hospitable country homes round about his camping places, where he and Sweeny, his banjo-playing familiar, were always welcomed for an evening of gaiety—sandwiched in, perhaps, between two days of hard riding and battle. Young John Morton, the boy who left college to become at twenty-one Forrest's Chief of Artillery, has left for us a running record of the homes he visited, the suppers he ate, the dances he danced, and the songs he, and the young ladies, sang. There was the song of *The Homespun Dress*, whose ending,

> "Three cheers for the homespun dress
> The Southern ladies wear,"

was, perhaps, compensation to the ladies who had to wear them. And then there was the antiphonal duet wherein the soldier sang,

> "Lady, I go to fight for thee
> Where glory banners wave;

To fight for thee, and, O perchance,
To find a soldier's grave,"

to which the lady replied:

"Soldier, I stay to pray for thee,
A harder task is mine;
Which is a long and lonely grief
That victory may be thine."

And that, no doubt, sung in the half-light of candles glowing on some ancient square piano of rosewood, was a mighty sentimental and satisfactory song. War, famine, pestilence, death—but living goes on.

There were to be tremendous military events in 1864, a concerted, unrelenting ring of pressure about the Confederacy, under the direction of one military mind, but the year opened with politics.

The Republicans, still a new party, and the Democrats, were due to nominate candidates for President in the summer, and the electors were to choose between them in the fall. In northern theory, at least, the states calling themselves "Confederate" were still in the Union. In fact, Union armies held almost all of one of them, Tennessee, and the most considerable and substantial parts, including the capitals, of two others, Arkansas and Louisiana. The convention votes of those states might be needed in the Republican Convention, and their electoral votes would certainly be useful in the November election. A state government, headed by Andrew Johnson as Military Governor, was already in being in Tennessee. Steps were taken to set up civil governments, of a sort, enough to have convention and electoral votes, at least, in Louisiana and Arkansas.

Another state, weak and exposed, which might reasonably be added to the roll, was Florida. The settled portion of Florida, then, except for Key West and a few isolated points on the keys and coasts of the Peninsula, stretched only from St. Augustine and the territory along the St. John's and St. Mary's Rivers, on the east, to Pensacola, on the west, with

Tallahassee, the capital, about half-way between. Key West, away to the south, had never been given up by the Union. Other seaports, Fernandina, St. Augustine, Jacksonville, Pensacola, had been occupied early in 1862.

President Lincoln, on January 13, 1864, wrote to Major-General Gillmore, commanding troops on the South Atlantic coast, calling his attention to the fact that "an effort is being made by some worthy gentlemen to reconstruct a loyal State government in Florida," and bespeaking his aid in the movement. The most practical aid seemed to be a military expedition, which was fitted out at Hilton Head, the Union base at Port Royal, and dispatched by sea to Jacksonville, early in February—seven thousand men under General Truman Seymour, convoyed by five gunboats. From Jacksonville there ran westward a rickety railroad, with one wretched little engine. Along this line General Seymour was ordered to advance, with intent to establish himself in the interior, in the neighborhood of the Suwanee River settlements, and from there to obtain and send out cotton and naval stores, and recruits for the negro regiments being organized at Port Royal, and "to inaugurate measures for the speedy restoration of Florida to her allegiance."

General Seymour, who disapproved the plan which he was called on to execute, found no real desire on the part of the Floridians to come back into the Union, and warned against "frittering away the infantry in the interior." After a cross-fire of reports and orders, however, he started in to cut off communication between East and West Florida. At Ocean Pond, on the Olustee, thirteen miles east of Lake City, Confederate Brigadier Joseph Finegan drew up his force—largely Georgians, for the Florida troops were away in the armies to the north, more of them than there were white men of voting age in the state—and prepared to resist Seymour's advance.

The Battle of the Olustee, fought on sandy plains among sparse pine woods, on the afternoon of February 20, 1864, resulted in a complete victory for Finegan's men and a repulse of the Union forces, with a loss of one-third their number in a three-hour fight. Seymour fell back to the St. John's, leav-

ing half a dozen field-guns and sixteen hundred much appreciated muskets in Confederate hands.   The project of the
invasion of interior Florida was ended for the war.

About the same time that General Seymour was advancing
from Jacksonville to the west, General Sherman, returned to
Vicksburg after playing his great part in raising the siege at
Chattanooga, set out eastward from the Mississippi River with
twenty thousand infantry, to proceed along the railroad through
Jackson to Meridian, doing a thorough job of wrecking as he
went.   At the same time he ordered Major-General William
Sooy Smith, with a brigade of infantry, seven thousand cavalry
and twenty guns, to march out of Memphis, strike across country
to the Mobile & Ohio Railroad, and follow down that line
to Meridian, for a junction with the main force.   Smith was
to have left Memphis on February 1, 1864, with instructions
to make his meeting at Meridian by the tenth.

From Meridian there were railroad lines east to Selma,
where the Confederates had an arsenal and gun foundry, the
only one in the South capable of casting cannon except the
Tredegar Iron Works at Richmond; and southeast to Mobile,
the only important port on the Gulf left to the Confederacy.

What Sherman would have done after General Smith joined
is not known.   He was at Meridian on the fourteenth, having
been twelve days on his march across the state of Mississippi,
and there he waited for Smith—waited and waited until the
end of the month, and heard no word, when he gave up and
went back to Vicksburg.

General Smith had run into trouble.   He had been eleven
days late in his start, for a variety of reasons, and then had
advanced cautiously, finding no enemy of consequence in his
front, but slowed up by his orders to do a good thorough job of
devastating the country as he came, which takes time, and by
the growing mob of "contrabands" which attached themselves
to his column.   As he pushed forward, slowly and dubiously,
having come more than half-way to Meridian, he began to find
a little resistance in his front.

The troops in front were, mostly, very new troops.   Nathan

Bedford Forrest, their commander, had raised them, some as volunteers, some as conscripts, within the Union lines in West Tennessee and West Kentucky during December of 1863; had brought them safely out and back within the Confederate territory south of the Memphis & Charleston Railroad just at Christmas time; had armed and equipped them with captured Union supplies; had organized, disciplined and trained them in January, and now, in mid-February, was putting them against a Union column of three times their own strength.

As Smith got farther away from his base at Memphis, the resistance stiffened. Finally, at the crossing of the Sakatonchee Creek, below Okolona, on the afternoon of February twentieth— by coincidence the same afternoon that the Union column advancing into Florida was to strike trouble—he found a bridge strongly defended. That night, perplexed and unhappy, he considered his situation; the next morning he started back to Okolona, a "retirement" which Forrest, by front and flank attacks of his two thousand five hundred men, soon turned into a "retreat" and then into a "rout"—at any rate, a rapid movement to the rear which ended only with safety at the Union base of Memphis. To Forrest himself, however, the victory brought his greatest personal loss, the death in battle of the youngest of the seven Forrest brothers in the Confederate service, a posthumous child whom the General had raised as a son.

The campaign against William Sooy Smith made soldiers of Forrest's new troops. Almost immediately, in mid-March, he moved north with them, to carry organized Confederate troops to the Ohio River, for the last time, with the seizing and holding for several hours of Paducah, where a store of government horses were captured for the mounting of Abram Buford's Kentucky recruits who did not join the army to walk. The expedition remained within western Kentucky and Tennessee for more than a month, collected recruits and horses, arms and supplies, captured Union garrisons and broke up Union communications. Finally, late in April, Forrest brought out his command, enlarged and strengthened.

During this sojourn within the territory held by the Union a part of Forrest's command stormed and captured Fort Pillow, on the Mississippi River forty miles above Memphis. The "Massacre of Fort Pillow" became *the* "atrocity" of the Civil War—which had "atrocities," North and South, quite in the modern manner of the late war. The fort was defended by a garrison of colored soldiers and of Tennessee Unionists, of the sort known in West Tennessee as "home-made Yankees." Forrest and his men stormed the fort; incompetent defense, prolonged beyond any possible hope, made of the storming a horror of unnecessary bloodshed; a Congressional Committee of Inquiry, appointed with special reference to the massacre of colored soldiers, made of it an "atrocity."

More of the defenders were killed than should have been, under ordinary circumstances, but that there was no general "indiscriminate slaughter" after surrender, as charged by the Congressional Committee, is clear now from the very evidence on which it relied. The committee's report was political, for political consumption. President Lincoln, however, writing on April 18, 1864, about the rumor that there had been a massacre of colored soldiers at Fort Pillow, said, "if there has been the massacre of 300 there, or even the tenth part of 300, it will be conclusively proved; and being so proved the retribution shall as surely come."

Secretary Stanton wired to General Sherman, in command in the West, to "investigate and report minutely the facts in relation to the alleged butchery of our troops, at Fort Pillow." General Grant, too, wired Sherman, "If our men have been murdered after capture, retaliation must be resorted to promptly."

Whatever Sherman's investigation may have shown, it evidently did not sustain the political findings of the Committee of Congress, for no retaliation was ever ordered—and Sherman was not a man who would have hesitated to order it had he thought that the facts justified.

In these winter and early spring months of 1864, while the major armies of the Union and the Confederacy faced each other in Virginia, looking across the Rapidan "frontier," and in North Georgia, with the Valley of the Chickamauga between Chattanooga and Dalton separating them, there were stirrings of military activity at places as widely scattered as Florida, "the Purchase" in Kentucky, the prairies of eastern Mississippi, the Sounds of North Carolina, the coasts of Texas, and the Red River country in Louisiana. And always, as an undertone to the war, there went on the intermittent pounding siege of Charleston, met by Beauregard's skilful and stubborn defense.

The first aggressive movement of the Confederacy during the year, the effort to clear the Sound Country of eastern North Carolina, which had been held by Union forces since early 1862, was not happy in its results. On January thirtieth, Major-General George E. Pickett set out from Kinston to capture New Bern, most important of the Sound ports, to which light-draft blockade runners could come and from which a railroad ran into the interior. Accompanying General Pickett's force of some four thousand five hundred men, were three hundred men in rowboats, armed with cutlass and rifle, under command of President Davis' aide, John Taylor Wood, who had been a naval officer. They quietly paddled down the river into New Bern harbor on the night of February first, and boldly boarded and captured the nearest of the Union vessels of war, the *Underwriter*, lying under the guns of Fort Stevenson, only to find that its fires were out, its boilers cold, and that it could not be moved. Setting fire to the vessel, Wood and his men in darkness and confusion of battle escaped in their rowboats. The land forces, finding the defenses too strong to storm, abandoned the attack after three days—as another Confederate expedition against New Bern was to do later in the spring, on May fifth.

Before then, however, the Confederates were to take another of the Sound ports, the quaint little town of Plymouth, on Roanoke River eight miles above the head of Albemarle Sound. Confederate forces under Major-General R. F. Hoke surrounded the town on the land side, while the iron-clad ram *Albemarle*, which had been quietly building all winter on the

Roanoke River, backed down-stream to engage the Union navy on the river-side. During the night of April eighteenth, the *Albemarle* dropped down to the town, rammed and sunk the *Southfield*, and drove the *Miami* out of the river and into Albemarle Sound, after a fight at such close quarters that one shell fired by Commander Flusser of the *Miami* struck the iron shield of the Confederate vessel, rebounded, exploded at the gun from which it had been fired, and killed the man who had pulled the lanyard.

The next day, after a stubborn resistance, Hoke's men stormed the fortifications of the town and captured the post and its garrison, under General Wessels.

The submarine, then as now the resort of the side of less naval strength, was first used in this defense of Charleston. The one used was a curious craft, fish-shaped, about twenty feet long, manned by a crew of seven or eight who drove it with muscle power, applied through an arrangement of cranks, screws and fins. The *H. L. Hunley*, named for her inventor, was an unreliable death-trap, which drowned two crews, the second commanded by the inventor himself. Raised from the bottom of the harbor, a third crew—an incredibly gallant crew, commanded by an Alabama infantry lieutenant, George E. Dixon— took her out once more, and, at the price of destroying the boat and themselves, torpedoed and sank the *U. S. S. Housatonic*, on February 17, 1864.

On May fifth, while the last attempt at New Bern was under way, the *Albemarle*, with two unarmed steamers carrying troops, steamed out of Plymouth, down Roanoke River and into the broad reaches of the Sound. To meet her came a Union squadron: four "double-enders," light draft boats of quick maneuverability, armed with six heavy guns each, and three smaller gunboats. Of the "double-enders" the *Albemarle* sunk one, disabled another, and appeared to be in a fair way to clear the Sound of Union ships-of-war when the *Sacassus*, one of the swiftest of Union ships, managed to ram her at full speed. The *Albemarle* was still afloat, however, and after driving off the Union ships retired to Plymouth, there to remain, a constant threat to Union vessels on the Sounds, until her destruction late in October, 1864, by Lieutenant W. B. Cushing, of the United States Navy, who, with fourteen men in a small launch equipped with a spar torpedo, slipped up the river at night, boldly steamed over a protecting boom, and, in face of almost certain death from his own explosion or from Confederate guns, coolly placed and fired his torpedo and sank the *Albemarle*—all with a loss of two men drowned and eleven captured. Cushing himself and one other escaped by swimming.

The major military activity of the Union in the early months of 1864, however, was west of the Mississippi. On January fourth General Halleck issued orders for an invasion of the great cotton-growing sections of Louisiana, eastern Texas and southern Arkansas, to be made by advancing along the Red River.

The expedition was conceived and planned in the grand manner. Banks, who was to be in command, was to march on Alexandria, almost in the center of Louisiana; there to be joined by troops to be sent by Sherman from Mississippi, and by a great river flotilla under Porter; the combined force to march on to a junction with Steele, moving down from Arkansas; and so, with the three columns of troops and the cooperating fleet, to sweep up through the Valley of the Red to Shreveport, where Kirby Smith had his Confederate headquarters of the trans-Mississippi; and so, perhaps, on into Texas.

General Banks, under the orders issued in the late summer of 1863 when the government at Washington wanted to put the flag in western Texas, had spent November and December on the Texas coast with the Thirteenth Corps, under Major-General Cadwallader C. Washburn, on a fleet of transports convoyed by three vessels of war. They had occupied Brownsville, the Confederate port at the mouth of the Rio Grande, through which a considerable blockade-running commerce with Mexico had passed, and had then worked back eastward along the coast, occupying Point Isabel, Corpus Christi, Aransas Pass, and Port Cavallo at the entrance to Matagorda Bay. From that inlet, seized on December thirtieth, Banks planned to move his expedition to the mouth of the Brazos and so clear on to the mouth of the Sabine, between Texas and Louisiana, a point which a surprise gunboat and land expedition in September had signally failed to capture, when it ran afoul of Lieutenant Dick Dowling's determined band.

Banks' progress up the coast was interrupted, however, by orders for the difficult Red River expedition. The expedition had no military importance—except, as it turned out, to deprive the armies of Grant and Sherman of a good many men whom they needed later in the spring—but great things were expected of it in the way of catching cotton.

Running through all the latter story of the war was this thing of cotton trading. The stuff had become enormously valuable in the hands of those who could get it to Europe or to the mills of New England, and worth but little in the hands of holders in the interior of the Confederacy. The Confederate Government sought, earnestly, to confine its export to Confederate channels—which, by 1864, had become reduced to but two of consequence, the swift blockade runners slipping out of the mouths of the Cape Fear River by night, carrying cotton brought to Wilmington by rail, and the channels established by General Kirby Smith through Galveston or across the Rio Grande and through Mexico. The law of the Confederate States required that cotton, and naval stores as well, be destroyed before being allowed to fall into the hands of the enemy.

The Government of the United States, having in mind its own cotton textile industries, and anxious, too, to mitigate the effect of its blockade of the South on the mills of Europe, diligently sought to capture and get out cotton by channels other than those legitimate from the Confederate point of view. The potential profit in the cotton trade is indicated by General Kirby Smith's statement that he was receiving, in Mexico, fifty cents a pound gold for cotton that cost but three or four cents in the interior of the Confederacy.

General Kirby Smith's shipments were for the account of the Confederacy, which, by that time, was able to do but little directly for the troops and territory he commanded, but all along the line of contact between the armies through a cotton country there was more than a trickle of trade, sternly for· bidden but irrepressible. "Out-post officers would violate the law, and trade," wrote General Dick Taylor, who for more than two years commanded in the principal cotton-producing states. "In vain were they removed; the temptation was too strong, and their successors did the same. The influence on the women was dreadful, and in many cases their appeals were heart-rending. Mothers with suffering children, whose husbands were in the war or already fallen, would beseech me for permits to take cotton through the lines. It was useless to explain that it was against law and orders, and that I was without authority to act. This did not give food and clothing to their children."

The evil was as troublesome on the Union side. Columns invading cotton territory were followed by a flock of specula-tors, usually armed with passes from Washington secured by political influence, and engaged in picking up here and there the cotton that was supposed, when seized by the armies, to be turned in through the Quartermaster Department to a special agent of the Treasury Department designated to receive it. Through these official channels tens of thousands of bales of cotton passed the Union lines to the world, but there were a great many other thousands which went to the enrichment of cotton speculators—sometimes, it was charged by honest soldiers who detested this particular breed of camp followers, being hauled in government wagons that should have been mov-ing supplies for the troops.

Cotton was one of the prime purposes of the great Red River expedition. Another, it would seem, was elections, to be held in the interest of the reconstituted "free state" of Louisiana, whose delegates and electors might be needed in the summer and fall. There was, doubtless, some military purpose, also, for such a grand expedition—one, really, too grand. It had in its plan too many close junctions, too many *ifs*—and, always, the fickleness of the river itself.

The start was delayed until March to take advantage of the

spring rise in the river, which that year did not come. The naval part of the expedition, under the active and resourceful Porter, included some of the same iron-clad and "tin-clad" gunboats which had done such stout service for the Union at Fort Henry and Fort Donelson, at Vicksburg and Port Hudson, and a great many more as well—in fact, the greatest of all river fleets, twenty armed and armored vessels, more than twice that many transports, tenders, supply ships and the like.

Besides the immense naval force there were three converging columns, forty thousand men in all, directed toward Shreveport. To meet them Kirby Smith had about half as many, scattered about under Price in Arkansas, Magruder in Texas and Taylor in Louisiana.

The first of the converging Union columns to go into action was that from the Mississippi, under A. J. Smith, with divisions commanded by Mower and Kilby Smith—not to be confused with the Confederate Kirby Smith. Keeping the run of Smiths who commanded in both armies is not always simple. There was a Melancthon Smith and an M. L. Smith on each side; in the fighting about Chattanooga there were four Union Generals Smith, including three commanding brigades in the same division, while three different Union Generals of that name marched against Forrest. A. J. Smith's column, on the afternoon of March fourteenth, promptly carried by assault Fort De Russy, the unfinished Gibraltar of the Red River, upon which Alexandria depended for protection.

On the fifteenth and sixteenth, with Smith in the town, the fleet tied up there, to await the coming of Franklin's column, marching over land from the Bayou Têche, and of Banks himself. Meanwhile Taylor fell back toward the old Spanish-French town of Natchitoches, where he began to concentrate his forces. The Union columns were delayed two weeks at Alexandria, for a variety of causes; among them, the seeds from which sprung the bitter quarrels among the Union commanders after the unhappy expedition. It was a most fortunate delay for the Confederates.

Finally, with thirteen gunboats and thirty transports successfully through the rapids at Alexandria, and the others left at that point, the advance toward Shreveport was resumed. Above Natchitoches Taylor's reenforcements began to come in—the Texas horse, under General Tom Green, the same whose marine cavalry had stormed Galveston the year before, in advance. Taylor continued to fall back, picking up reenforcements as he went, until finally, at Mansfield, he made his stand, covering the three roads to Shreveport and the road to Marshall, Texas, which diverge from that place.

General Kirby Smith, back at Shreveport, was having an anxious time. With Steele moving down from Arkansas, he had had to withdraw the most of Price's force to meet Banks, and now had Price's infantry as a general reserve, half-way between Mansfield and Shreveport, about twenty miles from each place. Taylor, at Mansfield, had perhaps the most cosmopolitan command gathered by the Confederacy. It included John G. Walker's brigade of Texas infantry, and another small brigade of Texans, temporarily commanded by Prince Charles Polignac, a Frenchman of ancient Bourbon lineage, who after serving as a brigadier in the Confederate Army returned to his native country. Among Green's devoted Texas horse was a regiment raised in the German settlements at New Braunfels, commanded by Colonel Buchell, formerly of the Prussian Army, drilled in the European fashion, and armed with the saber, which most of the Confederate cavalry discarded in favor of revolving pistols. There was a Louisiana French brigade, also, commanded by Alfred Mouton, son of the former Governor of the state, until his death at Mansfield, and then by Prince Polignac.

Taylor, at Mansfield with less than nine thousand men, found coming against him a force of at least twenty thousand—but they were strung out along a single road, with twelve miles of wagon train mixed in with the troops, and the whole column, from head to rear, more than twenty miles long. Drawn up in good defensive position, covering all the diverging roads to the rear, Taylor waited very comfortably until, late in the afternoon of April eighth, the head of the long column struck the Confederate position. What was intended to be a defensive battle became a decidedly aggressive one when Mouton's troops left the lines, rushed forward and attacked, supported by the whole Confederate line. By dark the head of the Union column was in flight, a flight complicated by a wild panic among the teamsters of the wagon trains, so that the road and the open spaces in the sparse pine woods on both sides were filled with a tangled and confused mass of negroes, cavalry, camp followers, wagons, ambulances, everything.

Five miles in rear Emory's division managed to preserve a battle line which, as night came on, stopped the pursuit and allowed the routed front of the column to pass through.

That night the reserve divisions of Churchill and Parsons marched forward twenty-five miles to Mansfield, and on the next day, April ninth, Taylor's whole force pushed on to find Banks' troops well drawn up in strong position at Pleasant Hill. An attack resulted in sharp repulse, but that night, again, the Union forces retreated, making their way back to the river at Grand Ecore. The army's retreat left the fleet in an exposed position, from which they succeeded in escaping to Grand Écore, but not without a sharp brush with the cavalry, in which the gallant Tom Green was killed, to be succeeded by John A. Wharton, who had taken a regiment of Texas Rangers to Tennessee at the very beginning of the war, and there had earned much reputation fighting under Albert Sidney Johnston, Forrest and Joe Wheeler.

And now, from Grand Écore, where but a few days before General Banks had held an election among the people, of whom he had reported that they were touchingly devoted to the Union, the whole army, beaten and discouraged, began a weary and difficult retreat, with the naval flotilla anxiously steaming alongside, wondering what would be the stage of water at the rapids above Alexandria. General Kirby Smith, after Pleasant Hill, made what seems now, and to some seemed then, a mistake in handling his forces. There were too many opportunities in front of him—to pursue the beaten Banks, or to crush Steele, who had advanced below Camden. He undertook to do both.

To that end he stripped Taylor of all but a handful of troops to go after Steele.   After a final Confederate victory at Jenkins' Ferry on the Saline, on April thirtieth, Steele retreated to Little Rock, while Kirby Smith's forces marched again to join Taylor for the final blow to Banks.

They were too late.   Taylor, able to do nothing more than worry Banks' flanks and rear, and harass the operations of the fleet in the river, followed them down to Alexandria.   There it seemed as if the river itself would give the Confederates a great prize—one fleet of gunboats and transports, caught by falling waters above the shoals.   But a young Wisconsin engineer, Lieutenant-Colonel Joseph Bailey, devised the scheme to meet the desperate danger; thousands of men of the army worked at it, toiling in the forests and half-submerged in the waters.   One week before the Confederate troops got back from Arkansas, the Union vessels floated over the rocks above Alexandria, rushing through a narrow gate into which the waters had been raised and forced by a most ingenious system of wing dams, cribs and chutes, all built in record time.

Between the eighth and thirteenth of May all the vessels were safely passed, the troops reembarked and the grand expedition steamed its way back to the Mississippi, but too late to be of service to Grant in Virginia or to Sherman in Georgia in the opening of those great final campaigns which had been conceived, planned, ordered and started during the ten weeks in which they had been pushing out toward Shreveport, and wearily struggling back.

CHAPTER XXVII

From the Rapidan to the James

On March 4, 1864, after three years of hostilities, Major-General Grant, commanding west of the Alleghanies, was summoned from his headquarters at Nashville to Washington.

There, on March ninth, he received at the hands of President Lincoln his commission as Lieutenant-General and his assignment to the supreme command of all the armies of the United States, under the President. From that day, as the war went into its fourth year, there was a new intent and direction to the Union efforts.

The grand strategy of the final year was simplicity itself—concentration; continuing simultaneous pressure on the main Confederate armies; disregard of the "side-show" operations which required so many men and so much material, and produced so little real result; maintenance of the blockade.

The execution of such a design, which meant relentless pounding, with disregard for losses that even in 1864 shocked the northern people, and in earlier years would have sickened them, required a General of dogged and determined temperament, and one who possessed the confidence of the President and the nation. In Grant, for the first time, the Union found him.

To carry forward his design for ending the war by crushing weight rather than by sparring maneuver, Grant created three major armies, spread in a grand line from lower Chesapeake Bay to Chattanooga; strengthened them by stripping down unnecessary garrisons and calling back troops from scattered operations; and prepared them for a simultaneous advance when the spring should open.

The Army of the Potomac was his center, charged with the duty of seeking, and ceaselessly attacking Lee's army. Meade, of Gettysburg, was to remain in command.

The Army of the James was the left, charged with the direct attack on Richmond from the southeast. Benjamin F. Butler, who had been out of active service for nearly a year after Banks superseded him in New Orleans, was in command in this sector, and Grant, after a visit to his headquarters at Fortress Monroe, decided to leave him.

Burnside's Ninth Corps, still at Knoxville where Longstreet had besieged them in the December before, was brought back East, reorganized, strengthened and encamped at Annapolis, whence it might be moved to reenforce either Meade or Butler. No man but the secretive Grant knew which it was to be.

Forces in the Valley of Virginia, under Franz Sigel, and in the Kanawha Valley in West Virginia, under Crook and Averell, were to move forward in cooperation with the main advance in Virginia.

On the right of the line Grant had his friend Sherman, now commanding all the West and concentrating under himself at Chattanooga a powerful mobile wing, to be used for the gigantic flanking movement through the South which finally sealed the fate of the Confederacy.

One other simultaneous advance, that of Banks from New Orleans to Mobile, contemplated in Grant's original plan, was blocked by disasters up Red River.

There was about Grant's plans none of the grandiose quality of early Union projects for magnificent expeditions "sweeping" through the South, capturing cities and gathering in armies as they went. The objective of each of the Union armies was limited, but they were to be undertaken all at once and carried out all together.

To meet all this the Confederacy had its two major armies: Lee's Army of Northern Virginia, on the south bank of the Rapidan; and, at Dalton, in North Georgia, the Army of Tennessee, now under Joseph E. Johnston. General Bragg, at his own request, had retired from the command after Missionary Ridge, and turned it over to Hardee, who, with rare modesty and generosity, declined the tender and held the place only until another could be chosen. Everything and everybody pointed to Johnston, whom the President, perhaps grudgingly, named to the place just before Christmas of 1863. General Bragg, on February 24, 1864, was "assigned to duty at the seat of the government, and, under the direction of the President, is charged with the conduct of the military operations in the armies of the Confederacy"—in short, a Chief-of-Staff for the President. Not the least admirable of President Davis' qualities was the strength and steadfastness of his devotion to the friend to whom he had once given his confidence.

Besides the major armies of the Confederacy there were the men in the fortifications about Richmond, and a scattering of troops in the Carolinas and in Virginia south of the James, a territory committed to the care of General Beauregard on April 20, 1864; a still smaller scattering in the Valley and in southwestern Virginia, the department commanded by Breckinridge; and the garrison of Mobile and other small commands in Alabama and Mississippi, the department commanded by Stephen D. Lee, who succeeded Leonidas Polk, when that militant churchman went back to the Army of Tennessee to lead a corps.

West of Chattanooga there was but one Confederate force which gave concern to Grant and Sherman, Forrest's cavalry in northern Mississippi, a little command which might have been so used as to become a major factor in the politico-military situation of the summer of 1864—but was not.

The Confederacy elected to stand on the defensive—indeed, with little choice in the matter, although General Longstreet, from his winter quarters in upper East Tennessee, had gone to Richmond to urge a plan by which Beauregard was to gather up scattered garrisons in the Carolinas; move them through the mountains to Abingdon, in southwestern Virginia; join forces with Longstreet in East Tennessee; the combined force to join with Joe Johnston, advancing from Dalton; and the whole to push forward up the railroad through Tennessee into Kentucky. The plan got scant consideration from President Davis and his adviser, General Bragg, wrote Longstreet, who attributed this to the President's distrust of Beauregard, as a commander, and his dislike of Johnston. The plan itself, audacious enough, was scarcely practicable, certainly nothing like so feasible as the similar ones proposed the year before.

Instead of such combination for offensive purposes, Longstreet was ordered back to Virginia, in the early spring, to rejoin Lee's army on the banks of the Rapidan. A. P. Hill's corps was along the river, near Mine Run where Meade had made his abortive crossing and attack five months before, with Ewell's corps farther up-stream. Longstreet was held about Gordonsville, some thirty miles away, in reserve. With the three infantry corps, Stuart's cavalry and the artillery, commanded by General W. N. Pendleton, an Episcopal minister turned artillerist, Lee had a little more than sixty thousand men.

Before dawn of May 4, 1864, while the Union armies were advancing on all fronts, the sixth "On to Richmond" drive was put under way—a drive that was never to let up until, after eleven months of fighting, it ended in the capture of the southern capital that had baffled McDowell, McClellan, Pope, Burnside and Hooker. The new drive started with one hundred eighteen thousand men of the Army of the Potomac, crossing the river on bridges at Germanna and Ely's Fords, a year after and almost exactly at the same place as Hooker's crossing.

Like Hooker's, the crossing was unopposed—for it led into the Wilderness, and that was Lee's chosen field of battle.

Through the Wilderness, from Orange Court House where Lee had his headquarters, there run two roads east: the old Turnpike nearest the river, the Orange Plank Road, from two to four miles south of the Turnpike, and roughly parallel to it. Nearing Chancellorsville, the roads turn toward each other, to a junction near the ruins of the mansion house burned in the battle of the year before. From Germanna Ford, where Grant's center and right corps crossed, the Germanna Plank Road runs southeast to cross the Turnpike at the old Wilderness Tavern, thence to run on, under the name of the Brock Road, across the Orange Plank Road, and southeast to Spottsylvania Court House and Richmond. On this road, all that day of the fourth, the corps of Warren and Sedgwick marched, unopposed.

Lee, waiting for Grant with his one hundred eighteen thousand troops, and his train of four thousand wagons, which took up sixty-five miles of road space, to get across into the Wilderness, made no attack on the fourth. On the morning of the fifth he sent Ewell's corps, on his left, forward along the Turn- pike; Hill's, his right, on the Plank Road, marching at right angles to the direction of the Union advance. Orders were not to bring on a general engagement, but to develop the march and position of the enemy.

By afternoon, however, not one but two serious battles were in progress, with no close connection between them. The dis- turbance of the Union march was such that Hancock, whose corps had crossed farther east at Ely's Ford the day before and was already stretched out on its march toward Richmond by way of Chancellorsville and Spottsylvania Court House, was called back and, at four o'clock in the afternoon of the fifth, thrown against the divisions of Heth and Cadmus Wilcox, on the extreme Confederate right.

There was fighting, hard, desperate, close fighting, in the tangled Wilderness all that afternoon and until eight o'clock. During the night Burnside came forward, to strengthen the Union left. The Union troops were busy, too, throwing up log breastworks—a precaution which the commanders on the Con- federate right did not take because, as was explained, the men were exhausted and it was expected that they would be replaced by Longstreet's men, who had been marching a night, and a day, and now another night to take over the position at day- break.

Daybreak of May sixth came, with Longstreet's men still three miles from the field when the overwhelming Union attack struck the scattered and disorganized brigades of Heth and Wil- cox. The Confederates were giving way, in confused retreat westward along the Plank Road, when there swung into view Longstreet's corps, moving at the trot, in double column of fours, Kershaw's division leading on the right, Field's on the left, filling the road from side to side, magnificently advancing to the battle. As they came into the zone of fire the brigades obliqued off the road, right and left, into the woods and formed battle line with scarcely a moment's delay—and not a minute too soon.

Lee, waiting just off the Plank Road, watched a battle which, without these men, was lost. On they came, cheering Lee as they spied him standing beside a battery. As the splendid Texas brigade which had been Hood's and was now commanded by Gregg swept by, the commanding general himself rode forward to go with them into the attack—when the men, divining his intent, cried out to Lee, "Go back! go back! We won't go on unless you go back!"

While Longstreet's left fought and checked the Union front, General M. L. Smith, of the engineers, led troops along an unfinished railroad way, to the south, and threw them upon Hancock's left flank—another movement of the Chancellorsville sort. Four brigades, piled against the exposed end of the Union line, rolled it up and threw it back to and beyond the Plank Road.

And then, when it seemed as if the battle on Longstreet's front might go as Chancellorsville had gone, Longstreet was shot down by a mistake of his own men, as his two columns approached at right angles, in the dense and tangled woods— shot down, much as Jackson had been the year before, and within a mile or so of the same place. General Micah Jenkins, with him, was killed. Longstreet, terribly wounded, with a ball through his throat and into his shoulder, propped against a tree, with bloody foam bubbling from his lips, ordered the battle on before he was carried to the rear, but there was no one there to handle and direct the movement of troops in the difficult country in which they were entangled. After a delay of hours, when they attacked again, they found that the flight of the Union troops through the woods had been checked; that new breastworks facing the flank attack had been built; and that there was to be no more hope of Union rout on that flank.

Away on the other flank, just as darkness fell, Ewell sent part of Early's division, the Georgia brigade of Gordon and Johnson's North Carolinians, against Sedgwick's exposed right flank. The movement, undertaken too late to be of real service, caused considerable confusion, with the capture of several hundred prisoners, including two brigadiers. General Gordon relates that the opportunity for it had been open throughout the day, and had been so reported, but that General Early's fixed belief that Burnside's corps was in the woods back of Sedgwick's exposed right, prevented the attack being made until General Lee, riding to the Confederate left to ask for a diversion to help the right, learned from Gordon of the opportunity, and personally ordered the assault.

By the morning of May seventh, with both battle lines entrenched through the Wilderness, with the ditches and thickets of that gloomy woodland choked with Union dead—more than two thousand two hundred of them and nearly six times that many wounded, thousands of them wondering whether the stretcher-bearers or the fires burning in the underbrush would reach them first—it became apparent to General Grant that he was not going to "walk by" Lee on his way to Richmond. To General Lee, whose losses, more than half those of General Grant, were an appalling drain on his smaller army, it became apparent that he would not be able to hurl his new opponent back across the Rapidan.

"As I remember," wrote Sergeant-Major George Cary Eggleston of the Virginia artillery, after the war, "surprise and disappointment were the prevailing emotions in the ranks of the Army of Northern Virginia when we discovered, after the contest in the Wilderness, that General Grant was not going to retire behind the river and permit General Lee to carry on a campaign against Washington in the usual way. . . . We had been accustomed to a programme which began with a Federal advance, culminated in one great battle, and ended in the retirement of the Union army, the substitution of a new Federal commander for the one beaten, and the institution of a more or less offensive campaign on our part. This was the usual order of events, and this was what we confidently expected when General Grant crossed into the Wilderness. But here was a new Federal general, fresh from the West, and so ill-informed as to the military customs in our part of the country that when the battle of the Wilderness was over, instead of retiring to the north bank of the river and awaiting the development of Lee's plans, he had the temerity to move by his left flank to a new position, there to try conclusions with us again. We were greatly disappointed with General Grant, and full of curiosity to know how long it was going to take him to perceive the impropriety of his course."

While Grant's move to Spottsylvania was a surprise to most of Lee's soldiers, it was not to Lee himself. Scouts reported that Grant's wagons were going north toward the river, but Lee correctly divined that these were but ambulance trains, or empty supply wagons, with the necessary guards. Later in the day Stuart's cavalry reported the movement of Union supply trains southward, but before that time Lee, working out the probabilities of the case in his own mind, had determined what Grant's next move would be and put himself in readiness to make the apt counter-move.

Lee knew what his soldiers did not—that Grant, determined and tenacious, had the whole of the immense resources of the United States and the entire confidence of that government at his command; and that this time there was to be no letting go, no giving up, no going back. The conditions of the problem pointed to Spottsylvania Court House, behind and beyond Lee's right flank on the way to Richmond. And there, even before General Grant had issued the order for his secret movement, Lee was fixing his attention.

On the night of May seventh Grant began the first of the series of "sidling" movements by the left flank, which were to take him from the Rapidan to the James, across that river, clear around to the south of Petersburg and on to Appomattox Court House—eleven months later. On the morning of May eighth when the Union advance reached the cleared field north of the quaint little white columned court-house of Spottsylvania, on the road from Fredericksburg to Richmond, there was Longstreet's corps, now commanded by R. H. Anderson, deployed and waiting for them.

During that day both armies were pushing troops to Spottsylvania, crowding them forward on roads roughly parallel, with the Confederates having somewhat the longer route, but making the better speed, probably because they had less to carry.

Spottsylvania was the beginning of "trench warfare" in the modern sense, twelve days of it, from May eighth to twenty-first; nearly two weeks with all the familiar sound of a 1916 communique. There was a day of marching in; three days of maneuvering and entrenching, without decisive results; a day of general assault all along the line. Hancock's Second Corps, concentrating most heavily on the salient north of the court-house, held by Johnson's division of Ewell's corps—the Bloody Angle, it was to be called—carried it and captured its defenders, only to be stopped by a desperate counter-attack by others of Ewell's men under Rodes. A week longer they fought about the lines of Spottsylvania, the Confederates holding the new and shorter line across the base of the Bloody Angle, and all the rest of their original position; the Union armies maneuvering and thrusting here and there, and waiting for reenforcements on their way from Washington. Nearly three thousand Union soldiers were killed, nearly fifteen thousand wounded, more than two thousand captured in the fighting. The wounded lay outside the Confederate lines, untended, while General Grant, as at Vicksburg, would not ask truce to care for them and to bury the dead, and no man could go into the no-man's land between the lines and live. Confederates watched one wounded Union soldier, lying in front of the trenches on the left, try feebly for two days to brain himself with the butt of his own musket. On the third day he was dead.

Lee's losses at Spottsylvania were scarcely more than a third those of the Union army—but a man lost to Lee was irreplaceable, while Grant could draw to himself men from all the world. The pounding policy of attrition was beginning to work. To the Confederate soldiers, in their way as much logicians as their statesmen who could not understand how any one could fail to see the utter unreasonableness of an attempt to coerce the Southern States into remaining in a Union which they had a clear paper right to leave, there seemed something subtly unfair about this method of Grant. Why couldn't he fight them with just the armies with which they started out? They could engage to whip that many, just two to one, but this persistent new General kept bringing in fresh ones—and that wasn't fair. But it was war, and Grant was out to win the war.

While the infantry of the armies was at stalemate in the trenches about Spottsylvania, the cavalry was whirling down toward Richmond. Grant had reorganized the cavalry corps of the Army of the Potomac, along with a great many other things, and had put in command of it young Phil Sheridan, an infantryman and a ferocious and relentless fighter. On the night of March eighth, as the battle lines were forming about Spottsylvania, Grant started Sheridan on his first raid to Richmond. There had been several attempts to raid Richmond and its environs—Stoneman's the year before, while Hooker was fighting Chancellorsville; and the one of Judson Kilpatrick and Ulric Dahlgren, only two months before, which had penetrated within five miles of Richmond, had accomplished little, and had resulted in the death of young Dahlgren and the loss of many of his men. This raid by Sheridan, however, was on a different scale. It was strong enough to accomplish results in the way of railroad breaking and the like, and even to go into Richmond had not Sheridan's good sense told him that if he went he could not stay there engaged in desperate street fighting.

Its main purpose was to suck Stuart's cavalry away from Grant's flanks, where they were embarassingly observant of his movements and projects, a purpose in which it succeeded beyond all hope.

Sheridan started south on the morning of May ninth, with ten thousand horsemen, a column thirteen miles long. Two hours after the start, the Confederate cavalry overtook and began to harass the rear, but the main column kept moving south. During the night, while Sheridan was busy destroying railroad tracks and trains at Beaver Dam Station, Stuart collected what cavalry he could and passed beyond him, to attack at dawn of the tenth, in his front. All that day they obstructed Sheridan's advance as best they could, sending urgent messages for reenforcements. The next day, skirmishing about Yellow Tavern, six miles north of Richmond, General Stuart received a pistol ball in the abdomen, and was carried to Richmond to die, while Fitzhugh Lee took command and kept up the fight.

During occasional hours of delirium the following day Stuart fought again his raids and battles; or wandered with that eldest daughter who, just the year before had died while her father was fighting on the Rappahannock. In clearer moments he called for his wife, hastening to him, to arrive too late—the Virginia girl whose husband was the most famous of southern cavalrymen, and whose father, Major-General Philip St. George Cooke, of the United States Cavalry, was one of the Virginians who served the Union. While his old troopers, under Fitzhugh Lee, were fighting Sheridan away from Richmond Stuart died— aged thirty-one. "I can scarcely think of him without weeping," said Lee, face to the enemy at Spottsylvania.

While Lee was checking Grant in the Wilderness and holding him at Spottsylvania, Beauregard, in command south of Richmond, succeeded in neutralizing Butler's Army of the James—corked him in a bottle, to use General Grant's simile. Butler had advanced promptly on the same night that Grant crossed the Rapidan, with his army of thirty-six thousand men afloat in all manner of craft, under convoy of the war vessels of the North Atlantic Blockading Squadron, moving from their base at Hampton Roads up the James River.

Butler's movement was made very promptly, as far as City Point, where the Appomattox falls into the James, and on to Bermuda Hundred, a wide area jutting into the angle between the two rivers, the "bottle." Over land from the James at Trent Reach to the Appomattox at Port Walthall, the neck of the bottle, was but three miles. From this neck to the railroad and turnpike between Richmond and Petersburg was but three miles more.

This important base Butler seized on May sixth, while the Army of the Potomac was fighting in the Wilderness, and then

seems to have spent several days in self-congratulation, or perhaps perplexity.   Petersburg was lightly defended, but to reach
it along the railroad required the crossing of two unfordable
streams, Swift Creek and the Appomattox River, in the presence
of the enemy, and Butler's orders were for Richmond.   Toward
Richmond, less than a dozen miles away, he moved a week
later, to strike the Confederate fortified lines at Drewry's Bluff
on the James River, which he attacked on May thirteenth and
fourteenth.   On the sixteenth, after he had made some lodgment
there, Beauregard, with his little mobile army, attacked Butler
fiercely and forced him to retire within his entrenchments along
the neck of land between the James and the Appomattox.   General Butler carefully fortified himself in a strong position.
Beauregard, skilful engineer, threw a Confederate line of
trenches across the same neck and there the General was, neatly
corked in his own bottle, while General Grant was yet trying to
fight or find his way past Spottsylvania.

In the same weeks, Sigel's operations in the Valley had come
to grief.   There was a triple advance in the mountain regions:
Sigel himself straight up the Valley toward Staunton; Crook,
from the Valley of the Kanawha, against the East Tennessee &
Virginia Railroad; Averell, who had made a locally successful
railroad-breaking raid in the same region in December, against
the lead mines at Wytheville and King's Salt Works at Saltville, in far southwestern Virginia.

Only Crook's force reached its objective.   Defeating the
little cavalry command of Albert Jenkins at Cloyd's Mountain
on May ninth—Jenkins himself being mortally wounded—
Crook pressed on to the railroad, destroyed a depot of supplies
at Dublin Station and burned the long bridge over New River,
at Radford, an achievement that would have meant more
earlier in the war when the Confederates yet held the Tennessee
end of this important interior line.

Averell, after a difficult advance across the mountains,
reached the neighborhood of the lead and salt mines.   There,
confronting him, was John H. Morgan, who, confined in the
Ohio State Prison at Columbus after his capture in Ohio the

July before, had escaped by tunneling through stone floors, across the prison yard and under the outside walls, to make his way back to Confederate territory. At Crockett's Cove, on May tenth, commanding a small cavalry force, including a thousand of his own old troopers, Morgan succeeded in repulsing Averell, who with Crook fell back into West Virginia.

Meanwhile Franz Sigel, starting in the lower Shenandoah Valley with an expedition of about eight thousand infantry, cavalry and artillery, undertook his part in the simultaneous advance of all the Union armies. To oppose his advance up the Valley the Confederates had only the enterprising Imboden and some one thousand five hundred of his men. Lee could spare no reenforcements—the battles were on in the Wilderness, and the race to Spottsylvania—but John C. Breckinridge, commanding the department, was gathering up detachments and pushing forward with them. Imboden retreated slowly, harassing Sigel's advance, and even ambushing and capturing or scattering two large cavalry flanking detachments which Sigel sent out, east and west, across the Blue Ridge and the North Mountains.

Finally, on May fifteenth, at the beautiful little valley village of New Market, while Lee's men fought at the Bloody Angle, Breckinridge was up and joined forces with Imboden, a total of about five thousand men, including a battalion of two hundred and twenty-five gallant boys from Stonewall Jackson's school, the Virginia Military Institute, the oldest of them under eighteen, to strike Sigel, front and flank, and drive him back down the valley.

That done, Breckinridge, leaving Imboden to hold the Valley, marched his two thousand two hundred and fifty infantry to the railroad, put them on the cars, and started for Lee.

Lee was still at Spottsylvania. Grant, having thoroughly tested the possibility of going through or over him, found it not to be done; again sidled to the left, on the night of May twentieth, and started for a crossing of the North Anna River, to Lee's right and rear.

Within a few hours of Grant's start Lee was on his way,

too—leaving the blasted lines of Spottsylvania, where great trees had been brought down by the constant chipping of bullets, and where the Confederate ordnance detachments had gathered up more than one hundred and twenty thousand pounds of precious northern lead, to be recast and fired back at the Union troops before the war was to end.

By night of May twenty-second Lee's whole army was below the North Anna, with its center holding the south bank of the river between Jericho Mills Ford and the Chesterfield Bridge, where the Telegraph Road direct from Fredericksburg to Richmond crosses, and with flanks drawn back in entrenched lines running to Little River in the rear.

Grant's men appeared on the north bank of the river the next morning, to begin an immediate crossing, without real opposition. That day and the next, the twenty-fourth, Grant threw his corps across the stream, to left and right of the narrow center front held by Lee—to discover, when it was too late, that he had split his army on the head of the spear held toward him by Lee; that the Army of Northern Virginia was in an impregnable position between the Union wings, which could reach each other only by a long detour and two crossings of the North Anna; that, in short, he was in a badly disjointed and exposed position.

Lee, with his greatest opportunity of the campaign at hand, was sick, confined to his tent, anxious, impatient, fretting. "We must strike them! We must not let them pass us again! We must strike them!" he muttered in his fever—but the opportunity was lost.

Grant, with nothing for it but to recross the North Anna, withdrew his wings on the night of May twenty-sixth, gathered his army and started sidling again to the east and south, down the Valley of the Pamunkey, which is formed by the junction of the Annas, North and South. At Totopotomoy Creek he found Lee in front of him once more, and again started his side-slipping, this time toward the Chickahominy, last natural obstacle in the advance to Richmond, and there, after a trying march through weather hot and muggy, over roads inches deep in dust, with heavy skirmishing for the cavalry in front, when the Union army reached Old Cold Harbor, at the northern edge of the old battle-fields of two years before, they found, as ever, Lee's army drawn up and waiting, with the Chickahominy at their backs and beyond that, not ten miles away, Richmond.

The Confederates had been somewhat reenforced as they drew nearer to Richmond—Breckinridge's little division from the Valley; Pickett's division, recalled from side-show operations in North Carolina to rejoin its old First Corps; Hoke's division sent up by Beauregard from the lines south of the James. Grant had been reenforced, also, by the Eighteenth Corps under W. F. Smith, sixteen thousand men, sent from Butler's bottled and corked army at Bermuda Hundred, across the James and by water around to McClellan's old base at the White House.

The first fighting, cavalry affairs, was on the night of May thirty-first. On June first there were heavy Union infantry attacks, repulsed. June second both armies used to perfect their positions—lines facing each other, extending from the Chickahominy above Grapevine Bridge, past Gaines' Mill with its memories of the earlier battle, and on six miles or so northwestward beyond Bethesda Church and Pole Green Church, almost along the route by which Jackson's Corps had marched into the battles of the Seven Days when last the Union armies had been in sight of Richmond, back in 1862.

There was no more room for maneuver, if General Grant was to go to Richmond. There was the way, short and direct, straight across the Chickahominy, but across the way stood Lee and the Army of Northern Virginia. Against that army, at five o'clock on the morning of June third, Grant hurled his army in a direct frontal attack against entrenchments. The actual duration of the first advance all along the line was less than a quarter of an hour; its result, fields and slopes covered with men dead and wounded, ten thousand of them; and with sound men, on the ground among the dead and wounded, unable to rise in that withering fire to advance or to retreat. Except spots where one or two gallant spirits dashed forward to die on the breastworks, and one place where Barlow's division got into the line, only to be driven out by Finegan's Confederates, the attack never reached the Confederate lines; no other assault that day was able to get started. Soldiers, hearing that another was to be launched, quietly sat down to sew on their coats bits of cloth with their names, so that they might not lie on the field as unidentified dead.

And then began another of those three days of horror when stubborn Grant would not ask for truce to treat his wounded or to bury his dead—three days of Virginia summer, with Union dead decomposing in the sun and Union wounded dying in agonies of thirst and fever. The dead did not move, but among the not entirely helpless wounded there was enough of movement to give the slopes before the Confederate positions, seen at a little distance, a peculiar *crawling* effect—a creepy thing to add itself to the moans, lower and lower as strength failed and death came with its mercy, and to the stench of the unburied, for three days, until there was no longer much use to succor the wounded, and only need of urgent haste in burying the dead.

CHAPTER XXVIII

HAMMERING

FROM the third of June, when the last assaults were so bloodily repulsed, until the fourteenth, while the Army of the Potomac was busy with pick and shovel, working at night on trenches to protect themselves from the terrible fire of the Confederate sharpshooters, making zigzags and parallels to the front and communication trenches to the rear, the General commanding all the armies was considering what to do.

On May eleventh, while the troops were gathering at Spottsylvania and the night before the massed attack on the Bloody Angle, he had written to General Halleck a phrase that became famous: "I propose to fight it out on this line if it takes all summer." And now, with the summer scarcely started, in the one month from the crossing of the Rapidan to the slaughter at Cold Harbor, Grant's army had lost fifty-five thousand men— not far from the total number with which Lee started the campaign—and of those lost, forty-six thousand were dead or wounded. And, after all that, the General stood, blocked and repulsed, right where McClellan had been two years before, looking across the Chickahominy toward the church spires of Richmond.

The distinct military achievements of General Grant are four. He captured Vicksburg, by a bold and original campaign in which he was aided to no small extent by the uncertainties of Confederate policy and the division of Confederate command; he raised the siege of Chattanooga, somewhat helped by the lack of confidence of the Confederate soldiers in their hapless General; he coordinated the 1864 efforts of the Union armies, pressing at the same time on all fronts, a triumph of common sense and dogged determination; and, for three days, he gave the slip to Robert E. Lee, an achievement in which he was aided by nothing but his own perception of his problem and its correct answer, and his own good management of the movement from the north to the south bank of the James River.

After Cold Harbor it became necessary for the Union commander to change the line on which he was to fight the remainder of the summer. It was manifestly not possible to go into Richmond through or over the Army of Northern Virginia, nor to destroy that army in its fortified lines before the city. There was not room to go around Lee's right flank again, while to attempt to go around his left meant a retrograde movement toward Washington, not to be thought of.

But there was Petersburg, the key to the capital, for the army which held Petersburg controlled Richmond by commanding its rail communication with the South. And Petersburg, but twenty miles south of Richmond, was almost undefended and could be reached by Grant's army, so long as the control of the Rivers James and Appomattox was held, with no more difficulty than it could by Lee's.

While the Army of the Potomac was at work on its trench system, General Grant was working out his plans for the movement that was to begin on the morning of June fourteenth; to be conducted so quietly and skilfully that General Lee could never be certain that Grant had indeed left his front, and so swiftly that Petersburg must surely have fallen but for the desperate and devoted defense of the handful of troops and home guards who for four days held the place until Lee and the Army of Northern Virginia shifted to the south bank of the James to meet Grant's movement.

During the days while the shift toward Petersburg was being planned and executed, Union armies were again advancing through the Shenandoah Valley, aiming at Lynchburg, another vital spot in the rail communications of Virginia. Major-General David Hunter, who had replaced the unfortunate Sigel, was moving up the Valley with eight thousand five hundred men. To meet him was the active Imboden, with about one thousand cavalry. Everything else had gone to Lee immediately after the victory at New Market, and none could now be sent back.

Imboden fell back up the Valley, as slowly as he could,

gathering in detachments. The "reserves" of the valley counties, boys and old men, were called out; Brigadier-General William E. Jones, commanding in southwestern Virginia, collected and brought up his scattered garrisons; Vaughn's brigade of Tennessee horse, a thousand of them, marched in from the south, and, finally, on the night of June fourth the newly gathered army of some five thousand was organized into brigades, with Jones in command. The ten-hour battle of Piedmont, fought the next day, was a complete Union victory with a Confederate loss of one thousand five hundred, including General Jones, killed.

Hunter made a short march to Staunton, where he was joined by the column which had advanced across the mountains from the Kanawha Valley, under Crook and Averell, making a total Union force of eighteen thousand men. The Valley, at last, was open to them, with only the remnants of the little Confederate force that had fought at Piedmont hanging on to the gaps in the Blue Ridge.

Cold Harbor had been fought meanwhile, and Lee was able to send reenforcements. Breckinridge's small division—not so large as a brigade of the early days of the war—came first.

Hunter's orders from Grant were to march from Staunton to Lynchburg by way of Charlottesville, but with Breckinridge's Confederate force holding the Rockfish Gap, through which he must pass, he decided to forego that part of his march, move straight up the Valley to Lexington, and then cross the mountain to Lynchburg.

General Grant, not knowing of the change in his subordinate's plans, dispatched Sheridan and the cavalry from their camps in rear of the trench lines at Cold Harbor, to meet Hunter at Charlottesville and join with him in a thorough break-up of the Virginia Central Railroad, which connected Richmond with the Piedmont and the Valley and, through Lynchburg, with the southwestern section of the state. Sheridan, with eight thousand men, started on June seventh with his usual vigor. On the eleventh, after a day of confused mounted and dismounted fighting about Trevilian Station, in which both sides claimed tactical victory, Sheridan yielded his purpose of going to Char-lottesville to meet Hunter and returned to the main army.

The Confederates had a new chief of cavalry—Wade Hamp-ton, of South Carolina, promoted to Stuart's place. Lieutenant-General Hampton was one of the great grandees of the South. His grandfather, of the same name, had fought as a General in the Revolution and in the War of 1812. The third of the name, owner of vast plantations in South Carolina and Miss-issippi, was said to have been the largest slaveholder of his time, and one of the wisest. His only public service of note before the war, had been a term or so in the Legislature of South Carolina, where he had strongly opposed any measures looking to the reopening of the African slave trade. He had been an outspoken Unionist, but with the outbreak of war he organized and equipped the Hampton Legion, infantry, and served with them from Manassas through the Peninsula campaign before he was made a brigadier and transferred to the cavalry. Five times wounded, with rifle ball, grape-shot and saber cut, he fought on to the end.

The day after Hampton turned Sheridan back at Trevilian Station, Lee detached Jubal A. Early and part of the Second Corps to meet Hunter's threatening advance. Early moved promptly at two o'clock in the morning of June thirteenth, marched out of the lines at Cold Harbor and shoved forward to Charlottesville and Lynchburg. As Hunter's men approached from the west, leaving a broad track of burning and destruc-tion behind them, including Stonewall Jackson's Virginia Mili-tary Institute at Lexington, Early's men marched in from the opposite direction. Hunter, for lack of ammunition as he explained afterward, decided not to attack the town he had come so far to reach, and turned for a rapid retreat into West Virginia, with Early after him. After three days of pursuit, seeing him safely into the mountains, "Old Jube" on June twenty-second moved into the upper Valley, headed to the north and to the Potomac.

During these days while Early was expelling Hunter's huge Union raid from the Valley. John Morgan had gone on his last ride into Kentucky. He started from southwestern Virginia. after the repulse of Crook and Averell, at the last of May, with two thousand men, of whom nearly half were on foot foɪ lack of horses. They marched across rugged and broken mountains two hundred miles to their old home territory of the Blue-Grass, and there began to meet disaster. Morgan himself rode into Lexington on the morning of June tenth—his last sight of his home town—but that afternoon his dismounted men, carelessly encamped near Mt. Sterling without proper pickets and too far from support, were cut off and captured. Morgan, turning toward the Ohio River once more, marched to Cynthiana on the eleventh, fought a brisk skirmish that afternoon with forces of about his own strength, and a pitched battle the next day, with forces four times his own. With ammunition almost exhausted, Morgan was driven off and out of Kentucky, in a weary broken march across the mountains—so much higher, so much steeper, so much more trying than they had been a week before as Morgan's men gaily marched into Kentucky. Back in Southwest Virginia and East Tennessee, Morgan entered upon a season of small affairs, to end on September fourth, when, surprised and surrounded in a home at Greeneville, he was shot to death in his attempt to escape.

During the same night in which Early's troops left Lee's lines at Cold Harbor, General Grant began his delicate movement away from Lee and toward Petersburg. Smith's corps moved first, slipping away from the lines in front of Lee, passing the rear of the Union army, and ferrying the James by afternoon of June fourteenth. Hancock's corps was crossing the same day. That night the pontoon bridge was up, across the wide river securely commanded by the Union Navy, and the movement was speeded forward, with a continuous column of marching men and animals on the bridge, and ferry-boats scuttling back and forth on the water. Everything was hurrying south for the immediate capture of Petersburg.

Beauregard was in command of the Confederate forces south of the James, a commander almost without forces, but alert, vigilant, determined, and toward the last of the four

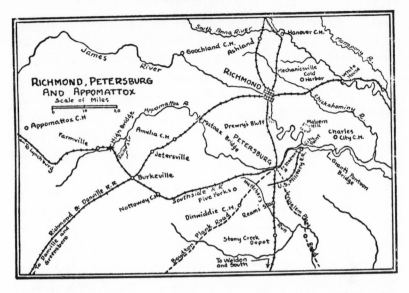

days just beginning, desperate. On June fourteenth, he discovered that Smith's corps had returned to Bermuda Hundred. He telegraphed Bragg, the President's Chief-of-Staff at Richmond. No answer. That night, from a deserter, he learned that another corps had followed Smith. This time he telegraphed Lee. No answer, again. Before morning he sent an aide to General Lee to tell what was afoot on the south bank. The General felt that the troops were only some of Smith's men returning to their proper command as part of the Army of the James, but he did order Hoke's division of North Carolina troops, which he had drawn north during the heavy fighting, returned to Beauregard.

That morning, June fifteenth, General Beauregard occupied the lightly fortified lines about Petersburg, more than four miles long, with but little more than two thousand troops, including militia. In the city itself fiery Governor Wise, of Virginia, a Confederate brigadier throughout the war, was in command of a mixed force, mostly "Junior Reserves," armed with cast-off equipment and hardly uniformed at all. The Governor, who had had poor success in West Virginia and less than that at Roanoke Island, was to have his chance in the early days of the great Petersburg siege.

The attack opened early in the morning of the fifteenth, to the north, where Beauregard was. By ten o'clock it had spread to the city. Wise was calling for help—of which there was none, except Hoke's division, hurrying south but still miles away. All that day the handful of Confederates, old, young, trained and untrained, hung on to the lines. Just at dark, as the Union forces made a lodgment, Johnson Hagood's South Carolina brigade came in at the double-quick and stopped the break, with Hoke's whole division right behind them.

General Smith, in charge of the Union advance, failed to exploit his advantage that night. With Hancock's corps on the field he had nearly forty thousand men; Beauregard, not more than one-fifth as many. Never again, until the end three-quarters of a year later, was Richmond in such peril as on the night of June fifteenth. At dawn of the sixteenth, Beauregard began to abandon some of his more exposed front, and to shorten his lines. The Confederate lines across the neck at Bermuda Hundred were given up—there were not enough men to hold them and the Petersburg lines, too—and Bushrod Johnson's fine little division was added to the defenders of the city. All that day, while Beauregard confronted them with ten thousand or so men, the Union army crossed the rivers and marched toward Petersburg. By five in the afternoon, Grant had more than fifty thousand men across and in his lines ready to attack.

Twice during the day Beauregard reported to Lee—in the morning that he had captured a prisoner from Hancock's corps of the Army of the Potomac; in the afternoon, that his scouts had seen ferry-boats and transports of the enemy crossing the James. So well had Grant's movement been conducted that General Lee still could not believe that the main army was swiftly slipping away from his front. "The transports you mention have probably returned Butler's troops," he wired Beauregard. "Has Grant been seen crossing James River?"

Late in the afternoon of June sixteenth the Union forces, after their strange delay, attacked Beauregard's thin line. There was a fierce fight of three hours, ending with the Con-

federate line broken again, on the right, where constant extending to meet the enveloping Union left had thinned it. While
the fight went on Warren's corps began to feed in on the Union
side. There were more than sixty-five thousand of them now.
More dispatches to General Lee that night. The General, in
the absence of "more definite information about Grant's movements," did not "think it prudent to draw more troops" to the
south side of the river.

The seventeenth was a day of battle, all day and until
eleven that night. There was no longer any hope of holding the
extended Petersburg lines, but a new, shorter and stronger
line in rear was staked out carefully and officers of each unit
were taken back and shown their places. Just after midnight,
on the morning of the eighteenth, Beauregard's handful of
men slipped out of the lines they had held so tenaciously, fell
back to the new position, and through the rest of the night,
with every sort of digging tool they could lay hands on, entrenched themselves.

The evening before Beauregard had wired General Lee
that prisoners, taken from the corps of Hancock, Burnside and
Smith, said that the whole Union Army was on the field or
coming. At midnight, he wired, "prisoners report Grant on
field with his whole army." And then the desperate Beauregard, knowing that a great army was pressing upon him, and
apparently the only man in high position in the Confederate
service who did know it, took steps to impress General Lee
with the seriousness of his situation. Three staff messengers
were sent, an hour apart, to Lee's headquarters at Drewry's
Bluff. The first reached him before two in the morning, found
him lying on the ground, awake, stated his message and the
facts supporting it, and failed to convince him that any large
part of Grant's army had crossed the James. The second
messenger, coming in half an hour later, was denied admittance
to Lee by his aides. The third, coming about three in the
morning, almost forced his way into the General's tent and
laid before him such further evidence as satisfied him that
Grant's army had been across the James two days.

Before three-thirty in the morning Lee, now all activity, was starting his movement to meet Grant in front of Petersburg. Most fortunately, in fact, he had started Kershaw's division of five thousand men the evening before, on the strength of Beauregard's representation, although at that time he was "not yet satisfied as to General Grant's movements."

Beauregard's insistence and the fortunate start of Kershaw's Carolinians saved Petersburg—and Richmond—for yet nine months more of bitter warfare. The first reenforcements reached the hard-pressed Petersburg lines early on the morning of June eighteenth; Field's division followed; Lee himself came in just before noon. The "grand attack" by the Union forces started at dawn; found the old Confederate trenches empty; halted to reorganize. Toward noon, the attack was launched, with four Union corps and part of a fifth, some ninety thousand men in reach—but Beauregard had twenty thousand now, and more coming. The assault was repulsed, with heavy loss. Other assaults were tried during the afternoon. That night the assaults died down, the Siege of Petersburg began.

The Army of the Potomac, which from the Wilderness to Petersburg, had lost more men than the sixty thousand with whom Lee started the campaign, settled down to the pick and shovel. Richmond, to the uninitiated, appeared to be as unassailable as ever; the end of the war as remote.

"There was at this time great danger of the collapse of the war," wrote Swinton. "Had not success come elsewhere to brighten the horizon, it would have been difficult to have raised new forces to recruit the Army of the Potomac, which, shaken in its structure, its valor quenched in blood, and thousands of its ablest officers killed and wounded, was the Army of the Potomac no more."

It required, to sustain the spirit of the North, all the great prestige that General Grant had won at Fort Donelson, at Vicksburg and at Chattanooga; all the confidence which the President had in his fighting quality; all the explanation of the newspapers that this was but the way chosen by the Great Hammerer, as they named him, to bring the war to an end.

There were those thousands of dead, hastily buried in Virginia soil; those tens of thousands of wounded, choking the hospitals, the foul hospitals of the days before antisepsis, harboring the unseen and unsuspected germs of pus infection; and the thousands of prisoners. The exchange of prisoners had been stopped by the North when relentless attrition became the policy to end the war. To hold every southern prisoner caught, rather than to exchange him to return with his rifle to the wasting Confederate ranks, was to shorten the war— even though it meant that for each one some northern soldier must remain in a southern prison. Stories of privation, suffering and, as was to be expected, of barbarity in these prisons filled the land, as like stories of northern prisons filled the South.

Food was scant in southern prisons, too, as it was in southern armies, for that matter. Medicines, and especially the indispensable quinine, specific for the "chills and fever" of malarial districts, were even scarcer, for southern field and forest roots and herbs could not supply the places of everything cut off by the blockade. These things the government at Washington knew, and knowing, it adopted the cruelly wise and merciful policy of speeding the end of the war by condemning those of its soldiers who were captured to the life of the southern prisons.

The ultimate humanity of the policy is unquestioned, but it does seem that one of the least justifiable of the tragic injustices of the period of vengeance after the war was the hanging of Major Henry Wirtz, commandant of the great prison camp at Andersonville, in Southwest Georgia, who did what he could for the thirty-odd thousand men in his charge with the food, blankets and fuel which his government could furnish him.

In May, in the same letter to Halleck in which he had outlined his fighting intentions for the summer, Grant had added, "I am satisfied that the enemy are very shaky, and are only kept up to the mark by the greatest exertion of their officers." But here it was only June, the best campaigning months of the year just ahead—and the same army was at Petersburg, its fighting quality unimpaired, its soldiers still filled with faith in Lee's ability to meet any assault, any movement, to find a way out of any difficulty.

And yet the methods of the Great Hammerer were beginning to tell. Lee's own losses had been great—relatively as large as Grant's, and far more serious, because they were men who could not be replaced. "What's the use of killing those fellows?" asked one of Lee's irreplaceables. "Kill one and half a dozen take his place."

CHAPTER XXIX

STRIKING AT THE HEART

ON THE morning that General Grant crossed the Rapidan, May fourth, his great lieutenant Sherman moved out from the fortified position about Chattanooga, to turn Joe Johnston's Army of Tennessee out of Dalton; to flank and fight them back to Atlanta; to capture that nerve center of southern communication, and so to furnish the stimulant of visible victory which braced the North for one more winter of war, and was the most potent of campaign arguments for the reelection of Lincoln.

Victory in war is not always a matter of arithmetic. There are always considerations of politics, and the politics of the Northern States during that anxious summer of 1864, with Grant blocked before Petersburg after his appalling losses, cried for victory, manifest and indisputable victory such as those of July, 1863. Atlanta was that victory.

The War between the States was the first railroad war. The South had no other communication of consequence, with harbors blockaded and inland rivers controlled and patrolled by Union gunboats, but it did have two "interior" lines of railroad connecting its East and its West. So long as those lines could be held and kept open the South could mobilize its strength and supply its armies. The loss of Chattanooga cut off one, the line through the valley of upper East Tennessee and Southwest Virginia to Lynchburg and Richmond. The capture of Atlanta cut the second, from Mobile and Montgomery, through Atlanta, to Charleston, Wilmington and Richmond. The holding of the key positions on these two lines more effectively dismembered the Confederacy than even the loss of the Mississippi River. Between the two great sections of the South there remained but one round-about and feeble line of rail communication, a collection of end-to-end branch roads, which did not always fit. With Chattanooga and then Atlanta gone, the power of resistance went out of the South; only the spirit and the will remained.

When Sherman, as his part of the great simultaneous advance, started to drive back the army of Johnston he found ready to his hand a connected line of railroad from his base in the Ohio Valley to the Southeast, cutting at right angles the two vital east and west lines of the Confederacy. Most modern of Civil War soldiers, he made of that line his most indispensable ally. Opposing him was one of the South's ablest soldiers—"No officer or soldier who served under me will question the generalship of Joseph E. Johnston," wrote Sherman—but Sherman had such an advantage of strength, about two to one, that he felt confident of his ability to flank or fight Johnston back, if that lengthening line of rails back through Chattanooga and Nashville to the Ohio River could be kept in operation.

"That single stem of railroad 473 miles long supplied an army of 100,000 men and 35,000 animals for the period of 196 days, viz: from May 1 to November 12, 1864," he wrote. ". . . The Atlanta campaign was an impossibility without these railroads, and possible only then because we had the means and the men to maintain and defend them in addition to what were necessary to overcome the enemy."

Another of the ironies of this most ironic war is that the citizens of Charleston were more than any one else responsible for the existence of that railroad connection. From the earliest days of railroad building in America, the proud Carolina city had pioneered. The first railroad in the United States designed from the beginning for the use of the locomotive, without a horse-path between the rails, being the same railroad which first in the world attained the length of one hundred miles, was Charleston-built. It reached the Savannah River, opposite Augusta, Georgia, the first step in the linked lines which Charleston sought to throw into the Mississippi Valley to bring to herself its trade in corn and pork and provisions.

From Augusta to a spot in the woods which is now Atlanta, the Georgia Railroad and Banking Company built on into the West; from Atlanta to a landing on the Tennessee River, which became Chattanooga, the state of Georgia itself, under the corporate name of the Western & Atlantic Railroad, threw its line; from Chattanooga to unobstructed steamboat navigation on the Cumberland at Nashville, the Nashville & Chattanooga Railroad, a private company built, but so interested were Charleston and Carolina in the completion of this link across the mountains that the city itself bought and for many years held half a million dollars of the stock of the railroad. Not even in Charleston was the life of the Old South quite the idyllic mixture of moonlight and mint juleps to which we look back with longing. The Carolinians—John C. Calhoun was their leader in this as in so many things else—were tremendously ambitious to bring to their city and port the flow of commerce from what was then "the West." With the courage of their convictions they spent their money in the untried field of railroads, to bring to them in peace commerce—and then, in war, after they had so long and gallantly stood off every attack from the seaward side, to bring to them from the rear devastating conquest.

Sherman's major concern during the four months of marching and fighting that ended in the occupation of Atlanta, was the maintenance of his life-line to the rear. The chief threat to the safety of that line was Forrest and his few thousand cavalry. As an essential part of the preparation for the advance, Sherman sent Major-General Samuel D. Sturgis, who had fought in Virginia and in Missouri, "to take command of the cavalry and whip Forrest," who was then in West Tennessee on the prolonged expedition of March and April, 1864, collecting and organizing his command and supplying their wants from the generous stores of the enemy. Forrest, ready to leave, passed out of West Tennessee, almost in sight of Memphis. Following him but a short distance into Mississippi, Sturgis turned back to Memphis. "I regret very much that I could not have the pleasure of bringing you his hair," he wrote to Sherman, "but he is too great a plunderer to fight anything like an equal force, and we have to be satisfied with driving him from the State. He may turn on your communications— I rather think he will, but I see no way to prevent it from this point with this force."

For that very purpose Sherman, now pressing on to Georgia, ordered a concentration against Forrest that by keeping him busy in Mississippi, would keep him out of Tennessee, where the all-important rail line ran.

The Army of Tennessee, against which Sherman moved, was the same that had broken back from the heights of Missionary Ridge the autumn before—but not the same, either. In the autumn, declared a private letter published in the Mobile *Advertiser,* it had been "disheartened, despairing and on the verge of dissolution"; in April, it was "a regenerated army. I can find no word but that to express the extent of the transformation." General Johnston, coming to command at the last of 1863, had improved the winter at Dalton. Desertion had been reduced, partly by a liberal and sensible system of furloughs, partly by the execution of deserters, lined up before the army, formed in half-square, to be shot, each man at the foot of his own grave.

For minor offenses there was a variety of punishments, depending somewhat on the customs of the locality from which came the various commands. In some of the units, the pillory was in use; in others, "bucking and gagging." Two cavalry-men convicted of stealing saddles, were sentenced to parade before their commands all day, carrying the saddles and labeled "Thief." The final part of the sentence, directing that they be transferred from the cavalry to the infantry as punishment, was emphatically disapproved by the corps commander, General Hood, who rightly observed that the infantry was an honorable arm, of more importance than all others, in which men could not be "sentenced" to serve.

Besides punishments, and drill, there was a deal of recreation in the winter camps about Dalton—rough recreation, perhaps, but it served. There were, for example, "gander pullings," whereat the bird with greased neck and head was hung, head down, from a rope stretched between two trees, the object of the game being for a mounted man, dashing under the rope with bystanders lashing and striking at his horse, to catch the squirming, jerking head of the gander. Less difficult, perhaps, and certainly less trying on the feeling of the ganders of that section, were the "tournaments," in which men raced down the lists to lift small rings on the points of their lances.

Most memorable of all recreations, though, was the great snowball battle, following a freak snow-storm in March. "It was the biggest fight—for fun—I ever saw, and there was so much rivalry between the troops that a number of soldiers had their eyes put out," writes one of the participants.

There was, too, the revival of religion that became almost an inevitable part of the long encampments of the southern armies. At outdoor preaching, one Saturday night in the spring, a dead tree fell across the altar and the mourner's bench, crowded with penitents. Ten men were killed, another mortally hurt—deaths that made far more impression on the army than would a hundred times as many in battle.

Early in the year there began in this army a most private discussion of a subject that was finally to come to light and increasingly to engage the attention of Confederate generals and statesman and, at the last, diplomats—the enlistment of slaves as Confederate soldiers. Lieutenant-General Hardee called the corps and division commanders to meet at General Johnston's headquarters on the night of January second. There they were presented with a memorandum prepared by Major-General Pat Cleburne, urging the enlistment and arming of the negro troops, with freedom as a reward for their service. This plan, described by at least one of the generals present as a "monstrous proposition," met with sharp and violent opposition, and for the time was dropped by its proponent. No copy of the plan was sent officially to Richmond, but Major-General W. H. T. Walker did submit one, privately, to the President, who replied, "Deeming it to be injurious of the public service that such subject should be mooted or even known to be entertained by persons possessed of confidence and respect of the people, I have concluded that the best policy under the circum-stances will be to avoid all publicity, and the Secretary of War has therefore written to General Johnston requesting him to convey to those concerned my desire that it should be kept private. If it be kept out of the public journals its ill effect will be much lessened."

General Cleburne was, so it seems, thoroughly squelched, but the idea did not down, as will appear. Meanwhile the direct and practical-minded Forrest had already met the problem, so far as his negroes and his armies were concerned. For the last two years of the war forty-five of his own slaves acted as team-sters in his army—free after 1863 when, fearing the possibility of death in battle, he emancipated them.

Johnston's army occupied Dalton, and the wide valley which stretches back from there through North Georgia fifty miles south to the Etowah River. Between the Confederates and Sherman's Army was Rocky Face Ridge, the last of the series of high, narrow, precipitous parallel ridges which form the watershed between the Tennessee and the Coosa-Alabama River systems. Dalton lies close under the eastern foot of the ridge. Seven miles north, at Buzzard-Roost Gap, where the railroad passed through the mountain in a tunnel, was a strong Con-federate outpost, strengthened, just back of the mountain, by closing up culverts under the railroad track and so converting Mill Creek into an artificial lake. Still farther north, at the end of Rocky Face, was a wide opening around which Sherman might pass into the valley of the Connasauga, in which Dalton lies. Confederate cavalry under Wheeler were out on this flank. Five miles south of Dalton is another opening in Rocky Face, a mountain road through Dug Gap, lightly held by Con-federate forces. Still farther south, some fifteen miles from Dalton, the wider and more practicable Snake Creek Gap was not guarded. From Dalton south to the crossing of the Oosta-naula River at Resaca, the railroad and wagon roads lie close to the eastern foot of Rocky Face.

In the early days of May, Sherman, with just over one

hundred thousand men organized into three "armies," commanded by Thomas, McPherson and Schofield, demonstrated against Tunnel Hill and along the crest of Rocky Face at

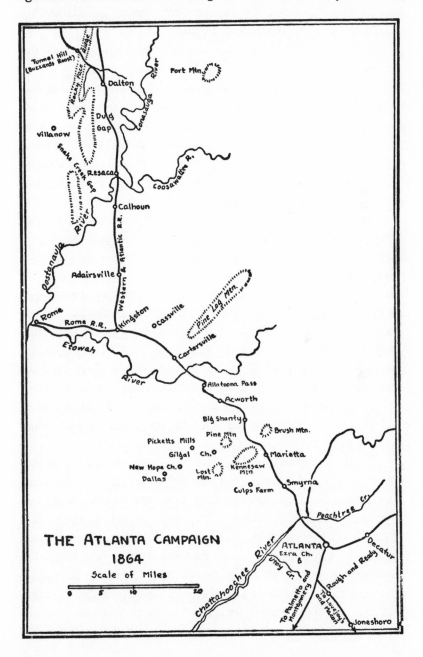

THE ATLANTA CAMPAIGN
1864
Scale of Miles

Buzzard Roost and Dug Gap, while McPherson's army marched down the narrow valley to the west of the ridge and filed through the unguarded Snake Creek Gap, away to the south. The process of outflanking Joe Johnston by extending the lines beyond his power to reach had begun.

As McPherson's men filed through the Gap and into the valley, facing the little railroad station and the bridges over the Oostanaula at Resaca, on May ninth, Grigsby's brigade of Kentucky Confederate cavalry rode in from the north. After a lively skirmish, McPherson halted his men at the mouth of the gap, and threw up the hasty entrenchments which became a feature of the closing campaigns of the war. Lieutenant-General Polk, on the way with his troops from Mississippi to Johnston's army, and moving up the railroad from Atlanta to Dalton, was halted at Resaca and charged with the defense of the place until the main army could fall back on him.

General Johnston could not afford to risk a great battle, with a hundred miles of open and undefended country between him and Atlanta, in case of defeat, while Sherman, if defeated, might fall back through the gaps in Rocky Face to his near-by fortified positions at Chattanooga. Aided by McPherson's halt, and the timely arrival of Polk's troops, he did the next best thing—fell back "in one of his clean retreats, leaving nothing behind," to face and delay the enemy, to inflict on him the heavy losses that the attacking party must suffer, and to watch warily for an opportunity to strike him while divided or unguarded.

The three-day battle of Resaca followed on May thirteenth, fourteenth and fifteenth, a hard-fought affair in which the Union attacks on the Confederate entrenchments were heavily repulsed—but which ended with word, on the fifteenth, that other Union troops were crossing the Oostanaula on pontoon bridges at Lay's Ferry, below Resaca, and so in rear of the Confederate left. At midnight of the fifteenth, Johnston's forces fell back across the Oostanaula, destroyed their bridges and took up their march southward to meet this new menace.

From Resaca south for twenty-five miles the railroad and

the wagon roads cross a wide valley, the angle between the Oostanaula and the Etowah Rivers, which flow together at Rome to form the Coosa. Across this open and exposed valley Johnston marched, Sherman close behind. On the seventeenth, at Adairsville, there was a sharp skirmish, which checked the pursuit. From Adairsville south to Cassville there are two wagon roads, some five miles apart at their point of greatest separation. Anticipating that Sherman would divide his force to march on both roads, Johnston laid an ambush to trap and punish one of his columns. Lieutenant-General John B. Hood, on an unconfirmed report of an enemy to the east, faced his corps the wrong way, in disobedience of orders, and the trap was not sprung. The retreat continued to Cassville.

There Johnston took up position on a bold ridge, facing across the wide valley through which they had come, and awaited attack. During the night, Polk and Hood, fearing that Union artillery could take them in flank, urged the abandonment of the position. Hardee, commanding the other corps, was for making the stand. Johnston, believing that if two of his corps commanders thought the position untenable, the feeling would spread to the army, decided to retreat—"a step that I have regretted ever since," he wrote afterward.

On May twentieth, the Confederate troops passed the Etowah, abandoning the elaborate fortifications to protect the railroad and wagon bridge near Cartersville, and moved into the broken Allatoona heights to the south of that stream. Three days later, while Grant was moving from his trenches at Spottsylvania toward the field of Cold Harbor, Sherman began crossing the Etowah at Stilesboro, again below and to the west of Johnston's position. On the next day, as Sherman stretched away on the road from Stilesboro to Atlanta, well to the west of the railroad, he found the Confederate corps in front of him again. Three days of battle northeast of Dallas, about New Hope Church—"Hell Hole," the Union soldiers called it— followed on May twenty-fifth, twenty-sixth and twenty-seventh. It was in this fight that three brothers manning the same gun in Fenner's Louisiana battery were killed, one after the other as they took over the dangerous post of "rammer." After the repulse of the Union forces, two little boys in blue uniform, exactly alike and obviously twins, apparently not over fifteen years old, were found on the field, dead, hand in hand. Not all the boy soldiers were in the Confederate Army. On the twenty-eighth, the Confederates attacked, to be driven off with heavy loss from the Union field entrenchments.

General Sherman, having left the railroad well to his left, decided to sidle back that way, with the idea of regaining the rail line and leaving Johnston to hold his entrenched positions about Dallas and New Hope Church. The movement began on June fourth. Johnston, not to be caught off guard, moved eastward as Sherman did. When Sherman established himself on the railroad, at Acworth, there was Johnston just to the south, holding the slopes in front of Kennesaw Mountain, with his center about Gilgal Church, an outlying flank on Brush Mountain to the right and on Lost Mountain to the left, and an advance post to the north on Pine Mountain.

From Dalton to the pause before Kennesaw, the campaign had lasted just a month—the same month in which Grant had fought and flanked Lee back from the Rapidan to Cold Harbor and the Chickahominy. Away to the west, from North Mississippi, during the same month, was launched a little cavalry expedition that promised results for the Confederacy, with Forrest in command, aimed at Sherman's rail line.

"I wish we could make an accumulation of supplies somewhere near," Sherman wrote from his lines north of Kennesaw to his wife. "The railroad is taxed to its utmost to supply our daily wants. . . . This far we have been well supplied, and I hope it will continue, though I expect to hear every day of Forrest breaking into Tennessee from some quarter. John Morgan is in Kentucky, but I attach little importance to him or his raid. Forrest is a more dangerous man. I am in hopes that an expedition sent out from Memphis on Tupelo about the first of June will give him full employment."

When the letter was written the expedition that was to give Forrest "full employment" was streaming back toward

Memphis in utter rout. It had been a fine expedition, "everything in complete order, and the force consisted of some of our best troops," as Major-General Washburn, department commander reported. The ardent Sturgis, lusting for Forrest's scalp, was in command; under him, Grierson, who had made such reputation with his raid through Mississippi at the beginning of the Vicksburg campaign, commanded the cavalry, armed with breech-loading carbines. There were twenty-two guns, the whole force more than double in numbers anything that Forrest could bring against them, and still more superior in equipment.

The Sturgis expedition met disaster at Forrest's hands on June tenth, at Brice's Crossroads—from the Confederate standpoint, a military masterpiece of marching, of planning and of fighting. On the Union side, in Sturgis' language, "order gave way to confusion, and confusion to panic." Nine days it took the expedition to march out from Memphis; two days and a half to get back, minus everything with which it had started.

It had, however, achieved its major object. It had caused Lieutenant-General Stephen D. Lee, who succeeded to the command of the Department when Polk went back to the Army of Tennessee as a corps commander, to recall Forrest from the start on his expedition to Tennessee, and it had kept Forrest busy for a while.

During the greater part of June, while Grant was making his move to Petersburg and starting on the weary siege of that city, Sherman was sparring with Johnston, with almost continuous fighting. There were short movements, shifts of position, adjustment of lines, skirmishes, reconnaissances. On one of these, on June fourteenth, brave old Bishop Polk, exposing himself on the slopes of Pine Mountain, was "sniped" by a Union field piece. No death could have more affected the army than that of the Bishop-General, who, except for his few months in Mississippi, had been with it since those far-off early days at Columbus.

General Polk combined ecclesiastical power and dignity with military ardor. Sometimes the combination was difficult.

Certain resources of language available to other commanders were denied to the Bishop, but he made out. Major-General Frank Cheatham was known throughout the army for his rallying cry to his Tennessee division: "Give 'em hell, boys, give 'em hell!" The Bishop-General, in a moment of stress, encouraged the same division by a simple paraphrase: "Give 'em what Cheatham says, boys, give 'em what Cheatham says!"

When he rejoined the Army, just from Mississippi, Polk told Johnston of the strength of the cavalry in that section under this new man Forrest, who had never been to the military schools, who knew nothing of what the books said about how to fight battles, but who had the gift of fighting them and winning. During the month of June, while he was sparring with Sherman, the Confederate commander suggested to President Davis, both directly and through General Bragg, "that an adequate force commanded by the most competent officer in America for such service (General N. B. Forrest) could be sent for the purpose of breaking the railroad in Sherman's rear. . . . This cavalry would serve the Confederacy far better by insuring the defeat of a great invasion than by repelling a mere raid." Lee advised the President, also, that "it would be better to concentrate all the cavalry in Mississippi and Tennessee on Sherman's communications." Generous Joe Wheeler, Johnston's chief of cavalry, urged it also, and even offered to waive his own rank and subordinate himself to Forrest, if the move were made.

This move the shrewd and far-seeing Sherman planned to avert, by working on the well-known unwillingness of the Confederate Government to abandon territory.

During June, he ordered another expedition from Memphis into Mississippi, this one to be on a still larger scale and to be commanded by Major-General A. J. Smith, back from the Red River disaster, with Brigadier-General Joseph A. Mower second in command. To President Lincoln Sherman wrote, "I have ordered General A. J. Smith and General Mower from Memphis to pursue and kill Forrest, promising the latter, in case of success, my influence to promote him to a major-general." To Smith and Mower, Sherman issued instructions "to pursue Forrest on foot, devastating the land over which he has passed, or may pass, and to make the people of Tennessee and Mississippi feel that although a bold, daring and successful leader, he will bring ruin and misery on any country where he may pass or tarry. If we do not punish Forrest and the people now, the whole effect of our vast conquest will be lost."

Here was no instruction to destroy public property, or private supplies of potential military use. The destruction enjoined was not necessarily for military purposes, but was punitive—to "punish Forrest and the people"—such a policy as General Sherman denied when imputed to his own subsequent campaigns below Atlanta and in the Carolinas.

On June twenty-seventh, after nearly three weeks in front of the lines, Sherman made his great frontal attack on the Confederate position on the flanks and slopes of Kennesaw— to meet repulse, as had Grant at Cold Harbor. As fire swept through the underbrush, close in front of the Confederate breastworks, Lieutenant-Colonel W. H. Martin, of the First Arkansas, left his safe position, climbed the parapet before him, waving a handkerchief on a ramrod, and declared a quick and informal truce: "Get these wounded men away from the fire. We won't fire a gun till you do. Be quick." Confederate soldiers left their lines to help in the rescue work, and then returned to resume battle. The day ended, with little loss on the Confederate side, heavy loss among Sherman's men, and the lines just where they were before.

Once more Sherman moved to the right to pass around Johnston. By July second, his right was nearer Atlanta than was Johnston's left, with only a handful of cavalry and some two thousand Georgia state troops, hurriedly collected to defend the soil of Georgia, between him and the bridges over the Chatta- hoochee. With his flank and his vital river crossing protected only by such slight forces, there was nothing for Johnston to do but fall back again, cross the Chattahoochee, which he did on the night of the Fourth of July, and occupy the partially built entrenchments about Atlanta.

Three days' heavy skirmishing up and down the Chatta‹ hoochee convinced Sherman that nothing was to be gained by a direct attack on Johnston's strong bridge-head positions on the south bank. It was another case for flanking movement, to be made this time by the Union left, several miles up-stream from the railroad bridge, where there were fords practicable in July. On the seventh, Schofield's command made the first crossing; by the ninth, three pontoon bridges were laid at different points and the whole army was on the way over; by the tenth, Johnston was once more forced to abandon his position and fall back, this time to the last fortified lines about Atlanta.

There was much popular and official dissatisfaction with Johnston's long retreat, as he gave back repeatedly to face Sherman in his new positions. The officials of Georgia, especially, seeing slices of their territory given up and their principal inland city threatened, strenuously urged the removal of Johnston from command. President Davis, at length, sent his adviser, General Bragg, to visit Johnston and report on the situation, thereby reversing the situation of the winter when Johnston had been sent to report on Bragg's command of the same army. Bragg, after two days with the army, wired the President:

"He has not sought my advice, and it was not volunteered. I cannot learn that he has any more plans in the future than he has had in the past."

Whereupon the President, by wire, demanded, in effect, to know whether or not Atlanta was to be given up without a battle. Johnston's plan from the beginning had been to give battle after he had withdrawn to the neighborhood of his place of refuge in Atlanta, whenever and wherever he was able to catch Sherman off balance. That opportunity he was hoping to find now, when Sherman undertook to cross the valley of Peach Tree Creek, and advance against the town itself, but even while he was laying his plans for the fight he returned to President Davis' inquiry a reply that the President considered evasive—as it was. There was that old distrust be‹

tween two of the South's ablest leaders, whose great abilities were too much alike, in some ways, for them to harmonize.

On the evening of July seventeenth there came a wire from Richmond:

". . . as you have failed to arrest the advance of the enemy to the vicinity of Atlanta, and express no confidence that you can defeat or repel him, you are hereby relieved from command of the Army and Department of Tennessee, which you will immediately turn over to General Hood."

Turning over the command as directed, General Johnston telegraphed the Secretary of War:

"Your dispatch of yesterday received and obeyed. Command has been transferred to General Hood. As to the alleged cause of my removal, I assert that Sherman's army is much stronger, compared with that of Tennessee, than Grant's compared with that of Northern Virginia. Yet the enemy has been compelled to advance much more slowly to the vicinity of Atlanta than to that of Richmond and Petersburg, and penetrated much deeper into Virginia than into Georgia. Confident language by a military commander is not usually regarded as evidence of competence."

President Davis and General Johnston lived to be old men, and wrote books, each devoting much space and many words to the circumstances surrounding this transfer of command, and its wisdom or unwisdom. To the soldiers of the army, and to most of the officers, there was no doubt then or later that it was a mistake—a mistake to have made the change at all; to have unwittingly timed it just before what was planned for the deciding battle; and to have chosen as Johnston's successor Hood, rather than either of the other corps commanders, Hardee or A. P. Stewart.

Hardee, having graduated at West Point in 1839 and gone through the French cavalry school at Saumur, had first crossed into Mexico and fought there under Taylor, and afterward Scott. By the direction of Secretary of War Jefferson Davis, he had prepared *Hardee's Tactics; or, the United States Rifle*

and Infantry Tactics, 2 vols., and was the senior. The command had been offered to him in the December before, however,
and had been declined—a fact which, averred Hardee, was
not to be taken as meaning that he never would take it.

Stewart, "Old Straight" his men called him, was next in
age, though junior in rank, as he had just been made a
Lieutenant-General to take command of Polk's old corps. After
graduation from West Point in 1842, he returned to the
Academy to teach mathematics. Poor health forced him from
the Army to join the faculty of Cumberland University at
Lebanon, Tennessee, where the outbreak of war found him—a
middle-aged college professor, quiet and modest, who in his
youth had roomed at West Point with the self-assertive Longstreet and the bumptious John Pope.

Either of these corps commanders, believed Johnston, would
have been better than the one chosen—the brave and devoted
John B. Hood, a dozen years their junior, suffering from the
disabling of an arm at Gettysburg and the loss of a leg at
Chickamauga. A long, high, narrow head, deep-set eyes under
strong brows, a beard of patriarchal proportions—these features in the portraits of Hood make it impossible to realize
that he was but thirty-three years old when he became the
eighth and last of the full Generals of the Confederacy.

Most of the soldiers who look out at us from behind the
whiskers of Civil War portraiture were not old. Jackson and
Stuart, in spite of the venerable seeming of their beards, were
killed in their thirties, A. P. Hill when he was barely in his
fortieth year; Pat Cleburne, dead on the breastworks at Franklin,
was thirty-six. Most of the bearded leaders, Beauregard, Bragg,
Longstreet, Ewell, Forrest, Hardee, D. H. Hill, Early, among
them, were in their early forties. The time of the Civil War
was the day of the beard—a style followed by almost every
commander of note on either side except Samuel Cooper, the
New York man who became the Adjutant-General and ranking
officer of the Confederacy; and David Farragut, the Tennesseean
who became the first ranking Admiral of the Union Navy
Both were more than sixty years of age.

"I feel the weight of the responsibility so suddenly and unexpectedly devolved on me," said General Hood, in taking command—and it was a crushing weight. During the long retreat of one hundred miles from Dalton young Hood had become severely critical of what he considered the ruinous policy of the timid defensive. And now, with a troop strength of not more than half Sherman's and with the last ditch behind him, he was called on to demonstrate his own better way. He must fight, and with an army that, he believed, was greatly impaired in morale and fighting quality by its repeated stands behind breastworks, followed by retirements to evade flanking movements.

"Hood was known to us to be a 'fighter,'" wrote Sherman, "a graduate of West Point of the class of 1853, No. 44, of which class two of my army commanders, McPherson and Schofield, were No. 1 and No. 7. The character of a leader is a large factor in the game of war, and I confess I was pleased at this change."

At Atlanta there centered, in 1864, four railroads: the Western & Atlantic, along which Sherman had come down from the north; the Georgia, running east to Augusta; the West Point, southwest to Montgomery; and the Central, south and southeast to Macon and Savannah. Sherman's plan was not to attack the fortified lines—"I was willing to meet the enemy in open country, but not behind well-constructed parapets," he wrote—but to cut these rail lines and so force the evacuation of the city. To that end he began again, on July seventeenth, his movement by the left, toward the railroad east from Atlanta.

McPherson was on that line on the eighteenth, at a point thirteen miles east of the city, and the next day turned toward Atlanta, destroying the railroad as he came. Thomas, with the larger fraction of Sherman's army, crossed Peach Tree Creek on the nineteenth, and so, for a time, was separated by several miles and by the valley of the stream from the other wings.

It was Hood's opportunity to strike. An assault on Thomas' lines, ordered to be made at one o'clock in the afternoon of July twentieth, before formidable entrenchments could be got up, was delayed until four o'clock by confusion in getting into position—caused by Hardee's negligence, said Hood; by Hood's indefinite and incorrect orders and his absence from the field of battle, said Hardee. The assault was to be made by Stewart's corps on the left and Hardee's on the right, with Frank Cheatham, temporarily in command of Hood's old corps still farther to the right, to guard against the coming of McPherson from that flank. Stewart's corps attacked savagely. Hardee's men, reported Hood, accomplished nothing, got up against breastworks and "lay down." Hardee reported that the action of Hood in depriving him of Cleburne's fine division just as the attack was launched caused the failure. So began the first of a series of unfortunate misunderstandings, disagreements and controversies between General Hood and his subordinate commanders.

The battle, known as Peach Tree Creek, whatever the cause, was a decided check, with losses that could not be spared. Thomas completed his advance across the creek, connecting with Schofield and McPherson and filling up all the space across the north and east of Atlanta, in the angle between the Chattanooga and the Augusta Railroads, with McPherson's left south of the latter line.

Hood, on the twenty-first, determined on a "Chancellorsville" move. Stewart's corps and the state troops of whom there were now something more than five thousand, with G. W. Smith in command and Robert Toombs, who had resigned his Confederate commission, as chief of staff, were left to hold the lines facing north toward Thomas; Cheatham's corps, was to face east along the Augusta Railroad; while Hardee, with the strongest of the corps, was to make a wide swinging night march of fifteen miles and come in clear behind McPherson's left flank, and attack from the rear. As Hardee's men attacked, Cheatham was to take up the action, which was then to be carried along the Confederate line from right to left.

The conception was good, considering that an army which has but half the numbers of its enemy must take the risks. The execution failed. Hardee, said Hood, failed to get far enough out and struck McPherson's entrenched flank, instead of his open rear. More nearly what happened in this fight of July twenty-second, known as the Battle of Atlanta, was that two divisions of Dodge's corps, which had been held in reserve behind McPherson, were marched out to extend the left flank during the same night and morning on which Hardee was making his movement, and so, by pure chance, plugged the hole into which Hardee was driving.

In heavy battle, from noon to night, Hardee's men completely dispelled any idea that they would not fight, while Cheatham's men, somewhat delayed by uncertainties of the fight in their front, sallied out in the afternoon and made a sharp attack. There were heavy losses on both sides, including the brilliant young McPherson, of the Union army, and W. H. T. Walker, of the Confederate, but the end of the fighting saw Hood back in his lines and Sherman in his. The Confederate Army could not afford such days.

With the Confederate check of the twenty-second, the siege of Atlanta may be said to have begun. Sherman, with the city closely invested on the east, started his movement down the valley of the Chattahoochee to reach the West Point Railroad to Montgomery. On July twenty-eighth, southwest of the city, Hood sallied out of his fortified lines again, advancing down the Lick Skillet Road to Ezra Church, once more to meet repulse with heavy loss. The railroad to the southwest was broken, not only by Sherman's main column, but farther out by a cavalry command under Lovell Rousseau, Kentuckian who fought for the Union, which had raided southeast all the way from Decatur, Alabama, for that purpose.

From the battle of Ezra Church on July twenty-eighth, the siege settled down for a month—a pause interrupted only by the unsuccessful efforts of Sherman's cavalry to break the last line of railroad left to Hood, the Central road south to Macon. The expedition of Stoneman and McCook was dispersed and its leaders captured; another, under Kilpatrick, succeeded in getting on the road and doing some damage, which was enthusiastically reported to Sherman as a complete break-up, but almost before the report was made the whistle of Confederate engines operating over the line was heard. And all this while Sherman's own rail line had to be guarded from Confederate attack.

Wheeler, with four thousand five hundred of his cavalry, detached by Hood and sent around Sherman's army and back north along the railroad early in August, made a wide and sweeping raid which carried them clear beyond Chattanooga into the mountain valleys of Tennessee, to return through Alabama. The raid resulted in temporary damage to the railroad, including the burning of the Etowah River bridge, but no such break-up as would cause any serious delay in supplying the Union army. There were in Sherman's army no men more important, better organized or better equipped than the operating and repair forces of the United States Military Railroads. His rail line was well and heavily guarded, also.

The most effective security for the line, however, was the great expedition under A. J. Smith and Mower, slowly working their way down from Memphis through Mississippi, to "punish Forrest and the people," and to keep Forrest away from that railroad.

By July eleventh Smith was into Mississippi nearly as far as Okolona, where William Sooy Smith's expedition had met disaster early in the year. On that morning Lieutenant-General Stephen D. Lee, the department commander, came up and took command of the Confederate forces. Smith changed the direction of his march, at right angles, and started east, with Lee hanging on his flank and rear. After two days of skirmish fighting Smith found the position he was looking for, at the little village of Harrisburg, just west of Tupelo. It was a strong position, and defended by nearly twice the number which the Confederates could bring against it. Neither Lee nor Forrest wanted to battle Smith in such position, but Lee, needing his troops to repel other expeditions threatening his department, felt that he could no longer hold together even the little force that he had gathered to oppose Smith, and that the fight must be made at once.

On the morning of July fourteenth, while Sherman was arranging his forces south of the Chattahoochee, the attack was made—a frontal assault across open ground against breastworks. The very eager bravery which gave the attack its one chance of success defeated it. Before the whole line could be made ready one Kentucky brigade charged, and precipitated a piece-meal attack, which was repulsed in detail.

The affair was a source of much gratulation, especially as Forrest was wounded in the foot a day or so later, and reported dead of lockjaw, but there was something about it that made General Smith uneasy in the mind. That night he burned Harrisburg and started on his retreat to Memphis. He left so hurriedly that he abandoned two hundred and fifty of his seriously wounded, their wounds undressed, to be found by the Confederates in Tupelo, a ghastly sight with open wounds fly-blown and festering. As Smith retreated the Confederate forces, with Forrest again in command, harassed his movements. It was a strange spectacle, an army which had just won a pitched battle drawing back from an enemy of half its own size which it had just beaten. When the report reached him, Sherman, who had been much relieved at the news of the scotching of Forrest, was not satisfied with the final result. Smith thought that his victory was not appreciated, and said as much to Sherman, through Washburn, the district commander, explaining that he had gone back to Memphis only to get supplies.

Sherman at once ordered Smith out again, with an even larger and more elaborate expedition. "He must keep after him till recalled by me or General Grant," he wrote, "and if Forrest goes toward Tennessee, General Smith must follow him. . . . It is of vital importance that Forrest does not go to Tennessee."

CHAPTER XXX

Victory Just in Time

IN THE August of 1864, before plain and unmistakable victory had come as a political portent, and when, indeed, to the unknowing it appeared that the vast concerted effort to crush the South on all fronts was failing of its purpose; with Grant, for all his hammering, apparently as far from Richmond as ever; with Sherman's main armies at pause before Atlanta, and his cavalry getting itself lost in middle Georgia; with Sheridan, who was to have shooed away Early's buzzing about Washington, and cleaned out the Valley, pushed back against the Potomac; with Forrest, defending Mississippi by raiding into Memphis—with such a military situation, and with formidable political opposition, within and without his party, President Lincoln had reason for doubt of the success of the Union cause, for political reasons, if not military.

"This morning, as for some days past," he wrote on August twenty-third, "it seems exceedingly probable that this administration will not be re-elected. Then it will be my duty to so cooperate with the new President-elect as to save the Union between the election and the inauguration, as he will have secured his election on such ground that he cannot possibly save it afterwards."

General Grant was still about Petersburg trying to find the hole in Lee's armor. One most ambitious attempt, the explosion of a great mine under Elliott's Salient in the Confederate lines on July thirtieth, had brought on the battle of "The Crater"— a great hole one hundred and seventy feet long, sixty feet wide, thirty feet deep, filled with dust from the explosion, with tumbled and broken blocks of clay, with a scattering of broken guns and carriages, and men blown up and buried. Into this Crater rushed a Union division, to be supported by a flanking division on either side. The defenders of the trench line, after momentary surprise, promptly and effectively anticipated the modern tactics for such a situation, pulled back their lines, faced inward toward the break and opened fire on the mass of men struggling to cross the great hole and come up into the Confederate trenches.

More troops were pressed forward by the Union commanders, jamming the hole worse than ever, and making it impossible for Confederate fire to miss. Finally, after two hours of the struggle, Ferrero's division of colored troops were sent into the Crater to reenforce Burnside's three white divisions already in and about the hole. The colored division—which had been intended to lead the assault, in the original plans, and had been specially drilled for that—did make its way around the edges of the Crater, and reached the Confederate lines beyond, to be driven back by the concentrated fire from front and flanks, and thrown for refuge among the disorganized men jammed into the Crater. And there they stayed, all or parts of four divisions, crammed into a hole whose every approach was commanded by Confederate fire.

Burnside planned to leave them there until night, when they could be withdrawn, but staunch William Mahone, organizer of the Confederate defense, had other plans. In the afternoon of that long hot day the Confederates advanced to the attack, and drove the crowded mass before them, at the point of the bayonet, out of the Crater and back to their own lines. The mine that made the Crater had taken more than a month of anxious, expectant labor. On it great hopes had been pinned. Its results were a huge hole in the ground and a loss of nearly four thousand men for the Union armies.

During the month that the Crater mine was being made ready there had been excitement in Washington. "Old Jube" Early, when he had finished driving Hunter's Lynchburg raid back into West Virginia, turned the head of his column down the Shenandoah, back over the old familiar track of the Valley Pike. There was a two-day halt at Staunton to lighten weight for the dash toward Washington, and to try to get up some

shoes, which did not come until after the march north had
started, with nearly half the men barefoot. On the Fourth of
July Early's men were at the Potomac once more; on the fifth
and the sixth they crossed above Harper's Ferry, demonstrated
against that place and turned east to march by the old fields
of Antietam and Boonsboro, through the passes of South Mountain and into Frederick City, with its memories of the first
"invasion," when the whole army was there, at the crest of
the Confederate tide in the summer of 1862.

It had been a hard march on the barefooted men, but there
were still eight thousand muskets in line. At the Monocacy,
east of Frederick, Major-General Lew Wallace appeared with
a force gathered from the garrisons of Washington and Baltimore. On July ninth Early's men crossed the river, flanked
Wallace and drove him back. Two days later they were in
the suburbs of the capital itself, advancing from the north down
the Seventh Street pike past Silver Springs.

Early's instructions had been to "threaten Washington,"
not to take it. That was all he could have done, for as he
came into sight of the town, with the recently completed dome
of the Capitol looming ahead, the Sixth Corps, detached from
Grant's army and sent back for the purpose, and the Nineteenth
Corps, which had just arrived by sea from New Orleans, were
filing into the formidable ring of forts which surrounded the
city. The night of the eleventh and all day of the twelfth
Early "threatened," and that night took up his march back to
Virginia, unmolested by any serious pursuit. On the morning
of July fourteenth, he crossed the Potomac east of the Blue
Ridge, and marched over the ridge and on into the Valley, to
remain for a season.

On July twenty-fourth Union forces under Crook and
Averell came up with him at Kernstown, to meet smashing
defeat and to withdraw. McCausland, commanding Early's
cavalry, followed their withdrawal, crossed the Potomac again,
rode for Chambersburg, the first considerable town in Pennsylvania, captured the place and burned it—an act which aroused
great resentment in the North, and no little condemnation in

the South, although it was, in its intent, but a reprisal for the wanton burning of private homes by Hunter on his raid up the valley to Lexington and Lynchburg. The Colonel of McCausland's leading regiment, William E. Peters, afterward to serve for nearly half a century as a professor in Virginia universities, when ordered to fire the court-house and other buildings in the town firmly refused and was placed in arrest for disobedience of orders—an arrest from which he was afterward released without the formality of trial.

Early remained in the lower Valley through the rest of July, and until the second week in August. On the seventh of that month, President Lincoln and General Grant sent to the Valley the rising star of the Union armies, young Phil Sheridan, with large reenforcements and with orders to dispose of Early and make it impossible for the Confederates again to use the Valley as a "covered way" to advance against the capital. Sheridan, admonished by his superiors to do nothing rash, started off cautiously. The very size of his force, however, forced Early to withdraw slowly as far as Fisher's Hill, near the north end of bold Massanutten, the mountain which divides the middle Valley into narrow halves. In that neighborhood General Early received reenforcements from Lee, Kershaw's infantry and the cavalry of Fitz Lee, and it was Sheridan's turn to retire. Finally, by August seventeenth, Sheridan had been pushed to and across the Potomac, and "Old Jube" and his men, on August seventeenth, had possession of the lower Valley once more, with troops posted about Winchester, obstructing the Baltimore & Ohio Railroad and the Potomac Canal, and threatening Maryland and Pennsylvania. And there, for one solid month, they stayed.

During the month after the miscarriage of the attack at the Crater, General Grant tried a new tack at Petersburg. The Weldon Railroad, almost due south from the town, was its direct connection with the Carolinas and Georgia. In mid-August, after throwing a force back across to the north side of the James to threaten Richmond as a demonstration, General Grant dispatched a heavy expedition against this line. From the eighteenth to the twenty-first there was sharp fighting along the Jerusalem Plank Road, southeast of the town, and about Globe Tavern, a station on the railroad to the south. Union local successes were gained, at a loss of more than four thousand men—enough to have distinguished the affair as a great battle earlier in the war. During the following week the movement against the Weldon road was extended to the southward, about Reams' Station, where the Confederates, with light losses, drove off a Union attack, with a loss of nearly three thousand men.

And all this while, the campaign for the election of a President of the United States was going on in the North.

The Democrats of the North had nominated General Mc-Clellan, "Little Mac," the old idol of the Army of the Potomac, who, so many believed, had been treated most shabbily by the Lincoln Government. It was easy for them to shake their heads over the management of affairs by that government. Here it was late August. The Great Hammerer had been pounding away since early May, with losses of more than eighty thousand men by now, and still he was not so close to Richmond as the Democratic nominee and his army had been in 1862—and there was the crack of Early's rifles, in ear-shot of the Capitol itself. And in the West, there was Sherman, with a hundred thousand men, way down in Georgia, most precariously dependent for ammunition and daily bread on nearly five hundred miles of exposed single-track railroad, and Atlanta still uncaptured.

That was the surface picture which campaign orators could paint, and there was about it enough truth to give the President the utmost concern. There were under the surface facts which showed that the shell of the South was crumbling, that its wasting armies were not being recruited and could not be, that victory was surely coming if the will of the North to war would but hold out. But these facts were not the shining and dramatic victory which was so needed for its political effect—and there was always the anxious possibility that Sherman's audacious enterprise might end in disaster and starving retreat, if ever the Confederate Government should come to realize what might be done by seriously concentrating on his life-line of steel rails.

Sherman himself realized, far better than did the government at Richmond, what might be done, and had a more just appreciation of the commander who could best do it. That commander he proposed to keep busy elsewhere than in the neighborhood of his railroad line.

Early in August, while the main Union army in the West was holding its lines about Atlanta and attempting to cut Hood off from the south, A. J. Smith and Mower started from Memphis again, under Sherman's peremptory orders to follow Forrest, with an expedition of seventeen thousand men of all arms. They followed the Memphis & Charleston Railroad, which the army had put in running order again, eastward to Grand Junction, and there turned south along the Mississippi Central, repairing the line after them as they went. This time they were not going to get caught out without supplies, and they intended to hold the country they occupied.

In front of them was Forrest, going about his duties as a dashing cavalry commander in an old farm buggy, with his wounded foot carried on a rack projecting over the dash-board. He had less than five thousand cavalry, the force with which three invasions had been turned back. To turn this one back by any ordinary means, was obviously beyond their powers, but Forrest was no ordinary commander.

Leaving half his force under Chalmers to demonstrate before Smith, he took two thousand picked men, gathered them quietly in the dusk of August eighteenth and set out from the little college town of Oxford, on a ride of a hundred miles to Memphis. At three in the morning of the twenty-first he was in the outskirts of the city with fifteen hundred of the men with whom he had started.

Memphis had been securely held by Union forces for more than two years. It had acquired, through the presence of large numbers of officers and soldiers, of sutlers, army contractors, and speculators in cotton or in government vouchers and pay claims, something of the air of a northern center of business. New York houses, and those of St. Louis, Chicago, Pittsburgh and Indianapolis, filled the newspaper columns with announce-ments of their Memphis branches or offices, or with advertise-ments of sutlers' goods, or Chesapeake oysters from Baltimore, of Madeira, or Sherry, of Moselle or Rhenish wines, of French brandy or cognac, of cigars from Havana, and of coffee— especially coffee.

The city seemed perfectly secure from interruption of all this pleasant and lucrative commerce, especially when the cor-respondent of the Memphis *Review* accompanying the Smith expedition reported the defeat of the "rebels 10,000 strong," with "The Rout Complete, Our Cavalry Pursuing." The *Review* containing this dispatch was printed on the evening of Saturday, August twentieth. "Sunday, with its sacred duties, was about dawning upon us," reported the *Review* in its next issue, "and unhaunted by the calls of a business day all were resting in the folds of Morpheus, when, stealing through the deep fog, about one thousand rebels fell upon our soldiers and the roar of musketry startled our citizens from oblivion." Forrest was in the town.

The immediate object of the raid, the capture of the three Union Generals known to be in Memphis, failed, although the uniform of one who escaped in what the reporter of the *Review* would doubtless have called his "nocturnal habiliments" was nabbed. The ultimate effect on the imaginations and apprehen-sions of the Union commanders, however, was just what Forrest expected. Smith's column was recalled to protect his base, and immediately fell back to Memphis, after burning Oxford.

Forrest, for the fourth time that year, had managed to turn back an invasion of Mississippi, but Sherman also had gained his object. Forrest was being kept busy and off his rail line, a result whose importance to Sherman's great plans may be judged from his exasperated dispatch to Secretary Stanton that he was ordering Smith and Mower to "go out and follow For-rest to the death, if it costs ten thousand lives and breaks the Treasury. There never will be peace in Tennessee until Forrest is dead!"

President Lincoln's note of deep discouragement was penned

on August twenty-third. On the twenty-fifth Sherman began the last of his long series of movements against Atlanta, to end this time only with the evacuation and surrender of that Confederate nerve center, in time to save the election of which Mr. Lincoln so nearly despaired. When Sherman moved, there came a sudden end to the bombardment which had been going on intermittently for more than a month; the old men, women and children might safely come out of their little underground burrows and bomb proofs; the lines immediately about the city were vacated. One corps was left, entrenched across the Western & Atlantic Railroad. With the rest, Sherman started another grand wheel, to pass to the southwest of the city and strike in on the Central Railroad, to Macon, in the neighborhood of Jonesboro twenty-two miles south of Atlanta.

The railroad south from Atlanta runs on the ridge dividing the headwaters of the Flint River from those of the Ocmulgee. Hood pushed his troops down the railroad, Hardee in the lead, to meet the menace from the west across the Valley of the Flint. Stephen D. Lee, who had been transferred from his department command in Mississippi to take Hood's old corps, followed. The rest of the army was still about Atlanta. The plan for the battle of August thirty-first was that Hardee should face westward from Jonesboro and "drive the enemy, at all hazards, into Flint River, in their rear"; that in the event of success Lee's force was to draw back to Rough and Ready, a station on the railroad half-way between Jonesboro and Atlanta, and there make contact with Stewart's corps and the state troops, the whole to move forward on the morning of September first down the Valley of the Flint, from the north, while Hardee drove in from the east.

Hardee's attack on the afternoon of the last day of August, the Battle of Jonesboro, an attack against breastworks, was a failure. Feebly made, said Hood, although, in truth, it was an impossible task, the old story of an inferior force going against entrenchments. The same force, on the next day, from behind their own breastworks, repulsed Sherman's advance on Jonesboro Regardless of cause, the repulse of Hardee at Jonesboro ended any hope of saving Atlanta. Hood's problem now was to march out, pass across the front of Sherman's victorious army, and reestablish himself somewhere on the railroad below Jonesboro—a problem that was successfully solved by retreat to Lovejoy's Station, protected by the battle fronts of the corps of Lee and Hardee. Sherman's first intimation of the evacuation of the city was the sound of the explosions of ordnance and ammunition that could not be carried away, about two o'clock in the morning of September second. That day Sherman's troops occupied the city; the Union had its clear and indisputable victory that all men might see.

The anxious August through which Mr. Lincoln had just passed had been lightened by one other victory, that of Farragut and his ships in lower Mobile Bay—a victory of no immediate consequence, except that it more effectively closed the last but one of the major ports of the Confederacy, but a fight whose bold and picturesque features heartened the North.

Farragut, after months of weary tossing on the Gulf off the entrance of Mobile, secured a reenforcement of iron-clad monitors in July and immediately planned his long deferred movement to cross the bar, silence the forts, with the cooperation of the army, and take up his position in the bay. On the morning of August fifth the attack was made with thirteen wooden ships and four iron-clad monitors. In command was Farragut, on his famous old wooden *Hartford*, with, as his chief of staff, Fleet-Captain Percival Drayton, the courageous South Carolinian whose first duty, as he saw it, was to the Union.

Ashore, on the right as the ships steamed in, was Fort Morgan, one of the old-styled brick casemated works, with ports for three tiers of guns; on the left, at the end of Dauphine Island and too far away to take any effective part in the naval battle, was the smaller Fort Gaines. Opposite Fort Morgan were torpedoes, home-made affairs of the sort that the Confederates used in their harbor defenses, beer-kegs or glass demijohns, tin cones, filled with powder, to be exploded on contact by fulminate in priming tubes, or perhaps by percussion caps.

Above the torpedoes, in the bay, was the Confederate naval

force, three improvised wooden gunboats, and the ram *Tennessee*, most powerful of Confederate ironclads. The *Tennessee* had been built during the winter and spring in the Alabama River, above Selma, of pine and oak cut from near-by forests; she was plated with iron rolled in the Confederate mills in Atlanta; armed with six guns cast at the Selma foundries, under the superintendence of Commander Catesby ap Roger Jones, the same who had armed the *Virginia*, first of ironclads; and engined with puny affairs taken from a Mississippi River steamboat, converted to turn a propeller instead of a paddle wheel, and capable of driving her at only six knots an hour in still water. She was, for all that, a formidable ship, and she was commanded by old Admiral Franklin Buchanan, the same who had first taken the *Virginia*, which had once been the *Merrimac*, into battle at Hampton Roads.

As Farragut's vessels steamed in, raked by the guns of Fort Morgan, the *Tecumseh*, one of his monitors in the lead, struck a torpedo and went down. The *Brooklyn*, leading ship of the wooden battle line, halted. Old Farragut, lashed to the rigging in his *Hartford*, swung past the *Brooklyn*, and ordered full steam ahead, ram or no ram, and "Damn the torpedoes!"

Above the torpedo obstructions came down the little Confederate fleet to engage the whole Union armada. The gunboats were soon captured or driven out of action. Only the *Tennessee* remained. Once she charged the Union line of battle, pouring in shot and receiving them on her iron turtle-back sides. Again she turned and followed back up the bay, to close with the whole group, ships-of-war and iron-clad monitors alike—a terrific battle in which her armor served her as well as her engines served her badly, until, after an hour or more of ramming and striking, with her funnel shot away, the draft of her engines down to where she could not keep up steam, and her rudder chains broken, she drifted helplessly. The hopeless battle ended with her surrender. Buchanan, wounded, and his officers and men were taken to the Union naval base at Pensacola.

On the next day the navy cooperated with the troops under

Gordon Granger, landed on Dauphine Island, in the reduction of Fort Gaines, to be followed by a transfer of forces across the mouth of the bay to Fort Morgan, the investment of that post, and its surrender on August twenty-third, after a three-week siege. The city of Mobile itself, with its rail lines running north into Mississippi and northeast to Montgomery, was safe behind a barricade of piles driven into the narrow Mobile River. It was garrisoned by troops under Major-General Dabney H. Maury, nephew of Commodore Matthew Fontaine Maury, father of the science of oceanography, discoverer of the Gulf Stream, once the great scientific light of the United States Navy and now, while his nephew was holding the lines about Mobile, in Europe as one of the three naval commissioners through whose zeal and efforts the Confederacy was able to secure the ships that became her cruisers, and her only mobile Navy.

In the summer of 1864, however, that resource of the Confederacy was failing. It was become more and more difficult for the naval commissioners, Commodore Samuel Barron in Paris, Commander Maury and Captain James D. Bulloch in London, to contract for ships, either armored or unarmored, and those that were already at sea were giving out. The *Nashville*, which was Confederate built, had been sunk on a mud-flat in Ossabaw Sound the year before; the *Florida*, again on cruise after her long tie-up in Brest, was soon to come to her end in a Brazilian harbor in October of 1864; the *Georgia*, which had gone out in April of 1863 to cruise the North Atlantic, lacking sail-power to supplement the coal that was so difficult for a Confederate cruiser to get, had finally put into Liverpool in May, 1864, and been disposed of.

At that moment, besides the *Florida*, but one other Confederate cruiser kept the seas, the famous *Alabama*, which even then was nearing Europe after a cruise of nearly two years which had well-nigh destroyed the carrying trade in United States bottoms. It had taken her into the Atlantic, the Gulf of Mexico, the Caribbean Sea, south to the Cape of Good Hope, across the Indian Ocean to the China Sea and back through the Malacca

Straits to the Arabian Sea and the Mozambique Channel, around the Cape once more, and now north along the Brazilian coast, to strike a long diagonal across the North Atlantic to the English Channel.

On June 11, 1864, Semmes sailed his battered and creaking ship into the port of Cherbourg, to ask hospitality and repair at the Imperial docks there. While he waited advices from the government at Paris as to what was to be done, the United States ship of war *Kearsarge* steamed into the port, remained a day and left. Semmes communicated to Captain Winslow, of the *Kearsarge*, his intention to come out and fight him as soon as necessary arrangements could be made. Captain Winslow courteously waited for the fight.

On Sunday morning, June 19, 1864, the *Alabama* went out past the heights about Cherbourg, lined with spectators come to see the battle. The two ships came on parallel courses, and then, steaming slowly around each other in seven complete circles, starboard broadsides on, firing into each other at short range, they drifted westward with the current. The *Alabama* opened with shell, to find that it dropped harmlessly from the sides of the *Kearsarge*. Solid shot was tried, when it was discovered that the *Kearsarge*, under deal boxing on the sides, had chain-armor covering her more vulnerable spots. That protection, together with the inferior ammunition of the *Alabama*, which had deteriorated during her long stay at sea, and the excellent handling and gunnery of the *Kearsarge*, brought the spectacular Sunday morning battle to an end with the sinking of the graceful *Alabama*, stern foremost. The English yacht *Deerhound*, two French pilot-boats and boats from the *Kearsarge* rescued the crew.

On August sixth, another Confederate cruiser slipped out from Wilmington, the *Tallahassee*, a converted blockade-runner. Commanded by the enterprising John Taylor Wood, she went up along the North Atlantic seaboard as far as Halifax, hovered off the port of New York, eluded the cruisers sent out to capture her, and made her way back into Wilmington, having taken and destroyed more than thirty vessels, mostly small.

But two other Confederate cruisers were to take the sea, be-fore the end, the *Shenandoah*, originally a merchant vessel built for the London-Bombay trade, armed and equipped at Madeira in the same manner as the *Alabama*, and dispatched in October for the Pacific, to attack northern commerce in those seas, from Australia to the Behring Strait; and the *Stonewall*, commissioned in the English Channel January 30, 1865, to hold the sea until she was given up in Havana in mid-May, after the war was over.

Against these gallant but almost futile efforts of the Confederacy to keep the seas, the United States opposed its great and growing Navy, maintaining, from the bases which it had established all along the southern coasts, its relentless, strangling blockade.

That the end was near must have been seen by all save the infatuated—but the Confederacy fought on, and even, for one last despairing effort, took the offensive and once more marched north.

CHAPTER XXXI

CONFLICT AND CONFUSION

BY THE autumn of 1864, through the fire of more than three years of conflict, the old ideas with which young men had gone to war in 1861 were burned out. War was no longer a matter of martial glory to be won in brilliant campaigns, a chivalric game to be played intermittently according to knightly notions. It had become a grim business, a life-struggle between peoples, unceasing, practical, hard—in a word, modern.

President Lincoln had found in the tenacious Grant and the soundly imaginative Sherman the right combination to make this modern sort of war. Through that last dreadful winter of hopeless war, Grant, with unshakeable grip, was at the throat of the Confederacy, while Sherman's army, whose Atlanta campaign had broken its back, flowed through its body.

General Grant, settled solidly in his entrenched lines before Petersburg, with a force which, in spite of the wastage of the campaign, of furloughs, and of demands for troops in Washington, was kept up to double the strength of that of Lee, was not a figure according to the romantic tradition of knighthood, but his method made to shorten the war, and whatever shortened a war wherein deaths by disease outnumbered deaths in battle was, in the long run, a mercy to both sides.

City Point, the deep-water base on the James through which the replacements, reenforcements, ammunition, supplies and equipment of this great force flowed, became the "busiest place in the United States." To its wharves came craft of every description, bringing everything the great army could need; from it, by mid-September, ran a military railroad to carry these supplies to the entrenched line of investment, a line which ran from the Chickahominy on the north, across the James and the Appomattox, past Petersburg and across the Weldon Railroad south of the town.

Petersburg, which had jealously protected the interests of its teamsters by refusing to permit the joining of the ends of the railroads entering the town from the north and the south, found a new use for teamsters when Union armies closed the Weldon Railroad late in August. Supplies from the south, brought up as far as possible by rail, were hauled by wagon into Petersburg by a round-about and precarious way, to the west of the railroad. Farther to the west, in spite of occasional cavalry interruptions, the Confederacy still held the South Side Railroad which reached Lynchburg and Danville, and connected with the South.

To seize and close this line, and so to complete the investment of the city, General Grant began late in October the extension of his lines around to the south of Petersburg and so on to the west, toward Hatcher's Run and the Boydton Plank Road. Through the fall and winter this extension was a slow and intermittent movement, partly because of the heavy detachments from Grant's army to the Army of the Shenandoah, the overwhelming force with which Sheridan moved in mid-September to relieve Washington of the threat of Jubal Early's continued presence in the lower Valley, to recover the use of the Baltimore & Ohio Railroad and, having done those things, to harry and desolate the Valley so that no Confederate force could use it again.

To oppose Sheridan's army of about fifty thousand men, Early had four small divisions of infantry, a little cavalry and artillery, less than twenty thousand all told. They were scattered through the pleasant towns in the wide lower reaches of the Valley. Against the headquarters town of Winchester, Sheridan sent his heavy columns on the morning of September nineteenth. The result was to have been foreseen, except that the Confederates, by hard marching to the place of concentration and hard fighting after they were there, managed to inflict on the attackers a loss of five thousand men, mostly in killed and wounded. Finally, when Union cavalry burst through on the Confederate left flank, a hasty retreat began, covered by Ramseur's division drawn up across the pike—the old Valley Pike, pathway of the armies, up which the Confederates now marched for the last time.

Early's men retreated—it was not far from a rout—as far as Fisher's Hill, in the narrow valley west of the Massanutten Mountain, whose mass separates the forks of the Shenandoah and divides the middle Valley. There they made a stand, formed line of battle and awaited the onslaught of Sheridan's overwhelming army. Three days later, on September twenty-second, the attack came. Again the Confederate line was flanked on the left, and once more it was driven along the Pike, up the Valley to Woodstock and on to New Market. There Early left the Pike, turned east to Jackson's old camp ground at the foot of the Blue Ridge, and made a stand to await reenforcements.

Sheridan, pursuing no farther, turned to the latter part of his mission, the devastation of the Valley. From Staunton back to Winchester his great army marched, with its cavalry spread wide across the Valley, from wall to wall, burning and destroying not only the granaries, the hay-stacks, the corn in the shock, and all else that might be useful to an army, but also the houses, the barns, the agricultural implements with which to make the next crop, the mills to grind the corn, everything that was or might be useful to the Confederates. The tale of the ravishing of that fair valley is best told in the boast that even a crow flying across would find it needful to carry his rations with him.

As Sheridan fell back, busy in his work of destruction, Early, to whom Kershaw's division and some artillery had come as reenforcements, followed closely behind. Sheridan halted and camped at Cedar Creek, just below the bold northern end of the Massanutten Mountain, supposed to be impassable for troops. There, in the security of a strong position, his men rested, while their General went to Washington to confer with the Secretary of War and General Halleck about future plans.

John B. Gordon, commanding one of Early's brigades, was not what was usually called, in those days, an "educated soldier," but he was a most aggressive one. From the bold headland of Massanutten he saw Sheridan's camps spread out below him in the Valley, and saw that their left flank was weak and could be turned. Across the mountain he marked out a rough track over which troops could, with the utmost effort, be moved. To General Early he urged his plan, and from him secured approval. He was given three divisions, his own and those of Ramseur and Pegram, with which to cross the mountain and attack the Union flank and rear, while Kershaw and Wharton were to attack the front. The attack was to be made just at daybreak of October nineteenth.

Through the night before, quietly and secretly, the flanking column filed over the steep mountain. Gordon and Stephen Ramseur, young North Carolina Major-General, sat on a bluff overlooking the movement, through the night. Ramseur had married since the war began; to him had been born a daughter, whom he had never seen. He talked that night of the daughter, and of the young mother, and of his deep longing for a pause that he might go home. As dawn approached he rose and started to his place in the battle line. "Well, Gordon," he remarked quietly and with perfect assurance, "I shall get my furlough to-day." Before the battle was old he had it, a furlough for ever.

The death of the inspiring Ramseur, however, did not slacken the charge of his division, nor that of the other Confederate flanking forces. Their attack was irresistible, sweeping the field of their surprised and routed enemies, until but one of the Union corps held its organization and showed resistance. And then, for reasons that are matters of controversy, the rushing Confederate advance halted and for hours rested on its arms. "Ordered by Early," say subordinates. "Silly story. Bad conduct of the troops and a propensity for plundering in the captured camps," replies the General. "Nothing of the sort," retort the men who were with the leading divisions.

Whatever the cause the delay of hours was fatal, for it was during those hours that Sheridan, on his black horse, made the ride from "Winchester, twenty miles away" which became the subject of poetry and declamation; rallied the broken and fleeing elements as he came; and brought them back into battle, to turn the tables on Early, just as night fell. The Confederates, driven from the field, lost most of their artillery, much of their train, many prisoners who could not be spared.

The last of the Valley campaigns, so different from that first one in the long-ago spring of 1862, was ended. There was some small skirmishing through the winter, until the spring of 1865 when the most of both armies were to be found in the last heavy fighting about Petersburg. Except for the constant wearing losses of that siege, the major operations of the last winter of the war were to be fought, and marched, in the lower South and in the West.

Sherman, safely in Atlanta early in September, drew his troops back into entrenched lines, began the longed-for accumulation of supplies, considered what he might do and where he might go, and left the next move up to Hood.

That General, encamped thirty miles south of Atlanta, immediately wired Richmond asking for reenforcements, without which he felt that he could not again engage Sherman from the front. "Every effort has been made to bring forward reserves, militia and detailed men for the purpose," answered President Davis. "No other resource remains." There was no prospect of reenforcement for Hood from Confederate sources, then, while at the same time he was to lose his Georgia state troops, whom Governor Brown, by proclamation, withdrew from his command and granted blanket furloughs "to return to their homes and look for a time after important interests"—furloughs from which the Confederate Government was never able to recall these state troops.

With Governor Brown's action, and the bitter quarrel which ensued, there flared up, openly and never again to be downed, the conflict between the authority of the states and of the Confederate States. From the beginning, in the theory of the sovereignty of the states, the new government had carried within itself the seeds of destruction, and now, with disasters crowding, disintegration began.

There had been premonitions of the conflict as early as the summer of 1861, when the new Confederate Government,

charged with the defense of the whole, needing arms and equip-
ments for willing recruits and having nothing itself, turned to
the states for their supply—to find, in most instances, that each
state government, fearing invasion and anxious about its own
local self-defense, was not willing to give up to the general
armies of the Confederacy the rifles it had. Albert Sidney
Johnston at Bowling Green, concealing his weakness from the
world, needing men and especially arms for the men he might
get, made his appeal not so much to the War Department at
Richmond as to the Governors of the Southern States whose
advanced frontier he was guarding, and made it, for the most
part, in vain. Men were wasted by the thousands in armed local
defense forces, while other men, in the main armies, were without arms.

The Conscription Act of the spring of 1862, which put under
the government at Richmond all men of military age, with
certain exemptions, ended that situation for a time, but it
introduced another conflict between the jealous states and the
new nation they had created. It was an unnecessary law, said
the objectors, and it stifled the volunteer spirit which would
keep the armies of the Confederacy filled. It put too much
power in the hands of the President, said the logical state's
rights extremists, some of whom, at least, had conceived the
darkling suspicion that Jefferson Davis was aiming at auto-
cratic power, perhaps through the use of "his Janissaries, the
regular army." The power of conscription in the Confederate
States, moreover, was destructive of the state militia, and might
even, it was feared, destroy the state governments by dragging
their personnel into the Confederate armies.

To men entertaining such views of the Confederacy and its
President, resistance to the encroachments of that government
on the rights and reserved powers of the states became a sacred
constitutional duty. This resistance expressed itself in two
major ways: by the passage of state exemption laws, under
which all manner of petty minor officials, justices of the peace,
deputy sheriffs or clerks, policemen, even notary publics, were
declared necessary to the operation of the state's civil govern-

ment and so exempt from military service except in the state's own militia, and by stern, or even frenzied, resistance to the passage by Congress of Acts declaring a public emergency and authorizing the suspension of the writ of *habeas corpus*.

A notion about the Confederacy widely held, and often expressed, is that it early became and remained a military despotism in which all freedom of discussion or expression of opinion unfavorable to the government was sternly suppressed. The tenacity, and the success, with which the opponents of the government resisted its efforts to suspend the writ of *habeas corpus* shows the error of such notions, if any proof other than the unrebuked diatribes of the opposition newspapers were needed. The government constantly sought to secure passage of laws authorizing the suspension of the writ, but with all its efforts was able to secure such statutes for limited times only, and for a total of less than sixteen months during the four years of the struggle. Through the whole of the critical year 1863, with its great battles and disasters, and from August 1, 1864, to the end, the constitutional guaranties of the writ were in full force.

There were judges in almost every state to whom the war-weary soldier could apply for release from his conscripted service, and secure it on grounds sometimes so flimsy as to be fantastic—as in the case of the two Virginia soldiers who put themselves within the class of the "exempts" by securing contracts as carriers of the mail at an annual stipend of one cent in one case, and of one-fourth of that amount in the other, and so secured their release from the army by the writ of *habeas corpus*. There were judges, toward the end, who protected actual deserters from the armies by the cover of the great old common law writ. And constitutional bigots, while the house burned, screamed imprecations upon the firemen who sought to extinguish the blaze except by rule and rote. "Centralized despotism" they abhorred, whether at Washington or at Richmond.

It so happened that just as Governor Brown was furloughing all his Georgia state troops, the Confederate Secretary of War requisitioned them for the campaign against Sherman's rear planned by Hood. The two documents crossed each other in the mails between Georgia and Richmond. Governor Brown, receiving the letter of the Secretary of War just after the issue of his own proclamation, was roused to wrath. He demanded that the Confederate Government reenforce Hood's army for the defense of Georgia, or, failing that, threatened to recall the troops of his state from Virginia, and to command "all the sons of Georgia to return to their own State and within her own limits to rally round her glorious flag."

The Governor of Georgia achieved a considerable degree of distinction by the vigor, not to say violence, of his resistance to Confederate "encroachments," but his attitude, in fact, represented nothing more than the logical extreme of the Confederate doctrine of state sovereignty. While he went farther in action than any of the others, he was not alone. The theory found support for various causes, and in varying degrees, with Rhett of South Carolina and his son, editor of the *Mercury* at Charleston; with Governor Zebulon Vance, of North Carolina, who proposed to use North Carolina resources to supply North Carolina troops, and none other; with Clark, the Governor of Mr. Davis' own state, and with Henry S. Foote, who had long been Mr. Davis' bitter opponent in the politics of Mississippi, and now as a Confederate Congressman from Tennessee, was one of his most venomous critics; above all, with the "Georgia group"— Alexander Stephens, whose accuracy of thought and honesty of purpose were beyond question, but whose fine mind was like a powerful engine working perfectly in a vacuum of theories untouched of fact; Linton Stephens, his adoring younger brother; generous, hearty Bob Toombs, who had tried both the civil and military arms of the Confederate Government, and had come back to his beloved Georgia.

To Governor Brown, Georgia was his country; its direct defense on its own soil, his chief obligation; the maintenance of a government at Richmond, with the help of Georgia rifles in far-off Virginia, merely secondary—a local point of view which affected many another leader. Even of Robert E. Lee, perfect in his subordination to the civil government of the Confederate

States, it might be said with much truth that the country he defended was Virginia.

So many and such difficult problems were pressing in Georgia that President Davis left his capital and made a hurried trip to that state, to attempt to compose the difficulties with the state government, to inspect Hood's army and to consult about the future operations of that force.

General Sherman, meanwhile, was busying himself with converting Atlanta into a fortress, pure and simple. To do that, and to relieve the army of the necessity of policing and supplying them, he ordered all non-combatants to leave the city, with the choice of going North or South. There was a truce between the armies for ten days while this pitiful exodus was under way. Those families who elected to go South were moved by the Union troops as far as Rough and Ready, bringing with them such clothing and bedding as they could carry. There they were taken in charge by specially detailed guards from Hood's army and transferred across the fifteen-mile gap in the railroad to Lovejoy's, and passed on within the southern lines.

By the time the truce ended General Hood had determined on his next operation—to swing around Atlanta to the west, pass north and attack Sherman's communications, attempt to draw him back into the mountain section of North Georgia, and there seek favorable opportunity to attack.

As a first step in the plan he shifted his army to Palmetto, a station on the West Point Railroad southwest of Atlanta, where, on September eighteenth and nineteenth, President Davis visited them, conferred with Hood and his corps commanders, reviewed and addressed the troops. "Be of good cheer," he said to Cheatham's division of Tennesseeans, "for within a short while your faces will be turned homeward, and your feet pressing Tennessee soil"—a statement greeted with loud and prolonged cheering. Howell Cobb, who had been President of the first Congress of the Confederacy, and who, with Senator Ben Hill, headed the opposition in Georgia to the particularist policies of the Governor, followed the President with happy remarks.

From Georgia President Davis went on to Montgomery,

where, in the capitol on whose portico he had been inaugurated back in the gay and hopeful beginning of things, he addressed the Alabama Legislature, in special session to consider the failing state of affairs. The President was still hopeful—so much of the bad news, and of the deep discouragement and bitter disillusion of the people never reached him—but there were thoughtful men in the armies who for months had known that there was no more hope.

One of them was the level-headed Lieutenant-General Richard Taylor, the President's brother-in-law and friend, who had been transferred to command the Department of Alabama and Mississippi after Stephen Lee went to Hood's army as a corps commander. After a day of speech-making and official reception, the President took Taylor into his room at the hotel, locked the door and put in the night at work, before starting back to Richmond the next morning. Taylor, just from the trans-Mississippi, damped the President's hope of any reenforcement from that quarter. It was impossible to cross organized bodies of troops over the great river, patrolled by gunboats, he said, and even if they could be brought, they would not come. Instead of sending more men to the East, they "clamored for the return of those already there." He added, "Certain senators and representatives, who had bitterly opposed the administration at Richmond, talked much wild nonsense about setting up a government west of the Mississippi, uniting with Maximilian, and calling on Louis Napoleon for assistance."

From the rich black lands of the Alabama River country about Selma there ran a new railroad to the northeast, terminating at Blue Mountain, in Alabama, some sixty miles west of Sherman's line of communications and at right angles to it. Taylor suggested that Beauregard be put in command of the Army of Tennessee—his real preference was Joe Johnston, but he knew better than to suggest him just then—and that the army be moved to the country east of Blue Mountain, where they could cover their own line of supply from Selma and whence they could operate against Sherman's line.

One other thing, already done, he reported to the President.

He had, as almost his first official act, taken Forrest off his duty of "repelling raids" in North Mississippi, and sent him with some four thousand five hundred cavalry into Middle Tennessee to operate against Sherman's rail line. Forrest had crossed the Tennessee River on September twenty-first and by the twenty-seventh had broken up the railroad over which Sherman's returning trains were operated from Stevenson through Decatur to Nashville. On the night of the twenty-seventh, he slipped away from Rousseau's force opposing him at Pulaski, and started across to reach the direct railroad between Nashville, Stevenson and Chattanooga. That night he dispatched General Taylor that the "enemy is concentrating heavily against me." It is doubtful if he knew, however, that thirty thousand men, all told, were being drawn back from Sherman's army or thrown forward from Nashville and the north to crush his little force. Sherman's greatest lieutenant, George H. Thomas, was sent back from Atlanta "to look to Tennessee." Two divisions of infantry, Newton's and Morgan's, were sent from Georgia; Steedman's division came up from Chattanooga; two brigades were started east from Memphis to get on Forrest's flank; Cox, Rousseau and Gordon Granger assembled the commands in North Alabama and Middle Tennessee; Washburn started from Cairo up the Ohio and the Tennessee Rivers with a division on transports. Stanton, Secretary of War, wired the Governors of the Middle Western States to hurry forward every available man to Nashville, "to guard General Sherman's communications, without an hour's delay."

Forrest's movement, which could cause so much commotion even with Sherman safely in Atlanta, no longer closely engaged with an enemy and with an accumulation of reserve supplies, came too late. Had the raid been made during the months when Sherman was fighting his way to and into Atlanta, with a powerful and alert enemy in his front, with the trains barely able to meet his daily requirements of ammunition and subsistence, and with the fate of the administration in the fall elections almost hanging on the fighting about Atlanta, it is hard to calculate what might have been the results.

As it was, with forces pressing on all sides, he achieved much and escaped the net which, dispatched Thomas, "should press Forrest to the death. . . . I do not think we shall ever have a better chance than this." That was on October third. Three days later Forrest ferried safely across the unfordable Tennessee River, having killed, wounded or captured as many men as he had with him, taken nine guns and an immense amount of stores, and put one of Sherman's rail lines out of commission for three weeks.

While Forrest was in Tennessee and President Davis was in the South, consulting and considering how to deal with Sherman, indomitable old Sterling Price marched once more, and for the last time, to Missouri. While the troops in Indian Territory demonstrated against Fort Smith, he crossed the Arkansas River at Dardanelle, below that point, with the divisions of Fagan, Marmaduke and Shelby, in all about twelve thousand men, and headed northeast. After an all-day fight at Pilot Knob, on September twenty-seventh, he pushed on to the outer fortifications of St. Louis itself, in charge of General Rosecrans, who had for so long commanded the Army of the Cumberland. An important part of the garrison was the infantry corps of A. J. Smith, which since the beginning of the year had been on its way to join Sherman. It had been detained by the Red River disaster. With that over, it had started once more for Georgia, to be stopped at Memphis and twice sent out after Forrest in Mississippi. Again it had started, by river steamers from Memphis, only to be caught at Cairo and diverted to St. Louis.

Price, repulsed from the fortified lines of St. Louis, turned westward up the Missouri, toward Jefferson City. Driven off there, he pushed on up the rich valley to Lexington, which he reached on October twentieth. There he found Curtis, who in the early days of the war had been the victor at Pea Ridge, and who now commanded the Union forces in Kansas. Price drove his old opponent across the Little Blue River. Curtis made a stand on the Big Blue, farther west, and was again being driven back when the cavalry sent out from St. Louis, under Alfred Pleasonton, the same who had once commanded the horse of the

Army of the Potomac, attacked in the rear. On the next day, October twenty-third, at the battle of Westport, Price was attacked by the forces combined against him, from two sides, and was driven southward along the state line. Smith's infantry, which had followed the movement all the way from St. Louis, angled south to head him off, but failed. Price made stands to protect his crossing of the Marais des Cygnes River, again at Mine Creek in Kansas, and on October twenty-eighth, at Newtonia, in southwestern Missouri, where the active pursuit ended, and with it the last of heavy hostilities in the trans-Mississippi.

President Davis, before his return to Richmond, created a new command for Beauregard—one of vast territory, cruel responsibilities, small resources and slight power. He was given a department which stretched from the Carolina and Georgia coast over to the Mississippi River. He had the department, but not the troops, as the Army of Tennessee, the only considerable body available, was still under Hood, subject only to a certain vague supervision from Beauregard.

Before Beauregard reached his new territory, Hood, feeling the imperative need of doing something about Sherman, snug in Atlanta, started north to operate against Sherman's communications, at the beginning of October. On the second of the month his army was again on the railroad between Atlanta and the Etowah River; on the third, detachments captured Big Shanty and Acworth; on the fifth, French's division attacked the fortified post at Allatoona Pass.

Sherman, as soon as he was sure of Hood's plans, left Slocum's corps to hold the fortress that Atlanta had become and moved rapidly north with the rest of his army. From the top of Kennesaw Mountain, on the fifth, he signaled to Major-General John M. Corse, gallantly defending Allatoona, to hold the fort, as relief was coming—a message that became the basis of P. P. Bliss' revival hymn, "Hold the Fort, for I am Coming."

Corse held the fort; Sherman's army came. Hood swung away to the westward in a wide circle, crossed the Coosa River below Rome, and again struck the railroad, from Resaca north to Dalton, captured the latter place, with its garrison, on

October thirteenth, and on the next morning marched away through Snake Creek Gap to camp grounds nine miles south of Lafayette, where the army had been before Chickamauga, a year ago.

Three days the army remained in bivouac, while Hood meditated drawing Sherman into battle. He gave up the plan, he wrote, when his corps commanders assured him that the troops were not in condition to risk battle with an army of such number as General Wheeler's cavalry reported Sherman having. On the night of October sixteenth General Hood decided on his campaign into Tennessee; on the morning of the seventeenth, the troops were in motion toward Gadsden, Alabama, on the Coosa, and not far from the northern end of the Blue Mountain railroad, where supplies could be accumulated.

There Hood met Beauregard, and secured his approval of the attempt to draw Sherman back from Georgia by the desperate venture of the march into Tennessee. It was decided, however, that Wheeler's cavalry should be left in Georgia, to watch Sherman and to operate against his marching columns should that bold commander decide to move south from Atlanta, instead of north. Wheeler's place was to be supplied when the army reached the Tennessee River with the cavalry of Forrest.

A happy army, homeward bound, shouting, joking, swinging along almost like the early days, set out from Gadsden on the morning of October twenty-second, to march over the low range of Sand Mountain and cross the Tennessee River at Guntersville. Before they reached the river, came the first mischance of a campaign of mischances. Forrest's cavalry which had gone into West Tennessee on another raid before Hood's march was decided upon, was more than three hundred miles away and could not be got back in time to join at Guntersville. It was on this last of their raids that Forrest's men captured a gunboat and transports on the Tennessee River; manned them with volunteer crews, literal horse marines; lost them in a floating fight with the rest of the gunboat flotilla; finally, marched up along the west bank of the wide flooded river which they could not cross, and with artillery fire alone, burned and sank nineteen vessels, gunboats, transports and supply boats, tied up at the wharf at Johnsonville, as well as immense store of Union supplies accumulated there by steamboat for transshipment by rail to Sherman's armies.

The operation was brilliant, indeed unique, but was unwittingly costly to Hood's movement. Hood changed his plan, marched down the Tennessee River from Guntersville, to cross at Florence, in the Muscle Shoals region, where Forrest was to join him. This change and other unexpected obstacles delayed the movement into Tennessee for three weeks, so that not until November sixteenth was the whole army across the river and stretched away for the march to Nashville.

During the two months since the end of the truce below Atlanta, while Sherman was working at his problem, there had been much speculation, North and South, as to what he would do. The southern newspaper editors were fond of comparing his situation in Atlanta with that of Napoleon at Moscow. They quoted the saying of the Czar that "General January and General February" would be his best allies. The comparison was faulty. The climate of Georgia is not that of interior Russia, nor was Sherman dependent solely on local supplies or those brought in by wagon train. Not only had he been able to accumulate a surplus ahead of his daily needs, after active large-scale hostilities ceased, but he found that the corn had ripened in the Georgia fields, turned from cotton-growing to raising feed supplies; that the harvest was in, the hogs fat, the cattle plentiful; that there was an untouched country to the south of him, with an abundance of subsistence for an unopposed army which could march light, spread on a wide front, intensively foraging all the country in between.

That was the sort of army that he proposed to have for his bold and daring movement. As early as October ninth, convinced of the impossibility of maintaining his rail line with Forrest, Wheeler and now Hood, loose "without home or habitation," as he put it, he wired Grant, "I propose we break up the railroad from Chattanooga and strike out with wagons for Savannah."

Grant approved. Thomas, much to his disappointment, was ordered to remain in Tennessee. To him were returned the corps commanded by Schofield and Stanley. Four infantry corps were retained by Sherman, with Kilpatrick's cavalry, a force totaling about sixty-eight thousand men. On November twelfth, the telegraph line to the North was broken, the railroad again destroyed, the army that was to go with Sherman to the sea concentrated in Atlanta. On the night of November fifteenth, Atlanta was burned. Sherman's orders were that all buildings and property which could be of the slightest use to the forces of the enemy should be destroyed. The orders were broadly construed, there was naturally some carelessness, some inevitable spreading of the fire, with the not unexpected result that the town was ruined.

Early on the morning of November sixteenth, as Hood was starting in earnest on his march toward Nashville, Sherman's army marched out of Atlanta, spread wide on roads to the south and east, with bands playing and men singing *John Brown's Body*. Sherman, from the top of a rise on the Decatur Road, looked back. "Behind us," he wrote, "lay Atlanta, smouldering and in ruins, the black smoke rising high in air and hanging like a pall over the ruined city"—a fitting beginning for the march from which was to spring another song, *Marching through Georgia.*

CHAPTER XXXII

SHERMAN TO THE SEA; HOOD TO TENNESSEE

AND now, through the last months of 1864, with the armies about Petersburg blocking each other for a winter in the trenches, with Sheridan's work of desolation done in the lower and middle Valley of the Shenandoah, with Price driven out of Missouri for the last time, the attention of both nations was riveted on a sight remarkable in war.

The two great armies in the West, which from Shiloh to Atlanta faced and fought, had turned their backs and were marching away from each other. Each movement, if successful, promised vast results; if a failure, colossal disaster. Sherman was going to the sea, there to establish a new base from which he could turn north and march to Grant and Richmond; Hood was going back to Tennessee, and if successful there, on to the Ohio River at Louisville or Cincinnati, with a remote idea, even, of crossing the mountains and marching to Lee and Richmond. Sherman, with the larger and better equipped army, and with incomparably the easier task, succeeded; Hood, dashing his slight forces against the immovable Thomas, failed. With his failure, the last flicker of hope for the Confederacy died.

Sherman, with the intellectual honesty which was one of that great soldier's most engaging traits, never rated the "March to the Sea" as the great feat of arms so fulsomely represented by his eulogists, but did claim, and rightly, that his march, coupled with Thomas' successful defense of Tennessee against Hood, and followed by the march north through the Carolinas, was "vastly important, if not actually conclusive of the war."

The real triumph of Sherman's march lay in the imagination which conceived the movement, and the very practical planning which preceded the execution. The almost unopposed march itself was more like a "grand military picnic," as one officer described it,—the army marching usually on four roads, with wings spread wide, threatening at the same time Macon on the south and Augusta on the east; gathering in again, for a brief season, about the state capital at Milledgeville, where soldiers held a mock session of the Georgia Legislature; spreading out again and pressing down the ridge of land between the Savannah and the Ogeechee Rivers toward Georgia's principal seaport; "foraging liberally on the country" by order, and still more liberally by individual initiative, as the "bummers" spread right and left over the country, stealing and plundering.

Sherman's orders were that soldiers should not enter private houses, except as members of organized and official foraging parties, but there was more than a little laxity in the enforcement of the order—especially after the army marched into South Carolina, against which there was a peculiar vindictiveness because of the part played by the state in leading the secession movement. Moreover, there were cases where pillage and destruction were expressly authorized—as at places where the advance of the army might be resisted or obstructed. Such perversity on the part of the inhabitants or the soldiers of the enemy was to be punished by systematic devastation, "more or less relentless, according to the measure of such hostility."

The organized military opposition to the march was negligible. General Bragg had come down from Richmond to Augusta, where he was trying to accumulate forces to hover on Sherman's left flank; G. W. Smith and Howell Cobb had a force of about three thousand Georgia state troops at Macon, making such attempt as they could to worry the right flank; Wheeler, with the cavalry of the Army of Tennessee, skirmished along in front, a hopeless undertaking whose principal result was more devastation under the retaliatory orders.

There was one sharp little skirmish on the right flank, at Griswoldville, where Kilpatrick's cavalry drove Howell Cobb's state troops off the line of march and back into Macon, on November twenty-first. The next night Sherman spent in General Cobb's plantation home, which was left in ruins, with everything that could be moved or destroyed carried away or burned.   There was no military reason for this destruction of private homes, unless in this particular case it was the unworthy one of punishing Cobb for his contumacy in resisting invasion, nor for much else that went on.   At best, it is difficult to restrain the lawless tendencies bound to exist among an invading soldiery; it would have been too much to expect nice discrimination among the soldiers of an army marching under the avowed purpose of making war terrible, and to whom so much of licensed pillage was authorized.

As Sherman marched into the interior of Georgia, lost to the world for more than a month, Hood's Confederates went north, to assail strongholds that had been in Union hands since early 1862.   Anxiety at the North for the safety of Sherman was matched by apprehension of the results of Hood's "invasion" of Tennessee, which was not an invasion at all, but to many of his army a home-coming.

As Hood started from the Muscle Shoals crossings toward Nashville, carrying high the last hopes of the Confederacy, Thomas began his concentration to meet him.   Schofield, commanding his own corps and that of Stanley, was called back from his advanced position at Pulaski.   The cavalry under Forrest, thrusting in from the southwest, was crowding his rear when he crossed the formidable Duck River at Columbia, with scarcely an hour to spare.   After three days' sparring across the river, Hood sent Forrest forward, on November twenty-eighth, to cross the Duck by remote fords above Columbia and to ride again for Schofield's flank and rear.

Stephen Lee's corps was left on the south bank of the river at Columbia to keep up a noisy demonstration and engage Schofield's attention until the rest of the army could get behind him.   Cheatham, who had Hardee's old corps, and Stewart followed Forrest across the river and started for Spring Hill, twelve miles north of Columbia and a critical road junction on Schofield's line of retreat.   With Spring Hill strongly held by the Confederates, Schofield's troops, who made up the largest and best part of Thomas' available forces, would be stopped, surrounded and captured.

Schofield, not yet sure that Hood was crossing the river in force, started his train of eight hundred wagons back to Nashville on the morning of the twenty-ninth, with Wagner's division as train guard. The rest of his army he kept in line facing Lee's corps, while two-thirds of the Confederate army was marching around his flank.

At noon of the twenty-ninth, Forrest's cavalry approached Spring Hill from the east; at the same hour, Stanley, in command of the train and its guard, came up from the south, forming line of battle on the run as he came. The road back to Columbia was filled with crawling wagons. There was fighting about Spring Hill all afternoon between detachments of Confederate cavalry and the infantry of Wagner's division, until, about four o'clock, Cheatham's infantry corps reached the neighborhood. There followed, between that hour and midnight, another of the fatal misunderstandings that marked the history of the Army of Tennessee. With but one Union division on the ground, with a road blocked with wagons, with Hood himself in the lead, planning and directing the operations for the rest of the day, and with two Confederate infantry corps up or close behind, no attack was made. Schofield's army, in a hopelessly exposed and perilous position, was allowed to escape.

Hood's plan for the destruction or capture of Schofield was excellent; its execution was a total failure for reasons that are involved in heated controversy and endless detail between Cheatham and Hood and their supporters. The fundamental reason for the failure, thought Hood, was that the army had been made so timid by Johnston's strategy of retreat that even "after a forward march of 180 miles, it was still, seemingly, unwilling to accept battle unless under the protection of breastworks"—a thought that the events of the next afternoon at Franklin should have erased from his mind for ever. The real underlying reason, as now appears, was lack of clarity in the giving of the orders, and even more, a lack of efficient supervision of their execution.

Whatever the reason, by ten o'clock, or a little later, in

this night of fatal misunderstandings, contradictions and varying recollections, two corps of the Confederate army were in
position, in line of battle, ready to strike, while Schofield's
escaping troops were hurrying by in the darkness on the pike
from Columbia. So close together were the armies that stragglers from the Union column wandered into the Confederate
camp-fires. The story is told that one such straggler came
up to a little fire where two soldiers were munching cold corn-
pone.

"What troops are you?" he asked.

Being answered "Cleburne's division," he turned and
walked off in the darkness.

"Say, wasn't that a Yank?" asked one of the Confederates.
"Let's get him."

"Aw, let him go. If you want any Yankees go down to the
pike and get all you want."

More than half the night, while the Confederate army was
in line stretched out four miles along the pike, Schofield's
wagons creaked along, his guns rumbled by, his men hurried
past, undisturbed except for the enterprise of individual Confederate soldiers who caught Yankee stragglers for the con-
tents of their knapsacks. It was daylight before the last of
Schofield's wagons got away from Spring Hill, creaking north.
Hood's Tennessee campaign was lost that night at Spring Hill.

The next day at Franklin, strongly situated in a bend of
the Harpeth River, Schofield made his stand, occupying
and strengthening the old entrenchments of 1862 and 1863.
That afternoon Hood's army marched over Winstead's Hill
and deployed across the wide plain south of the town. Forrest,
in advance with the cavalry, urged upon the commanding general
a flanking movement, which subsequent events and study show
to have been the one chance of success. Hood declined to
wait for it, and ordered a direct frontal attack against the lines
of the enemy. Lee's infantry corps, marching at the rear, was
not up in time to join in the battle; Forrest's cavalry, unwisely
divided, was frittered away; the battle fell upon the two infantry corps of Stewart and Cheatham.

The battle began not long before dark on November thirtieth, a still, windless, hazy Indian summer day, when the smoke of battle hung low. If General Hood had doubted the courage of his soldiers the night before, he could not now. They swept across a mile of open country, without protection, against well-covered troops, charging with desperate bravery, but little coordination. Brigades were thrown forward singly as they came on the ground, in an attempt to take the works in the short hour of daylight that was left. The charging Confederates reached the works, and in a few places were able to make lodgments which they held by hand-to-hand fighting far into the night. Some Union officers report as many as thirteen separate assaults made on their positions. In the middle of the night, with scattered fighting still going on, Schofield withdrew from Franklin, crossed the Harpeth and took up his retreat to Thomas at Nashville, eighteen miles away.

The Confederate loss was appalling, forty-five hundred killed and wounded in less than an hour's general fighting. Major-General Pat Cleburne, Irish-born Arkansas lawyer, educated at Trinity College, Dublin, trained in the British Army, brave intelligent soldier, beloved commander, was dead at the foot of the breastworks. Hanging on the breastworks was the horse of Brigadier-General John Adams, dead, with his dead master fallen by his side. A little way down, in the trench before the parapet, was Brigadier-General Otho Strahl, piled about with dead men, wedged upright, dead, in position of command. Gist and Granbury, brigadiers, were dead, Carter mortally wounded, six other Confederate general officers wounded in front of the breastworks at Franklin. Even more disastrous than the losses, was the loss of confidence in the command. The slaughter at Franklin grew out of the failure at Spring Hill the disaster at Nashville out of both.

Schofield fell back to Nashville; Hood followed. Nashville had been strongly fortified in the three years of Union occupation. Thomas had collected for its defense an army about double the strength of that of Hood. The Confederate commander was in desperate case. He could not attack; he could not pass around and leave the formidable Thomas in his rear; he could not retreat, he felt, without the disintegration of his army; he had not enough men to engage in siege operations; he could not long stay where he was. He encamped his troops along a line of hills four miles south of the town; sent Forrest with part of his cavalry and Bate's infantry to Murfreesboro, thirty miles southeast, where there was a considerable Union garrison under Rousseau, and sat down to await developments—indulging the illusory hope that reenforcements might come to him from the trans-Mississippi.

So matters stood for the first two weeks of December. Here was stout Thomas, taking his time, imperturbable, not to be hurried into premature fight before he was ready to do the job well and completely. The conditions under which he was working were not known to the War Department or to Grant, and to their anxiety about Sherman, still "lost" in Georgia, they added a petulant impatience toward Thomas.

Thomas was hard at work, organizing into an army the varied reenforcements that were coming to him. A. J. Smith's Sixteenth Corps, steamed in on transports from St. Louis, a most welcome reenforcement. Young James H. Wilson, sent out by Grant from Virginia, to command the cavalry corps, was busy remounting his twelve thousand men, and, for that purpose, seizing horses where he might find them in Tennessee and Kentucky, not only from farms, but from wagon circuses, from street-car companies, and even the carriage horses of Andrew Johnson, military Governor of Tennessee, and Vice President-elect of the United States.

With all this bustle of preparation Thomas was being bombarded daily from Washington with urgings and admonitions, and finally with threats of removal from command if he did not move to attack Hood. On December ninth an order was written in Washington removing him and naming Schofield. Before sending it, however, General Halleck wired him, "Lieutenant-General Grant expressed much dissatisfaction at your delay in attacking the enemy." Thomas had seen that sort of wire before, in those early days of the war when he was offered the command held by Buell, but he was not to be hurried off his balance. "I feel conscious that I have done everything in my power, and that the troops could not have been got ready before this," he answered. "If General Grant should order me to be relieved, I will submit without a murmur." The order for his removal, written out, was not sent that day.

That was the day of the great ice storm about Nashville, sleet and frozen rain, covering all the roads, the fields and the hills with a sheet of ice. "Yankees brought their weather with them," said the Nashville people. Movements of armies on such footing, and especially of horsemen, were manifestly impossible, but peremptory orders for immediate attack kept coming from the East. "They treat me as though I were a boy and incapable of planning a campaign or fighting a battle," Thomas remarked to Wilson, his chief of cavalry. "I will not throw the victory away nor sacrifice the men of this army by moving till the thaw begins. I will surrender my command without a murmur, if they wish it; but I will not act against my judgment when I know I am right, and in such a grave emergency."

To the usual qualifications of a good soldier, Thomas added those moral imponderables which make one great. Fortunately for the Union, he commanded at Nashville, and not a lesser man who might have yielded to popular impatience or official pressure, of which there was plenty. Thomas waited for the thaw, which he knew would come soon in that climate. Grant sent Logan to Nashville armed with orders to supersede Thomas, and then became so impatient that before Logan could reach Nashville, he himself started from City Point. Their movement was arrested, Logan at Louisville and Grant at Washington, by news from Thomas at Nashville.

When all things were ready, and the ice was melted, Thomas started out to drive Hood away from Nashville, on December fifteenth. Two days the battle lasted—a battle finely planned and perfectly executed by the Union troops. On the first day, while Thomas' left demonstrated against the Confederate right and center held by Cheatham and Stephen Lee, his right made a great wheel against the Confederate left, where Stewart's corps was. That night, with his advanced line broken in, Hood withdrew some two miles, crossed Cheatham over from the right to the left of his army, and took up a new, shorter and stronger line at the foot of the Brentwood Hills, through which run the Franklin and the Granny White Pikes to the South.

The next afternoon, after a day of hard fighting, Schofield's Union infantry and the great cavalry command of Wilson overlapped, folded in and broke the Confederate left. As darkness fell the Confederate army was in rout, the two roads choked with the army in flight—men, guns, horses, wagons, everything hurrying south in a haste that was made more frantic by the occasional bursting of a long-range shell. Not everything, however. There were stubborn rear-guards of infantry and cavalry, maintaining organization and blocking the way to the all-important gaps through the high Brentwood Hills toward which Hood's men were hurrying.

During the night of December sixteenth the Confederates passed the gaps, and took up their weary and disheartened retreat, one hundred and twenty-five bitter miles through a frozen and flooded country. It had been Hood's first plan to stop south of Duck River and winter in Tennessee, but the defeat was so crushing, the loss so heavy, the demoralization so great that nothing less than the broad Tennessee itself would protect the shattered fragments from the implacable pursuit of Thomas. The retreat was continued, with an indomitable rear-guard organized under Forrest, who had not been at the battle of Nashville but had marched from his detached position at Murfreesboro to connect with the retreating army above Columbia. With his cavalry, and with eight improvised brigades of infantry under young Walthall of Mississippi, Forrest's rear-guard of five thousand men fended off the pursuit from Duck River to the Tennessee, seventy-five miles.

"Ragged, bloody, without food and without hope," this rear-guard fought on, "undaunted, firm and doing its work bravely until the last," as Thomas reported. When pressed too closely, the barefoot infantry, placed in wagons to save their poor feet from the cutting of the frozen roads, would dismount and hobble into action. They left their wagons, too, when they would pass the carcass of some poor mule or steer lying beside the road. Mule hide or steer hide, even though freshly skinned from a body not yet cold, could be fashioned into a pretty tolerable moccasin. A felt hat, too, could be made into a fairly serviceable wrapping for one foot, and a man needed foot wrappings a lot worse than he did a hat on his head. Sleeves torn from jackets could serve, too, to case a bleeding and frozen foot. An infantryman will do a great many things to help his feet.

Hood's retreating army, crossing the Tennessee River in the three days after Christmas, was not so dispirited that it did not sing—a new song, made up for the purpose, and sung to the tune of *The Yellow Rose of Texas:*

> "And now I'm going southward,
>   For my heart is full of woe,
> I'm going back to Georgia
>   To find my 'Uncle Joe.'
> You may sing about your dearest maid,
>   And sing of Rosalie,
> But the gallant Hood of Texas
>   Played hell in Tennessee."

The tremendous news of Nashville—the first and only rout of a major Confederate army—went north to meet the great news that Sherman had, on the evening of December thirteenth, captured Fort McAllister, the Confederate work at the mouth of the Ogeechee, where the fleet, with mail from home, and supplies and everything the army needed, awaited him.

The port of Savannah, which Sherman wanted for his new base, was not yet reduced, however. Hardee, who after Atlanta had requested and secured release from command of a corps under Hood, was in charge there, with a fortified line across the neck of land between the Ogeechee and the Savannah Rivers. With great difficulty he had collected a garrison, the original Savannah garrison, some Confederate reenforcements gathered and sent down from South Carolina, a couple of thousand Georgia state troops under G. W. Smith, little more than fifteen thousand in all.

To collect even this force Hardee had been hard put to it. The Georgia state troops had been cut off at Macon, after Sherman passed that point, but had been brought to him by the enterprising Smith and Toombs by a round-about way, by railroad, of a sort, to Albany, across country to Thomasville, rail again to Savannah. Before the troop trains arrived there, in the early morning hours of the last day of November, General Hardee had ordered them sent on to South Carolina, to meet a Union force advancing from the coast against the Savannah-Charleston railroad, over which Confederate reenforcements were expected.

It was against state law to take the militia outside Georgia, but General Smith was persuaded to take his men into South Carolina, on condition that the troops would be brought back as soon as the emergency ended.

Many of the Georgia troops objected to leaving their state to aid South Carolina, whose militia, they said, had remained for months on the heights of Hamburg, across the river from Augusta, refusing to come over and relieve the Georgians so that they might march to oppose Sherman. General Smith, however, managed to sidestep this interesting expression of the theory of state sovereignty. The purpose of their going to South Carolina, he pointed out, was not so much to defend that state as it was to help keep open a railroad by which re-enforcements could be brought for the defense of the Georgia city of Savannah. That sounded reasonable all around. The troops, consenting to serve beyond the borders of their state, gave a good account of themselves at the small battle of Honey Hill, which saved the railroad line from capture. After one day's service in a foreign state they returned to their native soil, to take their place in Hardee's Savannah lines.

After the capture of Fort McAllister and the junction of the Union army and fleet, it was apparent that Savannah could not long be held. Hardee prepared a pontoon bridge over the river, anchored with old railroad car wheels, over which on December twentieth he evacuated his army to the Carolina shore. On the next day Sherman marched in, to send to President Lincoln the famous dispatch presenting to him as a Christmas gift the city of Savannah.

While Hood was struggling back to the Tennessee River, and Hardee making ready to evacuate Savannah, the Confederacy suffered one more loss, inconspicuous among greater events but nevertheless serious. The salt mines and works in southwestern Virginia, the objective of Union cavalry raids for two years, were destroyed on December eighteenth by an invading column marching up from East Tennessee. Another like attempt, just after John Morgan was killed at Greeneville on September 4, 1864, was turned back early in October by skilful maneuvering and severe fighting by Colonel Giltner and General Breckinridge. In the December invasion, while Breckinridge's force, reduced to less than two thousand men, engaged the main body of the Union troops in a stubborn fight at Marion, detachments marched to Saltville, destroyed the works and cut off the Confederacy's principal salt supply.

There was, however, one little bit of Christmas cheer for the Confederacy, of a negative sort. Fort Fisher, the wide-flung earthwork guarding the Cape Fear River, entrance to the port of Wilmington, was not captured on Christmas Day. It had been under attack by a combined naval and land expedition since December twentieth. On the twenty-third the "powder ship," a contraption in which General Butler, commanding the expedition, had much faith, was towed alongside the fort and exploded, without result. Two days later, under cover of a bombardment from the sixty Union vessels standing offshore, the army commanded by Butler and Weitzel was landed on the sandy peninsula on which the fort stood. Before it became seriously engaged, however, news of reenforcements approaching from the direction of Wilmington and the formidable appearance of the defenses caused withdrawal of the Union forces during the afternoon of Christmas Day.

Wilmington, the last port, was to be saved yet a little while longer. To blockade it had been most difficult. The Cape Fear has mouths widely separated, with Smith's Island and the Frying Pan Shoals between. In practise, it required two squadrons to close the harbor effectively, and there was near by no such great deep-water refuge and base as the waters of Port Royal Sound afforded to the Union ships standing off Charleston. On the land side, the town had railroad connections north and south, advantages which made it one of the great centers of the business of blockade running.

CHAPTER XXXIII

AFFAIRS OF STATE

DURING those months of hastening ruin the Congress of the Confederate States, shadowy behind the great figures of the men who fought, was holding its last session.

So many problems confronted them, and such insoluble problems, about which there must be so much talk, that substantially nothing was done.

President Davis' message, submitted at the beginning of the session on November 7, 1864, made a short step toward enlisting slaves in the Confederate armies. "I must dissent from those who advise . . . arming of the slaves for duty as soldiers," he said, but he did urge that the government of the Confederacy be authorized to purchase from their owners not to exceed forty thousand of them, to be used as army cooks, teamsters or labor troops.

The proposal drew fire from all sides. There were the constitutionalists who took the technically correct position that only states could legislate on the domestic institution of slavery. That had been the position of the President himself, but exigencies had changed his way of thinking, and were to change it still more.

Others, fearing "centralized despotism," saw behind the plan horrid visions of the unscrupulous use of such a force belonging to the central government for the subversion of the states. And there may have been some among the editors who screamed vituperation at Davis during these weeks whose underlying reason was that the President sought, in the same proposal to increase forces, to do away with the exemption of editors from military service.

Before Congress acted on the proposals in his first message, events had hurried the mind of the President far beyond. Hood's crushing defeat in Tennessee, Sherman's resistless march through Georgia, the threatened collapse of the whole military effort of the Confederacy, cried for reenforcement. There were the "exemptions," the "detailed men," the numerous state militia, which the President wished, in vain, to have placed under Confederate control; and there were the slaves. Before Christmas President Davis had come to the full view of arming them.

Meanwhile, William Smith, the sound and practical Governor of Virginia, took up the matter with his Legislature, earnestly recommending that Virginia arm the slaves for her defense, and give them freedom. With two hundred thousand negro soldiers already in the Union Army, the Governor asked, "Can we hesitate, can we doubt, when the question is, whether the enemy shall use our slaves against us or we use them against him; when the question may be between liberty and independence on the one hand, or our subjugation and utter ruin on the other?"

The matter immediately became the foremost topic of discussion not only in Virginia, but in the whole South. General Lee, by now recognized for the great figure that he was, was pressed for his views, and on January 11, 1865, spoke out clearly for arming the slaves, "accompanied by a well-digested plan of gradual and general emancipation."

"It is the enemy's avowed policy to convert the able-bodied men among them into soldiers, and to emancipate all," he wrote. "His progress will . . . destroy slavery in a manner most pernicious to the welfare of our people. . . . Whatever may be the effect of our employing negro troops, it cannot be as mischievous as this. . . . I think, therefore, we must decide whether slavery shall be extinguished by our enemies and the slaves be used against us, or use them ourselves at the risk of the effects which may be produced upon our social institutions. . . .

". . . The best means of securing the efficiency and fidelity of this auxiliary force would be to accompany the measure with a well-digested plan of gradual and general emancipation. As that will be the result of the continuance of this war, and will certainly occur if the enemy succeed, it seems to me most advisable to adopt it at once, and thereby obtain all the benefits that will accrue to our cause.

"I can only say in conclusion, that whatever measures are to be adopted should be adopted at once. Every day's delay increases the difficulty. Much time will be required to organize and discipline the men, and action may be deferred until it is too late."

That large numbers of the slaves would have fought with their masters, if given the chance, can not be doubted. It was the law of the Confederate Congress that negro Union troops captured should be returned to their masters, a requirement that could not always be complied with. Several hundred such negroes, captured by Forrest in his last Middle Tennessee raid, were in camp on Mobile Bay, working on fortifications there largely for the purpose of keeping them healthy by employment.

"Give us guns and we'll fight for you, too," said a leader among them to General Dick Taylor. "We would rather fight for our own white folks than for strangers."

Action was finally taken by the Virginia Legislature and then, away along in March and at the end of all things, by the Confederate Congress; but neither law included the essential of emancipation as the reward for service, as urged by Davis and Lee and Governor Smith.

The President, having once accepted the idea of emancipation, prepared to act in the field of diplomatic relations, under his own control, while Congress spent weeks in debate.

On December 27, 1864, with Sherman in Savannah and the last of Hood's army making its painful way across the Tennessee River, bound for Mississippi, with Confederate affairs most obviously in desperate case, Judah Benjamin, Secretary of State, penned a dispatch to Mr. Slidell and Mr. Mason whose under-scorings and emphasis indicate his agitation and the momentous import of what was not disclosed in the text.

"What is the *policy* and what are the *purposes* of the *western powers of Europe* in relation to this *contest?*" he wrote. "Are they determined *never to recognize* the *Southern Con-*

federacy until the United States *assent* to such action on their part? Do they propose under any circumstances to give other and more *direct aid* to the *Northern people* in attempting to *enforce* our *submission* to a *hateful* union? If so, it is but just that we be apprised of their purposes, to the end that we may then *deliberately consider the terms, if any,* upon which we can *secure peace from the foes* to whom the *question* is thus *surrendered,* and who have the *countenance* and *encouragement* of all *mankind* in the invasions of our country, the destruction of our homes, the extermination of our people. If, on the other hand, there be *objections* not *made known* to us, which have for four years *prevented* the *recognition of our indepen- dence* notwithstanding the demonstration of *our rights to assert* and our *ability* to *maintain it, justice* equally demands that an *opportunity* be *afforded* us for *meeting* and *overcoming* those *objections,* if in our power to do so. We have given ample evidence that we are not a people to be appalled by danger or to shrink from sacrifice in the attainment of our object. That object, the *sole* object, for which we would ever have con- sented to commit our all to the hazards of this war, is the vindication of our rights to self-government and independence. For that *end no sacrifice* is too great, *save that* of honor. If, then, the *purpose of France and Great Britain* has been, or be now, to *exact terms* or *conditions* before *conceding* the rights we claim, a *frank exposition* of that purpose is due to *humanity.* It is due *now,* for it *may enable* us to *save* most precious lives *to our country* by *consenting* to such *terms* in advance of *another year's campaign."*

The dispatch was to be handed to the Commissioners abroad by Duncan F. Kenner, a member of Congress from Louisiana throughout the war, and during much of the time Chairman of the Finance Committee of the House. The Secretary of State, after commenting on the standing and character of Mr. Kenner, added this significant statement:

"It is proper, however, that I should authorize you officially to *consider* any *communication* that *he may make* to you *verbally* on the subject *embraced* in this dispatch as *emanating* from this Department under the instructions of the President."

Mr. Kenner, after a secret journey of alarms and escapes,

in disguise, which took him through New York, reached Europe with his verbal messages.   Meanwhile Mr. Mason, Mr. Slidell and Colonel Mann, assembled in Paris, had studied their copies of the Secretary's dispatch, had divined the meaning between the lines, and arranged to undertake the delicate task of suggesting to the foreign governments, without suggesting it, that the Confederacy might, to gain recognition and independence, enter upon a program of emancipation.   On March thirty-first Mr. Mason reported the results of their negotiation in a dispatch which never reached the Confederate Government—for, by the time it reached Richmond, there was none.

Mr. Slidell saw the Emperor of the French first.   "On the matter we had in reserve being suggested to the Emperor, he said that he had never taken that into consideration; that it had not, and could not have, any influence on his action; but that it had probably been differently considered by England."

Whereupon Mr. Mason went to London, where on March 14, 1865, he was received by Lord Palmerston, Her Majesty's Prime Minister.

"The occasion impressed me as being one of great delicacy," he said, "my extreme apprehension being that if the suggestion were made in distinct form, which was the subject of the private note to Mr. Kenner, no seal of confidence which I could place on it would prevent its reaching other ears than those of the party to whom it was addressed, and it would then get to the enemy.   And if not accepted, the mischief resulting would be incalculable. . . .

"From the general tone of the interview I felt it impossible that the Minister could misunderstand my allusions."

The "allusions" were set out in a memorandum of the conversation, attached to Mr. Mason's dispatch.   Mr. Mason inquired, by inference, if there were

"some latent objection or hindrance which Her Majesty's government had not disclosed, but which yet governed its policy. If such be the case, had we not a right to know it in a matter so momentous to us—that thus, if it stood a barrier to recognition, we might remove it if in our power to do so; and if not, govern ourselves accordingly? . . . I impressively urged on Lord P. that if the President was right in his impression that there was some latent, undisclosed obstacle on the part of Great Britain to recognition it should be frankly stated, and we might, if in our power to do so, consent to remove it. I returned again and again during the conversation to this point, and in language so direct that it was impossible to be misunderstood; but I made no distinct proposal, in terms, of what was held in reserve under the private note borne by Mr. Kenner.

"Lord Palmerston . . . assured me that the objections entertained by his Government were those which had been avowed, and that there was nothing (I use his own word), underlying them. . . .

"It will be seen that I made no distinct suggestion of what the President considered might be the latent difficulty about recognition in the mind of the British Ministry . . . and while there was no committal on my part, I do not doubt that Lord P. understood to what obstacle allusion was made; and I am equally satisfied that the most ample concessions on our part in the matter referred to would have produced no change in the course determined by the British government in regard to recognition."

Twelve days after his conversation with Lord Palmerston, Mr. Mason had an intimate social chat with the Earl of Donoughmore. The Earl

"remarked that but for slavery we should have been recognized two years ago. I told him that in my former intercourse with the Government here, while fully aware that slavery was deplored among us, I had never heard it suggested as a barrier to recognition.

"He replied that in his opinion it had always been in the way, and after Lee's successes on the Rappahannock and march into Pennsylvania, when he threatened Harrisburg, and his army was at the very gates of Washington, he thought that but for slavery we should then have been acknowledged.

"I told him that what he said interested me greatly, as giving new impressions, and asked him: 'Suppose I should now go to Lord Palmerston and make a proposition—to wit, that in the event of present recognition measures would be taken satisfactory to the British government for the abolition of slavery; not suddenly and at once, but so as to insure abolition in a fair and reasonable time—would your Government then recognize us?' He replied that the time had gone by now, especially that our fortunes seemed more adverse than ever."

And so, on the despairing note of "too late," ended the history of Confederate diplomacy.

Arming and freeing slaves was but one of the questions which agitated the Congress of the Confederate States that last winter. Another was the allotment of tonnage space in the blockade-running ships. By 1863 running the blockade had been organized as a business. There were sizable corporations engaged in it, whose profits, though speculative, were apt to be enormous. Ships left the southern ports with cotton, delivered on board at perhaps twelve cents a pound, to be sold in Europe at four times that amount; they returned to the southern wharves, not with full cargoes of arms or army supplies such as the government so desperately needed, but with cargoes of liquors, wines, millinery, fine clothes, articles of luxury of small bulk, to be sold at high prices to speculators.

The Governor of North Carolina, whose opposition to Davis bespoke no luke-warmness in prosecuting the war for North Carolina, went into the blockade-running business for the state, with the purchase and operation of the *Ad-Vance,* which carried cotton, tobacco, rosin and turpentine to Europe and brought back army supplies and manufactured goods for the North Carolinians. Other states chartered all or part of ships for like purposes.

In February, 1864, the Confederate Government passed acts to regulate the growing evils of the blockade-running business. Importation of certain luxuries was prohibited, while it was required that one-half of the space on every ship, except those operated by the state governments, should be reserved for charter to the Confederate Government—an immense saving to the government on the price it received for its cotton, the price it paid for its supplies and on carriage, but a sad blow at the profits of the blockade-running companies.

Through the spring of 1864, with the armies of Grant and Sherman engaged in their great simultaneous push on all fronts, with the Confederacy needing desperately everything that could be brought in, there was a "strike" against the new government regulations among owners of the blockade runners. When it became apparent, however, that the government would not relax, and that increased advantages were not to be obtained, the vessels resumed their operations, carrying a portion of their cargo at the charge and for the account of the government.

Through the latter years of the war there was a natural desire on the part of the seaboard states to improve the condition of supplies of their own troops and people—a laudable enough purpose which they felt might be achieved by engaging in the blockade-running business, as Governor Vance had done, or by the simpler method of contracting with one of the companies for a part of their cargo space. After the sordid affair of the "strike" against the regulations the companies found a better way—to put the states into competition with one another and with the Confederate Government for ship space, with the idea that the space so chartered to a state should come out of that reserved by the regulations for the government. Against this plan President Davis set his face, which brought him again into conflict with the Governors of several states and with delegations in Congress. Finally, in March of 1865, the Congress overruled the President and removed all restrictions from the blockade-running business—an act of no moment, then, because there was no longer a port of consequence from or to which they might run.

A second attack had been made against Fort Fisher in mid-January, with a great fleet under the redoubtable David Porter, and some eight thousand troops under Major-General Terry. Butler, after his final fiasco three weeks before, had been retired and sent back to Massachusetts. Defending the fort was young Colonel William Lamb, to whom there came as a volunteer Major-General W. H. C. Whiting, who, by his inspiring valor and his mortal wound at Fort Fisher atoned for his failure to cooperate in Beauregard's promising operation against Butler the spring before. In general command was General Braxton Bragg, come down from Richmond to Wilmington, ten miles up the river from the fort.

The story was soon told. While the great fleet shelled the fort with six hundred guns, eight thousand troops and two thousand sailors and marines advanced to the attack of the works, designed more for resisting heavy bombardment than direct attack. For two days, while Whiting and Lamb called and hoped for reenforcements from up the river, the place was held, to be yielded on January fifteenth. Wilmington itself was not captured for another month, but with the fall of Fort Fisher its usefulness as a port came to an end. There was to be no more running of the blockade.

The South's dependence upon the blockade runners is brought into sharp relief by the curious story of the Great Seal of the Confederacy. The Great Seal, authorized by House Joint Resolution No. 13 on April 30, 1863, was designed to symbolize the importance of agriculture to the Confederacy, and the devotion of the new nation to the principles of Washington, whose birthday was chosen as the date for the inauguration of its permanent government. The seal was to "consist of a device representing an equestrian portrait of WASHINGTON (after the statue which surmounts his monument in the Capitol Square at Richmond), surrounded with a wreath composed of the principal agricultural products of the Confederacy (cotton, tobacco, sugar-cane, corn, wheat and rice), and having around its margin the words 'The Confederate States of America, 22 February 1862,' with the following motto, '*Deo Vindice.*' "

The Seal itself, a beautiful affair of silver and ivory, designed by a London sculptor and executed by a London engraver, reached Richmond during the fall of 1864, brought there from England through the port of Wilmington by Lieutenant Chapman of the Confederate Navy in a special lead-weighted valise which would be sure to sink if cast into the sea to avoid capture. The Seal was never used, however, for the press by which it was to be affixed to documents, consigned by blockade-running freight, was sunk at sea. Before another could be had, the end came.

There was much talk of peace by negotiation that winter, also, and more than one well-meaning effort to bring it about. Vice-President Stephens had proposed in the Senate, at the beginning of the year, that steps be taken to call a general convention of all the states to work out a new basis of government, but one preserving the old idea of state's rights as understood in the South. During the same month, January, 1865, the venerable figure of Francis P. Blair, Senior, enters into the peace picture. He had been one of the right-hand men of old Andrew Jackson; of his sons, one was Postmaster General in the Cabinet of Lincoln; another had done more, perhaps, than any other man to keep Missouri in the Union, and was now a Major-General commanding one of Sherman's corps in Georgia. By arrangement he visited Richmond, where he suggested to President Davis a reunion of the states to enforce the Monroe Doctrine by driving Maximilian out of Mexico. Davis was non-committal, but Blair returned to Washington with the way open for further conference.

Meanwhile, throughout the month, there were concerted attacks in Congress on the President, his policies and especially his Cabinet. Secretary of War Seddon, focal point of the hostility, resigned to save the President embarrassment, although Davis, loyal to his friends, wanted to keep him and to defy Congress. General Breckinridge was called to Richmond to become the sixth and last Confederate Secretary of War.

This first month of 1865, while Lee's men froze and starved in the forty miles of trenches that ran from the old battle-grounds along the Chickahominy away to the southwest of Petersburg, the Congress wrangled over the creation of a new office, that of a General-in-Chief of all the armies. The President's friends in Congress—and, it is said, the President's wife—resisted the proposal, bitterly, construing it as an attack on Mr. Davis as the proper constitutional Commander-in-Chief. The combined strength of those who disliked Davis, and of those who saw the genuine merit of a centralized command, secured the passage of the Act, which was approved by the President on January 23, 1865. The President at once named for the office the only man any one had considered—Robert E. Lee; the Senate very promptly confirmed him; and on February sixth, by General Orders No. 3, his appointment as General-in-Chief was published to the armies.

Lee, loyal to his chief, pointedly ignored the part that Congress had played in his elevation to supreme command. "I am indebted alone to the kindness of his Excellency, the President, for my nomination to this high and arduous office," he wrote, in accepting the appointment.

While the Congress argued, the preliminaries for the "informal conference" which was to grow out of Blair's visit moved forward. Finally, on February 3, 1865, after five days of the exchange of rather quibbling messages back and forth, the three Commissioners for the Confederate States, Alexander Stephens, Robert M. T. Hunter, of Virginia, President pro tem. of the Senate, and Judge John A. Campbell, of Alabama, formerly of the Supreme Court of the United States, met President Lincoln and William H. Seward, his Secretary of State, on board a government steamer at Hampton Roads.

Of the meeting there has been much written, and much romancing. The most engaging and widely spread romance is that President Lincoln, writing on a sheet of paper the one word "Union," handed it to the Confederate Commissioners to fill in other terms to suit themselves.

In fact the President took the only position possible for him—that there could be no cessation of war until the Confederate armies should disband and the authority of the United States be restored in all the states, and that there could be no recession from the policy of the Proclamation of Emancipation and the Thirteenth Amendment, then in process of adoption.

In effect, the large and hopeful peace-by-talk party were informed that nothing short of a surrender at discretion would bring peace. So far as Mr. Lincoln was concerned there was an intimation that this discretion would be exercised in a "spirit of sincere liberality," but the final power of dealing with the states lay not with the President but with the Congress, a body where already the Vindictives were showing their colors and their strength.

Except for one more futile effort to arrive at some sort of basis of accommodation through a "military convention," a movement wherein it was proposed to bring in the wives of officers of the old Regular Army now fighting on opposite sides as a link of contact, there was no more talk of a negotiated peace after the Hampton Roads conference. Thenceforward, for the little while that remained, the story of the Confederacy is that of its President, his mind set on the illusory hope of maintaining a dying war; and of the armies in the field, fighting on without hope, but with valor steadfast to the last.

CHAPTER XXXIV

THE LAST DESPERATE DAYS

AND now all things ran down quickly to the end. Sherman, in the far South, moved first. After a month of rest and refitment in the charming old city on the Savannah, he turned his hardened army of sixty thousand men northward on February 1, 1865, cut loose from his base once more, and struck into the interior, to move like a devouring flame through the Carolinas, toward Grant's army, holding Richmond and Petersburg in the grip of its long investing lines.

Sherman's men, in crossing the streams of South Carolina, had more hard work than in marching through Georgia, but even less fighting, and much less restraint on any plundering propensities which might show themselves. There appears in their accounts of the march a certain gleam of gleeful satisfaction that, at last, they were making South Carolina "feel the utmost severities of war."

Hardee was in command in South Carolina with some twenty thousand Confederate troops and a third that many state militia. With him, as chief of cavalry, was Wade Hampton, who, by chance, was at home on leave of absence when the invasion threatened. Against them, with wings spread wide, threatening Charleston on the one flank and Augusta on the other, swept Sherman's great force. Three-fourths of the available Confederate troops were in the garrison of Charleston. That garrison, insisted Governor Magrath, must be kept in place and intact, for if Charleston should fall the Confederate cause would be lost. Hampton, sound in his sense of war, dryly remarked that, important as Charleston was, the little town of Branchville, where the railroads from Charleston, Augusta and Columbia joined, was far more so. He urged prompt concentration of troops there, and an attack upon one or the other of Sherman's separated wings as opportunity offered, but even in extremity the Confederate policy of the dispersed defensive of local points was followed.

Sherman's men made their way across the Salkehatchie Swamp, struck the Charleston-Augusta Railroad, closed in toward Branchville and advanced to Columbia, capital of the state. Columbia fell—there was no one to defend it—and that night it was burned; "totally ruined," in General Sherman's expressive phrase. On the same night that the capital was burned, February seventeenth, Charleston, about to be cut off from the rest of the Confederacy, was evacuated. Last of the troops to march out were the garrison of the much battered Fort Sumter.

With all his men out, in their boats alongside the island waiting the word to pull for the mainland, Captain Thomas Huguenin, last Confederate commander of Sumter, went the rounds of the fort, garrisoned now only by ghostly shadows thrown by his swinging lantern as he walked through echoing vaults and galleries.

As Sherman's devouring army moved from Columbia 'hrough Cheraw and into North Carolina, the Confederate concentration, such as it was, was under way. There were but three forces of even slight consequence which could be brought against the invasion rolling up from the south. There was Hardee's command from Charleston, softened by long garrison duty, painfully marching toward Fayetteville, in eastern North Carolina; there was Bragg's Army of Wilmington, which evacuated that port five days after the fall of Charleston, and was now about Kinston, facing the Union forces advancing into the interior; and there was the Army of Tennessee.

That second of the major armies of the Confederacy, reduced to less than twenty thousand men after the disaster at Nashville, had wintered at Tupelo, in Mississippi, the same camps from which in the glorious spring of 1862 it had struck out on the march that was to carry it, victorious, within striking distance of the Ohio River. At Tupelo poor brave Hood, cast for a part beyond the strength of his crippled frame, retired at his own request. When Sherman's march northward started,

the brave and battered old army, by corps, started from Mississippi to the Carolinas—a long, slow and difficult movement
across the scarred and ruined face of the South.   Using the
wrecked and worn railroads of the one devious route left to
the Confederacy, through Mobile, Montgomery and Macon to
Augusta and from there footing it across upper Carolina, to take
rail again at Charlotte and pass beyond Sherman's marching
columns, finally, late in February, they joined the other Confederate forces about Smithfield, in eastern North Carolina.

And there, in the words of their song, they found their
"Uncle Joe" Johnston, recalled to service by Lee, the new
General-in-Chief, assigned to the command of his old Army of
Tennessee, and of all other troops in the Carolinas, and charged
with the mission of stopping Sherman.

While Sherman marched and Johnston worked on his con-
centrations, both Grant and Lee watched events in Carolina,
narrowly and anxiously.   The winter in the trenches about the
Confederate capital and its lesser sister city, Petersburg, had
been quiet, except for a slow and gradual extension of the
Union lines to the right and left, which had to be met by stretching and thinning the Confederate line.   Lee still managed however to keep the enemy off the South Side Railroad, his one
communication for the supplies that he must have from the
South.   Even with that, such was the broken-down condition
of the railroads, and the demoralization of the Confederate
currency and of its system of impressment and supply, that
Lee's army, all through the perishing cold of winter, barely
escaped literal starvation.   Half-rations were looked on as a
feast; quarter-rations, which meant a quarter of a pound of
meat and a handful of meal each day, were usual; at times,
one-sixth rations had to do.   As serious, perhaps, as the lack
of the substantials was the lack of vegetables—"small rations,"
they called them in those days.   During the battles between the
Rapidan and the James the year before, Lee had advised his
men to gather sassafras shoots and buds from the wild grape-
vines as substitutes for the vegetables they needed, but in the
Petersburg trenches, where now they had been for more than

half a year, there were no such pitiful resources. Scurvy, fevers, infections of all sorts attacked men whose starving bodies had no power of resistance. And the cold! It would have been bad enough for men well-fed and well-clothed, as were those soldiers just over in the other trenches, behind whose lines ran a railroad, bringing to them from the whole world everything that men might need. To men on starvation rations, whose clothes were like that coat of which Sidney Lanier, poet, player of the flute and southern soldier, said that "it afforded no protection to anything but the insects congregated in the seams of the same," the cold must have been no less than agony, even though they burned the wooden abatis and chevaux-de-frise placed in front to protect from Union assault.

In those last trying days there was a great longing for Providential intervention. Even at the front, informal prayer-meetings, marked by deep and fervent petitions for guidance and support, became common. In this respect, perhaps, the army took some of its tone from the Commander-in-Chief, to whom peppery old General Wise once remarked that it was all right for him and Jackson to do the praying for the whole army, if they would just let him do the cussing for one' small brigade.

Not every informal gathering was a prayer-meeting, however, and sometimes it was difficult for a man to tell to just what sort of gathering he was invited. There is the instance of the General, name not given, who rode within sight of a small house near the lines behind the junction of Hill's and Gordon's corps, in which members of both corps were holding an informal prayer-meeting. General Harry Heth waved to him an invitation to come in and join.

"No, thank you, General; no more at present; I've just had some," he gaily shouted, riding on his way.

As the spring opened, Grant called to himself Sheridan's force, which had wintered in the Valley. Sheridan marched through that unhappy country; struck the remnants of Early's little army at Waynesboro, on March second; drove and scattered them, with large captures; crossed the Blue Ridge, destroyed miles of the Virginia Central Railroad and the James River Canal, and, with little opposition, marched eastward through Virginia to the White House on the Pamunkey. From there, on March nineteenth, he reported his troops for duty with the armies immediately under Grant. Of these there were two: the Army of the James, now under Ord, who had been named to succeed the difficult Butler, and the Army of the Potomac, still under the dependable Meade. With Sheridan's force added, Grant now had one hundred and twenty thousand men; Sherman's eighty thousand were irresistibly making their way up through North Carolina; Thomas, with the troops which had held Tennessee, could be brought up to help finish the job at Richmond. With more than two to one against Lee now, it was possible for Grant to increase the odds to three to one or more, almost at will.

During March the situation of the Confederacy was discussed by General Lee with President Davis and the civil authorities. Three courses were possible: to sue for terms, which the Hampton Roads Conference had made certain could be but an unconditional surrender; to abandon Richmond, and move westward and then south, by forced marches, to join Johnston in North Carolina, and with the combined forces to fall on Sherman, while still separated from Grant; or to keep up the fight in the trenches about Petersburg.

The only course offering any chance of military success, however slight, was the abandonment of Richmond. But the President and his advisers, with reason, looked on Richmond as a symbol, not to be given up. An established nation may lose its capital and live—as did the United States in 1814— but for a people in "rebellion" to do so, would mean the end.

No terms, then, and no giving up of the Petersburg-Richmond lines. One course was left to the Army of Northern Virginia: to fight where they stood, in obedience to the will of the civil authority over them.

And Sherman marched on. On March tenth, when he reached Fayetteville, at the head of navigation of the Cape Fear River, he was met by small steamers sent up from Wilmington, which had been in Union hands more than two weeks. They had supplies, and mail, and news from the northern world. Of greatest interest to Sherman was the news that Schofield's twenty-six thousand men, brought two thousand miles by rail and sea, after the final crushing of Confederate hope in the West at Nashville, had been landed at Wilmington and were on the way inland to join.

Sherman's columns rested four days at Fayetteville, where they destroyed one of the principal Confederate arsenals, and started northeast to meet Schofield. For the first time, they began to run into something more serious than the annoyance of Wheeler's or Butler's cavalry, but after a sharp little brush with Hardee's contingent at Averysboro, on the fifteenth, the resistless march rolled on.

"Old Joe" had but one chance to check Sherman, and it was scarcely a chance at all. At Bentonville he took it. Concentrating all his troops there he waited to attack Sherman's left wing, widely separated from the right, as it marched up. There was never a battle line where so much of "rank" commanded so little of "file." Johnston, a full General, was in command, with Beauregard, of the same rank, as second in command. Bragg, another General, commanded one wing, and Lieutenant-Generals Hardee and Stewart, the others. Lieutenant-General D. H. Hill, who had taught mathematics at Davidson College in that neighborhood before the war, commanded a corps; Lieutenant-General Hampton, the cavalry, with Major-General Wheeler, as his second in command. There were the Major-Generals, also: Hoke, of North Carolina; Taliaferro and Stevenson, of Virginia; Cheatham, Bate and Brown, of Tennessee; McLaws, of Georgia; "Old Blizzards" Loring, with one arm gone; Patton Anderson, of Florida; Walthall, of Mississippi; Butler, of South Carolina—and all of them together commanding but twenty thousand men, the faithful remnants of divisions and corps which had fought all over the South, for four years.

The fighting about Bentonville lasted three days. On March nineteenth the Confederate line successfully withstood and even attacked Sherman's left wing; a second day, with Sherman's right coming into action, they spread and extended their line, and withstood the attack of both wings; on the third day, they withdrew in good order for a retreat toward the center of the state, covering the withdrawal with one last desperate cavalry charge, made by the Fourth Tennessee and the Eighth Texas, accompanied by Lieutenant-Generals Hardee and Hampton. With the Texans was Hardee's sixteen-year-old son, to die on the field in the last charge.

Sherman, bringing his wings together, marched on to Goldsboro, where with the troops under Schofield and Cox he had more than eighty thousand men, liberally supplied by the railroads reaching the sea at New Bern and Wilmington, and ready to move against Johnston or to go to the aid of Grant.

General Grant needed no help to finish the job on which he had started from the banks of the Rapidan, nearly a year before. During the winter the Union lines about Richmond and Petersburg had been so strengthened that they could be held by light garrisons, especially of troops armed with the new breech-loading and repeating rifles, leaving an overwhelming mobile force to work westward and cut Lee's last life-line. That could not be done, however, until the bottomless winter roads should become passable. Meanwhile, the General apprehended that Lee might be ahead of him in moving out to the west. The situation might resolve itself into a foot-race or a fight, or both.

General Lee, however, after his Richmond conferences, was compelled to remain where he was and fight. The lines about Petersburg were prophetic of modern field entrenchments— strong points, connected with lesser trenches, and so arranged as to cover and protect each other with crossing fires. Against one of these points, east of the city, known as Fort Stedman, the Confederates were to launch their attack. If a true break-through could be made, and held, Grant's military railroad from City Point, through which his whole vast organization lived, might be cut, and the tables turned on the invaders.

It was a most forlorn hope, but the only one. Thirty-

ɯree-year-old Gordon, youngest of the corps commanders, was
selected to organize and command the attempt; arrangements
were made for an attack just before dawn, to be preceded by
axmen to cut away the wooden barriers, and to include picked
detachments to rush through and seize the critical points in the
second line of defenses.

At four in the morning of March twenty-fifth, Gordon with
one soldier, who was to fire the signal gun for the attack, slipped
out of the Confederate trenches. A few ears of last year's
corn hung to dried stalks between the trench lines. As Gordon
and his signalman moved forward, there was a slight noise made
by removing obstructions behind them.

"What are you doing over there, Johnny?" called out a
Union picket. "What's that noise? Answer quick or I'll
shoot."

"Never mind, Yank," answered the quick-witted southern
soldier. "Lie down and go to sleep. We are just gathering a
little corn. You know rations are mighty short over here."

"All right, Johnny; go ahead and get your corn," was the
generous answer. "I'll not shoot at you while you are drawing
your rations."

The Confederate first wave slipped out of their trenches
cleared the way for the men to follow and lined up for the
attack. Gordon turned to his signalman, and ordered him to
fire the shot that would launch the desperate venture. The
soldier hesitated, evidently feeling that even in war it was
not quite fair to take advantage of the picket who had let him
"draw his rations." Finally, before firing, he called out:

"Hello, Yank! Wake up; we are going to shell the woods.
Look out; we are coming."

The Stedman attack, prophetic in many details of modern
trench warfare, carried its immediate objective with a rush.
With that passed, however, details sent to take various other
points in the rear defenses were confused by the unfamiliar
terrain of holes and ditches, and lost; defending reserves poured
in for the counter-attack; the breakdown of trains bringing last
minute reenforcements to strengthen the assaulting columns

disarranged plans; and, before the morning was far gone, Gordon's men were driven back into their lines. The last phase of the Siege of Petersburg had begun.

After the affair at Fort Stedman the war, quiescent through the winter, broke loose again. Grant started in earnest his final effort to cut off Lee from the south. Sheridan, with overwhelming forces of infantry and cavalry, pushed out from the entrenched lines past Dinwiddie Court House, and toward Five Forks, where five dirt roads met some four miles west of the "lines." The infantry divisions of Pickett and Bushrod Johnson, sent out to meet the menace, attacked the Union columns fiercely, with the same old flaming battle spirit, on the last day of March and drove them back almost to Dinwiddie Court House. Pickett fell back to a position covering the Five Forks, entrenched and waited attack. Sheridan attacked promptly, on April first, with overwhelming forces and complete success. Pickett's men, almost surrounded, were driven from their entrenchments with heavy losses, especially in prisoners.

Grant, advised of the victory at Five Forks on the night of April first, ordered an immediate assault on the Petersburg lines themselves for the next morning. All that day there was desperate fighting about Petersburg, at every weak spot in the Confederate lines. It was on this last day of fighting in the trench lines that A. P. Hill, at the front of battle, met instant death—to go, perhaps, to join Jackson, whom in life he had followed, and who, dying, called for Hill.

To Mr. Davis, attending services at St. Paul's Church in Richmond, that Sunday morning, came a discreet messenger, with news of the situation at Petersburg: that it could be held no longer than through the day, and that with Petersburg gone, Richmond must follow. He quietly walked out, to begin preparations for the evacuation of the capital. Without official notification, the news spread through the city, as such news will. There was a day of intense activity and excitement, as the government, with its records and its treasury, its civilians and its garrison, evacuated Richmond. As night came on riotous groups, most of them more than a little drunk, began destruction and pillage. The police and a few hundred soldiers remaining in the capital through the night of Sunday restored a degree of order, but nothing could abate the excitement.

Confederate arsenals and warehouses in the capital, fired to keep their stores from falling into the hands of the enemy, blazed up here and there, along the canal and the railroad and across the river, in Manchester. Bursting bomb shells, or perhaps incendiaries, scattered the fires to other buildings. Boxes of paper cartridges, catching fire and exploding, added the rattle of musketry to the lurid night. Mobs formed to carry off the provisions and supplies in the government warehouses.

Before daylight of Monday Ewell's men, who had been stationed on the James below the city, marched through to cross to the south side on the Richmond bridges, and on to join Lee, moving westward from Petersburg in an attempt to reach the Richmond & Danville Railroad and escape along it to the southwest. As the last of Ewell's men crossed, the bridges, saturated with turpentine, were fired. Just after eight o'clock Union troops, under Godfrey Weitzel, marched in, took charge of the city, completed the restoration of order, and turned in with a will to stop the spread of the fires.

When Richmond fell and the Army of Northern Virginia began its last march, General Lee was cut off from the other armies of the South, to whom the tremendous events in Virginia came only as rumors. Bromfield Ridley, once private in Morgan's cavalry and now, with more than two years' service at the age of nineteen, a lieutenant of the staff of A. P. Stewart, commanding what was left of the Army of Tennessee, noted those rumors, together with the doings of his own army, in his journal. On the day after the evacuation of Richmond he wrote:

"April 3d: Peace rumors rife again but are laughed at here. Fighting supposed to be going on both at Mobile and Richmond."

On the Monday after they left Richmond and Petersburg Lee's men, almost literally starving, marched westward all day and a good part of that night, sustained by the word that at Amelia Court House, a station on the Danville Railroad, would be found a train load of provisions. On Tuesday they reached the station, to find that some zealous officer had sent the train on to Richmond to rescue the archives of the government, without stopping to unload at Amelia Court House. The priceless supplies, which Lee must have if there was any chance of winning the foot-race to the southwest, were in Richmond, being burned or scattered. The men, who had marched for the most part of two nights and a day to get them, could only halt, while for a whole day the country round about was scoured to collect even the most meager ration for the dwindling army.

Lieutenant Ridley's notations for that day deal with the last review of the Army of Tennessee, in which the men filed by "with tattered garments, worn-out shoes, barefooted and ranks so depleted that each color was supported by only thirty or forty men. . . . It is beginning to look almost like a lost hope when we reflect upon the review of today," said the buoyant youngster. His journal entry for the next day was still more gloomy, noting the rumor of the fall of Richmond.

By the time this rumor reached Johnston's army, General Lee had already found his way to Danville blocked by Union troops, and had turned the head of his worn-out columns toward Farmville and Lynchburg—a road that was to end at Appomattox. With the change in direction, Sheridan's men, who had been in front of Lee, were put on his left flank, while other forces pressed the rear of the Confederate march. The fifth was a day of continuous small fights, from hilltop to hilltop; brief lines of battle formed by men hungry, weary but dauntless; forays by Union cavalry into the marching columns, or the wagon trains; rapid action by the field batteries marching with the Confederate troops.

On the Thursday of this last week of life for the Army of Northern Virginia, Ewell's corps, fending off Grant's troops

from the High Bridge over the Appomattox River, almost surrounded at Sailor's Creek and assailed from three sides, was
broken and disappeared, most of them, including Ewell himself and Custis Lee, son of the General, captured. There were
but two corps left now, Gordon's marching in front, Longstreet's in the rear, with the wagon trains between and battle
all around.

On the day of Sailor's Creek young Ridley wrote in his
journal at Smithfield, in North Carolina: "It never rains
but it pours, and still the bad news comes—Selma, Alabama,
we hear officially has been given up to a raiding party.
'Tis said, too, that a column of nine thousand Yanks have
entered it."

The second news was correct. Major-General James H.
Wilson, Thomas' twenty-seven-year-old chief of cavalry, with
the finest cavalry force ever organized on the continent, had
started into Alabama from the north in mid-March; had driven
back the handful of cavalry and militia under Forrest, which
was all there was to oppose him, and on April second, the day
that Richmond was given up, had stormed and carried Selma,
second only to Richmond as a Confederate munitions center.
From Selma Wilson turned his march eastward to Montgomery,
to Columbus and to Macon—a well-conducted and successful
march of immense achievement—which came too late to affect
the result.

There was fighting about Mobile, also, where Dabney Maury
was still hanging on to the city itself, and Commodore Ebenezer
Farrand, with his tiny gunboats, to the upper bay, while the
Union fleet and army held the lower bay and the forts at its
mouth. By the beginning of April large Union forces, marching up from Pensacola, in northern hands since early in 1862,
and from Fort Morgan, captured the summer before by Farragut, laid siege to the Confederate works at Spanish Fort and
at Blakely, on the eastern side of Mobile Bay—works that were
to be held until the ninth of April, a day to be made memorable
by the more important Confederate surrender in Virginia.

Friday, the seventh, the armies in Virginia marched and

fought—Lee following out the last hope beyond its end; Grant, with his goal in sight. That night Mahone, the brave little blue-eyed Virginian who had defended the Crater the summer before, asked of Humphrey, the Union commander in front of him, an hour's truce to care for wounded. With the granting of the truce came a letter from Grant to Lee, asking surrender, the beginning of a correspondence under flag of truce that was to last through the Saturday and into the morning of the Sunday of this last week. In the earlier part of the exchange of letters Lee deprecated the suggestion that surrender was a necessity for the army immediately under his command. He suggested a willingness, however, to treat for the restoration of peace, hoping that satisfactory arrangements might be made for all the forces of the Confederate States, of which he was now General-in-Chief. Grant, under most positive and explicit instructions from his government to consider nothing that might affect the political status of the Confederate States or their government, and so unable to enter into negotiation of a scope so broad as that inferentially suggested by Lee, sent another note, early on Sunday morning, proposing a meeting to discuss only the Army of Northern Virginia, and its fate.

It was a proposal that Lee could do nothing but accept. On the day before there had come to him, as he stood on the back porch of a farmhouse, washing his face in a tin basin, old General Wise, peppery to the last. Wise, who had washed his face that morning with water from a roadside puddle, was streaked from crown to chin with dried red Virginia mud.

"Good morning, General Wise," said Lee. "I perceive that you, at any rate, have not given up this contest, as you are in your war-paint this morning."

Wise had not given up the contest, it is true, but it was only because Lee continued to fight on—and the men who were left with the army at that stage followed Lee, just as the soldiers of the Continental Line followed Washington, the man and the General.

"Situation!" he said to Lee, in response to questioning. "There is no situation. Nothing remains, General Lee, but to put your poor men on your poor mules and send them home in time for the spring ploughing."

To a remark of Lee's about the "country," Wise exploded in reply: "Country be damned! There is no country. There has been no country, for a year or more. You are the country to these men. They have fought for you. They have shivered through a long winter for you. Without pay or clothes or care of any sort their devotion to you and faith in you have been the only things that have held this army together. If you demand the sacrifice, there are still left thousands of us who will die for you. You know the game is desperate beyond redemption, and that, if you so announce, no man, or government, or people will gainsay your decision. That is why I repeat that the blood of any man killed hereafter is on your head."

General Wise did not know that Lee hoped through his correspondence with Grant to bring peace not just to the army in Virginia, but to the South. He saw only another day of weary, disheartened toil and marching, fighting and dying.

To Alexander, who pressed upon Lee the suggestion that there should be no surrender, but that the army should be disbanded "to scatter like rabbits and partridges in the bushes," and to reassemble, either with Johnston or with the Governors of their separate states, and there to keep up the struggle, the General answered:

". . . We must consider its effect on the country as a whole. Already it is demoralized by the four years of war. If I took your advice, the men would be without rations and under no control of officers. They would be compelled to rob and steal in order to live. They would become mere bands of marauders, and the enemy's cavalry would pursue them and overrun many sections they may never have occasion to visit. We would bring on a state of affairs that it would take the country years to recover from.

"And, as for myself, you young fellows might go to bushwhacking, but the only dignified course for me would be, to go to General Grant and surrender myself and take the consequences of my acts."

"He had answered my suggestion from a plane so far above it, that I was ashamed of having made it," wrote Alexander.

On the Saturday night of this last week, General Lee called a council of war. Pendleton, chief of artillery, was there, and Fitzhugh Lee, the General's nephew who commanded the cavalry, and Longstreet and Gordon, commanding what was left of the infantry. The conclusion of the council was that the Army of Northern Virginia should do everything that could be done, even to the last; that Gordon's infantry, with the cavalry under Fitz Lee and the batteries under Colonel Thomas Carter, should try at daylight to cut through the surrounding lines to the west, with Longstreet moving up to support the movement. Leaving the meeting, Gordon sent back to ask for specific directions where he should halt and camp for the night.

"Tell General Gordon," answered Lee, "that I should be glad for him to halt just beyond the Tennessee line"—a matter of two hundred miles.

At dawn the last attack began. The last charge carried the Union breastworks, and captured two Union guns, but it was apparent almost from the beginning that the movement could not succeed as other columns of the enemy advanced from front, right and left, and toward the exposed rear, where the wagons were. To Colonel Venable, of Lee's staff, sent as a messenger, Gordon reported that his corps "was fought to a frazzle"—but it fell back, still fighting, toward the little village of Appomattox Court House. There, just to the west of that cluster of houses, before nine o'clock in the morning of Palm Sunday, the ninth of April, the last battle line was formed. William R. Cox's North Carolina brigade, pressed too closely, turned, leveled their muskets as if on parade, and sent the last volley crashing across the little valley before them. Divisions, by then, looked like regiments; Cox's whole brigade was not so large as one of its regiments, the First North Carolina, had been when it fought first at Big Bethel, four years before.

The time for truce had clearly come. General Lee, dressed in his finest gray uniform—which was also his only one since the burning of his headquarters wagon in the retreat—rode to the rear to meet General Grant and secure terms for the inevitable surrender. General Grant, meanwhile, had ridden to the front, expecting Lee there. While the misunderstanding was being straightened out and arrangements made for the Commanders to meet, flags of truce passed, front and rear, and fighting died down.

While the flags were passing, Custer, with his long yellow locks, his flowing scarlet necktie, and a pistol in each high cavalry boot, demanded, in Sheridan's name, the immediate and unconditional surrender of the Confederate forces, first of Gordon and then of Longstreet. Gordon refused to surrender, and put the responsibility for hostilities while a flag of truce was out between the two commanding Generals up to Sheridan; Longstreet, still suffering from his wound of a year before at the Wilderness, and sore at heart, was less formal. He simply cursed Custer out of his lines. Meanwhile, the Union advance on the Confederate rear, moving under orders of the night before, was threatening a heavy attack, which, most fortunately, Meade took the responsibility of suspending until word could be had from the commanders.

It was after noon before Lee and Grant could come together at Appomattox. There, in the home of Wilmer McLean, the Virginia gentleman whose other house had been Beauregard's headquarters on the field of Manassas, away back at the beginning, the two Generals met, each, in his own natural and unstudied way, to rise greatly to a great occasion. Grant, intent on peace and reconciliation, offered terms of which Lee said, with truth, that they would "have the best possible effect. It will be very gratifying and will do much toward the conciliation of our people."

Officers and men of the army—there were about twenty-eight thousand of them left, of whom less than nine thousand infantry with muskets could be mustered for battle—were to be paroled, under obligation not to take up arms against the United States until properly exchanged; arms, artillery and public property to be turned over to proper Union officers; side-arms of officers, baggage and private horses to be retained; and then, "this done each officer and man will be allowed to return to his home, not to be disturbed by United States authority so long as they observe their paroles and the laws in force where they may reside."

General Lee, for himself and the officers and men of his army, accepted the terms, with the suggestion that in the Confederate service the cavalry men and artillerists owned their horses. While he was hesitating to make the specific request that they be allowed to retain them, General Grant hastened to offer the concession, with the suggestion that without these animals it would be difficult for the small farmers, who made up so large a part of the Confederate Army, to put in the crops "to carry themselves and their families through the next winter."

Lee's army was out of rations—Sheridan had captured the trains sent out from Lynchburg the night before—and both armies were out of forage for the animals. Grant supplied Lee's men with food, but for the starving horses, there was none.

Late in the afternoon Lee rode away from the McLean house to his troops, who broke ranks, crowded around their leader, pressed close to touch him or even his horse, to show him their love and loyalty. Cheering and the firing of salutes, started in some of the Union commands, was quickly stopped by order of General Grant—a delicacy of feeling that was even more apparent on the next day, when as the Confederate troops marched out in formal surrender, to stack their arms, park their furled battle flags and disband their organizations, the Union division lined up to receive them, snapped from the "order arms" to the "carry," the marching salute of that day. Had the spirit shown by General Grant and the officers and men at Appomattox prevailed, the nation would have been spared much of anguish and bitterness.

The surrender of the Army of Northern Virginia, while it ended serious active hostilities and all hope of southern independence, did not wind up the affairs of the Confederacy. There were still in the field armies of Johnston in North Carolina; the forces of Maury at Mobile, and of Forrest in interior Alabama; Kirby Smith's scattered forces in the trans-Mississippi; others here and there over the South. There was still a President and his Cabinet in the exercise of their functions, so far as their power extended.

During the week of Lee's retreat from Petersburg the "capital" of the Confederacy was at Danville, in Virginia, guarded by a provisional brigade commanded by the great sea raider, Admiral Raphael Semmes. With the surrender at Appomattox, the government passed on south to Greensboro, where it opened communication with Johnston.

On April tenth, the day after the surrender of Lee, Sherman began his advance toward Johnston, who retreated westward through North Carolina, still not knowing definitely of events in Virginia. Lieutenant Ridley, in his journal, notes the progress of the army, the state of its information, and the affairs of the country, from day to day.

"April 10th: The army was divided into three corps, under Stewart, Hardee and Stephen D. Lee. Different corps moving toward Raleigh. Enemy advancing on us rapidly.

"April 11th: Camped three miles west of Raleigh, on Hillsboro Road. Have heard nothing of enemy's progress. As we passed the female seminary in Raleigh the beautiful school girls greeted us warmly. Each one had a pitcher of water and goblet. We drank, took their addresses and had a big time."

To the elders the end of all things may have come, not to the Confederate boys such as Ridley.

"April 12th: Started this morning at sunrise and landed this evening one mile east of Durham Depot, eighteen miles from Hillsboro. General Johnston left Raleigh on the cars to meet President Davis at Greensboro. Rumors of Lee's capture in Virginia are rife, but not believed.

"April 13th: Camped this evening two miles east of Hillsboro. General Johnston returned from Greensboro. More rumors of Lee's capitulating, and some are led to believe.

"April 14th: Today we passed through Hillsboro. Saw a good many nice looking young ladies. . . . Saw a Doctor Brown directly from the artillery in Lee's army.

"April 15th: Our march today is only twelve miles in consequence of heavy roads, caused from rains. Passed old Chapel Hill University. The farther we go the worse the news we get from Lee's army. General S. succeeds in having a barrel of peach brandy and a half box of tobacco given him by a Mr. Vaughn. We are taking it along for medical purposes. Dr. Smepton invited the General and staff to his house this morning to partake of a mint-julep. To our surprise we found he had sugar, coffee and ice, things scarce in these times. Every time we get into a drive of this kind General S. destroys our prospects by telling these fellows that 'sometimes the older members of my staff partake, but the younger members never touch it.' We just had to look at that julep and sigh. Dibrell's cavalry had been suddenly transferred to rear. They say he has gone to Greensboro to repel a raid. It turned out that they were to escort Jefferson Davis farther south."

Faith in the invincibility of Lee and his army died hard with the South, but on the next day, it being one week after the surrender at Appomattox, young Ridley noted:

"April 16th. Marched eight miles and camped in four miles of Greensboro. Have just heard of Lee's farewell address, he and his army were captured. What next?

"April 17: We rest today; have been to town, sold ten dollars in greenbacks for one thousand in Confederate. Found all bustle and excitement there. Gloom and sadness pervades the whole land; subjugation stares us in the face.

"April 18: Beauregard and Breckinridge [the Secretary of War] went up to Hillsboro last night at the request of Johnston. 'Tis supposed that they are negotiating with Sherman for the surrender of this army. Desertion every night is frightful.

"April 19th: General Stewart just returned from town, states that Johnston has returned and brings news of the killing of Lincoln and the stabbing of Seward by some unknown persons in a Washington City theatre. In the recklessness of the times, some of the masses rejoice, yet our thinking gentry regard it as most unfortunate. General Johnston gets the information from Sherman, with whom he has been conferring for the last day or two, in which he has secured an indefinite truce. He is negotiating we all think, upon terms of surrender. Confederate money is worth nothing now—am sorry I let that ten dollar greenback go."

Sherman, most terrible in war, was most wise and generous in peace. As soon as he received definite word of Lee's sur· render, while his army was marching west through North Carolina, he stopped the destruction of railroads and private property, which his men had made an art. The orders of the War Department to Grant, not to "decide, discuss or confer upon any political question," had not been sent to Sherman. When he met with Johnston near Durham's Station, they agreed, on April eighteenth, on a tentative treaty—a document so broad and sound that it had no chance of being accepted in Washington in the dreadful days after the assassination of Lincoln. Sherman, with all his immense achievement for the Union, found himself denounced in the most scurrilous terms by newspapers and politicians, for his "leniency to the rebels." The immediate effect of the Sherman-Johnston convention, was an outburst of rage and villification, but it was on terms closely approximating those agreed on by the two great soldiers that the nation was finally reorganized and reunited, after a dozen years of political conflict more bitter than the years of the war.

The Confederate Government, now moving south by wagon train, through a land where the railroads had been broken up, promptly approved the convention. Awaiting word from Washington, hostilities ended in Carolina; in Georgia, where Wilson's cavalry had its last brush near La Grange on April sixteenth; and in Alabama, where Maury surrendered the city of Mobile on April twelfth, and drew his troops back into the interior to await developments.

On April twenty-fourth, Johnston's army received word that the tentative treaty had been disapproved, and that hostilities were to be resumed. "Every man had his eye turned homeward," wrote young Ridley, "and this suddenness of a proposed continuation of the struggle is more saddening than the news of the first surrender." Two days of that suspense, and then, on April twenty-sixth, the final surrender of Johnston's army on the same terms as that of Lee; to be followed, early in May, by a convention between Canby and Richard Taylor for the surrender of all the troops in the far South—mostly the com mands of Forrest and Maury; and finally, by the surrender of the last of the Confederate land forces, in the trans-Mississippi.

The fugitive Confederate Government, which was the President and his Cabinet, escorted by the remnants of five small brigades of cavalry, mostly Kentucky and Tennessee troops under the command of Breckinridge, made their way across the Carolinas, slowly and painfully.

It was a bitter journey of ruined men, to the last Cabinet meeting at Washington, Georgia, where it was decided that there should be no effort to keep up the struggle, whether east or west of the Mississippi; that the Cabinet and its escort should disperse to their homes, and about their own affairs—the end of the government of the Confederate States of America.

But not quite the end. There was the cruiser *Shenandoah*, under Waddell, isolated in the North Pacific, destroying commerce all through May and June, firing its last shot on June twenty-eighth, when captured newspapers told them of the end of their government. And then, through the summer and into the autumn, a lonely ship sailed seventeen thousand miles, flying the flag of a nation that was gone, to drop anchor in Liverpool, and there, on November 6, 1865, to haul down her flag, last vestige of the sovereignty of the Confederacy.

The Confederate dream of independence died—but not the story of the Confederacy. That story of a people who, overwhelmed, followed the last gleam of hope into black and starless night, and fought on; of Jefferson Davis, who, captured and imprisoned, the scapegoat for his ruined people, was enfolded by a love and loyalty such as had never been his as President of their nation; of great Lee, who lived for duty, and of young Sam Davis, who was not afraid, on a scaffold alone among enemies, to die for duty; of the men who fought, of the women who suffered; and of the youngsters, such as Ridley, even in the extremities of their last march to surrender taking note of the "nice looking young ladies," loving the past but looking to the future, to the rebuilding of their shattered states within a new Nation—that story is deathless.

THE END

A SYNOPTIC TABLE OF EVENTS OF THE WAR BETWEEN THE STATES

PRELIMINARY EVENTS

December, 1860

20th: South Carolina State Convention adopted Ordinance of Secession.

26th: United States garrison of Charleston Harbor moved from Ft. Moultrie to Ft. Sumter.

January, 1861

9th: U. S. steamer *Star of the West*, bringing reenforcements to Ft. Sumter, fired on by South Carolina state troops. Mississippi Convention adopted Ordinance of Secession.

10th: Florida Convention adopted Ordinance of Secession. United States garrison of Pensacola Harbor moved from Ft. Barrancas to Ft. Pickens.

11th: Alabama Convention adopted Ordinance of Secession.

19th: Georgia Convention adopted Ordinance of Secession.

24th: Referendum vote in North Carolina against calling State Convention.

26th: Louisiana State Convention adopted Ordinance of Secession.

February, 1861

1st: Texas State Convention adopted Ordinance of Secession.

4th: Provisional Government of Confederate States of America organized in Montgomery, Alabama. "Peace Convention," called by Virginia, met in Washington.

9th: Jefferson Davis elected Provisional President, and Alexander H. Stephens, Vice-President, of Confederate States. Referendum vote in Tennessee against calling State Convention.

13th: Virginia State Convention met.

18th: Confederate Provisional officers inaugurated at Montgomery.

March, 1861

4th: Abraham Lincoln inaugurated President of the United States. Arkansas State Convention defeated Ordinance of Secession.

11th: Constitution of Confederate States adopted by Congress.

16th: Confederate Congress adjourned.

April, 1861

11th: Final demand for surrender of Ft. Sumter to Confederate Government.

12th and 13th: Bombardment of Ft. Sumter by Confederate troops, under Beauregard.

14th: Ft. Sumter evacuated.

15th: President Lincoln called for troops to be used against Seceding States.

17th: Virginia Convention submitted Ordinance of Secession to referendum vote.

19th: President Lincoln declared blockade of Confederate ports.

24th: Virginia entered into military alliance with Confederate States.

29th: Confederate Provisional Congress met at Montgomery in called session.

May, 1861

6th: Arkansas Convention adopted Ordinance of Secession.

471

A SYNOPTIC TABLE OF EVENTS OF THE WAR BETWEEN THE STATES—Continued

PRELIMINARY EVENTS

May, 1861

7th: Tennessee Legislature submitted Ordinance of Secession to referendum vote; voted military alliance with Confederate States.

10th and 11th: Missouri militia at Camp Jackson, St. Louis, seized by Union forces, followed by rioting in city.

13th: Delegates to State Convention elected in North Carolina. Baltimore seized by Benjamin F. Butler's troops.

20th: North Carolina Convention adopted Ordinance of Secession.

21st: Confederate Congress adjourned, to meet next in Richmond.

23d: Virginia voters ratified Ordinance of Secession.

24th: Union troops entered Virginia. Kentucky Legislature adopted resolutions of neutrality and mediation.

29th: Capital of Confederate States transferred from Montgomery to Richmond; executive departments transferred during June.

June, 1861

1st: Captain John Q. Marr, Warrenton Rifles, killed in skirmish at Fairfax Court House, Va.; first Confederate battle death.

8th: Tennessee election ratified Ordinance of Secession. Buckner, commanding Kentucky state forces, entered into neutrality agreements with McClellan, for Union, and Governor Harris, of Tennessee.

OPERATIONS IN VIRGINIA	OPERATIONS IN CENTRAL SOUTH	OPERATIONS IN MISSISSIPPI VALLEY	SEA COAST AND "OUTSKIRT" OPERATIONS
		JUNE, 1861	
3d: Confederate outposts defeated at Philippi, W. Va. 10th: Union advance repulsed at Big Bethel, Va. 17th: Union reconnaissance defeated at Vienna, Va.		17th: Missouri state troops defeated by Lyon at Booneville, Mo.	

JULY, 1861

11th: Confederates driven from Rich Mountain, W. Va.

13th: Engagement at Carrick's Ford, W. Va.

17th: Skirmish at Scarey Creek, W. Va.

18th: Union advance repulsed at Blackburn's Ford, Va. (Confederate, Bull Run).

20th: Confederate Provisional Congress convened at Richmond.

21st: Battle of Manassas (Union, Bull Run).

5th to 26th: Engagements between Missouri state troops and Union army, at Carthage, 5th; Monroe Station, 19th; Millsville, 16th; Fulton and Martinsburg, 17th; Forsyth, 22nd; Blue Mills, 24th; Lane's Prairie, 26th.

27th: Ft. Fillmore, San Augustine Springs, N. Mex., and garrison captured by Texas forces under Baylor.

AUGUST, 1861

6th: Camp Dick Robinson, Ky., established by Unionists.

26th: Engagement at Cross Lanes, or Summerville, W. Va.

31st: Confederate Congress ended session at Richmond.

10th: Battle of Wilson's Creek, Mo., sometimes called Oak Hill or Springfield. Lyon killed.

2nd to 19th: Engagements between Union troops and Missouri state troops at Dug Springs, 2nd; Athens, 5th; Brunswick, 17th; Charleston, or Bird's Point, 19th.

29th: Fort Hatteras, N. C., and Hatteras Inlet, captured by Union fleet and army.

SEPTEMBER, 1861

10th: Engagement at Carnifex Ferry, W. Va.

12th and 13th: Confederate attacks on Cheat Mountain, W. Va., fail.

25th: Engagement at Kanawha Gap. W. Va.

3d: Confederate forces under Polk occupy Columbus, Ky.

4th: Union forces under Grant occupy Paducah, Ky.

12th to 20th: Missouri state forces besiege and capture Lexington, Mo.

17th: Union navy captured Ship Island, Miss.

Operations in Virginia	Operations in Central South	Operations in Mississippi Valley	Sea Coast and "Outskirt" Operations
		OCTOBER, 1861	
3d: Engagement at Greenbrier, W. Va. 16th: Skirmish at Bolivar Heights, Va. 21st: Union repulse at Battle of Ball's Bluff, near Leesburg, Va.		13th to 25th: Engagements between Missouri state forces and Fremont's Union troops in Missouri, at Monday's Hollow, 13th; Underwood's Farm, 14th; Potosi, 15th; Ironton, 17th to 21st; Springfield, 25th. 31st: "Rebel Legislature" of Missouri, at Neosho, voted to secede.	9th: Confederate attack on Santa Rosa Island, Pensacola Harbor, Fla.
		NOVEMBER, 1861	
12th: Outpost skirmish at Pohick Church, Va. 18th: Confederate Provisional Congress met. 26th: Cavalry skirmish at Dranesville, Va.	9th: Skirmish at Ivy Mountain, Ky. 18th: Kentucky convention at Russellville voted to secede and join Confederate States; elected Confederate governor of state.	7th: Grant repulsed from Belmont, Mo., by Confederate troops under Pillow and Polk.	7th: Capture of Port Royal Harbor, S. C., and establishment of South Atlantic base on Hilton Head Island, by Union fleet and army. 8th: Commissioners Mason and Slidell taken from Trent in Bahama Channel. 23d: Confederate attack on Ft. Pickens, Pensacola, repulsed.
		DECEMBER, 1861	
13th: Engagement at Buffalo Mountain, W. Va. 20th: Engagement at Dranesville, Va.	17th: Skirmish at Rowlett's Station, Ky. 28th: Cavalry skirmish at Sacramento, Ky.	3rd to 28th: Engagements between Missouri state and Union troops at Salem, 3d; Milford, or Blackwater, 18th; Mt. Zion and Hallville, 28th.	

JANUARY, 1862

4th: Bath, Va., captured by Confederates.

10th: Engagement at Middle Creek, near Paintsville, Ky.

19th and 20th: Union army defeated Confederates at Mill Springs, Ky., also called Fishing Creek, Logan's Cross Roads or Somerset.

8th: Cavalry skirmish at Charleston, Mo.

1st: Commissioners Mason and Slidell released.

FEBRUARY, 1862

6th: Ft. Henry, Tenn., captured by Union gunboats.

16th: Ft. Donelson, Tenn., and garrison captured by Union army.

23d: Nashville, Tenn., occupied by Union Army; southern Kentucky and Middle Tennessee lost to Confederacy.

17th: Confederate Provisional Congress adjourned.

18th: Confederate Regular Congress met in Richmond.

22nd: Confederate "permanent" Government inaugurated at Richmond.

17th: Skirmish at Sugar Creek, Ark.

20th: Confederate fortifications at Columbus, Ky., evacuated.

8th: Confederate fortifications on Roanoke Island, N. C., and garrison, captured by Union fleet and army.

10th: Confederate "Mosquito Fleet" destroyed at Elizabeth City, N. C.

21st: Confederate victory at Battle of Valverde, N. Mex.

28th: Confederate cruiser *Nashville* destroyed.

MARCH, 1862

8th: Morgan's cavalry raid suburbs of Nashville, Tenn.

8th: *Virginia* sinks U. S. ships *Cumberland* and *Congress*, Hampton Roads, Va.

9th: Battle between ironclads *Monitor* and *Virginia* (*Merrimac*).

23d: Confederate repulse at Kernstown, Va.

1st: Grant's Union Army begins concentration at Pittsburg Landing; Johnston's Confederate, at Corinth, Miss.

6th, 7th and 8th: Confederate defeat at Battle of Elkhorn Tavern (Pea Ridge) Ark.

13th and 14th: New Madrid, Mo., captured by Union troops.

14th: New Bern, N. C., captured.

26th, 27th and 28th: Engagement at Glorieta, near Santa Fe, New Mexico; Confederate retreat begun.

Operations in Virginia	Operations in Central South	Operations in Mississippi Valley	Sea Coast and "Outskirt" Operations
		APRIL, 1862	
5th: McClellan's siege of York-town, Va., begun.	12th: Union raiders capture engine "General"; recaptured by Confederates with engine "Texas."	6th: Confederates under Johnston and Beauregard win first day, Battle of Shiloh.	
21st: Confederate Congress adjourned, after passing Conscription Act.	29th: Union troops, advancing east from Huntsville, capture Bridgeport, Ala.	7th: Union troops, under Grant and Buell, defeat Confederates second day, Shiloh.	
		8th: Confederate fortifications on Island No. 10, in Mississippi River, and garrison, surrendered.	11th: Fort Pulaski, Ga., at mouth of Savannah River, captured.
		18th: Bombardment of Forts St. Philip and Jackson, guarding New Orleans, begun.	25th: Fort Macon, N. C., captured.
		24th: Farragut's fleet passed up river beyond forts, to capture New Orleans; followed by surrender of forts.	
		28th: Halleck opened Siege of Corinth, Miss.	
		MAY, 1862	
4th: Yorktown, Va., evacuated. Stonewall Jackson opened first Valley Campaign.	5th: Morgan's cavalry defeated at Lebanon, Tenn.	19th: Cavalry skirmish at Searcy Landing, Ark.	10th: Pensacola evacuated and occupied by Union forces.
5th: Battle of Williamsburg, Va.		29th and 30th: Corinth, Miss., evacuated by Beauregard; siege ended.	
7th: Engagement at Eltham's Landing, Va.			
8th: Engagement at McDowell, Va.			
9th: Norfolk evacuated.			
11th: *Virginia* destroyed.			
15th: Union naval advance up James River repulsed at			

476

Drewry's Bluff, eight miles below Richmond.

23d: Jackson defeated Banks at Front Royal, **Va.**

24th to 30th: Jackson drove Banks from Valley, with engagements at Middletown and Newtown, 24th; Winchester, 25th; **Charlestown, 28th.**

27th: Battle of Hanover Court House, Va.

30th: Skirmish, Front Royal, Va.

31st and June 1st: Battle of Seven Pines, or Fair Oaks, Va., J. E. Johnston wounded; Lee put in command.

JUNE, 1862

1st: Close of Battle of Seven Pines, Va.

6th: Engagement at Harrisonburg, Va., as Jackson retreated. Ashby killed.

8th: Battle of Cross Keys, Va.

9th: Battle Port Republic, Va.

11th to 14th: Stuart's raid around McClellan's army.

26th to July 1st: The Seven Days' Battles about Richmond—Mechanicsville, or Ellerson's Mills, 26th; Gaines' Mill or first Cold Harbor, 27th; Golding's Farm, 28th; Savage Station, 29th; Frayser's Farm, or Glendale, 30th; Malvern Hill, **July 1st.**

18th: Cumberland Gap evacuated and occupied by Union forces.

4th: Fort Pillow, Tenn., evacuated.

6th: Memphis, Tenn., occupied after destruction of Confederate River Fleet.

17th: Gunboat battle at St. Charles, White River, Ark.

26th to 29th: Farragut's fleet passed Vicksburg batteries to join Union upper river **fleet.**

10th: Skirmish on James Island, near Charleston, S. C.

16th: Union advance on Charleston repulsed **at Secessionville, S. C.**

Operations in Virginia	Operations in Central South	Operations in Mississippi Valley	Sea Coast and "Outskirt" Operations
	JULY, 1862		
1st: Battle of Malvern Hill, followed by establishment of new Union base on James River at Harrison's Landing.	4th to 28th: Morgan's first Kentucky raid, with engagements at Tompkinsville, 9th; Lebanon, 12th; Cynthiana, 17th; Gallatin, Tenn., 21st. 13th: Capture of Murfreesboro, Tenn., and Union garrison by Forrest.	7th: Engagement at Bayou Cache, or Cotton Plant, Ark. 15th: Naval engagement near Vicksburg, Confederate ram *Arkansas* against Union fleet.	
	AUGUST, 1862		
9th: Union repulse at Battle of Cedar Mountain, Va. 18th: Session of Confederate Congress opened. 23d to Sept. 1: Second Bull Run Campaign, with skirmishes on the Rappahannock, 23d to 25th; engagements at Bull Run Bridge and Kettle Run, 27th; battles at Groveton and Gainesville, 28th and 29th; second Battle of Manassas, August 30th; pursuit of Pope, and Battle of Chantilly, or Ox Hill, September 1st.	12th: Gallatin, Tenn., and Union garrison captured by Morgan. 23d: Skirmish at Big Hill, Ky. 28th: Bragg marched from Chattanooga on Kentucky Campaign. 30th: Kirby-Smith won battle of Richmond, Ky.	5th: Confederate attempt to recapture Baton Rouge, La., repulsed. 6th to 16th: Cavalry engagements in Missouri at Kirksville, 6th; Independence, 11th; Lone Jack, 16th.	24th: Confederate cruiser *Alabama* commissioned at sea near the Azores.

478

1st: Battle of Chantilly, or Ox Hill, Va.
5th: Lee crossed Potomac into Maryland.
10th: Engagement at Fayetteville, W. Va.
12th to 15th: Capture of Harper's Ferry by Jackson.
14th: Battles of Boonsboro and Crampton's Gap, South Mountain, Md.
16th and 17th: Battle of Sharpsburg, or Antietam Creek, Maryland.
19th: Lee crossed into Virginia.
20th: Engagement at Shepherdstown, Va.
22nd: Lincoln issued Emancipation Proclamation.

16th: Bragg captured Munfordville, Ky., and garrison.
19th: Bragg marched toward Frankfort.

19th and 20th: Price repulsed in Battle of Iuka, Miss.
30th: Confederates driven from Missouri in engagement at Newtonia.

6th: Engagement at Washington, N. C.

1st: Cavalry fight at Shepherdstown, Va. Stuart's first Pennsylvania cavalry raid.
13th: Confederate Congress adjourned.
26th: McClellan crossed Potomac into Virginia.

4th: Richard Hawes inaugurated Confederate governor of Kentucky.
8th: Battle of Perryville, Ky.
10th: Engagement at Harrodsburg, Ky.
17th: Cavalry skirmish at Lexington, Ky.

3d and 4th: Attack of Van Dorn and Price on Corinth, Miss., repulsed.
5th: Rear-guard action at Big Hatchie River, Miss.

22nd: Union attack on Pocotaligo, or Yemassee, S. Car., repulsed.

Operations in Virginia	Operations in Central South	Operations in Mississippi Valley	Sea Coast and "Outskirt" Operations
NOVEMBER, 1862			
1st to 5th: Cavalry skirmishes at Philomont, Bloomfield, Union, Barbee's Cross Roads and Chester Gap, Va. 28th: Cavalry skirmish at Hartwood Church, Va.		7th: Engagement at Marianna, Ark. 8th: Engagement at Hudsonville, Miss. 28th: Confederate repulse at Boston Mountain, or Cane Hill, Ark.	
DECEMBER, 1862			
13th: Union repulse at Battle of Fredericksburg, Va. 27th: Cavalry skirmish at Dumfries, Va.	7th: Morgan captured Hartsville, Tenn., and garrison. 25th to 28th: Morgan's "Christmas Raid" to Kentucky, with engagements at Green's Chapel, 25th; Bacon Creek, 26th; Elizabethtown, 27th; Bacon Creek, 28th. 30th: Engagement at Watauga Bridge and Carter's Station, Tenn. 31st to January 2nd: Battle of Stone's River, Tenn.	7th: Battle of Prairie Grove, near Fayetteville, Ark. 16th to January 1st: Forrest's first West Tennessee raid, with engagements at Lexington, 18th; Jackson, 19th; Trenton, 20th; Parker's Cross Roads, 30th. 20th: Grant's advanced base at Holly Spring, Miss., destroyed by Van Dorn. 28th and 29th: Sherman's attack on Chickasaw Bayou, Vicksburg, Miss., repulsed.	12th to 18th: Union expedition to Goldsboro, N. C., repulsed.
JANUARY, 1863			
12th: Confederate Congress met. 30th: Skirmish at Deserted House, near Suffolk, Va.	3d: Bragg withdrew from Murfreesboro to Tullahoma, Tenn. 24th: Skirmish at Woodbury, Tenn.	11th: Ft. Hindman, at Arkansas Post, captured by Union troops and gunboats. 14th: Land and water engagement at Bayou Teche, La.	1st: Recapture of Galveston, Tex., by Magruder. 11th: *Alabama* sank *Hatteras*. 15th: Confederate cruiser *Florida* sailed from Mobile. 31st: Raid of Confederate gunboats *Chicora* and *Palmetto State* on blockading fleet off Charleston Harbor.

FEBRUARY, 1863

3d: Confederate attack on Ft. Donelson driven off.

8th: Midnight raid on Fairfax Court House, Va., and capture of General Stoughton, by Mosby.

17th: Cavalry fight at Kelly's Ford, Va.

MARCH, 1863

13th to April 5th: Attempt of Union gunboats and army to pass through Yazoo River to Vicksburg defeated at Ft. Pemberton.

14th: Farragut's fleet ran past Confederate batteries at Port Hudson, La.

16th to 22nd: Attempt to reach Vicksburg by gunboat expedition through Steele's Bayou defeated.

28th: Engagement at Pattersonville, La., between Taylor's forces and Union gunboat.

4th and 5th: Engagement at Thompson's Station, Tenn.

20th: Engagement at Vaught's Hill, near Milton, Tenn.

25th: Forrest's raid on Brentwood and Franklin, Tenn.

22nd to 1st: Cluke's (of Morgan's cavalry) raid in Kentucky, with engagements at Mt. Sterling, 22nd; Danville, 24th; Dutton's Hill, 30th.

APRIL, 1863

1st: Confederate cruiser *Georgia* commissioned.

7th: Naval ironclad attack on Ft. Sumter repulsed; one monitor sunk.

12th to 14th: Engagement at Bisland, La.

17th to May 2nd: Grierson's Union cavalry raid from LaGrange, Tenn., to Baton Rouge, La.

26th: Repulse of Marmaduke's cavalry at Cape Girardeau, Mo.

27th: Attack of Union gunboat fleet on Grand Gulf, Miss., repulsed.

2nd and 3d: Cavalry skirmish at Woodbury and Snow Hill, Tenn.

10th: Confederate cavalry attack on Franklin, Tenn.

27th to May 3d: Streight's raid to Rome, Ga., captured by Forrest.

12th to May 4th: Siege of Suffolk, Va., by Longstreet.

27th to May 8th: Stoneman's Union cavalry raid in Virginia.

Operations in Virginia	Operations in Central South	Operations in Mississippi Valley	Sea Coast and "Outskirt" Operations
MAY, 1863			
1st to 4th: Union forces defeated at Battle of Chancellorsville. Stonewall Jackson mortally wounded. Battles at Fredericksburg and Salem Church on same days. 1st: Confederate Congress adjourned. 4th: Confederates raise siege of Suffolk.		1st: Grant captured Port Gibson, Miss., below Vicksburg. 12th: Confederate defeat at Battle of Raymond, Miss. 14th: Grant captured Jackson, Miss. 16th: Union victory at Battle of Baker's Creek, or Champion Hill, Miss. 17th: Confederates driven across Big Black River, Miss. 18th to July 4th: Siege of Vicksburg. 23d to July 8th: Siege of Port Hudson, La.	
JUNE, 1863			
9th: Cavalry Battle of Brandy Station and Beverly Ford, Va. 13th and 15th: Second Battle of Winchester, Va.; town and much of Union garrison captured by Ewell. 17th: Cavalry fight at Aldie, Va. 21st: Cavalry fight at Upperville, Va. 30th: Cavalry fight at Hanover, Pa.	4th: Confederate demonstration against Franklin, Tenn. 9th: Cavalry skirmish at Monticello, Ky. 16th: Cavalry skirmish at Triplett's Bridge, Ky. 23d to July 7th: Rosecrans' Tullahoma campaign, flanking Bragg out of his Middle Tennessee positions, to fall back to Chattanooga.	1st to 30th: Siege of Vicksburg and of Port Hudson. 6th to 8th: Taylor's attack on Milliken's Bend, La., repulsed. 20th and 21st: Engagement at La Fourche Crossing, La. 23d: Attack on Union garrison at Brashear City, La. 28th: Taylor's attack on Donaldsonville, La.	17th: Confederate gunboat *Atlanta* captured in Wassaw Sound, Ga.

JULY, 1863

1st to 3d: Battle of Gettysburg.
4th and 5th: Cavalry fights at Monterey Gap and Fairfield, Pa.; Smithsburg, Md.
6th: Cavalry fights at Hagerstown and Williamsport, Md.
7th to 9th: Cavalry fight at Boonsboro, Md.
10th: Rear-guard action at Falling Waters, Md.
16th: Rear-guard action at Shepherdstown, Va.
17th: Cavalry fight at Wytheville, Va.
21st to 23d: Cavalry fights at Manassas Gap and Chester Gap, in Blue Ridge.

2nd to 26th: Morgan's raid into Kentucky, Indiana and Ohio, with engagements at Lebanon, Ky., 5th; Buffington Bar, Ohio, 19th; Beaver Creek, near New Lisbon, Ohio, 26th.
14th: Rear-guard action at Elk River Bridge, Tenn.

4th: Vicksburg surrendered. Confederate attempt to recapture Helena, Ark., repulsed.
5th: Engagements at Bolton and Birdsong Ferry, Miss.
8th: Port Hudson, La., surrendered.
9th to 16th: Sherman's campaign against J. E. Johnston; Jackson, Miss., reoccupied by Union troops.
13th: Yazoo City, Miss., captured. Engagement at Donaldsonville, La.

10th to September 6th: Siege of Fort Wagner, Morris Island, Charleston Harbor, with bombardment of Ft. Sumter and the city.
17th: Cavalry engagement at Honey Springs, Indian Territory.

AUGUST, 1863

1st to 3d: Cavalry fights at Rappahannock Station, Brandy Station and Kelly's Ford, Va.
26th and 27th: Engagement at Rocky Gap, near White Sulphur Springs, W. Va.

1st to 31st: Bombardment of Fort Wagner and Fort Sumter.

SEPTEMBER, 1863

13th: Cavalry fight at Culpeper, Va.
19th: Cavalry fight at Rockville, Md.

9th: Cumberland Gap, Tenn., and Confederate garrison captured. Bragg evacuated Chattanooga.
19th and 20th: Battle of Chickamauga; Rosecrans retreated to Chattanooga.

10th: Little Rock, Ark., evacuated by Confederates.
27th to Oct. 28th: Shelby's cavalry raid into Missouri.

6th: Fort Wagner evacuated.
8th: Union attack on Sabine Pass, Tex., repulsed.
10th: Night attack on Ft. Sumter repulsed.

Operations in Virginia	Operations in Central South	Operations in Mississippi Valley	Sea Coast and "Outskirt" Operations
		OCTOBER, 1863	
14th: Battle of Bristoe Station, Va.	7th: Cavalry fight at Farmington, Tenn.	15th to 18th: Confederate cavalry attacks at Canton, Brownsville and Clinton, Miss.	
15th: Engagement at McLean's Ford, Va.	Cavalry fight at Blue Springs, Tenn.		
18th: Engagement at Charleston, W. Va.	20th and 22nd: Cavalry fights at Philadelphia, Tenn.	25th: Engagement at Pine Bluff, Ark.	
19th: Cavalry fight at Buckland Mills, Va.	28th and 29th: Battle of Wauhatchie, near Chattanooga, Tenn.		
		NOVEMBER, 1863	
6th: Engagement at Droop Mountain, Va.	6th: Cavalry fight at Rogersville, Tenn.	3d: Engagement at Grand Coteau, La.	6th: Brownsville, Tex., occupied.
7th: Battle of Rappahannock Station, Va.	14th: Cavalry fight at Huff's Ferry, Tenn.		16th: Corpus Christi, Tex., occupied.
Engagement at Kelly's Ford, Va.	16th: Engagement at Campbell's Station, Tenn.		
26th to 30th: Operations at Mine Run, Va., ending in retirement of Union army to north bank of Rapidan.	17th to December 4th: Siege of Knoxville by Longstreet.		
	23d to 25th: Bragg driven away from heights about Chattanooga. Battles of Chattanooga, Lookout Mountain, Orchard Knob and Missionary Ridge, Tenn.		
	27th: Rear-guard actions at Ringgold and Taylor's Ridge, Ga.		

484

DECEMBER, 1863

7th: Confederate Congress met.
8th to 21st: Averell's Union raid in southwestern Virginia.

2nd: Cavalry skirmish at Walker's Ford, Tenn.
10th to 14th: Engagements at Bean's Station and Morristown, Tenn.
28th: Cavalry skirmish at Charleston, Tenn.

1st to 4th: Engagements at Ripley, Moscow and Salisbury, Tenn.

30th: Engagement at St. Augustine, Fla.

JANUARY, 1864

3d: Cavalry engagement at Jonesville, Va.
29th to Feb. 1st: Cavalry skirmishes at Medley, W. Va.
31st: Engagement at Smithfield, Va.

16th and 17th: Engagement at Dandridge, Tenn.
19th and 24th: Engagements at Tazewell, Tenn.
27th: Engagement at Fair Gardens, or Kelly's Ford, Tenn.

FEBRUARY, 1864

6th: Engagement at Morton's Ford, Va.
17th: Confederate Congress adjourned.
28th to March 4th: Kilpatrick's and Dahlgren's raid on Richmond.

3d to March 5th: Sherman's expedition from Vicksburg and Jackson to Meridian, Miss.
10th to 25th: William Sooy Smith's cavalry expedition from Memphis to Meridian driven back by Forrest, from Okolona, Miss.
25th to 27th: Engagements at Buzzard Roost and Rocky Face, Ga.

1st to 3d: Confederate attempt to recapture New Bern, N. C., unsuccessful.
9th to 14th: Union advance into interior Florida.
17th: Confederate submarine Hunley sank Housatonic off Charleston.
20th: Union defeat at Olustee or Ocean Pond, Fla.

Operations in Virginia	Operations in Central South	Operations in Mississippi Valley	Sea Coast and "Outskirt" Operations
MARCH, 1864			
9th: Grant made commander of all armies.	9th: Sherman put in command in West.	14th: Banks' Red River expedition captured Ft. De Russy, La. 24th: Union City, Tenn., and garrison captured by Forrest. 25th: Forrest's raid, Paducah, Ky. 26th to 30th: Engagements, Longview and Mt. Elba, Ark.	
APRIL, 1864			
		8th and 9th: Banks' Red River expedition defeated and turned back at Mansfield and Pleasant Hill La. 10th to 30th: Retreat of Steele's Union expedition to Little Rock, with engagements at Prairie D'Ann, 10th; Moscow, 13th; Liberty and Camden, 15th and 16th; Poison Springs, 18th; Marks' Mill, 26th; and Jenkins' Ferry, Saline River, Ark., 30th. 12th to 24th: Retreat of Banks' Expedition to New Orleans, with Confederate attacks at Blair's Landing, 12th; Monetts' Ferry, Cane River and Cloutersville, La., 22nd to 24th. 12th: Forrest stormed Ft. Pillow, Tenn.	17th to 20th: Confederate troops and iron-clad ram *Albemarle* retake Plymouth, N. C.

2nd: Confederate Congress met at Richmond.

5th, 6th and 7th: Battle of the Wilderness.

8th: Cavalry fight at Todd's Tavern, Va.

8th to 18th: Battle of Spottsylvania Court House, including Bloody Angle.

9th and 10th: Engagement at Swift Creek, Va.

9th: Engagement at Cloyd's Mountain, Va.

9th to 25th: Sheridan's Cavalry Raid to Richmond; including engagements at Beaver Dam Station, South Anna, Ashland and Yellow Tavern. Stuart mortally wounded at Yellow Tavern.

10th: Engagement at Crockett's Cove, Va.

12th to 16th: Battle of Fort Darling, on Drewry's Bluff, Va.

15th: Union defeat at Battle of New Market, Va.

20th: Battle of Bermuda Hundred; Butler "bottled up."

23rd to 28th: Battles, North Anna, and Totopotomoy Creek.

27th and 28th: Cavalry battles at Hanovertown and Salem Church, Va.

30th: Cavalry engagement at Ashland, Va.

5th to 9th: Opening of Sherman's Atlanta campaign, at Rocky Face Ridge, Ga.

9th: Cavalry fight at Varnell's Station, Ga.

13th to 16th: Battle of Resaca, Ga; engagement at Lay's, or Turner's Ferry, Ga.

17th: Skirmish at Adairsville, Ga.

18th: Skirmish at Rome and at Kingston, Ga.

19th to 22nd: Confederate stand at Cassville, Ga.

25th to June 4th: Battles about Dallas, New Hope Church and Pickett's Mills, Ga.

26th to 29th: Cavalry engagements at Decatur and Moulton, Ala.

1st to 8th: Retreat of Banks' Red River expedition continued.

5th: Union gunboats at Dunn's Bayou attacked by Taylor.

18th: Engagement at Bayou de Glaize, or Calhoun Station, La.

5th: Confederate ram *Albemarle* engaged Union fleet in Roanoke River, N. C. Confederate attempt to retake New Bern, N. C., defeated. Confederate cruiser *Georgia* commissioned.

Operations in Virginia	Operations in Central South	Operations in Mississippi Valley	Sea Coast and "Outskirt" Operations
JUNE, 1864			
1st to 3d: Battle of Cold Harbor, Va.	9th: Morgan's last raid to Kentucky surprised at Mt. Sterling.	6th: Engagement at Lake Chicot, Ark.	
5th: Battle of Piedmont, Va.	9th to 30th: Kennesaw Mountain period of Sherman's Atlanta campaign, including Pine Mountain, Gilgal Church, Big Shanty, and general assault on Kennesaw Mt., 27th.	10th: Sturgis' invasion of Mississippi defeated by Forrest at Brice's Cross Roads, or Guntown, Miss.	
10th and 11th: Engagement at Lexington, Va.			
12th: Cavalry battle of Trevilian's Station, Va.			
14th: Confederate Congress adjourned.	10th: Morgan captured Cynthiana, Ky., and garrison.		
14th: Grant began crossing to south side of James River.	12th: Morgan defeated at Cynthiana, Ky.		
15th to 19th: Attacks on Petersburg, Va., met by Beauregard's force, reenforced by Lee on 18th. Siege of Petersburg began, to last until April 2, 1865.			19th: Confederate cruiser *Alabama*, sunk off Cherbourg, France, by U. S. ship *Kearsarge.*
18th: Hunter's army driven away from Lynchburg by Early.			
22nd to 30th: Engagements on Jerusalem Plank Road and Weldon Railroad, Petersburg, Va.			
JULY, 1864			
1st to 31st: Siege of Petersburg-Richmond continued. "The Crater" mine exploded under Confederate line, 30th.	2nd to 5th: J. E. Johnston's army flanked out of Smyrna Station lines, Ga.		3d: Engagement at Ft. Johnson, James Island, Charleston Harbor; Union attack repulsed.
	6th to 10th: Sherman crossed Chattahoochee River, Ga.		

488

5th to 7th: Union land attack on Charleston defenses repulsed.

4th to 20th: Early's Washington raid, including engagements about Harper's Ferry, 4th to 7th; Monocacy River, near Frederick, Md., 9th; Ft. Stevens, Washington, D. C., 12th; cavalry fights in Blue Ridge gaps and lower Valley, 17th to 20th.

23d and 24th: Third Battle of Kernstown and Winchester, Va.

11th to 22nd: Rousseau's Union cavalry raid from Decatur, Ala., to Sherman's army.

18th: Johnston replaced by Hood in command of Army of Tennessee.

20th: Battle of Peach Tree Creek, near Atlanta, Ga.

22nd: Battle of Atlanta, Georgia.

26th to 31st: Stoneman's Union cavalry raid to Macon, Ga.

28th: Battle of Ezra Church, near Atlanta, Ga.

28th to September 2nd: Siege of Atlanta.

14th: Battle of Harrisburg, or Tupelo, Miss.

27th: Engagement at Ft. Smith, Ark.

AUGUST, 1864

5th: Farragut's fleet entered Mobile Bay; destroyed Confederate Ram *Tennessee*; with cooperation of army captured Ft. Gaines and, on August 23d, Ft. Morgan.

6th: Confederate cruiser *Tallahassee* left Wilmington for three-weeks cruise.

17th: Engagement at Gainesville, Fla.

21st: Forrest's raid into Memphis to cause recall of A. J. Smith's expedition from Mississippi.

1st to 31st: Siege of Atlanta continued, with cavalry raids on railroads to rear.

31st and Sept. 1st: Battle of Jonesboro, Ga. (near Atlanta).

1st to 31st: Siege of Petersburg continued, including heavy engagements on Jerusalem Plank Road, at Globe Tavern and Reams' Station, on Weldon Railroad.

1st to 31st: Early remained in lower Valley, with engagements at White Post, Sulphur Springs Bridge, Berryville Pike, Snicker's Gap, Fisher's Hill, Front Royal, Winchester, Berryville, Halltown and Smithfield.

OPERATIONS IN VIRGINIA	OPERATIONS IN CENTRAL SOUTH	OPERATIONS IN MISSISSIPPI VALLEY	SEA COAST AND "OUTSKIRT" OPERATIONS
		SEPTEMBER, 1864	
1st to 30th: Siege of Petersburg continued; Union attacks on 28th and 30th repulsed.	1st to 8th: Wheeler's cavalry raid into Tennessee.	20th to October 28th: Price's expedition to Missouri, with engagements at Pilot Knob or Ironton, and Centralia, 26th and 27th.	16th and 18th: Skirmishes at Ft. Gibson, Indian Territory.
1st to 18th: Early remained in lower Valley, with engagements at Berryville, Lock's Ford and Sycamore Church.	2nd: Atlanta surrendered to Sherman.		
19th: Fourth Battle of Winchester, Va.; Early driven up Valley.	4th: Morgan killed at Greeneville, Tenn.		
22nd: Early defeated at Fisher's Hill, Va.	21st to October 6th: Forrest's Middle Tennessee raid.		
		OCTOBER, 1864	
1st to 31st: Siege of Petersburg continued, with engagements on Darbytown Road, 7th and 13th; Hatcher's Run, 27th; Fair Oaks, 27th and 28th.	1st to 15th: Hood's raid in force against Sherman's communications, with engagements at Big Shanty, Acworth, Allatoona Pass, Resaca and Dalton.	1st to 28th: Price remained in Missouri; with engagements at Glasgow, Little Blue River, Big Blue River, Westport and Newtonia.	7th: Confederate cruiser *Florida* sunk at Bahia, Brazil.
2nd: Expedition to Saltville, Va., salt works repulsed.	22nd: Hood started on Tennessee campaign.		8th: Confederate cruiser *Shenandoah* commissioned.
9th: Cavalry fight at Fisher's Hill, Va.			27th: Confederate ram *Albemarle* destroyed at Plymouth, N. C., by torpedo attack.
12th: Cavalry fight at Strassburg, Va.			
19th: Battle of Cedar Creek, Va.			

1st to 30th: Siege of Petersburg continued. Early remained in Valley, with engagements at Newtown, Cedar Springs, Rood's Hill.

7th: Congress met at Richmond.

4th: Forrest's cavalry destroyed Union base and boats at Johnsonville, Tenn.

16th: Hood crossed Tennessee River on Tennessee campaign.
Sherman left Atlanta for March to the Sea.

21st: Georgia state troops defeated at Griswoldville, Ga.

26th: Wheeler's cavalry engagement at Sandersville, Ga.

29th: Confederate attack at Spring Hill, Tenn., failed.

30th: Battle of Franklin, Tenn.

30th: Engagement at Honey Hill, or Grahamsville, S. C.

1st to 31st: Siege of Petersburg, with engagements at Stony Creek Station, Weldon Railroad, Hatcher's Run.

8th to 28th: Sheridan's Raid on Gordonsville, Va.

12th to 21st: Union raid from Bean's Station, Tenn., to Virginia salt works.

1st to 14th: Hood's army in front of Nashville, Tenn.

1st to 10th: Sherman marched to Savannah, Ga.

7th: Engagement at Murfreesboro, Tenn.

10th to 21st: Siege of Savannah, Ga.

13th: Ft. McAllister, Ga., captured by Sherman.

15th and 16th: Battle of Nashville.

21st: Savannah evacuated.

28th: Engagement at Egypt Station, Miss.

6th to 9th: Engagement at Deveaux's Neck, S. C.

25th: Ft. Fisher, below Wilmington, N C, repulsed combined naval and land expedition.

Operations in Virginia	Operations in Central South	Operations in Mississippi Valley	Sea Coast and "Outskirt" Operations
JANUARY, 1865			
1st to 31st: Siege of Petersburg.			15th: Ft. Fisher captured. 30th: Confederate cruiser *Stonewall* commissioned.
FEBRUARY, 1865			
1st to 28th: Siege of Petersburg, with engagements at Dabney's Mills, on Hatcher's Run, 5th to 7th. 3d: Hampton Roads "Peace Conference" failed. 6th: Lee made commander-in-chief. 27th to March 25th: Sheridan's cavalry raid in Virginia.	1st: Sherman started north from Savannah, Ga. 17th: Columbia, S. C., taken and burned, Charleston evacuated by Confederates.	22nd: Engagement at Douglas Landing, Pine Bluff, Ark.	22nd: Wilmington, N. C., captured.
MARCH, 1865			
1st to 31st: Siege of Petersburg, with engagements at Ft. Stedman, 25th; Quaker Road, 29th; Boydton Plank and White Oak Roads, and Dinwiddie Court House, 31st. 2nd: Early's command dispersed or captured by Sheridan, at Waynesboro, Va. 18th: Confederate Congress adjourned. 20th to April 6th: Stoneman's raid from Tennessee into southwestern Virginia and North Carolina.	10th: Fayetteville, N. C., and arsenal captured. 16th: Engagement at Averysboro, N. C. 19th to 21st: Battle of Bentonville, N. C.	22nd to April 24th: Wilson's Union cavalry raid from Tennessee River to Selma, Montgomery, Columbus and Macon.	26th to April 12th: Siege of Mobile, Alabama.

1st: Battle of Five Forks.
2nd: Petersburg and Richmond evacuated.
2nd to 9th: March of Lee's Army from Petersburg and Richmond to Appomattox Court House, with engagements at Amelia Springs, Sailor's Creek, High Bridge, Farmville and Appomattox.
9th: Army of Northern Virginia surrendered at Appomattox Court House.

2nd: Selma, Alabama, captured by Wilson.
13th: Montgomery captured.
16th: Last engagement east of Mississippi, at West Point, Ga.
Columbus, Ga., captured.
26th: Army of Tennessee surrendered at Greensboro, N. C.

12th: Mobile surrendered.

MAY, 1865

4th: Department of Alabama and Mississippi surrendered.
10th: President Davis captured at Irwinsville, Ga.

11th: Troops in Arkansas surrendered at Chalk Bluff.

11th: Troops in Florida surrendered at Tallahassee.
13th: Last land engagement of war, Palmetto Ranch, near Brownsville, Tex.
15th: Confederate cruiser *Stonewall* surrendered.
26th: Army of Trans-Mississippi Department surrendered.

JUNE, 1865

2nd: Galveston surrendered.
28th: Last shot of war fired by Confederate cruiser *Shenandoah*, isolated in North Pacific.

SOURCES

SOURCES for even the simplest general story of the Confederacy are overwhelming in number, mass, detail and variety—literally thousands of books, articles, pamphlets, publications of all sorts. From them, any particular event or incident in the vast story may be traced out as minutely as one wishes, usually in at least two differing versions, frequently with still other variants, as the view-points and opportunities of Union and Confederate observers differed not only from each other, but often among themselves. Somewhere among them lies the truth, if there be such a thing as "the truth" of what has been called the "haze of battle."

The aim of the book is to present a running narrative of the life of the Confederacy, with no more detail than seems necessary; with as much accuracy as I can achieve among conflicting accounts; with no intentional bias as to facts, certainly, but without pretending to an impossible impartiality of spirit.

Of the research of the historian, that is, digging out the hitherto unknown, there is little in the book, mostly occasional quotations from southern newspapers of the war period. The effort to keep the main story in focus does not permit elaboration of new angles or new details.

The *Official Records of the Union and Confederate Armies*, published by the United States, in 130 volumes, with 138,579 pages of text and 1,006 maps and charts; and the similar records for the Navies, 31 volumes, contain almost everything in the way of an official record of either side that has survived, and an immense amount of human material that is "official" only in the sense that it is included in the government's great collection.

Besides these official publications, seven other collections of military material are of special note: *Battles and Leaders of the Civil War*, 4 vols., New York, 1887, a splendid grouping of study and reminiscence from qualified observers of both sides; *Campaigns of the Civil War*, 12 vols., New York, 1883, prepared by Union writers; *Southern Military History*, 12 vols., Atlanta, 1899, prepared under the editorship of General Clement Evans; the *Photographic History of the Civil War*, 10 vols., New York, 1911, a magnificent collection of contemporary photographs, with accompanying text presenting the story from both sides and various angles; the series of publications of the Southern Historical Society, of Richmond; and the volumes of the *Confederate Veteran* (Nashville), which contain material of every sort, from the lightest of camp-fire stories to careful and detailed studies of engagements and campaigns by those qualified to write by both experience and study.

Individual military memoirs and reminiscences, ranging from the elaborate multi-volume works of some of the generals to the most ephemeral pamphlets of personal recollections, are abundant. Lee wrote nothing; nor, of course, did Albert Sidney Johnston, Stonewall Jackson, or J. E. B. Stuart, killed during the war. Books about Lee, however, fill shelves: General Long's *Memoirs*; Fitzhugh Lee's *General Lee*; Captain Robert E. Lee's *Recollections and Letters*; Jones' *Life and Letters*; Colonel Taylor's *General Lee*; and three more recent studies, Thomas Nelson Page's delightful *Robert E. Lee, Man and Soldier*; Gamaliel Bradford's *Lee the American*; and Major-General Sir Frederick Maurice's *Robert E. Lee the Soldier*.

Of the three great Confederate leaders killed in battle, the career of Stuart is covered by Colonel H. B. McClellan's *Life and Campaigns of Major-General J. E. B. Stuart* and William Allan's *The Army of Northern Virginia in 1862*. Colonel William P. Johnston's *Life* of his father is most complete. The work of Lieutenant-Colonel G. F. R. Henderson, of the British Army, *Stonewall Jackson and the American Civil War*, has become a military classic.

Of the southern military leaders, several wrote their own memoirs: Joseph E. Johnston's *Narrative*; Longstreet's *From Manassas to Appomattox*; Hood's *Advance and Retreat*; Semmes' *Memoirs of Service Afloat*; Richard Taylor's *Destruction and Reconstruction*; Gordon's *Reminiscences of the Civil War*; Early's *Lieutenant-General Jubal A. Early*; Dabney Maury's *Recollections of a Virginian*; E. P. Alexander's *Military Memoirs of a Confederate* (perhaps the outstanding of southern works of the sort), among them. Colonel Alfred Roman's *General Beauregard* lacks little of being a first person biography, while *Morgan's Cavalry*, by General Basil Duke, Morgan's brother-in-law and subordinate, is of much the same character. Satisfactory biographies of other leaders—Bragg, Forrest, Kirby Smith, Leonidas Polk, Wheeler—are available; while contemporary sketches of others are included in *Southern Generals*, by Captain William P. Snow, published in 1866, and *Lee and His Lieutenants*, by E. A. Pollard (1867).

Of the Union military leaders, Grant, Sherman, Sheridan and McClellan wrote elaborate Memoirs. T. B. Van Horn's and Piatt and Boynton's works on Thomas, and Captain A. T. Mahan's *Admiral Far-*

ragut present the part of those stout champions of the Union cause.

Of civil and political leaders, Lincoln, of course, wrote nothing in the way of a memoir, but books about Lincoln fill rooms. Jefferson Davis published, in 1881, his two volume *Rise and Fall of the Confederate Government,* followed by the *Short History of the Confederate States* in 1890. These works, besides giving much of the history of the government, present the southern reasons for secession, which are more elaborately set out in Alexander H. Stephens' *War between the States,* published in 1867. Postmaster-General Reagan's *Memoirs,* and biographies of Benjamin, Memminger, Yancey, Mason, Stephens and Davis give something of the non-military side of the Confederate Government.

The *Journals of the Confederate Congress,* and the *Messages and Papers of the Confederacy* (Richardson) are source material. Valuable works covering the civil field include Nathaniel W. Stephenson's *The Day of the Confederacy;* Professor Moore's *Conscription and Conflict in the Confederacy;* Professor Owsley's *State Rights in the Confederacy;* Edward Conrad Smith's *The Borderland in the Civil War;* Professor Schwab's *The Confederate States of America;* and *The Lost Cause,* one of E. A. Pollard's anti-Davis books, published in 1866.

Of works on life in the Confederate armies and the Confederate States there are hundreds, many of them published by the Neale Publishing Company of New York.

Private John Worsham's *One of Jackson's Foot Cavalry* stands out. An ancient work, *The Grayjackets,* published in 1867, is another. The *Journal of B. L. Ridley* is most interesting. Mrs. Mary B. Chesnut's *Diary from Dixie* gives glimpses of life behind the lines; T. C. de Leon's *Four Years in Rebel Capitals* is a racy, gossipy account of life in Montgomery and Richmond as a young man saw it; while the famous *Rebel War Clerk's Diary* of J. B. Jones gives a somewhat jaundiced view of affairs behind the scenes at the capital. Besides the numerous records by Americans, there are four English records: those left by Colonel Arthur J. L. Fremantle, who visited both western and eastern armies and saw Gettysburg; by young Garnet Wolseley, afterward to become Viscount Wolseley, Commander-in-Chief of the British Armies, who visited Lee's army, and whose studies of Forrest's operations, published in the *United Service Journal* in 1892, first directed professional military attention to that remarkable genius; by W. H. Russell, of the *Times;* and by an obscure William Watson, who served in and wrote a *Life in the Confederate Army.*

Of general military studies of the war, several are most helpful. John C. Ropes' *Story of the Civil War,* two volumes, completed after the death of Mr. Ropes by Colonel W. R. Livermore, four volumes, is a fine and fair study of the military campaigns. Colonel T. L. Livermore's *Numbers and Losses in the Civil War in America* is authority, although it would seem that his estimate of a total Confederate force of more than a million men in a nation whose military population did not exceed nine hundred thousand is above the mark. Mr. Walter Geer's *Campaigns of the Civil War*, 1926, and General Maurice's *Statesmen and Soldiers of the Civil War*, published in the same year, are distinct contributions to the study of the period, as are several of the recent biographies of its leading characters: Liddell-Hart's *Sherman; Soldier, Realist, American;* Thomason's, *Jeb Stuart;* Lytle's, *Bedford Forrest;* Young's, *Marse Robert;* Tate's *Stonewall Jackson, the Good Soldier* among them.

ROBERT S. HENRY

Nashville, Tennessee,
July 26th, 1931.

INDEX